ADVANCES IN LIBRARY COMPUTERISATION

ADVANCES IN LIBRARY COMPUTERISATION

Dr. Dattatray Narayan Phadke
Dy Librarian IIT Bombay (Retd.)
Consultant Librarian
Pillai College of Engineering
New Panwel, New Mumbai

Ess Ess Publications
New Delhi

ADVANCES IN LIBRARY COMPUTERISATION

ISBN : 978-93-87698-78-9

Price : Rs. 1700/-

First Published 2020

Published by:
Ess Ess Publications
4831/24, Ansari Road,
Darya Ganj,
New Delhi-110 002, INDIA
Phones: 23260807, 41563444
Fax: 41563334
E-mail: info@essessreference.com
www.essessreference.com

Cover Design by *Patch Creative*

Printed and bound in India

Contents

Preface vii

1 Information and Communication Technology (ICT) **1**

1.0 Introduction 1

1.1 What is ICT ? 1

1.2 Technologies Participating in ICT 2

1.3 Introduction to Technologies Involved in ICT 2

1.3.1 Computer Technology 2

1.3.1.1 Parts of Computers of Accessories 3

1.3.1.2 Mother Board 5

1.3.1.3 Central Processing Unit 6

1.3.1.4 Random Access Memory or RAM 6

1.3.1.5 Firmware 6

1.3.1.6 Removable / Moveable Media Devices 6

1.3.1.7 Internal Storage 6

1.3.1.8 External Connectivity 7

1.3.2 What is Information Technology? 7

1.3.2.1 Introduction to Internet 7

1.3.2.2 Internet Connectivity 8

1.3.2.3 Internet, Intranet and Extranet 8

1.3.3 Telecommunication 8

1.3.4 Mass Media and Supportive Technologies in ICT 9

1.4 Application of ICT Technology 9

1.4.1 Use of Traditional Computer Tools 9

1.4.2 Special Applications of ICT Technology 10

1.4.3 Networking / Networks 11

1.5 Understanding Data and Information 11
1.6 Data and Information 12
1.7 Information Resources in ICT 13
1.8 Information System in ICT 13
1.8.1 What is Information System? 13
1.8.2 Types of information systems 14
1.9 Types of Information Sources 15
1.9.1 Primary Sources 15
1.9.2 Secondary Sources 15
1.9.3 Tertiary Sources 16
1.10 Information Creation and Flow of Information 16
1.11 Quality of Information 18
2 Library Computerisation : Concept, Need and Background 19
2.0 Introduction 19
2.1 Library Computerisation: A Concept 19
2.2 Library Computerisation: Background and Need : A Comparative Review 20
2.3 Role of Librarian in Library Computerisation 21
2.4 Training Needs of Librarians in Computerisation 22
2.4.1 Higher Level IT Training for Librarians 24
2.5 Training Opportunities for Librarians in Library Information Technology 25
2.6 Advantages of Library Computerisation 27
3 Process of Library Computerisation 29
3.0 Introduction 29
3.1 Library Computerisation Planning and Preparations 29
3.2 Library Computerisation : System Development Process 30
3.2.1 Systems Study 30
3.2.2 Systems Development 32
3.2.3 System Analysis 32
3.2.4 Systems Design 33
3.2.5 Systems Test / Trial 33
3.2.6 System Implementation 33
3.2.7 System Maintenance 34
3.2.7.1 Generating Various Reports in the System 35
3.2.8 System Development Life Cycle 35

3.2.9 Flow Charting 36

3.2.10 System Documentation 39

3.3 Economics of Library Computerisation 42

3.4 System Performance 42

4 Library Computerization : Ways & Means 44

4.0 Introduction 44

4.1 Library Computerisation : A Historical Review 44

4.2 Library Computerisation : Main Methods 46

4.2.1 Categories of Library Softwares 47

4.2.2 Software Evaluation Characteristic 47

4.2.3 Indian Commercial Softwares 48

4.2.3.1 Use of Indian Commercial Softwares 48

4.2.3.1.1 e-Granthalaya 48

4.2.3.1.2 Librarian 49

4.2.3.1.3 Libsys 49

4.2.3.1.4 SLIM : Software for Library Information Management 49

4.2.3.1.5 SOUL : Software for University Library 49

4.2.4 International Library Softwares 50

4.2.4.1 Use of International Library Softwares 50

4.2.4.1.1 VTLS 50

4.2.4.1.2 CDS-ISIS, J-ISIS and ABCD 52

4.2.5 Library Computerisation with In-house Software 55

4.2.5.1 In-house Library Software Development Steps 55

4.2.5.2 Benefits in having in-house system 56

4.2.5.3 Difficulties in having In-house system 56

4.2.6 Process of Adopting Readymade Software. 57

4.2.6.1 Care to be taken while adopting external software 58

4.2.7 Library Computerisation with Open Source Softwares 60

4.2.7.1 Significance of having source code in O. S. Software 60

4.2.7.2 Open Source Library Softwares 61

4.2.7.2.1 Using Open Source Softwares 63

4.2.7.2.1.1 Using Koha Software 63

4.2.7.2.1.1.1. Koha Installation in Library 66

			4.2.7.2.1.2. NewGenLib	69
		4.2.7.3.	Use of cloud computing along with open source software	71
		4.2.7.4.	Service provider's Help in Adopting Koha (O. S.) Software	72
5	**Library Computerisation with Advanced Features (In Detail)**			**74**
	5.0	Introduction		74
	5.1	Computeried Acquisition		74
		5.1.0	Pre-Acquisition Information Service	75
		5.1.1	Significance of Acquisitions Policy	75
		5.1.2	Computerised Acquisitions	76
			5.1.2.1 Master Data Creation	76
			5.1.2.1.1 Master Data for Acquisition	77
		5.1.3	Handling Suggestions	77
			5.1.3.1 Online Suggestion Processing System	79
			5.1.3.2 Suggestion : Books on Approval Process	79
		5.1.4	Allocation of Budget	80
		5.1.5	Ordering	80
			5.1.5.1 Procurement Order	81
			5.1.5.2 Ordering Decision Making	81
			5.1.5.3 Ordering Conditions	82
			5.1.5.4 Book Approval Process	82
			5.1.5.4.1 Ordering Approval Books	83
			5.1.5.5 Direct Order Process	84
			5.1.5.6 Processing Donations / Gratis	84
			5.1.5.7 Reminders for Overdue Orders	85
			5.1.5.8 Cancellation of orders	85
		5.1.6	E-books Acquisition	85
			5.1.6.0 Introduction	85
			5.1.6.1 Definition of e-book	86
			5.1.6.2 Status of e-books Today	86
			5.1.6.3 Availability of scholarly titles as e-books	86
			5.1.6.4 e-book Formats	86
			5.1.6.5 E - Books Accessing Types	87
			5.1.6.6 E - Books Licensing	87
			5.1.6.7 E - books Available Offers for Library	88

5.1.6.8	E - Books Pricing Issues	88
5.1.6.9	Step to acquire e-books in library	88
5.1.7	Bill Processing	89
5.1.7.1	Accessioning of Books	90
5.1.7.1.1	Accessioning Process	90
5.1.7.2	Forwarding Bill for Payment	90
5.1.8	Advantage of Computerised Acquisition	90
5.1.9	Transferring Acquisition Data to TPS	91
5.1.10	E-bidding / E - procurement	91
5.1.10.1	Online purchasing of books	92
5.1.11	Acquisition Information services	94
5.2	Computerisation of Classification and Cataloguing	94
5.2.0	Introduction	94
5.2.1	Automation in Classification	95
5.2.1.1	Using Computer in Library Classification	95
5.2.1.2	Using Online Classification	96
5.2.1.2.1	Web Dewey 2. 0 (DDC - 23rd edition)	96
5.2.1.2.2	UDC Online	96
5.2.1.2.3	Online Library of Congress Scheme	97
5.2.1.3	Subject Heading Tools (LCSH, TEST, MESH, SHE and Sears List)	98
5.2.1.4	Experts/Intelligent Systems for Library Management	99
5.2.1.5	Colon Classification of S. R. Ranganathan	100
5.2.2	Computerised Cataloguing	100
5.2.2.1	Refining Entries as per AACR - II	101
5.2.2.1.1	Editing / Converting Book Data into MARC - 21 format	101
5.2.2.1.1.1	List of Important MARC – 21 Tags	101
5.2.2.2	Printing Catalogue Cards	104
5.2.2.3	Printing of Barcodes	104
5.2.2.4	Printing Spine Labels and Book Cards	104
5.2.2.5	Generating Online Computerised Catalogue	105
5.2.2.6	Cataloguing e-books and e-Journal	105
5.2.2.6.1	MARC Records Tags for e-books & e-Journals	106

5.2.3 Generating Computerised Accession Register 108
5.2.4 Uploauing / Integrating Book Data to Circulation 108
5.2.5 Collection Development of non Book Materials 109
5.3 Computerised Circulation System 109
5.3.0 Tasks Covered under Circulation System 109
5.3.1 Master Data in Circulation Section 110
5.3.1.1 Circulation Rules 110
5.3.2 Circulation Actions 111
5.3.2.1 Issue / Checkout of Library Material 111
5.3.2.2 Return / Check in 112
5.3.2.3 Reservation and Claims 113
5.3.2.3.1 Issuing e-Books 113
5.3.2.4 Circulation of Non Book Material 114
5.3.2.5 Overdue Charges / Fine Collection 115
5.3.2.6 No Dues Certificate 115
5.3.2.7 Tagging Book Status 116
5.3.2.8 Binding Process 116
5.3.2.9 Reminder and Messaging Systems 117
5.3.2.10 Book Bank and Study Room Collection 117
5.3.2.10.1 Study Room Collection 118
5.3.2.11 Reports and Statistics from Circulation Section 118
5.3.2.12 Advanced Circulation Automation Features 119
5.3.2.12.1 Instant Messaging Systems 119
5.3.2.12.2 Self Check Out and Online Renewal 119
5.3.2.12.3 Use of Biometric or Digital Signature Authentication 120
5.3.2.12.4 Providing Collection Location Features in OPAC 120
5.3.2.12.5 Virtual Browsing Systems 121
5.3.2.12.6 Library Physical Access Control System 121
5.4 Computerised Journals / Serial Management 122
5.4.0 Tasks Covered 122
5.4.1 Pre Subscription Information Services 122
5.4.1.1 Master Data Creation 123

5.4.1.2 Allocation of Budget 124

5.4.2 Menus in Journals Management (Serial's Control) 125

5.4.2.1 Handling Journal Subscription Suggestion 125

5.4.2.1.1 Journal Approval Process 125

5.4.2.1.2 Subscription and Renewal 125

5.4.2.2 Scheduling 126

5.4.2.2.1 Receiving / Recording Receipts of Issue 126

5.4.2.3 Sending Reminders for Non Receipt of Journal Issues 127

5.4.2.4 Journal Merger, Splitting and Discontinuation 127

5.4.2.5 Handling of Invoices 127

5.4.2.6 Binding Process 127

5.4.2.6.1 Preparing Sets for Binding 127

5.4.2.6.2 Generating Binding Work order 128

5.4.2.6.3 Receiving Bound Volumes 128

5.4.2.6.4 Payments 128

5.4.2.6.5 Accessioning, Classification and Cataloguing 128

5.4.2.6.6 Physical Verification of Bound Volumes 128

5.4.2.6.7 Updating Journal Holding Database 129

5.4.3 Subscription to E - Journals 129

5.4.3.1 Selecting E-Journal 129

5.4.3.2 E-Journal Subscribing and Renewal 129

5.4.3.3 License Agreement for E-Journals 130

5.4.3.4 Access Policy user Authentication and handling miss use 130

5.4.3.5 Downloading Journal Papers as per demand 130

5.4.3.6 E - Journals usage statistics 131

5.4.3.7 Advantages of Participating in Consortium 131

5.4.4 Circulation of Journal Issues and Bound Volumes 131

5.4.5 Information Services from Journal Management 131

5.4.5.1 Publishing Current list of Subscribed Journal 132

5.4.5.2 Publishing Updated Journal Holding Catalogue 132

5.4.5.3 Publishing Weekly Receipt of Journal Issues 132

5.4.5.4 Content page based SDI Services 132

5.4.5.5 RSS Feed Based Services: SDI Service 132

5.4.5.6 Information Service on Special Issues of Journals 133

	5.4.5.7 Providing Journal Union Catalogues	133
	5.4.6 Procuring Photocopies of Journal Papers	133
	5.4.7 Electronic Document Delivery Systems	134
	5.4.8 Resource Sharing of Journals	134
	5.4.9 Journal Management Reports and Statistics	134
5.5	Virtual Reference Service	135
	5.5.0 Introduction	135
	5.5.1 Virtual Reference Service: A Concept	135
	5.5.1.1 Software Tools used for Virtual Reference Services	136
	5.5.2 Virtual Reference Service Through Chat Server Websites	137
	5.5.2.1 Question Point Software-OCLC	137
5.6	Computerisation of Library Administrative Tasks	137
	5.6.1 Computerised Physical Verification	138
	5.6.2 Retrospective Conversion of Library Database	139
	5.6.2.1 Use of Online Tools for Retro Data Conversion	140
	5.6.3 Automating Librarian's Office	140
	5.6.4 Handling Multimedia, CD /DVD Collections of Accompanied CDS	142
	5.6.5 Digital Preservation of Library's Archival Material	142
	5.6.6 Other Administrative Tasks	143
5.7	Online Public Access Catalogue (OPAC)	143
	5.7.1 Need and Utility	143
	5.7.2 Types of OPAC	143
	5.7.3 Structure of OPAC	144
	5.7.4 Types of OPAC Searches	145
	5.7.4.1 Simple Search Method	145
	5.7.4.2 Advanced Search Method	146
	5.7.4.3 Using MARC Tags as Search Tool	147
	5.7.4.4 Facility to save OPAC Search	147
	5.7.5 OPAC for Searching Journals or Serials.	147
	5.7.6 OPAC Search for Non Book Non Print Materials	148
	5.7.7 Other Search Options in OPAC	148
	5.7.7.1 Increasing Quality of OPAC Search Retrieval	148
	5.7.8 Use of Z39. 50 Library Catalogue	149
	5.7.9 Collaborative Library OPAC	149

6 Management of Library Computerisation **150**

6.0 Introduction 150

6.1 Computerisation : Planning & Financial Management 150

6.1.1 Infrastructure Cost 151

6.1.2 Recurring Costs 151

6.1.3 Library System Development Cost 151

6.1.4 Financial Provisions: Income Generation 151

6.2 Manpower Needs, Planning and Utilization 152

6.3 Preparing Draft Proposal of Library Computerisation 154

6.4 Library Computerisation : Other administrative tasks 156

6.4.1 Designing Computer Network (LAN) Layout 156

6.4.2 Creating Inventory of Computer Hardware, Software and Peripherals 157

6.4.3 System's Security and Need of Uninterrupted Power Supply (UPS) 157

6.5 Use of Hardware and Software 158

6.5.1 Handling and use of Library Software 158

6.5.1.1 Handling Open Source LMS 159

6.5.1.2 Re-engineering Library Software 159

6.5.2 Management of Computer Hardware in Library 161

6.5.2.1 Use of Computer Hardware in Library 162

7 Introduction to BIBFRAME : The Future Cataloguing Standard **165**

7.0 Introduction 165

7.1 Historical Background of BIBFRAME 165

7.2 What is BIBFRAME Project ? 166

7.2.1 Think-tank behind BIBFRAME Concept 168

7.2.2 New Approach of BIBFRAME Project 169

7.2.3 Need of BIBFRAME 170

7.2.4 BIBFRAME - "The project Review" 170

7.2.5 Aim of BIBFRAME Project 171

7.3 Replacing Old MARC with Linked Data 171

7.3.1 Visualizing Bibliographic Data in Semantic Web 172

7.3.2 Significance of Linked Data in BIBFRAME 172

7.3.2.1 RDF Foundation 173

7.3.3 Inter linking Bibliographic Data 175

7.3.3.1 Interlinking Data : Graphical Mode 176

7.4	BIBFRAME Model	180
	7.4.1 BIBFRAME Organisation	181
7.5	How to BIBFRAME?	184
7.6	BIBFRAME Developments (Important milestones)	186
	7.6.1 BIBFRAME-Pilot	186
	7.6.2 BIBFRAME Vocabulary	187
	7.6.3 Zepheira	188
	7.6.3.1 Zepheira's Training Program	189
	7.6.4 LIB-HUB	189
	7.6.5 Linked data for Libraries (LD4L)	190
	7.6.6 BIBFLOW	190
7.7	Library Softwares Ready with BIBFRAME Structure	191
	7.7.1 What is Casalini's Share VDE (Virtual Discovery Environment) project?	191
7.8	How to get Involved in BIBFRAME Movement	192
8	**Migration of Library Management System-LMS Migration**	**195**
8.0	Introduction	195
	8.0.1 Migration of Library Management System: Concept and Nature	196
8.1	LMS Migration: Problem Examples	197
	8.1.1 Examples of Problems in Library Computerisation	197
8.2	Examples of LMS Migrations	199
8.3	Reasons behind LMS Migration	200
8.4	Data Conversion Issues in LMS Migration	200
	8.4.1 Data conversion case study in LMS Migration	201
	8.4.2 Use of UNESCO / ISIS Data Conversion Tools	203
	8.4.3 MARC-21 Editor	204
	8.4.4 Care and Precautions to be Taken for Data Conversion	204
8.5	Care and Precautions to Avoid LMS Migration Problems	205
8.6	Innovative Features of LMS – A Futuristic View	206
9	**Library Website Development : Techniques and Tools (HTML, CSS, Java Script, Ajax & PHP)**	**210**
9.0	Introduction	210
9.1	HTML Basic Programming Tool for Website Development	211
9.2	Cascading Style Sheet (CSS)	213

9.2.1 What is CSS? 213
9.2.2 Types of Style Sheets in CSS 214
9.2.2.1 Making Internal Style Sheet in CSS 214
9.2.2.2 Making External Style Sheet in CSS 214
9.2.2.3 Inline Style Sheet 215
9.2.3 CSS Syntax 216
9.2.4 Classes and ID's in CSS 216
9.2.5 CSS Comments 217
9.2.6 Setting Background Properties in CSS 217
9.2.7 Setting Background Image using CSS 218
9.2.8 CSS Setting 219
9.2.8.1 Setting Color Properties in CSS 219
9.2.8.2 Text Alignment Setting in CSS 220
9.2.8.3 Text Decorating Style 220
9.2.8.4 Letter Spacing Setting in CSS 220
9.2.9 Font of Letter Size Setting in CSS 220
9.2.10 Setting list Properties in CSS 221
9.2.11 Setting Border Properties in CSS 222
9.2.12 Setting Margin Properties in CSS 222
9.2.13 Setting Padding in CSS 223
9.2.14 Setting Outline Properties in CSS 223
9.2.15 Setting Table Properties in CSS 223
9.2.16 Setting Dimension in CSS 223
9.2.17 Setting Classification Properties in CSS 224
9.2.18 Setting Positioning Properties in CSS 224
9.2.19 Setting Pseudo Class in CSS 224
9.3 Java script 224
9.3.1 What is Java Script? 225
9.3.2 Difference between Java and Java Script 225
9.3.3 What can be Done with Java Script? 225
9.3.4 Introduction to Java Script 225
9.4 AJAX 227
9.4.1 How AJAX Works? 227
9.5 P.H.P (php) 227

9.5.1 What is php? 228

9.5.2 What we can do with php? 228

10 Content Management Systems (Joomla and Drupal) 230

10.0 Introduction 230

10.1 What is a Content Management System (CMS)? 230

10.2 Characteristics of Content Management System (CMS) 231

10.3 List of Available Content Management System 232

10.4 Joomla 232

10.4.1 Joomla Installation 233

10.4.2 Joomla Contents - Articles 234

10.4.3 Creating Sections in Joomla 234

10.4.4 Creating Categories in Joomla 234

10.4.5 Joomla Front Page Manager 235

10.4.6 How to Design and Customize your Website in Joomala 235

10.4.7 Plug-in, Modules and Templates in Joomla 235

10.5 Drupal 236

10.5.1 What we can do with Drupal? 236

10.5.2 Technical Features of Drupal. Following are the Technical Features of Drupal 237

10.5.3 Useful Available Sources for Drupal 237

10.5.4 Nodes and Taxonomy in Drupal 237

10.5.5 Experience of using Drupal 238

10.5.6 Advantages and Disadvantages in using Drupal 238

10.5.7 Drupal Installation Procedure 239

10.5.7.1 Drupal Modules 239

10.5.7.2 Drupal Nodes 240

10.5.7.3 Drupal Themes 240

10.5.8 Demos Available for Drupal 241

11 Development of Library Mobile Website : An Introduction 242

11.0 Introduction 242

11.1 Library Mobile Website Concepts 242

11.1.1 Development of Progress of Mobile Phone Technology 243

11.2 Development of Library Mobile Websites 243

11.3 Tips for Designing Mobile Library Websites 245

11.4 Examples of Contents Displayed on a Well Known Library Mobile Website 245

10.5 Guidelines for Developments of Library Mobile Website (Planning) 246

12 Use of Barcode and Scanning Technology in Library 248

12.1 Barcode Technology 248

12.1.1 Introduction 248

12.1.1.1 Barcode Technology : Background and Concept 248

12.1.1.2 Barcode Technology : Historical Background 249

12.1.2 Types of Barcodes Symbologies 250

12.1.3 Different Uses of Barcodes 251

12.1.4 Standardization in Barcode Technology 252

12.1.5 Use of Barcode Technology in Library Management 252

12.1.5.1 Advantages of Use of Bar-coding in Library 253

12.1.5.1.1 Significance of Types of Barcode Symbologies for Library Usage 253

12.1.5.2 Smart and Dumb Types of Barcodes 254

12.1.5.3 Where to Paste Barcodes on Books in the Library 255

12.1.5.4 Ways of Barcode Printing in Library 255

12.1.6 Barcode Readers / Scanners 256

12.1.7 Examples of Different Types of Barcodes 257

12.2 Scanning Technology 258

12.2.1 What is Scanning? 258

12.2.1.1 Layout / Design of a Scanner 259

12.2.2 Scanning Process 259

12.2.3 Scanning Resolution and Interpolation 260

12.2.4 Image Transfer Process 260

12.2.5 What is a Colour Scanner? 261

12.2.6 Types of Scanners 261

13 Networking Technology : Applications in Library Management 264

13.0 Introduction 264

13.1 Network - Concept & Objectives 264

13.2 Telecommunication Technology 266

13.2.1 Telecommunication and Networking 266

13.2.1.1 Telephone Network or Telephony 267

13.2.1.2 Telegraph Network 267

13.2.1.3 Telex Network 267

13.2.2 Telephone : Technical Background 267

13.2.2.1 Switching Systems 268

13.2.2.1.1 Switching Techniques 269

13.2.2.1.1.1. Message Switching Network 269

13. 2. 2.1.1.2. Packet Switching Network 270

13.3 Network 270

13.3.1 Networks Types 271

13.3.1.1 Computer Networks 271

13.3.1.2 Data Networks 272

13.3.2 Network Historical Background 272

13.3.2.1 Network Categories 273

13.3.2.1.1 Network Based on Usage 273

13.3.2.1.2 Network Based on Type of Users 273

13.3.2.1.3 Network Based on Topology (Geometric Design) 274

13.3.2.1.3.1. Simple Topology 274

13.3.2.1.3.2. Star Topology 274

13.3.2.1.3.3. Ring Topology 275

13.3.2.1.3.4. Distributed Bus Topology 275

13.3.2.1.3.5. Loop Topology 275

13.3.2.1.3.6. Tree Topology 276

13.3.2.1.3.7. Hybrid Topology 276

13.3.2.2 Network Based on Geographical Area 277

13.3.2.3 Network Based on Mode of Transmission 277

13.4 Information Networks 278

13.4.1 Bibliographic Information Network : Developmental Aspect 279

13.4.1.1 Development of International Databases 280

13.4.1.1.1 INIS Center in India 281

13.4.1.1.2 AGRIS center in India 281

13.4.1.1.3 Other International Information Networks 282

13.4.1.2 Information Service Networks in India 283

13.4.1.3 Integrated Services Digital Network 284

13.5 Library Networks 285

13.5.1 Library Network – Concept 285

13.5.1.1 Library Networks : Definitions 286

13.5.2 Library Networks: Background 287

13.5.2.1 History of Library Network Developments in India 288

13.5.3 Need and Objectives of Library Network 289

13.5.4 Library networks Types 290

13.5.4.1 Local Library Networks 290

13.5.4.1.1 DELNET (Developing Library Network) 290

13.5.4.1.2 CALIBNET 291

13.5.4.2 Regional Library Networks 292

13.5.4.2.1 INFLIBNET 292

13.5.4.3 Library Network Services 293

13.5.4.4 International Library Networks 294

13.5.5 Management of Library Network 295

13.5.5.1 Networks Management : Need of Human Resources 296

13.5.5.2 Adopting Network Topology 296

13.6 Collective Use of Library Resources Through Library Networking 297

13.6.1 Library Resource Sharing : Activities to Consider 298

13.6.1.1 Resource Sharing in Acquisition and Cataloguing 299

13.6.1.2 Exchange of Human Resources 300

13.6.1.3 Information Services & Database Development 300

13.6.1.4 Developing Specialized Book Collection 300

13.6.1.5 Developing Cooperative Warehouse Facility for Network 300

13.6.1.6 Inter Library Lending & Borrowing 300

13.6.1.7 Electronic Document Delivery System 301

13.7 Network Architecture 302

13.7.1 Introduction 302

13.7.2 Network Architecture: Protocol 303

13.7.3 Network Architecture: Objectives 303

13.7.4 Layered Network Architecture 303

13.7.4.1 Open System Inter Connection 304

13.7.4.2 OSI Reference Model 305

Index 306

Preface

I have great pleasure in presenting this book, "**Advances in Library Computerisation,**" to the readers. Library computerisation is the significant component of overall library automation project. Library computerisation needs to be completed first in all respects before library plans for taking up steps towards further automating library services. One may feel that automating library's housekeeping functions is a very easy task. Looking into the scenario with availability of readymade commercial softwares or so called LMSs one may say so. However, it is not at all an easy task. There are various ways and means to computerise a library. Despite all these means, it needs librarian's dedication and deep involvement in the entire process of library computerisation from planning to implementation. The librarian need not be a system designer or a programmer but the brain behind the entire process needs to be finally of the librarian and his staff, who are the actually end users of the system. Library computerisation concept has now been much stabilised, which goes through various stages. There is the need to have exact synchronisation between library's erstwhile manual but systematised functioning and with that of functions carried out with the help of computers. One therefore, needs adequate expertise and skills in achieving success in selecting a good LMS or making a dynamic library system.

This book would be more significant for the librarians and LIS professionals as it is based on the practical experience of computerisation of a large library like Central Library of IIT Bombay, gained by the author with his long association with it.

The book discusses, at length, computerisation using different ways and means e.g. by using in-house systems, by using available commercial softwares, or by using open source softwares like Koha. Now there is global trend of adopting Koha or other open source softwares. Koha being the standardised and internationally manufactured plus consistently updated LMS.

The book discusses computerisation of all library house keeping functions with special features in detail. The book also covers the process of migration of LMS if library decides to do so. It further discusses use of associated technologies like bar-coding & scanning technologies and networking. The library computerisation should always conclude with designing a library web based outlet viz. Library website, so this topic has been given good weightage in the book which explains the designing of library websites with formal programming techniques and tools as well as by using CMS (Content Management Systems) like Joomla and Drupal. The book has further introduced the concept of developing library mobile website. The book also covers the process of migration of LMS if library decides to do so. The book concludes topic of computerisation with the discussion on very latest topic on transforming library catalogues into future cataloguing format e.g. BIBFRAME (Bibliographic Framework) devised by LOC (Library of Congress) which is replacing an age old MARC data format by using Resource Description and Access(RDA) which is the revised version of AACR-2 style and by creating open linked data structures of the catalogue data using RDF (Resource Description Format). With this new format it would be possible to search library catalogue directly on the web, which had remained isolated only with the library and was away from web world before this.

Library computerisation forms one of the major parts of library automation project. As it becomes unwieldy to discuss the entire topic of library automation in a single book, for the convenience of readers, I have published a separate book on remaining aspects of library automation entitled "*Reinventing Libraries with Future Technologies*" (Ess Ess Publications, New Delhi, 2020) as a companion to this book ,which will be equally interesting to the readers of this book.

While accomplishing the task of writing of this book, I consider it my moral duty to express my gratitude to all those whose materials, mostly available in public domain has been referred or indirectly used in presenting review of use of future technology in future libraries. I am also grateful to the bloggers, professional home page owners ,authors of books, contributors of journal articles whose materials has been referred in terms of definitions, figures, tables or images with due acknowledgments. I am also grateful to Ms. Amber Billey the former Metadata Librarian at Columbia University Libraries, currently she is Systems and Meta Data Librarian at Bard College, Huston. While writing a chapter on BIBFRAME, I had mail correspondence with her and he got valuable explanation about the BIBFRAME project and its status at her place.

I would like express my gratitude towards Mr. Sumit Sethi, Chief Executive, Ess Ess Publications, New Delhi and thanks him and his team for enthusiastically considering the publishing this book at a short notice and extending all the cooperation in this regards. Thanks are also due to Mr. B P Juwale of Universal Prakashan, Pune for his cooperation and considerations.

I finally express my gratitude towards my family members for sacrificing their family life while I was busy in accomplishing the task of writing this book for the benefits of the readers.

I hope that the readers would appreciate the contents of this book ,read it patiently and look for more information on the themes. I further hope that the topics discussed in the book would help librarians, library professionals and LIS students to know the advances in library computerisation, they would try to adopt them and earn necessary expertise in it.

— Author

1
Information and Communication Technology (ICT)

1.0. INTRODUCTION

The present age is called an age of information technology rather the age of advanced information technology as information technology is at its much matured form than it was in first half of 21st Century. We are familiar with age old information technology. Information technology means converging effects of computer, telecommunication and internet technologies. Concept of information technology has always been expanding with time. This is because of fast developments and progress in technologies involved in it. In this chapter we are going to understand this broad concept. In short it is ICT i. e. Information and Communication Technology. Today ICT is in use in almost every field. ICT mainly relates to handling of information. With ICT technology it has become easy for everyone to handle information. ICT has gifted us many levels, systems and means to handle the information. In various ICT applications there has been emphasis on use of computer and telecommunication technologies in information handling. Present chapter intends to elaborate on what is ICT? And what are advanced means to use ICT.

1. 1. WHAT IS ICT ?

In short, ICT is a process of collective use of broader or comprehensive form of Information Technology. The term ICT is used many times synonymously with IT or Information technology. It is difficult to define ICT at any particular moment accurately as concepts, systems or technologies involved in it have been constantly evolving. ICT is a system or method of handling information due to which tasks such as storing information in digital or electronic format, to retrieve it or make changes in it, make it to flow or to obtain it are involved. ICT relates to processes such as storing data in digital format (parts of information), retrieve it, reformat it, communicate it or obtain it in a desired format. Computer and communication accessories and software are used for these processes. Information relates to flow of knowledge where as ICT relates to use of computer, telecommunication and internet technology tools in handling information. Information and

Communication Technology, in short ICT is collective effect of all the above processes in which information is obtained by use of information and communication technologies. In recent decades ICT has provided, in various ways, information communication capabilities for our society. For example, today any individual in present moment(real time) can exchange information, data or voice with other individual from any corner of the world through use of communication media. They can always keep in touch with each other by making use of modern concepts and technologies like instant messaging, voice over I. P., voice and video conferencing, social networking tools like Facebook. In the era of modern information and communication the world has come closer to form a global village, in which although the individuals are far away from each other but feel like as close as neighbours.

1.2. TECHNOLOGIES PARTICIPATING IN ICT

In ICT or Information and communication technology various technologies and techniques work together or they form a cohesive group. For example :

1. Computer Technology
2. Information Technology-Internet Technology
3. Telecommunication Technology
4. Mass media and Supportive Technologies.

ICT involved technologies provide us with various tools and means to handle information. Having ICT following things become possible :

a. To convert information into digital format. It has also become possible to convert printed text into digital form.

b. ICT makes it possible to obtain information online.

c. ICT facilitates networking of resources and use them co-operatively.

d. ICT makes us to improve quality in information handling techniques, which has facilitated increase in demand of fast and quality information retrieval.

1.3. INTRODUCTION TO TECHNOLOGIES INVOLVED IN ICT

1.3.1. Computer Technology

Computer is an electronic machine which receives information, processes it systematically and scientifically, preserves it and disseminates it when required in a desired manner and format. As compared to a human computer works faster, with at most accuracy and it never tires. However, it does not work on its own and it needs set of instructions i.e. programmes to process the given information. Computer machinery and its accessories are divided into two main groups such as :

Computer Hardware: Physically seen parts of computer

Computer Software : Intellectual part of computer.

Technically computer contains the following parts :

- Input devices

- Processing and memory devices
- Storage devices
- Output devices

Based on these parts of computer and accessories can be tabulated as shown below tables from table No - 1. 1 to 1. 9:

1.3.1.1. Parts of Computers of Accessories

A. Table of Computer Accessories

1. Input devices	Key Board, Mouse, Monitor screen, Scanner, Optical scanner, voice or optical recognition devices, laser scanner, RFID reader, smart card reader, quick response codes/ barcodes, digitizers etc.
2. Output Devices	Monitor or screen, Printers, (Dot Matrix, Inkjet and laser printers and plotters), barcode printers, voice and music synthesizes, FTP, e-Mail, Voices Mail, ROM, Worm and rewritable devices etc.
3. Storage Devices	Hard disc HDD, Diskette, Main drive, CD, DVD/CD network, magnetic disc, pen drive etc.

Table 1.1

B. Parts of Computers

Main parts of Computer	• Input and output • CPU Central Processing Unit • Storage
Parts of CPU	• Control Unit • Arithmetic or Logic unit

Table 1.2

C. Bit and Bytes

Bit	• Bit or Binary Digit Means 0 or 1
Bytes	• Byte (Binary) Contains more than one bit 4 Bits, 8 Bits, 16 Bits 32 Bits etc.

Table 1. 3

Binary Storage Units	
1 Kilo Byte	1024 Bytes
1 Mega Byte	1024 Kilo Bytes
1 Giga Byte	1024 Mega bytes
1 Tera Byte	1024 Giga bytes

Table 1. 4

D. Computer Peripherals

Ports	Parallel ports, Serial ports
Drives	CD / Video Drive, USB Drive, Pen Drive or other accessories Modem, LAN Cards etc.

Table 1. 5

E. Computer Languages.

Computer System Languages	Machine Language Assembly Language Higher Level Language
Old Languages	Basic, Cobol, Pascal, Fortran etc.
Web Based	C+, C++, Java, VB++, Perl, Oracle etc.
Languages of Internet	Hyper Text Markup Language HTML, SGML, JAVA, XML, PHP etc.

Table 1. 6

F. Computer Softwares

1. Operating Systems	• DOS (Disc Operating System) • Windows, Unix, • Open Source Software • Cent OS, Linux
2. Application Softwares	• SOUL, Koha, Tally etc.
3. Computer Utilities	Windows : Word, Excel, Access, Power Point, Outlook , Page Maker, Linux - Open office etc.

Table 1. 7

G. Types of Computers

Main Types of Computers	Digital and Analogue Computer
Capacity Based Computers	Main Frame, Micro, Personal
Depending on Usage	Desk Top, Palm Top, LAP Top, Tablet, IPOD etc.

Table 1.8

H. Computer Generation

Generation	Period	Technology
First Generation	1940 - 1959	Vacuum tubes
Second Generation	1959 - 1965	Transistors
Third Generation	1965 - 1971	Integrated Circuit
Fourth Generation	1971 - 1980	Very Large Integrated Circuits (VLSI)
Fifth Generation	1980 - on wards	Ultra Large Scale Integration

Table 1.9

I. Computer : Internal Hardware

Computer hardware and accessories which are physically seen and computer software is the intellectual part, in which operating systems or systems software are incorporated. Computer hardware accessories are generally not changed but application software keeps on changing or updating which makes necessary to upgrade the computer hardware. Normally computer main hardware parts remain the same in all types of computer, whether it is main frame or personal, only it differs in size, capacities and speed, one can name such accessories as :

- Power Supply(CMOS)
- CPU Cooling fan
- CD - DVD Drives
- Hard disc-HDD
- Graphic Card
- AGP, BUS, PCI, Buses and
- Mother Board

Now let us understand a bit about the Mother Board.

1.3.1.2. Mother Board

Mother Board is a computer's main unit. This is a Central Circuit Board in which complicated electronic devices are connected to Mother board, provides power to all parts of computer which makes these parts interfaced with each other and communicate. Inside mother board consists of

CPU Random Assess Memory (RAM) device, firm wares / External buses. Let us know about some other main parts of computer.

1.3.1.3. Central Processing Unit

Central Processing Unit or in short CPU which is also called as just processor. CPU is considered to be brain of the computer. It does four tasks such as :

- To Search (Fetch)
- Decode
- Execute and again
- Store or write back

During CPU operation, Arithmetic Logic Unit (ALU) and Floating Point Unit (FPU) are connected to each other which perform the desired function and finally result is given and displayed.

1.3.1.4. Random Access Memory or RAM

RAM is connected into mother board. In RAM, instructions are carried out and results are displayed. However unless the work is saved, if electricity is disconnected then the data in RAM vanishes and work done in RAM is lost.

1.3.1.5. Firmware

Firmware is a device in which computer's operating system is stored. It is connected to basic input output (BIOS) device. The contents of this information although are of software type but are stored in the hardware.

1.3.1.6. Removable / Moveable Media Devices

In a computer along with permanent type of accessories there are some devices which are of removable, that is replaceable type. i. e. CD & DVD drives. Today CD and DVD are of same size. Nowadays floppy like devices are no longer in use and have become obsolete. Instead of this, 3. 5 inch size diskettes are in use. They would also become obsolete soon.

1.3.1.7. Internal Storage

Data is stored in computer into internal storage, which is in Read Only Memory (ROM) form and it remains there with internal storage. There are various form or types of internal backup storage devices.

Hard Disk : HDD or Hard Drive stores data permanently. Data is recorded on revolving plates mounted on magnetic platform. Nowadays every type of computer contains HDD. A normal good desktop type of computer comes with hard disc having capacity of 120 to 400 G. B. (Gigabytes). In this type of hard disk, speed of revolving plates is 7200 RPM and with this speed data transfer speed is about 1 GBPS on higher. The data in HDD is retrieved through various buses in which contains serial and parallel bus / ports.

In computers other than above data storing devices there are various other devices called peripheral devices, among them are buses/slots like PCI, PCI Express, AGP, PPMCIA, etc.

Various Cards : Computer also contain other certain type of cards to provide specific capabilities like colour, sound, networking etc, and they are named as Video cards, Sound cards, Graphic cards, Network or LAN Cards.

1.3.1.8. External Connectivity

Computer can be connected to get information or data from external sources called USB (Universal Serial Bus), Fire Wire (For getting high speed Communication) PS - 2 keyboard or MIC Connecting parts, Sockets. In addition to CDs and DVDs there are booting devices. Booting devices are stored in computer memory however, if there is booting problem then the booting or start up signals are fed through external CDs / DVDs or accessed online through internet.

1.3.2. What is Information Technology?

In Information Technology, the Internet technology is the main technology which works on computer platform. Internet technology was invented by Tim Berners-Lee at ARPANET. Internet technology involves a computer with information source is called a server. The computer through which the information from server is accessed is called a client. Client is connected to server through communication media e. g. mostly telecommunication network. This way the information flows from server to client and to information seeker / end user.

1.3.2.1. Introduction to Internet

Internet works on client / server protocol. A Computer in which TCP / IP (Transmission Control Protocol / Internet protocol) is installed / configured can get connectivity to internet. When we try to know more on internet then we come across the term e. g. domain and specifically www or World Wide Web domain. In internet most of the time we try to browse internet pages and each address begins with www. However all such pages are governed by another protocol named http i. e. hyper text transmission protocol which means web pages are written in hypertext language. The well known among these languages is HTML – Hyper Text Mark-up Language. Hyper text is a technique which facilitates to write a word in hyper texted form to provide a link on front page to next page. The main technology in Internet pertains to web pages written in html or any hyper text mark up language. The Internet is therefore nothing but collection of web pages written in html on similar language. Each of these webpage has a unique web page address or called Universal Resource Locator (URL) and they exist independently on the internet. Through hyper texted words or links they are connected with each other. A group of web pages is called a Home page.

All web pages need to be uploaded on the internet in order to make them available worldwide. Internet Service Providers provide space to upload the web pages which requires fees. Once web pages or home page are uploaded it gets a domain name, which is normally seen in the web address.

Address of any web page has a specific structure i. e. www. amazon. com where amazon is a domain name provided by service provider. Web page once uploaded on internet is available for browsing in the entire world.

The internet in a broader sense is no doubt a collection of web pages but the significant part of Inte.net Technology is that it provides platform, which facilities to have access to various types of online resources such as e-Journals, e-Books, e-Data bases, e – Dictionaries etc.

1.3.2.2. Internet Connectivity

By just having a computer one cannot access the internet or Intranet or internet based e–resources. Computer needs first to be enabled by having TCP / IP protocol configured in it and by having internet connection. There are various ways to get internet connectivity such as :

1. **PC + Modem + Telephone line/ Telephone Broadband Connection
2. *PC + LAN Card + Internet cable
3. Lap top + Wireless software

   *PC and WIFI connectivity

   ** PC with TCP / IP

1.3.2.3. Internet, Intranet and Extranet

When we refer to internet terminology we come across terms with similar sound such as Intranet. Intranet also works on Internet technology. In an institution, information is distributed within the organisational geographic limit. It is done by using same internet technology. Such network is protected from outside world by a firewall security. In Intranet web pages are accessed in a same way as it is done for web pages but they are not uploaded on Internet so they are not accessible through Internet. Intranet pages could be accessed form outside but through a secured authentication (Login, password) and the technology is known by the term "Extranet". Intranet web page address does not start with 'www' domain words and the address begins with just http://e. g. http //etd. iitb. ac. in

So this is the difference among the terms Internet, Intranet or Extranet.

1.3.3. Telecommunication

Telecommunication Technology made its beginning with invention of telephony or telephone technology. This technology made speedy progress. Initially it was limited only for voice communication having manual exchange or with basic PABX System, then came switching system, electronic exchange and finally now we have packet switched switching system. Now in addition to voice transmission telephone technology is able to transmit digital data, video signal, and animation data also which has facilitated further to emergence of networking technology. Now each and every piece of data is carried forward and delivered without any leakage. With networking, now two computers can talk with each other using machine readable data. Networking capabilities of telecommunication has further facilitated to provide conducive situation to develop internet technology. Now various online information resources are available from commercial publishers through dedicated networks. Telecommunication remains a very vital media in the flow of information on Internet. People can communicate with each other via e - Mail, Video/Tele conferencing. Now information especially research type data is exchanged between individuals and institution beyond boundaries of nations worldwide. The telecommunication technology therefore forms the main support in ICT.

1.3.4. Mass Media and Supportive Technologies in ICT

Satellite Technology, Television Technology and all the media technologies plays a very good supportive role in making ICT a success. Geo Stationary Satellites receive signals from the base station and broadcast it back to earth to cover far more geographic area. These technologies are also parts of telecommunication, help to gather data which are useful for defence, environment, weather forecasting and also for spying or vigilance purpose. Now television technology provides television programmes Direct to Home (D2H) system from communication satellites in a digital form, which marks the success and progress of advanced telecommunication systems.

In ICT, other technologies are also in use as supportive technologies such as :

- Multimedia
- Barcode Technology
- LASER Technology
- Biometric and RFID Technology

1.4. Application of ICT Technology

There are two main applications of Information and Communication Technology e. g. :

1. Traditional Computer Based Tools.
2. Special application ICT.

Now let us elaborate these further.

1.4.1. Use of Traditional Computer Tools

In use of traditional based applications of ICT includes all those actions we performs with our personal computers, which are called data processing type of utilities. Windows platform has gifted us many such utilities, for example :

Word processing : By using this utility, we can prepare documents using Microsoft Word such as writing letters, preparing reports and presenting text in a desired presentable form.

Access : This utility is similar to converting text into data base.

Excel or Spread sheets : By using M. S. Microsoft excel utility, one can tabulate various types of data and analyse it and finally provide the results. Economical, financial analysis, preparing forecasting models, are feasible with this utility.

Presentation Utilities : Microsoft has helped us with various presentation aids to make the preparations meaningful and effective. They include power point and slides. In power points, information is presented in concise form on wide screen with the help of LCD projectors. With the use of Internet Technology online lectures webinars have become more attractive technique in e-learning educational programmes. This has largely helped in development of educational technology.

Desktop Publishing or e-Publishing : Generally it is called D. T. P. This technology has further becomes advanced with the use of other tools such as Adobe, In design, Quark Express as well as Microsoft publishing tools. Now it is possible to publish a newsletters, blogs or even scholarly e-Journals. With this appropriate technology it has become possible to bring out an Open Access Journal by an individual or institution (in house journals) very easily.

Graphic Software : Under these utilities like Adobe Photoshop Illustrator are used especially to handle image or pictorial data making logos, drawings pictures, figures. It has become easy and it further supports to e-Publishing.

Database software : With oracle, SQL servers one can handle data from databases with query utility very effectively to get desired output. Now a days open access software and servers (Apache) are also available to handle the databases, which are available online on internet.

Digitization Software : With development of digitization techniques it has made possible to digitize or convert printed page first into an image and further to a fully digitised page with Optical Character Recognition (OCR) technique. Finally this technology leads to preparing e-book. Audio files or musical data can also be converted into digital form. Geographic or spatial data can also be digitized using GIS (Geographical Information Systems).

1.4.2. Special Applications of ICT Technology

In special Application of ICT technology it includes development of special software keeping specific functions or purpose in mind, such as banking, railway / air reservation systems etc. Tally like packages are largely used for purpose of accounting, revenue, sales, purchase and management of pay roles. There are softwares to handle educational systems like admission, examination, process of conducting online exams and arranging the results. This group include mostly various packages such as.

- AutoCAD- Civil / Landscape and Architectural Designing
- Computer Aided Design (CAD), Designing simulation models
- Consumer selection management
- Data mining softwares are used to carry out market research and provide business forecasting input for commercial companies to attract customers effectively in a competitive environment.
- Application software such as SOUL or Koha are used for automating library functions which are also grouped in the special applications of ICT category. Open source softwares are found economical for libraries.

Artificial Intelligence : For higher level programming special software techniques are used to automate real life like situation. Attempts are also made to replicate human brain or to design a robot to perform various human related task such as help physically or psychologically disabled or aged people like care taker or an assistant.

e-Commerce / e-Governance : Packages under this category are used for ebanking or internet banking, online purchases, ATM Banking and for getting routine certificates from e-Governance kiosks which fall under special applications of ICT Technology.

1.4.3. Networking / Networks

In Information and Communication Technology information handling process includes sharing of data from local computer. Nowadays with the use of telecommunication media data is retrieved from computer located anywhere in the world. This process is carried out under networking environment. Networking Technology is difficult to understand as it contains complicated digital communication devices and circuits plus the networking software. However, using networking facilities is much convenient. Various types of networks are used for different purposes i. e. telephone network, banking network, television network, e-Mail network, mobile network and library network. All these types of networks are a part of our daily life. Networks are broadly grouped into two types.

LAN - Local Area Networks

WAN - Wide Area Networks or regional or international networks.

MAN - Metropolitan Area Network

1.5. UNDERSTANDING DATA AND INFORMATION

While learning about ICT it is interesting to clear our ideas about Data and Information. So let us understand them.

Data : Data is a raw or unorganised fact, that needs to be processed. It could be simple and random unless and until it is organised. Data are simply facts and figures. A bit of information is not information by itself. When it is processed, interpreted, organised, structured or presented in a desired manner so to make it meaningful or useful, which is finally the information. Information provides the context for data.

Data, original word comes from similar Latin word "Datum" which means something is given. It's usage is known since 1600s. Over the time data has become the plural of word datum.

Information : When given data is organised, processed and structured or presented in a expected manner, it becomes a meaningful information. Information is an older word and its origin is seen in 1300s. It relates to old French and Middle English in its origin. It is always referred to as the act of informing.

Examples

Data : Each student's test score is one piece of data.

Information : The average score of a class or of the entire school is information that can be derived from the given data.

- The history of temperature reading all over the globe for the last 100 years is data. If this whole data is organised and analysed to find that how global temperature is raising then it is information.

1.6. DATA AND INFORMATION

The number of visitors to a website of any particular international university is an example of data. Finding out from which country the students are more visiting to the website shows the interest of that country's students. Data is used as input for computer system, Information is output of data.

- Data is unprocessed facts & figures. Information is processed data.
- Data does not depend on information but information depends on data.
- Data is not specific but information is specific.
- Data is a single unit. A group of data entries is a data base which can provide news or meaning and is called information.
- Data does not carry meaning. Information must carry a logical meaning.
- Data is the raw material. Information is the product.

Information

- Information is the knowledge communicated or received concerning to a particular fact or circumstance. Information is a sequence of symbols that can be interpreted as message. It provides knowledge or insight about a certain matter. Information can be recorded as signs or transmitted as signals.

  Data is collected for various purposes i. e. for :
- Planning
- Recording
- Controlling
- Measuring
- Reporting
- Research
- For decision making to give strategic information
  - Tactical information
  - Operational information

  Data could be in the form of
  - Words or characters or text
  - Numerals or alphanumeric
  - Symbols, Images, Figures or animation
  - Sound, tone or voices. Data also relate with transactions or events of any item like maintaining of bank account or result of students etc.

1.7. INFORMATION RESOURCES IN ICT

There are broadly two types of resources such as :

1. Digital type of resources/databases : Websites, blogs, portals, Internet based resources such as :

- e-Resources, e-Journals
- e-Books, e-Databases
- Computerised catalogue of books in library, so also MARC database in LMS
- Open Linked Database

2. Open Access e–Resources e - journals and e - archives : However, printed books, journals, news papers, encyclopedias, reference sources, library's catalogue do not form the part of ICT. One can confine resources in ICT in the digital form only. Nowadays library functions are carried out with the use of ICT technology. If we review library functioning today then following resources would be considered in ICT.

- Library's e-books and e-Journals, Data base of library users etc.
- Transaction data of issue and return.
- Library employee's data base and database of dead stock items / furniture, library blog, library websites and digital library.

1.8. INFORMATION SYSTEM IN ICT

Various information systems are involved in ICT. Significance of any information system is that which type of data it handles or for which purpose it is used.

However, let us try to understand what information system is.

1.8.1. What is Information System?

An information system (IS) is a system composed of people and computers that process and interpret information. The term is sometimes used with restricted sense to only software used to computerise database or to only computer system / hardware.

An information system refer to collection of multiple pieces of equipment involved in dissemination of information, hardware, software, computer system connections, information system users and system's housing which are all parts of information system.

Information System many a times refers to a basic computer system but can also be described as a telephone switching system or environmental controlling system. Information system involves resources shared or processed information as well as people who manage the system. People are also considered part of system because without them system would not operate correctly.

Information system means Information + Communication Technology + Internet Technology and people / institutions who are responsible for a particular process and who take part in decision process. Information system involves tasks such as procuring data, filtering it, processing it, creating new data and presenting if finally.

There are various types of information systems depending on needs for which they are devised. An operation support system, such as transaction processing system which converts business data into valuable information. Similarly, management information system uses database information to output reports, helping users and business to make decisions based on extracted data. Information systems are specifically created to handle information for various fields such as :

Education : Information relating to students admission, educational programmes, exams results, quality analysis and information services to concerned people.

Business : Information about purchase, sales, profit, company management demand and supply, customer relation services.

Management : Information pertaining to company organisation, track record, reputation, employee data and information from corporate sector.

Any information system generally involves following parts :

1. Data or data bases
2. Hardware
3. Software
4. Employee
5. Guidelines and policies
6. Networks

1.8.2. Types of information systems

There are general types of information system. For example

Database Management Systems (DBMS) : It is a combination of data and software that makes it possible to organise and analyse data. DBMS Software is typically not designed to work with specific organisation or a specific type of analysis. It is a general purpose information system or software.

Electronic Spread sheet : It is also an another type of general information system or tool for basic data analysis based on formulas that define relationship among the data.

Special types of information system : In comparison to the above referred, there are a number of specialised information systems those which have been specially designed to support a specific process within an organisation or to carry out very specific analysis. Example:

Enterprise Resource Planning : Used to integrate the management of all internal and external information in an entire organisation.

Geographic Information System : Used to manage and analyse all types of geographical data.

Expert Systems : Expert systems is an artificial intelligence programme that has expert level knowledge about a particular domain and knows how to use its knowledge to respond properly.

Systems in Management : In management itself there are various streams of Information systems such as:

- Management Information Systems (MIS)
- Transaction Processing Systems (TPS)
- Decision Support Systems (DSS)
- Executive Information System (EIS)
- Knowledge Management Systems (KMS)

1.9. Types of information sources

We all generally know that there are three distinct types of information sources :

- Primary sources
- Secondary Sources
- Tertiary Sources

Many a times people confuse with their meanings . Let us understand them here.

1.9.1. Primary sources

Primary sources facilitate researcher to get as close to the original ideas, events and empirical studies as possible.

Such sources include the first hand exposure of creative ideas, first hand contemporary account of events, publication of the results of empirical observations or studies and items of research to form base for further research.

Examples :

- Novels, Plays, Poems, Arts Works, popular culture
- Diaries, narratives
- Autobiographies, Memoirs and speeches
- Govt. documents
- Patents
- Data sets, technical reports, experimental research results.

1.9.2. Secondary Sources

In secondary sources information is analysed, which is available from primary source or from another secondary sources. Even information source presenting facts or description of event is also a secondary source unless it is based on direct participation or observation. Many a times secondary source often rely on another secondary source and to reach the result they provide the principle source or analysis of primary source.

Examples :

- Biographies
- Review articles and literature review

- Scholarly articles that don't present any new experimental results, else it goes to primary category
- Historical Studies.

1.9.3. Tertiary sources

Tertiary sources provide overview of topics by synthesizing information collected from other sources. Tertiary sources often provide data in a convenient form and give the information in the context with the need to interpret it.

Examples :

- Encyclopedias
- Data books
- Chronologies
- Almanacs
- Text books

1.10. INFORMATION CREATION AND FLOW OF INFORMATION

It is rational that any individual or organisation must get right information at right time required to make right decision. It is also a fact that information can be created formally (connected) or informally (disconnected). It however lives within intellectual property (IP) and intellectual capacity (IC) of an individual. Information is evaluated in terms of three criteria :

- Relevance to end user.
- Impact on organisation
- Proximity to end user

Information life cycle is presented in the following points :

(A) How information is generated

Following table reveals how information is created and distributed (Table 1.9).

Process	Responsiblitity	Documents
Ideas generated Ideas studied and preliminary results presented to colleagues	Individuals, Authors, Scholars Information generated by a group of individuals in a formal organization or an informal community for the purpose of exchanging information and furthering the profession or trade.	Diaries Interviews Journals, Web Sites, Conference presentations
Ideas strengthened by research results and more widely reported to	Scholarly, or peer reviewed information shared with interested researchers or scholars for the	Journals, Books Dissertations

research community	purpose of exchanging research results and conclusions.	
Research reported to general public Implication of research integrated into public policy	Information produced for a general, mass reading audience Information generated by federal, state, or local governments for the purpose of keeping records, statistics and informing the public on government activities and policy.	Public Opinion Polls Government Documents Statistics Collections
Research synthesized and summarized, placed in larger cont xt within discipline subject area	Information compiled by staff writers and / or experts in a field of study, synthesizing history and trends; written for interested readers, usually non experts.	Encyclopedias, Handbooks

Table 1.9. Courtsey : Information Life Cycle by Scott & Ion

(B) How the information is delivered.

- One to many
- White paper presentation through website
- Frequently Asked Questions (FAQ)
- Subject websites or portals website
- Through website directed links sent via e - mail
- Application based delivery via managed expert systems
- One to one presentation
  - — word of mouth
  - — ad-hoc communication

(C) Types of information Created

- Tacit (Created and Stored Informally) remains with individual
- Human memory
- Local hard drive of computer
- Expert system (Moving tacit information into formalised structure)
- Explicit (Created and sorted formally) sharable information
- Network shared
- Network website / Intranet
- Informal Knowledge Management system.

- Document management system.
- Formal KM system

(D) Value of information source

- Age of information
- Proximity of information to its consumer.

(E) Stages of Information Creation

- Gain or achievements of ideas i. e. original information

— Input — Processing
— Storage — Retrieval
— Documentation — Data communication & Publication

1.11. QUALITY OF INFORMATION

Quality of information gazed on the fact that how much extent it impacts the decision making. Characteristics of quality of information are :

— Timeliness — Relevance
— Accuracy — Completeness
— Coherent — Format
— Accessibility — Compatibility
— Context — Expectations
— Security — Validity

Quality of information also depends on the following factors :

— Utility — Satisfaction
— Error — Bias

CONCLUSION

Information and Communication Technology or in short ICT is a very vast topic and consigning it in one chapter is just impossible. However, author has tried to cover it right from concept to its applications but in a hurried manner as he assumes that the readers are somewhat familiar with various terms discussed in the chapter. His purpose here is to just brush-up their old knowledge , add some facts in it and take to higher level of understanding. He further points out that the concepts here in abstract form are going to be discussed in full length in the subsequent chapters and feels that readers would bear with him.

REFERENCE

- Information Life Cycle by – Scott, Andersen and Ion Mandich: Microsoft Corporation, March 2007 (Accessed on 9th March 2016)

2
Library Computerisation : Concept, Need and Background

2.0. INTRODUCTION

Library Computerisation once upon a time was the buzz word of library world. However, basic computerisation has remained now of not much significance or relevant as libraries at least at international level are certainly looking forward beyond just computerisation. Any library develops or progresses further as new techniques of Information Technology are used in its functioning and services. Libraries abroad are in the state of well developed, as a lot of research and experimentation goes on constantly. It is observed that modern techniques and tools like Web 2. 0 are even being used in public libraries in USA. In contrast the situation in developing countries like ours is really alarming, as the progress in computerisation of various libraries is not at all a bright or encouraging and a lot needs to be done. Considering this situation it was felt that basic library computerisation has still good relevance to libraries in the developing countries , hence the chapter in this book.

2.1. LIBRARY COMPUTERISATION: A CONCEPT :

There are various assumptions among the librarians in India about - Library computerisation stages such as:

Examples 1 : Some people say that they have computer in their library used for word processing or doing correspondence, so our library is computerised;

Example 2 : Some other librarians have prepared book lists in access or excel and used them for issuing of books. They say we have computerised our library.

Example 3 : One library has bought as substandard (which does not have any future) software, they have created book and patron masters and it provides facilities of issue and return so they also say that their library is computerised;

Example 4 : Another library have scanned book chapters and saved files in folders of a PC or other library has provided internet access to readers and even they say we have computerised our library.

All above examples do show that there have been some attempts in the direction of computerisation but they are not permanent or long lasting scenarios or systematic efforts. Secondly, we may not find computerised catalogue (OPAC) in libraries for the readers, so their efforts fail to claim about library computerisation None of these libraries could be called a computerised library. In the true sense, concept of library computerisation refers to one, where most of library functions are carried out with the help of a standard computer software. Their routine or functions of housekeeping nature should be done in a computerised manner with a software. Functions or tasks of routine or of housekeeping nature include tasks like :

- Acquisitions
- Classification
- Cataloguing
- Circulation
- Serials or Journals Management
- OPAC
- Readers services

We are therefore, going to deal with the above true concept of Library Computerisation, in this chapter.

2.2. LIBRARY COMPUTERISATION: BACKGROUND AND NEED : A COMPARATIVE REVIEW

When we try to look at this aspect we need to pay attention to see what has happened in the outside world. We hear about globalisation, about competitions in world market and about progress and developments in developed countries and we read discussions in news papers and in mass media, radio, TV about it. When we consider these developments elsewhere we try to convince ourselves about how scientific, political and technological (IT) world has changed. The changes we see and read about them have been largely influenced in developing countries by use of Information Technology along with computer technology due to effective use of IT in industry, education, commerce, science and technology, in applied research and to some extent in social and political communications. In comparison to world progress and development we certainly realise that our country is really lagging behind and feel that we should also adopt the same path of development. We know that whenever we adopt any technology we have to pay for it. If we decide to use Information and Communication Technology (ICT) we need to provide a considerable amount for it and even if we do so we cannot directly measure the benefits of it in terms of money, still we need to spend for research and development. Benefits are assured but they are always notional. We can call it as National or world Benefits.

The emphasis of core aspect of modernisation is to computerise most of manual tasks or do them with computers although purpose here is to get the tasks done by computers which were performed by humans. We must accept that it is a universal fact that machines cannot replace humans entirely but computer pays a supportive role with humans.

In the beginning of 70s western countries started using computers in almost all fields. In India too, computers arrived in 1972 with the initiatives of Mr. Rajeev Gandhi, the then Prime Minister of India. Then onwards we saw developments on all fronts such as invention of super computers, proliferation of computers in various fields, research in software development etc. Today we have the strongest manpower in software development and we are now exporting softwares even to developed countries. There is equal progress seen in environmental science, nuclear power generation for civil purpose, space research Mangal Yan Mission of ISRO, research in CSIR, and defence labs. This was possible due to effective use of ICT by all these organisations. This progress followed with the beginning of use of information technology in other fields and applications like railways, air transport, and industry. Subsequently we noticed in use of personal computers, which have become almost part and parcel of our daily life. Due to availability cheap and efficient computer promoted automated manufacturing in India, which has created a sort of competition in adopting computerisation in almost all fields. The progress in Indian telephone industry has provided a supportive and conducive atmosphere for these developments.

Library and information field however, did not adopt computerisation up to the level of expectations. No doubt libraries attached to R & D organisations, national institutes, national labs and a few large university libraries are playing supportive role in the success of respective institutes or organisations. However, many small, medium size libraries and a considerable number of university libraries are yet to undertake computerisation in their libraries. This situation was mainly because of non availability of standard software, inadequate knowledge of computer technology and expertise with librarians and at the same time due to negligence of parental institutions about modernising their libraries. In recent years NAAC (National Assessment and Accreditation Council) and AICTE, the respective committees to evaluate academic and professional institutes performance in India, are recommending institutions to computerise their libraries with a view to enhance library service to the readers, which has helped to start computerisation process - However, these committees check only minimum level of use of computers in libraries and as such librarians too take few efforts in this direction. They do something to show that they have made the beginning. However, this stage does not improve any further and it remains the state of art for a number of years. This shows that most of the academic and professional institutes attached libraries are not seriously concentrating on true efforts of computerisation and improve services to their readers. There is a great need of computerisation in these libraries. In India public or school libraries concepts are yet to be emerged.

2.3. ROLE OF LIBRARIAN IN LIBRARY COMPUTERISATION

Role of librarian in functioning and services of library has been well recognised since ancient times. First of all librarian's job was recognised as a bibliographer. Then become librarian or custodian. As time passed his role and responsibilities kept on revising or upgrading the concept of library also got changed, which subsequently made him a facilitator or guide. Librarian's main responsibilities are about organising library in scientific and professional manner and provide library services to its users. Considering this, it is expected that librarian must have developed basic things or procedures of library i. e. acquisition, classification, cataloguing, journals control, card catalogue, reference service and readers assistance & training. Library computerisation certainly assumes that the basic library functioning have already been established. Although computerisation looks simple on its prima facie but it is a complicated and difficult task to do it. The librarian therefore, certainly has a vital role to play in the process of computerisation. We invariably see that computer experts and programmer understand and carryout computerisation without much difficulty even though they are not expert in library procedures. This happens because they very well understand basic logic of any task of library activity. However, it is seen that it is not true in case of librarians and we find that librarian remains bit apart from computerisation process as technically they are not that literate. Inspite of this situation it is expected that librarian must show his interest in proper development of his library system, as finally he and his colleagues are going to use it. He cannot therefore, keep himself away from actual practical process of computerisation. If computer experts without participation of librarian carry out computerisation then one can understand how embarrassing it would be for him and for his colleagues. Librarian should never keep computerisation for option and he must take active part in it. He must acquire necessary knowledge about it and keep it up to date. He needs to undergo some technical training to understand the process clearly which would facilitate him to talk to computer experts using computer terminology.

Computerisation process itself has undergone through drastic changes, moreover now it is at its advanced stage. The librarians therefore, need to take-up the challenge to acquire the advanced knowledge and expertise through participating in continuing education programmes or otherwise he could be isolated from this aspect of library development which could even set a threat for his further survival. We, therefore accept the fact that present day old librarians and newly educated library professionals are in great need of further training. Now let us understand what kind of training they would need.

2.4. TRAINING NEEDS OF LIBRARIANS IN COMPUTERISATION

In order for any librarian to take effective role in library computerisation he needs to first to change his attitude towards new change, accept his new role in taking library further and prepare to undergo necessary training.

List of General Understanding and Training for Librarians

Librarian needs to be positive towards use of information technology in upgrading present age old library functioning and services. His further understanding to include:

1. To understand need of computerisation and priorities of his library.
2. To understand manual procedure of library functioning, then he may do systems study of those functions. He should try to go for systems analysis. System study and analysis are initial steps of system development. Then redundant or unnecessary steps are to be removed from the existing procedures and library functioning need to be made systematic or logical, which could be a stage to go for computerisation.

4. To understand logical steps how each library software is designed. Basically it is the process of programming of logic of how each library function is carried out manually.

5. There are various softwares available in market useful for library computerisation. Library may try to carry out their comparative assessment, try to compare their performances and their up-to-date-ness. These steps would help the librarian in selecting suitable software for his library. He may further understand how a library software can also be designed e. g. in-house which are designed within the institute and with the assistance of programmers. It can also be done by adopting open source type of softwares.

6. To know hardware needs of computerisation and needs of other hardware, accessories and peripherals.

7. To acquire methodology of structuring database, use of protocol techniques of data formatting as well as meaning and importance of various types of library software manuals and guides.

8. Library webpage is the first interface of library software or an added product output available for users. Web pages are to be skillfully developed, maintained and upgraded.

9. To understand how digital library (library's own digital source) is developed, he may also need to know steps and procedure of adopting open source library softwares, where it is necessary to download free open source platforms, web services and ready to use softwares.

10. When any outside readymade software is to be adopted looking into library's local needs customisation needs to be done, the librarian should be able to visualize what minor changes required to be done if external software are to be adopted.

11. To know what exactly he is expecting by computerisation of his own library. He may be able to describe list of queries for which software would give desired output or answers. These queries are corresponding to queries of his library users.

12. The main characteristics of a standard software is that the software which is developed should be as per software standards. Secondly, the language in which it is written, should be the latest one and is of web based type. He needs to know what is back end platform (server) and what is front end type system clients. To check if the database developed is compatible to open source platform, so that locally it could be modified and maintained. Finally it should be possible to export data from current library software to next software without any difficulty. Librarian can acquire expertise to convert excel sheet based library data to MARC 21 format by using MARC editing tools.

13. One should take (at-most care) in designing OPAC (designed both for intranet and internet). One should make sure that it answers most of search requirements of readers of library and finally the OPAC must be integrated with all constituent activities related information services, which also should facilitate to search all types of library materials (books, reference books, journals) and non - book, printed or digital materials through one single window.

All points in above list are specific about understandings, and awareness that librarian should have in mind before going into process of computerisation. Following is the list of higher level trainings by which librarian by himself / herself could transform to be technical experts in developing and adopting systems and software:

2.4.1. Higher Level IT Training for Librarians

1. **Dealing with operating systems.**
   - Installation of windows platform and expertise to use all its utilities.
   - Installation of open source type operating systems i. e. Linux, Unix or cent OS and expertise in using all its utilities.
2. **Hardware and Networking :**
   - Configuring new P. C. or reformatting.
   - Able to assemble P. C and replacing / upgrading main hardware like hard disc, SMPS, RAM, Monitors, Printers, Scanners etc.
   - Creating server and client machines.
   - Designing a small LAN in library and maintaining it.
3. **Developing databases** for various types of library collections by using programming languages like C++ or by good web based language . To gain additional expertise to convert excel type data into MARC format is also required. (By using MARC Editor), Big data, Open linked data (Handling and Analytics).
4. **Techniques of Adopting Open Source Softwares**
   - Installation of LINUX or UNIX or Windows platforms and installation of open source software like Koha on it.
   - Downloading of web server Apache and customising it with local needs.
   - Uploading data of library collections, patrons and circulation rules.
   - Designing OPAC web page.
   - Configuring multi-location data of different libraries in one server and integrating it with one LMS. Writing queries in SQL / Oracle to retrieve output.
5. **Website designing and development.**

   Web designing is done in many ways.

   (a) By traditional way by writing web pages in HTML, Java or similar mark up languages - These web pages could be of static in nature.

   (b) By using several tools like Java scripts, Java style sheets one can create dynamic type websites but it requires knowledge and expertise to do it.

   (c) Web pages can be written without having web designing knowledge by using Content Management Systems (CMS) tools like Joomla or Drupal. These CMS tools give readymade templates or front page. This way designing web pages is found to be very easy and quick as compared to by using programming languages.

   (d) Designing of Mobile Library Websites and Library Apps.

6. **Development of Digital Library**

   Digital library development has been a recent feature added in library automation. Now days open source type digital library softwares are available. They are ready to use DL structures for making digital library (DSpace, Greenstone etc.). They require open access type of O. S. e. g. Linux. Digital Library is a library's own digital resource.

7. There are many things by which it is possible to bring further automation in library functioning and services, they include :

   (a) Knowledge of Library Electronic Security systems, products and services such as 3M electromagnetic security systems, use of RFID security system and use of CCTV surveillance system etc.

   (b) There is a new trend in library automation of giving information services using Web 2. 0 tool. Along with adequate knowledge of using internet now it is also expected that librarian should know using Web 2. 0 tool to provide services based on it.

While going through above paragraph on training need of librarians's readers have come across many new techniques or new terms of which they have not heard before and do not know the basic concepts about them. The purpose here is to present readers with current trend of librarianship and expectations from today's librarians by the library authorities. Many of the new concepts noticed above are not generally taught in the library schools or in their Graduation or PG level courses and therefore librarians and professionals need to take extra efforts in acquiring these skills and expertise. However, the author expects that readers would certainly get introductory and theoretical knowledge about these concepts in the subsequent chapters of this book.

2.5. TRAINING OPPORTUNITIES FOR LIBRARIANS IN LIBRARY INFORMATION TECHNOLOGY

The topic, "Use of Information Technology in Library and Information Centers" is taught in most of the university's library schools at graduation and PG levels. They are trying to incorporate this subject as per need of the present time. It is expected that the students going for this subject should have minimum level of competency of computer use. Having the computer basic skills and to undergone Information Technology related courses the students should also possess some introductory knowledge of use of IT in library. However, in reality ground level requirements/ expectations of librarian and library professionals differ from the knowledge and expertise gained by the students after passing out of library science courses, as their knowledge and expertise is not enough to handle advanced level of library computerisation. The librarians and professionals need additional amount of training to fill this gap. It is seen that the university departments do not take enough cognizance of this situation. Recently introduced integrated PG-M. L. I. Sc. Courses are slightly better than traditional courses of library and information science. Some university and private colleges do provide PG Diploma course with a view to give opportunity to old librarians and fresh professionals to undertake additional training in Library Information Technology applications in library. Examples are PGDLAN course of IGNOU or Post Graduate Diploma in Library Information Technology (PGDLIT) course conducted at Pillai Institute of Information

Technology at New Panvel, New Mumbai. These courses certainly help librarians and professionals to gain additional skills in making them expert is using these applicaticns. Many university conduct refresher courses for working librarians to give them opportunity to upgrade their knowledge and awareness about IT applications. However, since such courses are of mandatory type, which help librarians only to qualify and upgrade their career status to avail up-gradation / promotions, participants do not take them seriously and such opportunities are availed only for the sake of certifications. There are many organisations which provide training of short duration on various modules of IT applications in libraries, they include:

1. INFLIBNET Centre, Ahmedabad (www. inflibnet. co. in)
2. National Institute of Science, Communication and Information Resources (NISCAIR) - CSIR New Delhi (www. niscair. res. in)
3. Documentation Research and Training Centre (DRTC) Bangalore (ISI) (www.drtc.isibang. ac.in)
4. Delhi Library Network (DELNET) New Delhi (www. delnet. nic. in)

There are national associations in library science and computer fields such as:

- Indian Library Association (ILA).
- Indian Association of Special Library and Information Centers (IASLIC) Calcutta
- Society of Information Science (SIS)
- Computer Society of India (CSI)
- ISRO
- NISSAT (old DSIR Organisation no longer existing now)

News letters or programme bulletins of these organisations keep on publishing training programme schedules. The following list of programmes gives idea about nature of such trainings.

1. Library Computerisation
2. Adoption Koha based LMS
3. Development of Digital Library with Dspace and Greenstone
4. Website developments.
5. Content management systems (CMS) - Joomla, Drupal etc.
6. Internet Techniques.

If interested librarians and professionals keep visiting their home pages regularly they can certainly get updates about the forthcoming training opportunities.

In addition to the above there are websites specially meant for library professionals such as:

Infolibrarian (www.infolibrarian.com) : This site is bit more comprehensive which gives all necessary introduction to various library science terminology, it also gives information on conferences, trainings and even advertisements about new placements.

LISFORUM : This is like list serve group where you can remain connected with library world. Once registered one can get regular posts about happening in library profession direct in your mail box informing about discussions on various topics about new events and training announcements. You can also post information to publish among library science professionals in India on this platform. There is similar source of information for LIS professionals e.g. LISLINK.

Before going for any training in advanced knowledge or skills one should have basic or introductory knowledge about the subject of training which is available from one of the above organisation as knowledge level of all individuals may not be equal to effectively receive inputs in training programmes. Therefore, it is necessary especially for old librarians and fresh graduates to increase their knowledge level by reading professional literature and upgrade themselves in their profession skills. One should not wait when his own institute or organisation gives him / her opportunity to go for continuum education training. One can take his / her own efforts to spend time and own money for it as it has become essential to remain updated in professional knowledge in order to survive in it and build one's own career.

Computer's introductory knowledge could be gained by completing courses like MS-CIT. Many government and private agencies do provide advanced knowledge of programming, windows, Linux, web designing and on internet technology. Secondly, as one goes into series of sequential courses, he could become expert in using information technology and thus professional life becomes interesting and easy. There are free online, free to learn computer skills available like w3 school, which could be tried by librarians.

2.6. ADVANTAGES OF LIBRARY COMPUTERISATION

Since through this chapter we are concentrating on library computerisation it would be logical to know what advantages we can avail in computerising the library activities. Although library computerisation is a costly affair there are a lot of convenience and advantages especially for library users and also for library staff. However, such benefits cannot be measured in terms of money by carrying out cost benefit analysis as many advantages are of notional nature, which cannot be measured in terms of monetary advantages. List of all the advantages of computerisation is appended below :

1. Library computerisations brings sophistication in library functioning. It gives us feeling of to be advanced or being with the time and not lagging behind.
2. It helps in bringing sufficient discipline in procedures and operations as it requires to fulfill various conditions or checks built-in programmes of library software.
3. It helps in carrying out repetitive jobs faster and with at most accuracy.
4. The main advantage is for library users / reader as computerisation provides them with computerised catalogue, which facilitates them with easy accessing tool and which is also comparatively more comfortable than strenuous old card catalogue. In addition library website provides users with facility of linking them with every activity of library along with update information.
5. Computerisation relieves library staff from physical strenuous work of typing catalogue

cards. Now catalogue is available online for both staff and users and that too without preparing any catalogue card

6. Computerisation saves time and efforts in Catalogue Section especially it results in saving relieving manpower. However, with computer technology library is now in a position to introduce new facilities and information services where the relieved off man power could be reused.
7. Library can provide prompt library services to its users along with value added services.
8. Computerisation brings bibliographic control over all types of publication which promotes more use of library collections.
9. Computerisation brings good control on all library activities.
10. It can promote interlibrary co-operation and resource sharing.
11. It helps in avoiding duplication of work.
12. It helps to utilise available human resource more effectively.
13. With computerisation keeping control on budget expenditure and allocation of fund has become easy.
14. Use of barcode in functioning brings accuracy and speed, which helps in saving valuable time of readers
15. Computerisation brings transparency in work, which increases faith of users in library system.
16. Physical verification of library collections can be carried out in less time period and without disturbing library functioning if computerised method is adopted. Generally any good software provided this facility.
17. With computerisation library can take up Information Literacy and Library Literacy programmes.
18. Computerisation provides straights benefits to library users. They can get internet access and access to digital resources in library
19. Using computerisation in classification by creating authority files bring ease in this difficult task.
20. Library can prepare bibliographic data bases and provide bibliographic services to users.
21. Computerisation promotes automation of librarian's office activities
22. Computerisation elevates professional level of library, which helps parent institutes in gaining marks in evaluation process like NAAC and AICTE.

3
Process of Library Computerisation

3.0. INTRODUCTION

Librarian need to have many preparatory initiatives before the library takes up task of Library Computerisation. He is expected to first understand the computerisation process very clearly as :

- Understanding library computerisation concept broadly.
- Knowing library's need and priorities of computerisation.
- To have clear idea or study of all library manual procedures and functions
- Try to carry out systems study and analysis of current library functions.
- To understand hardware and software needs of library
- Know availability of library softwares or to explore feasibility of in house development of library systems.
- Having some idea of availability of funds for computerisation.

Initiation and completion of library computerisation depend on how librarian effectively and seriously takes the matter further. The responsibility of preparing library computerisation proposal remains solely with the librarian. He need not have to take full responsibility but need to have control on it. He could be side tracked in the process if IT personnel takes up the activity without librarian's role in it. It is therefore, necessary for him to be alert in these matters.

3.1. LIBRARY COMPUTERISATION PLANNING AND PREPARATIONS

In every computerisation process systematic planning is essential. Critical study of existing manual process needs to be done. Sequence of tasks in computerisation is the most important aspect. Secondly, the current manual processes need to systematised by removing redundant or unwanted steps, if there are any. The procedure needs to be logical and need to bring the improvement in it if required. All these tasks are covered in one scientific process called Systems Study Analysis and Design.

In Systems Study process the main task is divided into small or subtasks and they are critically studied, improvements are made wherever necessary and logical sequencing is done in these small subtasks.

Once the Systems Study and Analysis is performed then computerisation plan is to be prepared. In computerisation planning the following main things are involved:

1. If the library is large then planning of each constituting activities is to be done separately
2. Time management plan is prepared
3. Expenditure involved is assessed
4. Need of human resources is considered
5. Organisation of trainings programmes for staff as well as for users are planned and scheduled

3.2. LIBRARY COMPUTERISATION : SYSTEM DEVELOPMENT PROCESS

Designing and development of computerised system is the job of specialised person having specific knowledge and expertise. It is certain that librarian cannot do it but it is worthwhile to understand broadly the process of it. In librarian's point of view let us understand the process.

3.2.1. Systems Study

Systems study is the first step towards systems design. Before going into details let us first try to know what is the meaning of "system". The concept of system is described as: System means a group of subtasks/ mechanisms performed together to complete the main task. If it is seen in another point of view, then it is a group of subsystems which are interfaced or interlinked with each other. If a change is inserted in one, corresponding changes are also to be incorporated in other related tasks, because all of them work to achieve one single goal. Let us take one example : students, educational programmes, books and teachers form one educational system and each of them carry out single task i. e. imparting education among the students. Sometimes system is also defined in terms of human resources, machinery and processes. System could be small or big and they comprise of sub systems independently . Systems study of each sub system is possible.

If we consider the example of a library system, the library management is a big system consisting of various sub systems and all of them work for one goal i. e. 'Library Management'. In library management as a system there are sub systems or sub modules like shown in Fig. 3.1 :-

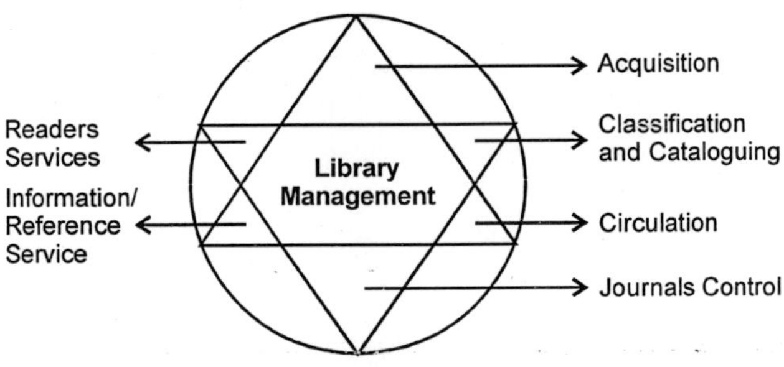

Fig. 3.1. Library System

Library subsystems

- Acquisition
- Classification and cataloguing
- Circulation
- Journal or serials control
- Information / Reference service
- Readers service

So each of these subsystems can be studied and analysed separately. If we visualise the Library System in terms of figures / picture it would look like as seen in above figure sketched.

Having understood the main basic concept of system and subsystem it would be easy to understand the importance of System Study and analysis in System Design and Development.

In order to achieve success in library computerisation a systematic study of each subsystems is carried out. After proper analysis, all sub-systems are structured on a logical base having inter connections among them. In each process it is critically checked how a task is performed in terms of flow of actions and flow of communication within the systems which gives an idea of flow charting of any task.

In pre-computerised situation library tasks are carried out for years together. In doing so each procedure is accepted as it was found suitable at that time. In the course of time attention is never paid to study the procedure of each task neither as of whole system. Many steps are done because they have been continued for years together, and no one have thought whether all the steps were essential or a few redundant steps could have discontinued to simplify the tasks. With library systems study attention is paid to this aspect. In library system study following points are considered :

- Review of main and sub activities of library.
- Study of procedures of each small and big tasks
- Simplify and systematise the tasks
- Consider links and dependency among small and big tasks
- Draw an integrated diagram of sub and main systems

It is expected that after having such study the tasks are restructured and improvised. This entire process is termed as systems study, analysis and design. System study analysis and design, and actual process of computerisation are independent processes. When any tasks is carried out by a human without use of any machines are called manual system. By just performing system study and analysis also it is possible to bring improvement and bring performance in them, whether to computerise the simplified tasks could be a matter of decision. However, logical and positive step after systemization is to go for computerisation. In library computerisation only those tasks which are feasible to go for computerisation are to be considered. Shelving of books is the task which is bound to be done only manually and is not to be considered for automation, although there are libraries where books are shelved and retrieved by robots. The tasks which are feasible and found better way to do them with the help of computer are only considered for systems study, analysis and design. The designing library management system depends on conclusion of systems study and analysis.

3.2.2. Systems Development

Any computerised system during the process of development goes through a series of processes, which is called as system development life cycle. In system development chain of steps like study, analysis and design first comes the systems study. In this phase each and every work process is closely examined. It is also ascertained that how much computerisation scope is available in those processes. Only such relevant tasks are identified and studied in detailed. This process works as follows :

- Information about each task and process which is worth computerisation is collected
- While the process is discussed face to face with people who have been part of manual task in the past or with people who are going to use the system in future with a view to know how exactly the process works and which part in their opinion was difficult to handle.
- Questionnaire is circulated in order to get relevant details from system end users

After collecting information through above steps, things are further sorted out to set objectives and expectations of computerisation. This way overall assessment of requirements of computerisation is done. All the data collected is further analysed to know the logic of the old process. Then attempts are made to find solutions to problems identified in the study of old process. By using the logic of old system along with solution found to overcome the problems the new system is designed. With this background now we would consider the steps in the system development processes as follows:

- Systems analysis
- Systems design
- Systems trial/test
- Systems implementation

3.2.3. System Analysis

In systems development steps like study and analysis of old procedures and defining of new system are involved. The steps of this process are as given below :

1. Structural flow of old process is identified.
2. Alternative to old manual process is found.
3. The model of new alternative process is prepared
4. Value of the new process, its usability and effectiveness are assessed.
5. The decision are converted in preparing new system

Supportive actions to above steps are also initiated such as :

(a) Preparing system work structure flow or flow charting.

(b) Logic of new process programme is written which is called source code.

(c) The newly devised system is again tested and evaluated to see its perfection.

This way old system gives birth to a new system in terms of computer programmes

3.2.4. Systems Design

After system analysis next step is to design the system by using findings of the analysis. The system design involves following steps.

- Logic thus identified in old system is converted into flow charts. Conditions and variations in flow chart are identified.
- Identify input which data information is to be put in to system.
- Out put of information fed to system is imagined.
- Decide selection of programming language
- Writing of programmes
- Providing necessary hardware and software.
- List out queries from the system as expectations.
- Actual implementing the system which is ready for use. Test it for it's expected output.

3.2.5. Systems Test / Trial

Once the systems in terms of set of programmes is devised, where in a series of old parts of process are converted to new procedures in terms of small programmes or scripts. In order to get desired output from combinations of all these tasks all relevant programmes are grouped and interlinked to complete the whole system. Now it is time to put the system for test/trail. The database is fed to programmes through forming a loop and resulting output or answers are obtained , which are tested for correctness. Any bug found in the process relevant corrections are made to respective programmes and again test is carried out until the system gives exact expected output. This is also called a dry run of the system.

3.2.6. System Implementation

Once the newly designed system(LMS) passes the test successfully then it becomes ready for implementation. New system implementation is done with some methodology. Generally it is done in a following way :

1. First to upload old transaction data into system and then start using new system.
2. Start from a cut off date which means from certain date only new transactions are recorded. In this case old transaction data is gradually loaded into new system.
3. Start fresh from scratch i. e. do not consider any old data and from a specific date new system would be put in to operation.

In case of library systems it is done like this: Once newly designed LMS is decided to implement then there are certain initial steps like:

- Uploading book data

- Uploading patrons data with their photo images.
- Upload circulation rules and overdue fine condition in the system.

Once this is done by adopting above methodology system is implemented and then onwards all operations would be done through computerised system and it is to be seen that no manual operations are allowed by library staff or insisted by the users / borrowers.

Just for precautionary measure the old manual system and new computerised system both are allowed to run parallel for limited time.

At the time of implementation of new computerised system it is an opportunity for library as well for users to settle old outstanding cases like.

- Loss of books by readers, which are settled as per policy of library.
- Clearing outstanding dues due to late return of books.

If these cases are kept pending then they could became complicated to settle in future or they might be forgotten with lapse of time resulting loss of books to library. Outstanding fine amounts could be waived-off as it is not the objective of library but lost book cases must be settled while system is at implementing stage.

3.2.7. System Maintenance

Once library software designed or accepted and put into operation then it becomes essential to maintain it 24 × 7. One can go further but there is no choice to go back. Moreover, it is the challenge for library and especially for the librarian of maintaining the new system. There are so many issues involved in it.

(a) Hardware used in the system and internal network used for software also need to be maintained.

(b) Maintaining software.

(e) Keeping back-up of system

(d) Keeping log of use of software in library.

Maintaining hardware is a routine task but maintaining continuous browsing services on intranet or on internet especially OPACs for library users is important aspect of hardware maintenance. Software maintenance is comparatively difficult task, as has to deal with database transaction and programme errors or bugs. There could be many break downs due to.

- Failure of electricity
- Discontinuation of net connectivity.
- Crashing of hard disc

Due to failure of electricity the operation of system could come to a halt. Unless there is battery backup or an UPS to server and clients, systems fails to function which may create embracing situation for the library. Especially failure of campus internet connectivity can also cause a short halt. However, if the library PCs are internally connected through LAN wiring with system server then system functions without interruptions but this additional connectivity need to be specially provided through LAN.

There are ways to have offline transactions saving standby arrangement when connectivity with server is lost or internet connectivity is also broken.

Crashing indexes or even hard disk could occur. In such situations previously saved back-up can help in restoring the system and putting into operation. It is always worthwhile to arrange to have back up automatically in the system itself but the backups need to preserved in two places and one of them need to be outside the server room and if possible at different location from the library.

The system maintenance requires continuous up-gradation of system or up gradation of its version. Bringing improvement is life long process, unless library decides to throw out the existing system and migrates to a new alternative LMS.

3.2.7.1. Generating Various Reports in the System

In report generation one can use the ready to use scripts to generate routine reports through menus in case the system is of open source type and there is a discussion groups existing online, where people keep on experimenting of writing scripts which are common in demand by system users. However, when the reports are required in different context which are not provided as readymade menus, then scripts need to be freshly written to satisfy specific query.

Frequent cross checking of backup of issue transaction, book card records with that of online data is also important to find out mistakes in issue and return transactions.

In LMS operations it becomes necessary to incorporate corrections in status of library books at any moment. These are due to following reasons:

1. Books are lost by users and costs are paid.
2. Books found untraced during physical verification
3. Books are damaged and are beyond any more use
4. Books found temporarily missing.
5. Books are sent for binding.

The status record of such books are necessary to be tagged in order to give factual positions of these books in library operations or shown in OPAC search. If sufficient care is taken in all the above points then maintenance of software becomes easy.

3.2.8. System Development Life Cycle

This is probably the last step in software development which is constantly assessed for :

- Whether system development objectives are fulfilled.
- The cross checking between expectations of system recorded initially with those of its actual performance.
- Whether it is suitable or any changes are required.
- If it is necessary to throw the current system and design all together a new system through re-engineering process

- When all the above points considered or chained together then it becomes a life cycle of software development. Now let us visualise the life cycle in terms of following diagram: (Fig. 3.2)

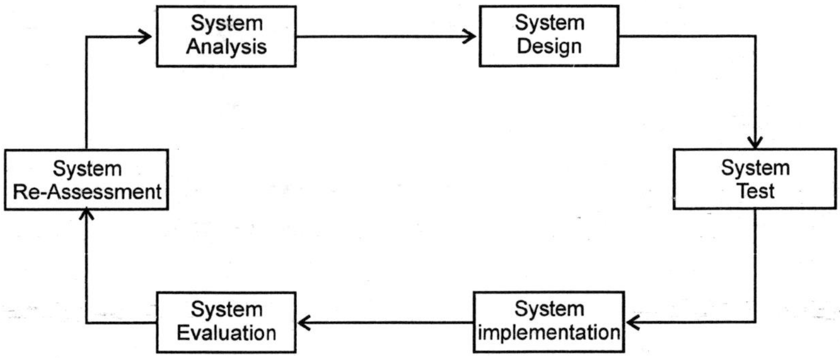

Fig. 3.2

In system development process there are two more most important steps such as :

- Flow charting of manual process
- System documentation

Now let us understand them in brief

3.2.9. Flow charting

Flow charting performs role of bridge between diagrammatical representation of system task operation reflecting to its corresponding manual operation. We have seen the step of system study and analysis. Experts understand the manual operation of any task by actual observation or through discussion with people participated in old manual operation. Flow charting help a lot to system developer for instructing programmers to write programmes corresponding to flow charts.

There are various types of symbols used in drawing actual flow charts such as show in table 3.1 below :

Symbol	**Name**	**Meaning**
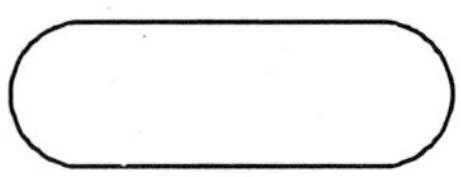	Start / End	Start / end of operation
	Arrow	Direction of system flow
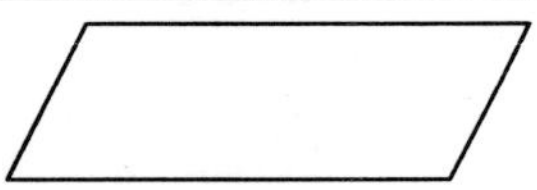 Parallelogram	Input / Output	Showing input output actions

Symbol	Name	Meaning
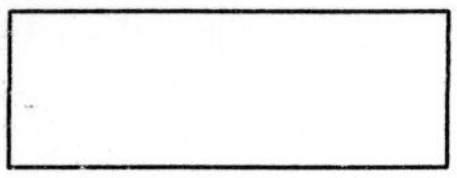 Rectangle	Process	Representing that a process in carried out
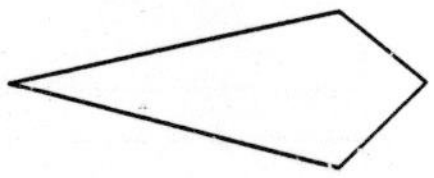 Diamond	Decision	Indicates step where decision taken with given condition

Table 3.1. Types of symbols in flow charting

There could be a comprehensive library of flow chart symbols comprising of main as well as secondary symbols such as shown in table no 3. 2:

Symbol	Meaning
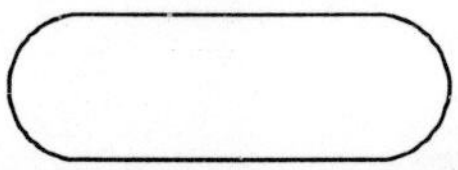	Start / End
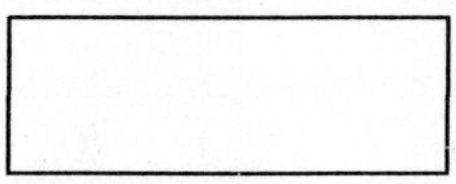	Action or process
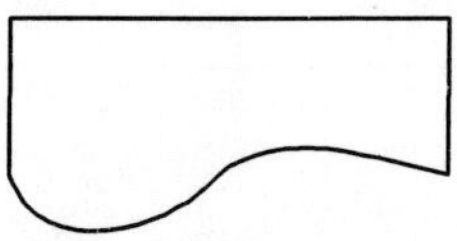	Document symbol
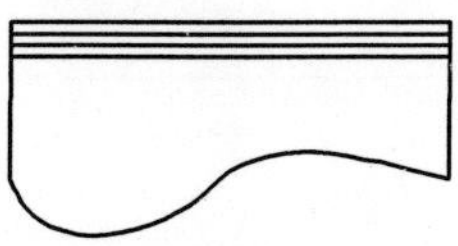	Multiple Documents
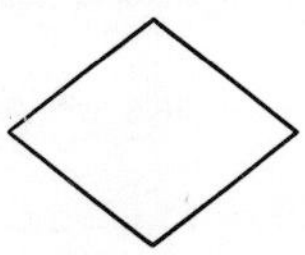	Decision Symbol
	Input / Output symbol

Symbol	Meaning
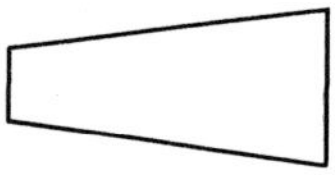	Manual input symbol
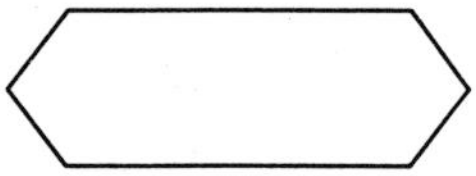	Preparation symbol
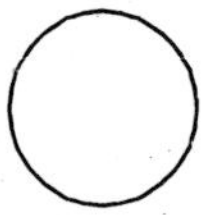	Connector symbol
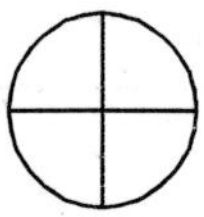	Or symbol
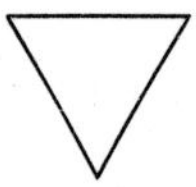	Merging symbol
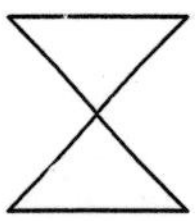	Collect Symbol
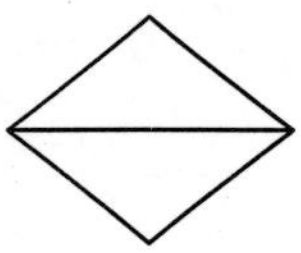	Sort Symbol
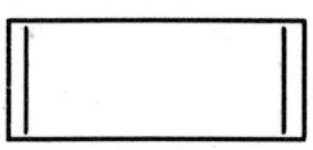	Sub routine symbol
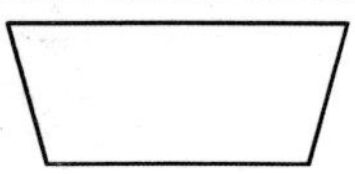	Manual loop symbol
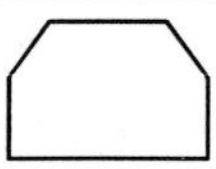	Loop limit symbol
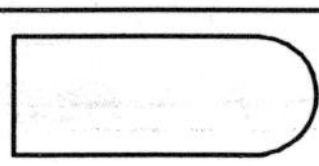	Delay symbol

Symbol	Meaning
	Data Storage symbol
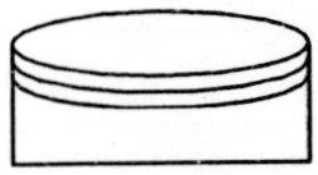	Database symbol
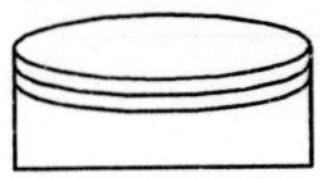	Internal Storage symbol
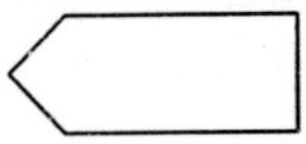	Display symbol
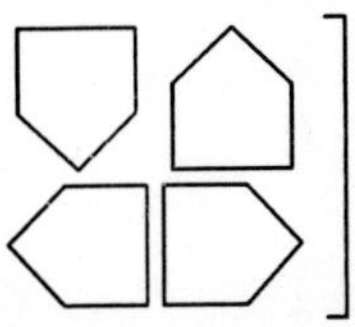	Off page - process continuation to next page symbol

Table 3.2. Library of flow charting symbols

We have understood various symbol used in flow chart diagram. Flow charting is useful for programmer to write a programme corresponding to actual task or operation. It gives sequence of operations along with flow of information in a given operation. In order to understand how flow chart is prepared let us take two examples of library operation which would give a fair idea in understanding the logic of any operation.

Example : Processing book suggestion to purchase of books, (Chart 3.1)

Example 2. Issue of book from counter. (Chart 3.2)

3.2.10. System Documentation

Designing a software, putting it in operation and to maintain it are the stages of system developments. Once this is achieved it is necessary to document the description how system works, what are subsystems, programmes details(source codes) of corresponding process, their inter connections. This type of documentation help in the situation when there is a change in the programmer which helps the next programmer to know source codes of systems programmes, so that if any problem arises the next programmer can rectify the programme in order to keep the system working smoothly. The librarian's role and responsibility is to insist system developer to prepare the documentation of entire system and handover it over to him otherwise it could happen that system developer can keep with him as his ownership and does not allow it to know anybody else. Such situation is very dangerous and it needs to be handled very meticulously.

Flow Chart of Book Purchase Process

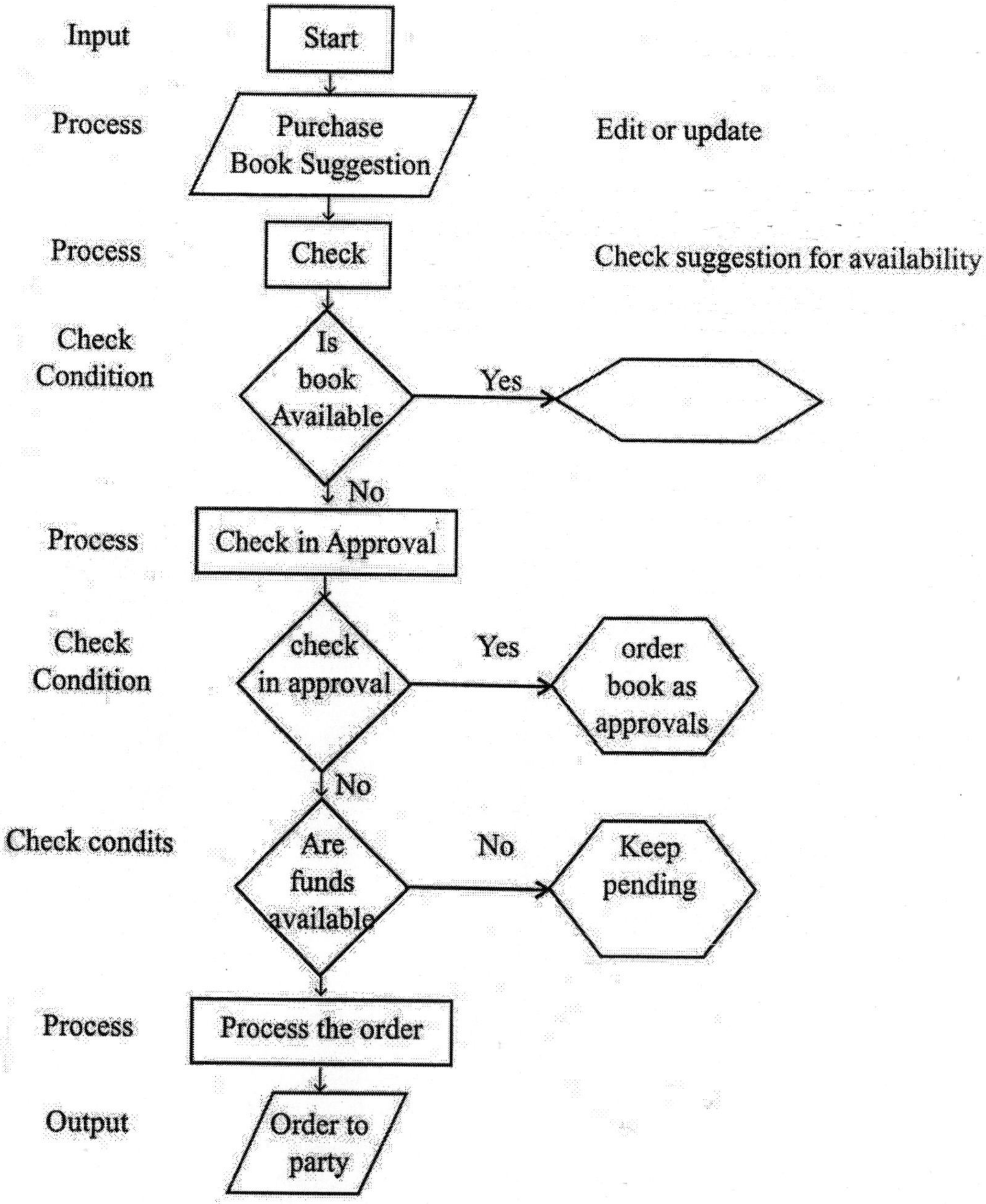

Chart 3.1. Book Purchase Process

Flow Chart of Book Issue Process

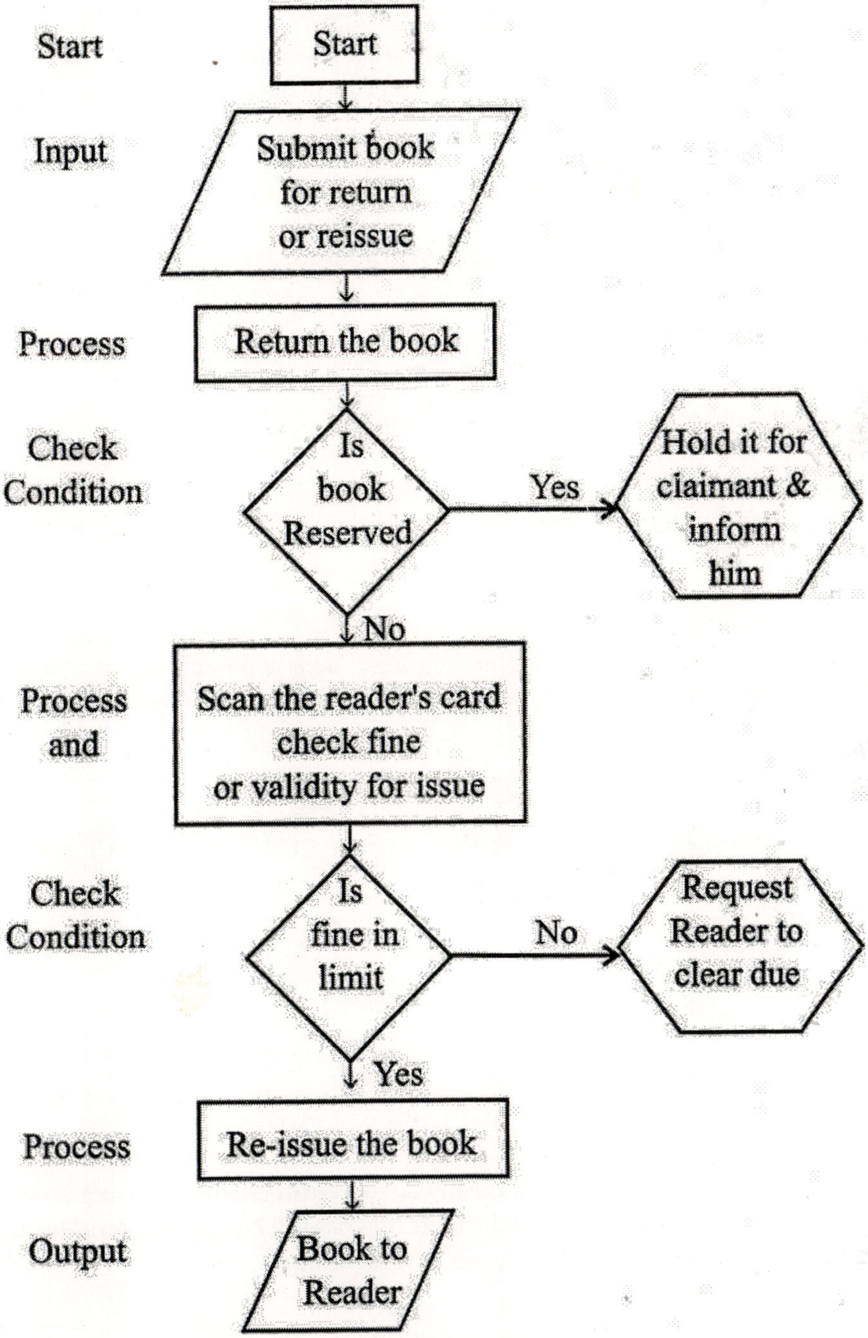

Chart 3.2. Issue of Books

3.3. ECONOMICS OF LIBRARY COMPUTERISATION

Librarian undertakes computerising task and completes it successfully. However, it is better if one understands the economics of the whole process of computerisation. We are aware that adopting any technology is a costly affair but it is better to have clear idea of costing of each and every constituating process. Let us try to understand costing of various stages of library computerisation.

The costing could be organised considering every head of it such as :

(A) System Development or System Purchase cost

- System study analysis and consultancy
- System Development
- Testing
- Cost of purchase of commercial software

(B) System Implementation cost

- Cost on ad hoc requirement of human resources (Data Entry)
- Cost of training to staff or system users

(C) Recurring cost

- Cost of system maintenance for making corrections and improvements in software and purchase of additional software of interfaces plus cost of electric consumption

(D) Capital & Overhead costs

- Cost of hardware: servers and client machines etc.
- Over head cost
- Cost of LAN Creation
- Cost of other accessories
- Cost of Air Conditioning

(E) Other Incidental costs

- Marketing of computerisation
- Information services
- Training to readers

The process of computerisation is a costly venture but it certainly gives expertise to librarian and library staff, which could be shared with other libraries to take up computerisation. This could be voluntary free service or it may be extended with consultancy charges

3.4 SYSTEM PERFORMANCE

It is equally interesting to know how the performance of any system is evaluated. It can be applied to library computerisation system also. Let us try to know now about how systems performance is evaluated. The system performance is evaluated with a definite method available to do this. Following parameters are kept in mind while evaluating or while measuring the system performance. Let us view the methodology in of library's point of view as :

1. Whether finally all the expectations have been fulfilled by the system?
2. How much it costed more to library as compared to cost of carrying out same operation manually?
3. What is the level of satisfaction of the staff ?
4. Time and speed response required to answer queries of staff or reader.
5. Accuracy of operation.

Qualitative and quantitative both methods are used to test the performance and reports are prepared. Logically cost effective analysis is done rather than cost benefit analysis as benefit in terms of money is not generally expected and only notional benefits such as user's satisfaction are more relevant than costing in terms of money, which always supplements benefits of computerisation.

4

Library Computerization : Ways & Means

4.0. INTRODUCTION

If we try to take a stock on how libraries around us are tackling the issues of library computarisation, we find that there are no similarities in their methodologies, as one library does it with the help of in-house software, whereas other libraries are seen adopting readily available software in the market. There are no similarities in choosing the softwares as they go for variety of commercially available softwares, where as some do it by adopting open source software available at international level. The above account shows that there are various means and ways available for library computarisation and any library is free to choose one such suitable way.

4.1. LIBRARY COMPUTERISATION : A HISTORICAL REVIEW

If we look into the past we find that "Library Computerisation" Concept was first emerged and founded in US in 1950. The main reason for this was decreasing cost of computers. However, the actual idea was geared up in subsequent decades only. The first significant step in this direction was an attempt of computerising library catalogues or preparing computerised bibliography which laid foundation or beginning of library computarisation. In order to prepare computerised catalogue it was logical that the library must be computerised. A lot of research in this area was done in US and UK. After World War II it got further momentum and need for library computarisation was seriously realised. The reason was, information explosion resulting emergence of various types of publications to represent knowledge like books, periodicals, reference books and non-books materials. The need was felt of having bibliographic control on these different types of publications which were published in a spontaneous manner. It was also felt necessary not only to have collection of all publication published in a nation available in country's national library but need was also felt to publish national bibliographies at international levels. International Federation of Library Associations and Institutions - IFLA came forward to provide a solution to this. With great efforts IFLA put forth ideas of Universal Bibliographic Control (UBC) and Universal Availability of Publications (UAP) to promote co-operation in exchange of bibliographic data internationally. These new concepts initiated library computerisation both at national and International levels. In the history of library computerisation we see some significant milestone developments such as :-

1. Dr. H. P. Loon prepared first Computerised Bibliography in 1957.
2. American Chemical Society (ACS) published first computerised list called "Chemical Titles" (1960).
3. MARC-standard was emerged in 1971.
4. Library of Congress made the beginning of computerisation of their library (1963).
5. In India, Indian Statistical Institute first used Computer Technology in their library (1995).
6. INSDOC (now NISCAIRE) started using computer in its library in which they prepared first Computerised Bibliography of Indian Science Abstract (Title and subject) in 1969.
7. INSDOC also prepared and published Regional Union Catalogue of Roster of Indian Scientific and Technical Translators (1965)
8. INSDOC subsequently published Regional Union Catalogue of Scientific Serials of Bombay-Pune region 1973. INSDOC also published National Union Catalogue of Scientific Serials in India (NUCSSI), which helped greatly in promoting resource sharing among the Indian Libraries.

Above events significantly show how library computerisation made its beginning at international level and in our country. However, it would not be correct to declare that only above referred events were responsible to promote library computerisation as there were other valid reasons also to create favorable situation for it Such as :-

1. There was a great need of computerisation in post World War II period.
2. Availability or proliferation of computer technology with their decreasing cost.
3. Government's policy of encouraging computerisation.
4. Competition created in using Information Technology in various fields including library.
5. Availability of trained manpower / human resources in the country and availability of opportunities for training for professionals.

Above and many more developments promoted / expedited further use of computer technology and computerisation.

In India, institutions like INSDOC (Now NISCAIR), DRTC, DESIDOC and network organisations like INFLIBNET- national library network and DELNET, CALIBNET like local library networks played significant role in promoting library computerisation by organising training programmes for working current librarians and library professionals. However, these efforts were inadequate against its demand in developing country like ours as no programmes or continuing education programmes for old libraries were organised or they were insufficient to train huge strength of old librarians. Even today situation is not much changed. This was the main barrier in expediting computerisation in libraries in our country. It was felt that as a part of evaluation process of accreditation committees like NAAC or AICTE the academic libraries (UGC) or libraries of professional institutions (AICTE) would try to computerise their libraries as these committees were insisting library computerisation. However it proved foul as only artificial shows are created to satisfy the committees. As such presently there is no stress or driving force either from government policies or from professional associations to expedite computerisation of libraries in the country. Unfortunately, there is no question of computerisation of public and school libraries as they do not exist significantly.

In spite of above scenario, it may be interesting to review progress of library computerisation in India. Due to the initiative of NISSAT library computerisation got initial momentum as they started distributing UNESCO's CDS - ISIS package to libraries (1980). Many libraries thus overwhelmingly accepted this package because it was available free of cost. Secondly, it facilitated libraries to create database of library collection that too as per international standard. NISSAT organised number of training programmes to motivate librarians to adopt the package and the result was very positive. In spite of this fact libraries did realise that it was not a complete solution to library computerisation as CDS – ISIS package had several limitations such as:

- It worked only in stand alone mode.
- It was requirin considerable computer space.
- It was not suitable to handle data of large libraries.
- It also did not have provisions to handle other essential library activities like acquisition, circulation or journal control.

In short CDS - ISIS package could facilitate only documentation of library collection especially of books and journals. So also facilities other than only preparing bibliographies as per international standard and searching them were not available in the package.

In due course of time all the difficulties in using CDS – ISIS package were resolved. Subsequently the network version of CDS – ISIS was also available with its windows version called WINSIS. It included circulation activity in CDS –ISIS. Further a package called "Sanjay" based on CDS – ISIS was introduced but there were not many takers for it. In spite of all these developments such packages could not proliferate further and search for good library software continued. Now the situation for library computerisation has changed considerably as many readymade commercial Library Management System (LMSs) are available in the market. Now let us try to review various Methods of library computerisation adopted by libraries in the following paragraph.

4.2. LIBRARY COMPUTERISATION : MAIN METHODS

In 1990 the situation was slightly favorable for library computerisation due to some pressure from evaluating committee, libraries (academic as well as professional) started realising importance of library computerisation. In panic however libraries started achieving the state of computerisation by somehow. Colleges and universities also started emphasising on library computerisation. In all there was some competition among college libraries to computerise their libraries. However, there was no standard software available. INFLIBNET took up manufacturing of library software called SOUL (Software for University Libraries) . However, speed of adoption of SOUL was very slow and was available in phase wise , keeping the university libraries waiting for their turn to get SOUL.

If one looks at library computerisation in a methodical way then it reveals that there are definite methods to do it. Generally there are two to three main methods to computerise library:-

1. Computerisation with in-house software.
2. Computerisation by using readily available commercial software.
3. Computerisation by adopting open source software like Koha

Each of these methods have certain advantages and disadvantages. It depends on situation existing in the respective institutions. If there are IT experts available to take up task of designing software then institution could very well go for in-house software. Now a days there is a boom like in US that throw the old systems and buy new readily available one. So naturally more institutions tend to go for adopting readily available commercial software. Designing in house system however requires considerable efforts and funding. The library which had that much credibility were going for it. In institutions where IT experts are not available librarian alone cannot go to do something in this direction. It is however true that either library goes for in-house library software or decides adopting commercial software, in both the cases support of IT experts is absolutely essential.

Presently there are many softwares available in market but which one to choose is really a big task. If the librarian has adequate knowledge then it becomes easy. There are many softwares developed locally in India, whereas there are softwares available internationally also. We would try to list them out and try to know some details, not of all but about some of them at a later stage. Before we look into various softwares, first let us see various categories of library softwares available for computerisation.

4.2.1. Categories of Library Softwares

There are different types of library softwares and each of them has different functionalities. Let us see various categories of library software as listed below.

(A) Library softwares based on functions.
   - (i) Database creation type CDS – ISIS.
   - (ii) Library house-keeping software
   - (iii) Proprietary / commercial library management systems (Libsys, OASIS, SLIM, SOUL etc)
   - (iv) Softwares to develop institutional repository / digital library (dSpace, E Print, Fedora and Greenstone).

(B) Open source type softwares which provide source codes to facilitate modification at local levels and which are freely downloadable. (Koha, Evergreen, Openbiblio, New GenLib, SOPAC (Social online Public Access Catalogue) Drupal based packages etc.

4.2.2. Software Evaluation Characteristic

We also need to understand the main characteristics or features of library software based on which we can evaluate them before making their selections.

Characteristics / Features

1. Barcode preparation and with scanning facility.

2. Acquisition
3. Catalogue Management
4. Circulation Management
5. Creation of customer / patron and library collection databases.
6. Handling of (customizable) queries.
7. Data base Integration
8. Fee collection
9. OPAC
10. Periodical and serials management.
11. Search functionality.
12. Self check- in, check- out and self online renewal.
13. Web services.
14. Compatibility to manage RFID security system.

4.2.3. Indian Commercial Softwares

There are good number of Indian library software available today. As listed below :

1. Autolib : Software system (www. autolib_india. net) - Chennai

2. Easy lib soft (www. easylibsoft. com) - Bangalore

3. e-Granthalaya (NIC) – (http: //egranthalaya. nic. in) – New Delhi

4. Librarian : Library Management Software (www. cr2. in) Ahmedabad

5. Library Manager : (www. safexindia. com) – Dhanbad.

6. Libsys : (www. libsys. co. in) - Gurgaon

7. New Gen Lib : (www. verussolution. biz) - Secunderabad

8. Rovan LMS : (www. rovan. in) - Shivkashi

9. SLIM : (http://slimkm. com) - Pune

10. SOUL : (Software for University Library) – (www. inflibnet. ac. in) – Ahmedabad.

4.2.3.1. Use of Indian Commercial Softwares

The list of Indian commercial softwares gives an idea that there are plenty of softwares available in Indian market today. Some softwares emerge, stay for some time and disappear. Some continue to remain and keep upgrading. We are going to see details of such softwares in detail in the next paras.

4.2.3.1.1. e-Granthalaya

e - Granthalaya is library automation software from National Information Centre, Deptt. of Electronics and Information Technology, Ministry of Communication and Information Technology, Govt of India.

- Gives OPAC interface on Intra / Internet.
- Covers most of common features.
- Current version 3. 0 uses windows platform.
- MS SQL server as backend.
- It is freely available. There are local vendors who help library for installation, data porting and further maintenance against some charge, website : http://egranthalya.nic.in

4.2.3.1.2. Librarian

Vendor : CRT Technologies Ahmedabad, India. (www. cr2. in)

Librarian : Provides all international standards like MARC - 21, Z39. 50, AACR - II style etc. It has multi lingual unicode data handling capacity which covers most of the features.

4.2.3.1.3. Libsys

Vendor : Libsys Ltd. - Gurgaon Haryana www.libsys.co.in

Coverage : Covers all common features of library softwares.

Development : Based on JAVA, J2EE works on windows and UNIX, uses N - Tire Architecture and RDBMS and Fire Bird LAN version, MS SQL server.

Characteristics

- Client server model.
- Z39. 50 cataloguing standards.
- Web OPAC
- Supports RFID security system at cost.

4.2.3.1.4. SLIM : Software for Library Information Management

Vendor : Algorithms, Pune. http : // www. slimkm. com

Coverage : It covers all common features of library software and facilities to manage all types of library collections including non book materials.

Development : Modular based.

Special Features : Multilingual data entry using Unicode : supports RFID based security system.

4.2.3.1.5. SOUL : Software for University Library

Vender : INFLIBNET, Ahmadabad. www. inflibnet. ac. in/ soul/index. php

Coverage : All common features of normal LMS like: Acquisitions, Cataloguing, Circulation, OPAC, serials control and administration. Supports bilingual entry/search. Works on windows as well as on Linux.

Version : SOUL. 2 based on International standards like MARC – 21

NCIP - 2 and Sip- 2 based protocol required for RFID.

Pricing : SOUL. 2 Full edition - Rs 80, 000. 00

Additional copy - Rs 50, 000. 00

Limited Edition (50000) - Rs 30, 000. 00

Prices may vary with time

Coordination : State wise coordinators are available.

Development : MSSQL server with RDBMS.

4.2.4. International Library Softwares

As compared to availability of library software in India there are a good number of softwares available at international level. Indian libraries, however may find it difficult to adopt them due to non availability of their representative/ agents in India who could provide assistance in installation, handling and maintenance. A few of them are actually used in Indian libraries. The list of international softwares is tabulated as below. in table no. 4. 1 There are over 70 such softwares available:

List of International Library Softwares:

Resource Mate	**OPALS**
Resource Mate	OPALS
KOHA-ILS	Alexandria
Insignia Library System	Mandarin Oasis
Soutron GLOBAL	Access - It Library
Aura Online	Auto Librarian
Bibliotheca	Circulation Desk system
Genesis G4	Lib portal
LibData	Liberty
Libman	Request Manager
School Key	Series – M
Small Library	VTLS – Virtua
Organiser pro.	CDS-ISIS, J-ISIS , ABCD (UNESCO)

Table 4. 1. List of International LMS

4.2.4.1. Use of International Library Softwares

4.2.4.1.1. VTLS

VTLS : Vision Technology in Library Solutions

Origin : VTLS Inc USA http : // www.vtls.com

Indian Representative : VTLS Library software Pvt Ltd. – NOIDA.

VTLS has been designed to carry out computerisation of most of the library functions or library related automation. It consists of seven modules such as :

- Virtua
- Vectors
- VITAL
- Vortex
- V. C. Commerce
- Verify
- Fast Track

Let us understand them in detail.

Virtua : This module facilitates development of database using ORACLE. It further covers computerisation of most of housekeeping functions such as :

- Acquisition
- Circulation
- Serials
- Reports

All the above functions have been integrated in one group. In doing so care is taken to fulfill all the needs of any library. It facilitates change of module and go to other in an easy manner.

Vectors : This module pertains to develop in a comprehensive OPAC, which gives integrated search facility. Secondly, it could be made accessible through any internet enabled PC.

VITAL : This module facilitates development of digital library collection and can provide classification, cataloguing and search facilities. It has inbuilt facility to create metadata of digital documents using related languages like XML, TEI, EAD and bibliographic software like Dublin core. It is also compatible for internet data communication formats of protocols like TCP/ IP, HTTP , SOAP and ITP. It can be interfaced with metadata standard like WSDL, web Services, OAI-PMH, MARC-21 and Z39. 50. Database in VITAL is handled by using open source server/Query languages like My - SQL, MICOL, FEDOR & APACHE VALET. This module facilitates providing document delivery services to other library using digital document collection of the library.

Vortex : This is a special module relating to digital library development which provides submitting of digital document from any remote location.

VC Commerce : This module is specially designed for library to facilitate online purchase of books. Journals and further facilitates e-resources collection development by handling all aspects including financial matters. This module is meant for handling and selling of in-house publications plus managing money transactions with the readers.

Verify : This is a modern feature given in VTLS which is not available with any other LMS so far i. e. facility to handle all aspects of e-resources collection development, for example handling date pertaining to e-Journals has made it easy such as :

- Subscription and renewal
- Payments
- Agreements contracts of licensing
- Access Restrictions
- Links to e-resources
- Copy-right restriction
- IP Address Registration

In addition, it is suitable to handle access right, optimum usage and usage statistics.

FAST TRAC : This is a very important module available in VTLS software for which it is famous for i. e. facility to interface with RFID Technology. This compatibility (Sip - 2) is already built in this software. Having this compatibility, the system provides further automation of library functions like

- Self check-out & check-in system.
- Fast carrying out physical verification.
- Navigation and finding of misplaced books on shelves.

Many Indian libraries are found adopting VTLS because of its built in RFID compatibility.

4.2.4.1.2. CDS-ISIS, J-ISIS and ABCD

In India a very few international software have been adopted because of practical difficulties faced by libraries in adopting them. VTLS was exception to this. While concluding this section it was felt necessary to take a note of initiatives taken by UNESCO in developing the CDS-ISIS, a software to develop library database as per ISO standard e. g. ISO-2709. Although CDS -ISIS is no longer in use in India but it is interesting to take a review about the further initiative taken by UNESCO in bringing out advanced version of CDS - ISIS and Open Source software called ABCD based on J-ISIS. Let us try to know about it.

CDS/ISIS : CDS ISIS stands for Computerized Documentation System - Integrated Set for Information Systems developed by UNESCO.

"Micro" CDS/ISIS was an advanced non-numerical information storage and retrieval software developed by UNESCO from 1985 to 2005, to satisfy the need expressed by many institutions, especially in developing countries, to be able to streamline their information processing activities by using modern (and relatively inexpensive) technologies.

The software was originally based on the mainframe version of CDS/ISIS, started in the late 1960s, thus taking advantage of several years of experience acquired in database management software development. Several partners contributed to its development through the years.

In 2009 BIREME/PAHO - Brazil, a historic major partner of UNESCO for the development of CDS/ISIS software, released ABCD a fully integrated Open Source Library Management System based on CDS/ISIS technologies developed by BIREME during these years. ABCD received financial support from VLIR, the Flemish Inter University Council (Belgium) as well as BIREME.

The last official release of CDS/ISIS for Windows, called WinSIS, was released in 2003 with a few updates until 2005. Since then, thousands of institutions worldwide have continued to download and install the UNESCO's software benefitting from the support of its worldwide community of users.

UNESCO has been also very active in capacity building for information professionals organizing or supporting a large number of training courses and workshops on CDS/ISIS solutions worldwide. Many other local or international organizations, including FAO and the UN have been providing courses and material to professionals for years. Many information systems in the UN have been built and some are still running on software based or derived from UNESCO's CDS/ISIS.

Also, till 2/3 years ago the approach of CDS/ISIS to database was considered by many disruptive, i. e. out of the classic relational database management system (RDBMS, SQL) model. In 2009 the emergence of a growing number of open source non-relational, distributed database systems was acknowledged and the term MySQL was finally adopted (the term was introduced for the first time in 1998). These developments confirm the long term visionary approach of UNESCO in the field of information storage and handling as well as the importance for the organization to work with continuous engagement (more than 20 years in this case) with a view to achieve concrete, grass-root results and impact the lives of hundreds of thousands of information managers and users worldwide.

J-ISIS : J-ISIS is a general purpose Open Source database system entirely written in Java and based on existing and solid FOSS software packages, such as Berkley DB and Lucerne, from the Apache Foundation.

The J-ISIS project's mission and goals are to develop a new Multiplatform Free and Open Source Software (FOSS) ISIS suite that would provide the same successful concepts and functionalities as the actual UNESCO ISIS suite while removing the restrictions, being Client/Server, UNICODE, and benefiting of the latest software developments. One of the objectives was also to keep the assets and experience of the users. But the main objective is to develop a long-term solution that would be modular, easy maintainable and extensible.

However, it seems that now the J-ISIS development has been looked after by Kenai (http://kenai. com/projects/j-isis)

ABCD : ABCD is an Open Source web-based integrated library management software developed by BIREME and VLIR (the Flemish Inter-universityCouncil, Belgium).

It comprises the main basic library functions, including:

- Cataloguing of books and serials
- End user search (OPAC)
- Loans circulation

- Acquisitions
- Statistics
- Library services like SDI, barcode printing, quality control, etc.

ABCD stands for "Automatizacion de Bibliotecas Centros de Documentation" (Spanish), which means: Automation of Libraries and document centers Its development was promoted and coordinated by BIREME, with the support of VLIR.

ABCD is web-based integrated library management software comprising the main basic library functions. This kind of library application is a long held aspiration for the ISIS community, since the first MS-DOS version came out more than 20 years ago. Several library automation systems were developed during this period and are still in operation worldwide. BIRME EMP previous system was limited to the circulation services. The main characteristics of ABCD are the coverage of the main library functions, its web centrality and its development and maintenance under the methodology of Free and Open Source Software.

Main functions

- Definition of any number of new databases (similar to WinSIS), which includes: FDT, PFT, FST, and worksheets directly on the Web, or copying from existing ones either from the Web or from WinSIS on a local hard disk,
- Cataloguing of books and serials, independently of the format: MARC, LILACS, AGRIS, etc.
- End-user searching (OPAC),
- Loans circulation,
- Acquisitions,
- Statistics,
- Library services like SDI, barcode printing, quality control, etc.
- Compatible with CDS/ISIS database technology for the bibliographic databases, i. e. reading ISIS-databases and making use of ISIS Formatting Language for producing output and indexing of records;
- Run on both Windows and Linux platforms;
- Use of MARC-21 cataloguing formats and other current standards or protocols (Dublin Core, NETS, Z39. 50...);
- Published as Free and Open Source Software (FOSS) with the accompanying tools for the developer community;
- Multi-lingual.

General Considerations

- **ABCD** is aligned with the CISIS/1660 version 5.2 platform, and will eventually be made compatible with later versions. This means that the inverted file entries are 60 characters long, and will increase in length in the ISIS-NBP based version.

- ABCD is compatible with programming languages accepted by the GNU licenses, i. e. PHP, Java, JavaScript, Python, etc. The current version **of ABCD** is written in PHP v. 5 and ISIS Script.
- The system is totally language independent. The product is available in Spanish, English, French and Portuguese and can be translated into other languages in the same way the CDS/ ISIS applications always does. (http://unesco. org)

4.2.5. Library Computerisation with In-house Software

We have already dealt this while discussing topic - Library System Development in Chapter No. 3. Let us refresh the same here. Developing library management system in-house within the institution is really a systematic method. However, its success depends on many factors like availability of IT experts, active participation of librarian in the process plus promotion and support from parent authorities. If one assumes all these factors then it is possible to do it. Many institutions have successfully showed that they could successfully design a library system. In this process library needs to handle many technical issues. Librarian's knowledgeable participation and with supports of IT people it is possible to achieve it. There are various steps involved in system development pertaining to library such as :

- System study
- System Analysis
- System Design & Development
- Systems Implementation
- Bringing Improvements
- Systems Evaluation
- System Maintenance

Secondly, it is very important to have time restricts in completing the project otherwise it gets delayed by several years. It is also necessary to provide benefits to users as early as possible.

4.2.5.1. In-house Library Software Development Steps

(i) To survey and study of existing functions and tasks.

(ii) To understand logic of manual work.

(iii) To refine work procedure and bring systemization by removing redundant steps in old procedure.

(iv) To prepare expectations of all functions from computerising them.

(v) To understand flow of information. Discuss with system developers, make them to understand logic of old system and draw flow charts.

(vi) System developer converts these preparations into a set of programmes or into source codes.

(vii) To interface various programmes to form an integrated system and sub systems.

(viii) Decision to be taken to adopt which operating system, programming language, database management system, query system, front end and back end servers are to be adopted.

(xi) Development of website and providing OPAC of library catalogue in it.

(x) Convert, reformat and import old database into newly designed systems or prepare fresh through data entry project.

(xi) Provide presentation of the system functioning and performance to authority, uses and seek their consent and acceptance.

(xii) Make system trial run. Test the system and make changes if any bugs are found in the smooth running of the system.

(xiii) Implement the system from a cut off date and transfer data of old transactions in it.

(xiv) To put computerised systems in operation by switching off all manual activities.

(xv) Bring improvements in running system.

(xvi) Upgrade, improve software and hardware.

(xvii) Provide training to staff and users to have familiarity with the new system

(xviii) Evaluate the system and accept system development life cycle to bring in quality in it.

4.2.5.2. Benefits in having in-house system

There are several benefits and conveniences in developing in house library software such as :

(a) If time management is prefect library can get system in a shortest possible time.

(b) System can be easily implemented.

(c) Maintenance of system is very easy and prompt as technical help is available. It doesn't require any money.

(d) System can be easily improved without additional spending.

(e) Library can own the copyright of the database.

(f) Migration to new system is very easy.

(g) Conversion of database is possible.

(h) Capacity and performance of system can be increased.

(i) No need to consider involvement of funds for designing whole or subsystem.

(j) User's satisfaction and convenience is at top priority.

(k) Librarians participation is assumed. He understands technical details of system development.

(l) Does not require much training in using the system.

4.2.5.3. Difficulties in having In-house system

If there is conducive atmosphere in the institute then in-house system development goes very smoothly with the cooperation of librarian and IT experts. The operation of system design and development also goes very smoothly. However, real difficulties start only after the system is put into operation because of following factors. :

1. Difficulties faced in coping up with fast development of information technology.
2. The knowledge of system developers or IT experts could become older or obsolete in course of time.
3. High mobility of software experts makes it difficult to hold the people to maintain the in-house system.
4. In the absence of system developer and maintenance staff, system could go into trouble or it could halt functioning as librarian cannot replace software experts due to inadequate IT knowledge.

Due to the above factors it becomes headache for librarian and institute authority. The idea of in-house software development is now no longer or cannot prolong for long time and hence decision to depend externally maintained software becomes inevitable.

4.2.6. Process of adopting readymade software.

Skipping the time and efforts required in developing in-house software and adopting a readily available commercial software looks apparently very easy and convenient. Unless proper care is taken in choosing a suitable software, library could come into great trouble in maintaining it. The following are some of the live examples of library's failures in adopting readymade software.

1. One library adopted the software of a reputed company. Initially the library did not face any difficulty but trouble started in maintaining it, as library is committed to pay minimum 10% of cost of software purchase to vendor. When library has incurred huge finance in purchasing and customization of new system, it becomes difficult to make provision for recurring cost of maintenance. Over and above the library need to pay to and from travel expenses to the software vendor staff. Someone comes forward to attend the trouble shooting in the system. But when he disappears and as system vendors refused to attend the system repair work without making payment the system stopped functioning making librarians position very embarrassing.
2. Library started functioning with newly adopted external software. After some time the library started realizing that the software is not performing as per expectations. Readers are not happy about it. Library wished to migrate to new and better system but the old system vender refused to allow exporting data to the new software as they claim that it is their copyright. It became very difficult to overcome such main hurdle in getting library database back.
3. Library decided to leave in-house software and go for external readymade software. Institute purchased new system on quotation basis. One company sold the software at lowest quotation. Knowing financial saving in deal, library decided to adopt new system on trial basis. Vendor presented the system to library authorities but it was totally rejected. The company promised to provide improvements in all sub systems. Library adopted software

on this status. The vendor started publicising purchase order to get more business and they kept on improving their old version. The customisation was not completed in five years time. As a result computerisation of library prolonged without having gained any benefits out of it.

There could be several examples of failures in adopting external softwares. In order to avoid such unfortunate situations librarian and authorities need to take utmost care and then only go into adopting software externally. Actually librarians fail to get necessary guidance in tackling this issues. The author has therefore made an attempt to list out all those care and precautionary measures to be taken up by library while selecting the software as bellow :-

4.2.6.1. Care to be taken while adopting external software

1. Understand technical details of new software and get it assessed by technical experts or by forming a purchase committee comprising of librarian and IT expert. They must check things such as -
   - If software language is modern, web based and compatible to latest internet technology.
   - If advanced data base management system is used?
   - Which networking architecture has been used?
   - What technology has been used for back end and front end hardware?
   - Which software standard has been used or has it been developed as per international standard?
   - Whether operating system used is licensed one and vendor has paid necessary fees?
   - Necessary system security measures have been incorporated or not?
   - It is suggested that a comprehensive legal agreement should be signed by both library and vendor so that things provided would not differ than they were promised.
2. Library should ensure that vendor has provided system as per special features highlighted in their offer.
3. Library may check if vendor has included costs of each sub modules while pricing the whole system. Library should not agree for unnecessary costing included in bill such as intranet and internet catalogue / OPAC priced separately. Vendor should not start freshly charging for any new subsystem demanded by library. As such costing needs to be done comprehensively without leaving any loopholes in it.
4. Whether vendor has made provision to take system back up and preserve it elsewhere to meet eventual situation if server crash/ hard disk crash situation arises.
5. Vendor's service unit location should be near the library so that unnecessary expenses on travel by technician are not claimed by vendor.

   Vendor is normally bound to provide free servicing, repairs and maintenance within one year of post sales period of the system. However, vendor takes long time in installation of software, data porting and putting system into operation and one year very shortly comes to an end.

The vendor then starts asking for maintenance payments which becomes unnecessary liability for the library. It is therefore advisable to sign agreement to maintain system for 3 to 5 years by negotiating after sales maintenance cost. It is possible to do it along with purchase of software but it is very difficult to do it afterwards.

6. Every vendor plays a trick by giving library older version of software and in no time they start insisting for adopting next upgraded version at additional cost. While adopting system it may be checked if vendor has given the latest version. Honestly adopting next upgraded version should not take time and money. However, the clause of provision of free upgraded version must be included in the legal agreement or it should not cost more than 10 to 20% of purchase cost.
7. Librarian must see whether vendor's technician is visiting library to do preventing maintenance of the system regularly. Situation of no preventive maintenance check for long time is not good for a smooth functioning of the system.
8. Vendor should be prevented publicising purchase of software to a specific library unless system is successfully installed and maintained by them.
9. If library staff want some modifications in software for making operations more simple (user friendly) then such modifications should be done without charging any additional fees.
10. Library should never give copy right of library database to vendor. Library should independently develop its database using available open source software platforms and preserve the same with itself. Vendor must agree to allow export of library database wherever library wishes so.
11. Librarian should verify while purchasing software that database development has been done as per latest standard and library practice or not e.g. the format of database should be MARC-21 or higher version. At the same time one it should ensure whether data convertibility which is compatible as per ISO-2709, Dublin core or Z39-50 has been provided or not, which facilitates data export and import. The presentation data style however needs to be as per AACR-II. Considering future need of software should be easily adoptable for the future open linked data standards like BIBFRME and RDA.
12. It may be checked that library OPAC and software based library services are actually accessible on intranet and internet or not. One should also check if circulation related services like reservation and reissue, have been provided, however they are generally available on site only.
13. Network arrangement should be done in such a way that client machines would be connected to system server by nearest way so that even if internet connectivity fails counter operation would continue uninterrupted as client remains connected with server through LAN.
14. Library must assess well functioning of all modules of softwares and also it should check response speed of the system. Although computer hardware processor capacity is responsible for this, having fast retrieval from system server is its performance test.
15. Institute may watch if there are cases of under dealing in software purchase deal.

16. In case the deal with software company comes into trouble due to some problem then losses incurred must be claimed in consumer forum/court.
17. Under any circumstances library software should never be purchased by quotation system.
18. Library should insist the vendor for user as well as technical manual of the system.
19. Clauses regarding system warranty to be scrutinised by a legal expert before agreement is signed.
20. If possible or if both sides agree system may be installed on open source platform and right to undertake minor repairs (trouble shooting) by an institute expert may be obtained from the vendor, which helps is running of the system smoothly.
21. Library may share their experience about adoption of any software and about performance of particular vendor with other libraries.

Above is a long list of do's and don'ts but it will certainly help library to take maximum precaution while purchasing of any library software. All systems may not be bad but it is expected that the library does not make a deal unknowingly with any substandard or non performer company and lands into trouble.

4.2.7. Library Computerisation with Open Source Softwares

Nowadays there is a new trend of using open sources software for library computerisation as it is convenient and economical for a library. The speciality of open source lies in its name i. e. source codes are open to any one who wishes to bring some modification in system programmes. At this point let us try to understand significance of source codes in system development.

4.2.7.1. Significance of having source code in O. S. Software

Every computer programme is written using programming language like C++, Java or Perl etc. The programmer includes somewhere text, giving details of programme for his information is called source code. Source code indicates source of programme containing variable declarations, instruction and function loops and other statement that tell the programme how system to function. Programmer also adds comments to his source code. These comments help others programmers in giving at least some idea of what the source code does without digging the programme. The comments help to original programmer or to their group programmers. The source code is converted into a programme in specific language and it is compiled to run the programme. Subsequently compiled programme functions in the system. Source codes and object codes refer to 'before' and 'after' versions of computer program which is compiled before it is ready to run in a computer. Generally any proprietary software system all the source codes are with original programmer or system vendor, which are not shared with customer or with any other programmer. In order to modify or repair the programmes of purchased system we need to call system vendor or original programmer only against payment of fees.

In contrast open source software comes to customer along with source codes of all programmes of the system. Having access to the source codes any other programmer available with customer library is possible to repair, modify programmes to upgrade or improve without even paying fees of license.

4.2.7.2. Open Source Library Softwares

There are various kinds of open source software used in library for example digital library, library catalogue and library management software. We are however going to concentrate only on open source LMS. Let us know which open source LMSs are available (Chart No. 1).

1. Evergreen	This is the highly-scalable software for libraries that helps library patrons find library materials, and helps libraries manage, catalogue, and circulate those materials, no matter how large or complex the libraries are. Evergreen is an open source software, licensed under the GNU GPL, version 2 or later. The Evergreen Project develops an open source ILS (integrated library system) used by over 1000 libraries around the world. The software, also called Evergreen, is used by the libraries to provide their public catalogue interface as well as to manage back off-house operations such as circulation (check-outs and check-ins), acquisition of library materials, and (particularly in the case of Evergreen) sharing resources among groups of libraries. The Evergreen Project was initiated by the Georgia Public Library System in 2006 to serve their need for a scalable catalogue shared by (as of now) more than 275 public libraries in the state of Georgia. After Evergreen was released, it has since been adopted by a number of library consortia in the US and Canada as well as various individual libraries, and has started being adopted by libraries outside of North America.
2. Koha	Koha is the first free software library automation package. It is in use worldwide, its development is steered by a growing community of users collaborating to achieve their technology goals. Koha's feature set continues to evolve and expand to meet the needs of its user **Full-featured ILS.** In use worldwide in libraries of all sizes, Koha is a true enterprise-class ILS with comprehensive functionality including basic and advanced options. Koha includes modules for acquisitions, circulation, cataloguing, serials management, authorities, flexible reporting, label printing, multi-format notices, offline circulation for when Internet access is not available, and much more. Koha works for consortia of all sizes, multi-branch, and single-branch libraries. **Multilingual and translatable.** Koha has a large number of available languages, with addition of more languages every year. **Library Standards Compliant.** Koha is built using library standards and protocols such as MARC 21, UNIMARC, Z39.50, SRU/SW, SIP-2, SIP/NCIP, ensuring interoperability between Koha and other

	systems and technologies, while supporting existing workflows and tools. **Web-based Interfaces.** Koha's OPAC, circulation, management and self-checkout interfaces are all based on standards-compliant World Wide Web technologies- XHTML, CSS and Javascript-making Koha a truly platform-independent solution. **Open Source / Free Software.** Koha is distributed under the Free Software General Public License (GPL) version 2 or later.
3. OpenBiblio	It is easy to use, open source, automated library system written in PHP containing OPAC, circulation, cataloguing, and staff administration functionality. The purpose of this project is to provide a cost effective library automation solution for private collections, clubs, churches, schools, or public libraries.
4. NewGenLib	NewGenLib is an integrated library management system developed by Verus Solutions Pvt Ltd. Domain expertise is provided by Kesavan Institute of Information and Knowledge Management in Hyderabad. India. NewGenLib version 1.0 was released in March 2005. On 9 January 2008, NewGenLib was declared an Open Source Software under GNU GPL[1] The latest version of NewGenLib is 3.0.4 Rl released on 13 September 2012. [2] Many libraries across the globe (mainly from the developing countries) are using NewGenLib as their primary integrated library management system as seen from the NewGenlib discussion forum It an outcome of collaboration between Verus Solution and Kesavan Institute of Information and Knowledge Management (Hyderabad). NewGenLib is developed and maintained by Verus Solutions and Kesavan Institute has provided the domain expertise. It provides many basic ILS functions as well as having several social media functions built-in.
5. SOPAC (Social Online Public Access Catalogue)	It is a module for the Drupal CMS that provides true integration of your library catalogue system with the power of the Drupal content management system while allowing users to tag, rate, and review the holdings. User input is then incorporated into the discovery index so that SOPAC becomes a truly community-driven catalogue system. The socialopac. net is the official website of the Social OPAC application suite-an award-winning, open source social discovery platfc..n for library bibliographic data. The purpose of this site is to build a cohesive community of users and developers around the SOPAC project suite.

Chart 1

4.2.7.2.1. Using Open Source Softwares

4.2.7.2.1.1. USING KOHA SOFTWARE

Koha is an Open-Source Integrated Library System (ILS). Koha is a web-based multilingual integrated library system to cater to computerization needs of medium to large libraries. It provides economical solution to library computerization as it is freely downloadable software. Koha satisfies all the functional requirements of a library management system. It is MARC based integrated library system and can be customized to cater to the needs of libraries. current Koha version is 16. 05. 18 (Oct. 2017)

History : In 1999 the Horowhenua Library Trust in New Zealand contracted with Katipo Communications to develop a new ILS as their existing system failed due to Y2K. During the proposal process, Katipo suggested to the library that the software they developed should be released under the GNU General Public License (GPL) to ensure the project lived on and would be able to be supported by other companies Koha is a 100% browser-based open source integrated library system; there is no need to install a desktop client to access staff/library functionality. As such, it is constantly growing and improving. The following list of features are provided as a brief overview of Koha.

FEATURES OF KOHA

Koha OPAC/Public Access Catalog

- Fully responsive LMS and would adjust properly on all devices
- Keyword and advanced searching
- Search filtering by location, item type, subjects and more
- Cover images from over five popular services
- Enhanced OPAC content from external products tagging, commenting and star ratings
- Availability and online resource links shown on search results
- Virtual shelf browser
- Social network share buttons
- Permanent URLs throughout
- Overdrive API Integration

Personalized patron experience

- Ability to place, suspend and cancel holds
- List of current and past checkouts
- Account history (fines and payments)
- Private lists
- Ability to register for a library card online
- Access to account information

- Subscribe/Unsubscribe to/from library notices via email, SMS and/or phone
- Make purchase suggestions

Circulation System

- Check in and out with a barcode scanner or manually
- Enter calendar of closings for calculating fines and due dates
- Book drop mode to backdate check ins
- Ability to forgive fines on check in
- Holds pull list generated on your schedule
- Course reserves
- Offline circulation for Windows and/or Firefox
- Place, suspend and cancel holds for patrons
- Transfer materials between branches
- Set circulation, fine and holds rules for each branch
- Perform collection inventory
- POS connectivity *(expected Spring 2014)*
- Communication with collection management companies
- Web-based self check out module
- Checkout by keyword, title, call number, etc

Patrons Processing

- Upload patrons in bulk
- Upload patron images individually or in bulk
- Create patron cards
- Batch modify patrons
- Run reports on circulation custom to your library
- Search patrons by phone, email address, name and more
- Browse patrons by name
- Connect children to guardians and see an entire family's current checkouts on one screen
- Set rules to prevent check out of inappropriate materials to children
- Add custom searchable fields to patron records

Koha Cataloging

- Add bibliographic and authority records by batch uploading
- Add bibliographic and authority records by copy cataloguing with a built in Z39. 50 search engine
- Add bibliographic and authority records using the OCLC Connexion client

- Add bibliographic and authority records using original cataloguing
- Add and modify items individually or in a batch
- Add and link to authority records
- Duplicate bibliographic records for sudo-original cataloguing
- Catalogue following AACR2 or RDA rules
- Create custom cataloguing templates with pre-set values for efficient cataloguing
- Built in links to Library of Congress cataloguing help
- Create spine and barcode labels
- Batch modify and delete item records
- Create public lists of records at the library

Reports in Koha

- Complete access to all data stored in Koha; write any report you want
- Custom reports shared publicly on the Koha wiki
- Easily run any saved report at any time
- Group reports by branch, category or any custom criteria
- Enter filters on reports to run them on for specific item types, branches, patron categories, time frames and so much more
- Search reports for easy access

Acquisitions in Koha

- Enter budgets and funds
- Duplicate budgets and funds for the following year
- Keep track of all vendor information
- Order from vendor files
- Order using EDI *(expected Fall 2014)*
- Order multiple copies
- Order copies of existing records
- Order by searching Z39. 50 targets
- Track order status
- Generate late reports and claim letters
- Track budget encumbrances and expenditures
- Create 'on order' items to allow patrons to place holds
- Accept purchase suggestions and keep patrons notified as the item moves through the Acquisitions process
- Importing and overlaying of pre-processing records *(expected in Fall 2014)*

Serials Management

- Create subscriptions with full prediction patterns
- Receive issues one at time or in bulk
- Barcode serials on receipt if desired
- Generate late issue reports and claim emails
- See full serial history
- Print routing lists for each subscription
- Duplicate subscriptions for multiple branches
- Library defined numbering frequencies and patterns

Koha Administration

- Full access to administrative functions
- Over 400 system preferences to make Koha run just the way you want
- Full circulation and fine rules matrix for each branch
- Define your own libraries , item types, shelving locations and more
- Create custom pull down menus for use in cataloguing, patron management and invoicing
- Enter/change Z39. 50 targets

Adoptable Systems in Koha

- Unlimited SIP2 compliance
- LDAP functionality
- MySQL database
- Works with RFID and self check-out products

Software and hardware required to adopt Koha Hardware Requirement

- Processor Pentium-4, 2. 6 GHz or higher
- RAM:2GB
- HDD :80 GB ;DVD Drive
- Software Requirement:

  Windows : Windows XP (Service pack 2 or 3) or higher for installation of Koha on Windows.

  Linux : Any flavor of Linux operating system (Ubuntu, CentOS, Fedora) for installation on Linux.

4.2.7.2.1.1.1. KOHA INSTALLATION IN LIBRARY

Facts: Koha is written in Perl, stores its data in My SQL database and is accessed via Apache web server. It can be installed on windows platform but Koha itself favors to install on any flavors of Linux. i. e UBUNTU, centOS, fedora etc.

It has presented general guidelines to adopt Koha as it can be installed either on Linux or

Windows platform. The installation involves handling for other supporting software or servers like:

- Perl
- Apache web server
- My SQL Database
- Z39. 50 server
- Koha latest version or Koha W32 install

When one is ready with platform like Linux and Windows the next steps are to install :

- Apache server
- My SQL
- Perl
- Z 39 - 50

One can follow instructions of each of their supporting software

1. Apache web server is available from site http: // apache. org / dist / php/ install it to c:\binaries program files \apache group
2. MySQL Database is available in different popular releases. The recommended installation package is My SQL 3. 23. 58 Zip (13MB). There are latest versions of My SQL My SQL V.3.23 XX or my SQLV4 at http: //www. myself. Com / downloads / mysql-4. 0 html. install to c:\mysql
3. Active state Perl is available from http://www. activestate. com/products/active prl/ install it to c:\\user\

Then actual installation of Koha could be taken up. Koha can be downloaded from its website(http://koha-community. org). The site recommends following.

- A Debian Linux server is mostly used by many people
- Apache
- MySQL
- Perl
- Root access to server

One should have better than average level of skills and command lines for Apache and MySQL tools. Koha is a free software and is licensed under the GNU -General public license either version 3 or any later version.

There are often two versions of Koha released.

1. Latest features - Every six months
2. Bug fixer is released every month

Downloading Koha from current stable release (tar. gz) from site : http // koha community. org / download. Koha. In addition we may need Z39. 50 client for downloading bibliographic records, which helps to develop database in a standard format.

Let us revise our steps to install Koha.

Step 1 : Install Windows or Linux on a PC which would be designated as server. If it is Linux then let it be sole server do not mix with windows etc.

Step 2 : install Apache to : c:\programfiles\apache group

Step 3 : install Perl to : c:\usr

Run files you downloaded. Be very careful to change path on the second or third dialog to c:\user Accept the default settings on the rest of the install dialog.

Step 4 : install Koha after it is downloaded from Koha site. Koha installation will first check to be sure of saving Apache, MySQL and Perl are installed in their proper locations. After a couple of dialog system will prompt you, if you want to pull custom install. One should choose a full installation on the backup 'Replace files' dialog, make a note of where backup files will be stored in case you need them again. Let process continue and installation be complete. At this stage verify these both Apache web server and MySQL databases are running.

Start your browser and access to Koha. Once Apache and MySQL are running, start the internet explorer and type either OPAC or Intranet on the address bar to check, access to Koha, OPAL. Default login is Koha\Koha.

Useful Tools for Managing a Koha server and database.

- SQL on – http:// www. webyog. com. This is a tool to manage your MySQL Database.
- MySQL Front - http: // my sqlfront. venturemedia de. Similar tool to massage SQL database.

Example : Create / drop / edit / add delete field /edit /insert delete record / execute sql/ script / created/ drop table replicate / import / copy/ manage upon / write sql queries / save and lot more.

Important Koha configuration files : Following are important configuration files to perform customization in Koha.

http.conf - It is the main configuration file for Apache server

Koha.conf - It is the main configuration file far Koha which tells which database to use and the location of all the files for the Koha program.

My.ini : It is the initialisation for MySQL database server and for MySQL admin database and other administration tools.

Some observations

Normal Koha installation procedure is presented in a friendly manner which gives impression as if it is very easy for any person having a good knowledge of computer but it is not so. Installation of Linux is the main and difficult part of beginning of installation. Librarian having awareness of Koha installation steps may not be able to do it alone. It is always better to accompany an IT person having good knowledge of hardware and networking. Just installing Koha in all respect is also not enough as subsequent Koha or Linux server as maintenance task is equally difficult. Library therefore should make sure that adequate IT assistance would always get to run the Koha system smoothly.

Installation of Koha using Live / CDs

Readers may be aware that there are many live Koha installable CDs available. Librarian can just insert CD do koha installation and start playing or browsing it. It looks very simple, one should however, note that such Live CDs or DVDs are to be used for only orientation purpose as they have limitations that the Koha in it cannot be upgraded. To do this one has to start from Zero. The live CDs are therefore, not recommended for permanent adoption of Koha for any library. Live CDs/DVDs sources.

- http://sourceforge. net / koha-live-dvd
- http : //kohageek. blogspot. com/
- http : // vimal 0212. wordpress. Com/ koha. live. dvd

LIBLIVCD

A live CD - Pre configured with library related software.

http :// 117. 240. 93. 3

4.2.7.2.1.2. NEWGENLIB

NewGENLib: Open source Library software is distributed in India

NewGenLib is an integrated library management system developed by Verus Solutions Pvt Ltd. Domain expertise is provided by Kesavan Institute of Information and Knowledge Management in Hyderabad, India. NewGenLib version 1. 0 was released in March 2005. On 9 January 2008, NewGenLib was declared Open Source Software under GNU GPL. [1] The latest version of NewGenLib is 3. 0. 4R1 released on 13 September 2012. [2] Many libraries across the globe (mainly from the developing countries) are using NewGenLib as their Primary integrated library management system as seen from the NewGenlib discussion forum. [3]

Modules and Functions in New GenLib

NewGenLib has following main modules:

- Acquisitions
- Technical Processing
- Serials management
- Circulation
- Administration
- MIS Reports
- Task to do today (daily scheduler)
- OPAC

Some advanced functional features:

1. Android mobile and tablet capable
2. Integration with Twitter helping to send messages of transactions directly to users' Twitter accounts.

3. Flexibility of defining own search field in OPAC.
4. Enhanced contents and interactive OPAC like availability of book jackets, Google preview, comments/ book review, tagging, favorite reading list, etc.
5. Zotero compliant OPAC
6. RSS Feeds in OPAC
7. Faceted Browsing (Refining search results)
8. Suggestion for other books in the rack
9. RFID supports
10. Provision for frequently used predefined templates along with freedom of defining own customized data entry template s in Cataloguing
11. Configurable SMS system - a proof of transaction.
12. Integration with Gmail or paid mailbox account. This enables automatic sending of email to patrons during issue /return.
13. Enhanced Report Module for generating in CSV format with a provision for wide customization.
14. Provision for integrating with Vufind SOPAC (Ex: OPAC of the Library of Bangalore University).
15. Catalogue can be harvested through Google site map, and thus the visibility of the library can be further improved.

Technologies Used and Standards Supported

NewGenLib uses a number of well supported and widely used, reliable and well tested open source components like PostgreSQL, Apache Tomcat, and Solr Lucene. It is entirely Java-based, platform-neutral, and uses the following major software technologies in its presentation, web server and database layers

- Java- SE
- Apache Tomcat Server
- Spring framework
- Hibernate framework
- Lucene and Solr
- JDOM for XML messaging
- Java Servlets, JavaServer Pages
- Java Mail
- OpenOffice. org for form letters
- JasperReports
- FreeMarker template (from version 3.04 R1)

NewGenLib is platform independent and can be installed on Linux and Windows operating systems.

Standards supported by NewGenLib

- MARC21 - For bibliographic data
  - — Import and Export in ISO-2709, MARC XML
- MARC21 - For authority files
  - — Import available in ISO-2709
- MARC21-Holdings
  - — Holdings data structures designed for MARC21 Holdings.
- Z39. 76 - Holdings statement display
- MODS3. 0, AGRIS AP
  - — Bibliographic records can be exported in MODS 3. 0 and AGRIS AP
- ISBD
  - — Record display and punctuations as per ISBD rules.
- OAI-PMH
  - — Allows harvesting (manual) from external repositories
  - — Create Open archive collections, and items, search the repositories and also act as data provider
  - — Metadata formats: MARC XML, DUBLIN CORE, MODS 3. 0 and AGRIS
- SRU/W
  - — Federated search engines can search bibliographic databases using this protocol
  - — Query language: CQL (Common Query Language), bench marking Level 1 compliance
  - — Profiles used: BATH, and DUBLIN CORE
  - —Metadata standards: MARC XML and MODS 3. 0
- Unicode 4. 0
- Z39. 50 Client for federated searching. Zotero compliant OPAC

4.2.7.3. Use of cloud computing along with open source software

Libraries get a lot of freedom and flexibility when they shift their computerisation using open source software like Koha and others. The first and for most thing they get is the chance to own the system server. Having this, library can manage its system application server. However, managing or rather maintaining servers is found to be very critical because of unreliability of computers hardware technology. We hear many times that due to heavy online search processes system goes into trouble. However, now time has given us a solution to it i. e. Cloud computing services. Thanks to information technology to make it successful. There are many cloud computing service providers such as Amazon (AWS), who take responsibility of managing your server at their place. Let us not bother what is this technology now but only try to understand it utility point of view. Readers may note that this book has separate chapter(No. 24) on

Cloud Computing. Now let us see how this service works for library. Normally when library is computerised it needs hardware like- server, client machines. The server is kept centrally say at the server room. The library jobs are carried out by client machines by having access to server. The main server and other servers are kept on all the time as through them library services are accessed online on internet. Server is any way machine works 24 X 7 and it is likely that it might fail some time. Once library opts services of cloud computing service providers then by paying fees we can shift all our data to a more efficient server of the service provider company. Library can also keep its application software in that server. Now with this library's LMS and server could be with service provider and library client machines can access it for day to day work. The transaction data also saved there. Library or parent institution is free from botheration of maintaining server or data on it. Open source software makes this aspect easy as each of their modules is accessed through internet. Although the library is far away from its server and available with cloud with present day fast internet technology makes us to feel as if library is very near to server.

4.2.7.4. Service provider's Help in Adopting Koha (O. S.) Software

In India library service providers have helped in popularising above referred concept of using cloud computing for library automation. This was probably main attraction for libraries to approach service providers. There are valid reasons why one needs assistance in adopting open source softwares which are freely downloadable. This is because adopting Koha in library involves some technical tasks such as:

1. Downloading Linux, Perl, SQL database and Apache web server and downloading Koha and configuring or customise it to match the local needs.
2. Converting, importing book and patron data into Koha system plus circulation rules.
3. Establishing server and putting Koha open source LMS into operation and finally
4. To keep the system running all the time, have back up and upload bulk data of users and books whenever they are added to library collection.

When we go through the above tasks we would find that it is a difficult task for any librarian especially for those who do not have specialised skills to handle all these tasks. Naturally one would look for a service provider to take it up. Fortunately there are many service providers in India who take up these responsibilities but at considerable cost. Examples are M/s Nucsoft- OSS labs and M/s Informatics Ltd. both at Bangalore. To have an idea one may consider the payments made to one of such service provider by a medium size library is as given below.

1. Estimated cost of data importing of 25000 titles or 40, 000 volumes and 3000 users and uploading it in the system along with circulation rules plus system maintenance for the first year and providing cloud facility and for maintaining the server plus necessary trouble shooting comes to around Rs 80,000/-
2. System maintenance cost of subsequent years comes to approx. ——— Rs 60, 000/ year.

In the above case the library had to spend almost Rs. 60, 000 – Rs. 80, 000 per year even to adopt a open source software and maintain it further , which otherwise is freely available.

However, there are good numbers of efficient librarians who have put their own efforts in acquiring all these skills and they are in a position to computerise their libraries using Koha like O. S. software in a very economical way.

In case of Koha software is freely available and there are many service providers to help libraries to undertake computerisation. In case of NewGenlib however situation is different as the open source software is itself provided solely by Kesavan Inst. of Information and Knowledge, Hyderabad and M/s Verus Solutions Put Ltd. Because of this the software NewGenlib has now become like an Enterprise company. Secondly, there is lot of difference in developing their software. Koha which is an international software has been kept constantly upgrading. There are many hackers/users or forums which are contributing to develop Koha further. Author opines that as compared to Koha NewGenlib is found to be slow in upgrading and customising as per satisfaction of libraries. There are however, good number of libraries in India who have adopted open source softwares like Koha, NewGenlib and others.

(Above facts are based on the actual experience gained by the author as consultant librarian in 2011 while reviewing various O. S. softwares. The current situation could be different now)

5
Library Computerisation with Advanced Features (In Detail)

5.0. INTRODUCTION

Library computerisation has been generally emphasizing automating library house-keeping function only. However, with the progress in Information Technologyespecially with advanced internet technology, the scope of computerisation is naturallyexpanding further by up grading functions and information services.

House-keeping functions in library refer to activities of routine nature like: acquisition, classification and cataloguing, circulation, journals control and a few other administrative functions like physical verification, retro conversion etc. Along with these traditional function now we also see many advanced features or rather value added features like 'virtual reference service' etc.

It would be ideal or rare case to see integration in computerisation of these housekeeping functions at once. However, due to availability of funds, manpower and time constrains the priorities are always kept in mind and possible integration is achieved to a maximum extent.

In addition to computerisation of routine functions, library could also upgrade its service by making use of information technology. With this let us take up discussion on computerisation of all the house-keeping function one by one.

5.1. COMPUTERIED ACQUISITION

Tasks Covered : Following tasks relating to acquisition are considered in this paragraph. Providing pre-acquisition information service, attending and handling suggestions, checking suggested materials in library stock and at various probable areas, ascertaining list of books to be purchased, selecting vendors in publishers point of view, placing orders to vendors, receiving materials along with bills, verifying bills, attending unfulfilled orders, accessioning new books, forwarding payments, updating budget and finally providing post acquisition information services.

5.1.0. Pre-Acquisition information service

In academic institutions, courses taught in classrooms, the subjects in which research project are taken up mainly help in generating need of purchase of newly published material. Every faculty, researcher and students need new literature pertaining to their work of teaching, study and research. If the library keeps a track of these needs then it would be possible to judge what would be the demands for new materials from the readers. Librarian can play a supportive role in providing information such as publishers's literature, new announcements, publishers's product literature and publishers's bulletins to academic community. Having done this library can certainly receive good response from them which would help in selecting good quality and latest materials. Normally such service is rarely provided to readers by the libraries but it has lot of significance in developing library collection. Now a day most of publishers try to present up to date information on their websites. Librarian can make effective use by downloading relevant literature and providing it to library users in selective manner. Moreover, if librarian thinks to compile such literature and brings out news letter periodically and electronically giving images of new books, faculty community would certainly appreciate it as they can get regular updates about new literature. In addition to books, it can also cover information about non - book material. One must consider the fact that faculty and research community is the main driving force in building library collection not only quantitatively but qualitatively too.

5.1.1. Significance of Acquisitions Policy

In library collection development point of view acquisition is a very important process. It gradually helps in developing good collection. In doing so, functions of directing readers to new literature and providing them with books of their own choice at the earliest are continuously carried out. Library must therefore, acquire relevant skill of purchasing and obtaining reading materials required by the readers. In the past library book publishing speed was very slow but now a days with information explosion the speed of information publishing has increased considerably. In this phase, selecting a relevant material becomes critical. Thus need of pre acquisitions policy guidelines is strongly felt. Acquisition policy directs librarian and library acquisitions team to purchase books and other material in a systematic and disciplined manner. Objectives of parent institution, subjects taught in the institute and research fields do impact in framing book acquisition policy. It can also help in conserving library funds and in utilizing financial resources available to library optimally. Acquisitions policy could generally guide Acquisitions Section in deciding on:-

- Fixing the formula of buying text books in multiple copies in context with book to students ratio, to decide limit of maximum multiple copies purchase.
- Purchasing books only in accordance with thrust areas of the institute.
- Purchase of original books (imported) as only reference purpose and need not buy them in multiples.
- It gives right to fill the gap in acquisition to fulfill overall need of reader groups.
- Guidelines to purchase of e-books, costly reference books, sets and serials.

- In having resource sharing arrangement with other libraries, in sharing resources of reference collection and out of print books.

In the modern times such acquisition policy could be built-in in the computerised acquisition system in such a way that various conditions can be set to facilitate librarian to take decision which will not violate limitations set by the acquisition policy.

5.1.2. Computerised Acquisitions

With globalization of education at the same time proliferation of literature, increase in number of courses and appropriately increase in number of faculty, researchers and students have prompted to publish more number of book, which has finally resulted in demand for more book. Librarians are now buying more number of books and also literature in non book and non print forms. In this situation task of selecting good books/materials, evaluating and purchasing them at competitive prices has become unwieldy, which makes handling book acquisition comparatively difficult. This vindicates idea of automating it. However, before the task is computerised like other processes, study and analysis of old system becomes absolutely necessary to systematize the old procedure and methods by removing redundant and unwanted steps. It has been proved that if computer is used for acquisition process it not only helps to work faster but it also brings accuracy and quality in it. It is now possible to provide better and value added pre and post acquisitions information services to the users.

Since libraries have now started adding non book and non print materials in their collection, automation would help the librarian to tackle this new trend efficiently.

Acquisition process begins with accepting suggestion to purchase new books and finally ends in obtaining and making them available to the readers. It involves various critical steps. With a view to handle each of them the whole process is broken down into small sub tasks as listed below:

- Accepting and handling suggestions
- Scrutinizing and approving them.
- Creating order by grouping them by publishers.
- Ordering by distributing, purchasing task of book procurement among the various distributers and book sellers.
- Received books with bills and verifying them.
- Accessioning
- Forwarding bills for payment.
- Making books and data available to next section i. e. to technical processing
- Providing information to indenters.

Now let us discuss all the above steps which are identified in computerized systems as menus

5.1.2.1. Master Data Creation

Before we start discussing the acquisition system sub-menus it is necessary to understand the importance of creating master data pertaining to acquisition. Master data relates creating files and codes of various types of data which are created once and used again and again. In acquisition the following master data would be required which makes further system to work smoothly.

5.1.2.1.1. *Master Data for Acquisition*

1. **Coding suggestion number :** Any particular suggestion received from department need to have a code number with the following structure.
   - Department code -
   - Faculty code -

     (Normally it is employee code)
   - Suggestion No -
   - Suggestion Sr. No. -

   Considering this suggested item would have number like

   Dept. code Faculty code Sugg. No. and Sr. No.

   Each suggested item be identified by this key.
2. Budget codes for:
   - General Book, Reference books, Text book, Book Bank Books etc.
3. Vendor Code
4. Currency Code
5. Order no. Codes
   - Procurement order number
   - Approval order number
   - Direct procurement order no.
   - Gratis or donated books orders
6. Bill forwarding number
7. Accessioning sequence
   - General Book sequence
   - Book Bank books
   - Non Book and non print material sequences.

Once the above master data is created picking them whenever necessary and processing further becomes very easy.

5.1.3. Handling Suggestions

This would be the first step in acquisition. The acquisition policy would prompt the suggestion handling system whether to entertain a particular suggestion or not. In any typical academic institute only faculty community would be privileged to suggest books for purchase. The suggestion entry would be done in a structure of suggestion number as specified in the previous para.

However, before the suggestion entry is made it is necessary to check whether indenter has provided all the required bibliographic data of item suggested, if not then the form needs to be updated by referring to bibliographic tools like books in print etc. Once this is complete, suggestion entry is done, as various codes are picked up the system would generate suggestion number for each suggested item, perhaps the output would bear all the necessary details of suggested item. A typical suggestion form would have the following details.

Author's Name - In a style as per AACR - II ....
Title - .... Edn No....................
Imprint - place : Publisher's name; year of publication - ....
Editor - ....
No. of copies - ....
Cost per copy with currency - ....
Course No. ....
Number of students - ....

Suggestion number is created by selecting values by drop down way from already fed data in the master file. Serial number would be assigned by the system.

Once the suggestion is fully entered and saved, next step would be to run a system check on it. This checking would provide the report as given below.

- Book is or copies of it are already available in library at call no. (s)
- Book available but previous edition.
- Library has already received the suggestion and book has been ordered with vendor having order no. ——————
- Book has been received as donation with details
- Book received on approval with details.
- Library does not have the book

In earlier days all the above checks were done manually, which was certainly a tedious as well as a repetitive task and seldom it used to leave some doubts as due to human errors finally was leading into unnecessary duplications. It could be done by devising separate module by taking into account all the conditions as specified above. It would be convenient to forward the system generated report to the indenter for his / her information. Making suggestion entry in a systematic way (in AACR format) in this step itself is crucial for further processing as same data flows through entire acquisition processing and the same is further transferred in the same form to the next module i. e.

technical processing, which need not have to enter it again and again and this is the great advantage achieved in the library computerisation.

5.1.3.1. Online Suggestion Processing System

In the suggestion entry task described above it is assumed that the entries are done by library staff after updating details of suggested books. However, the process could be furthei automated by providing data entry form online to the department, which is made available to each faculty. Whenever an individual wishes to suggest a new books for purchase he / she would fill it in a database structure sheet and forward it to the library, which eventually would be attended by staff in the library and saved to a new suggestion file.

This system can further be automated by making it online suggestion processing system. Once library receives any suggestion it is rational that the library would seek approval of the Head of Departmant as HOD normally does monitoring of spending funds available to the respective department. Secondly, the department should also ensure that requirements of all faculty is considered and it is not bias only to a few members of faculty.

Online suggestion processing system would also consider the completion of the above scrutinisation steps of each suggestion in the online suggestion system, in department itself. Such system to follow online document handling method. The steps of it could be as follows:

1. Faculty would fill all the details of new suggestion in a digital data entry form available on-line and submits it electronically to the system.
2. The form then is routed to HOD. HOD would be able to see the facts such as balance funds available for him to utilize. He would also know the funds already committed through the orders placed previously. He would also know the past history of the faculty's suggestion. He would then assess the usefulness of books for the course, approve it and would forward it to library for processing. Suggestions received this way would help the library to process them speedily as approval process is already completed by concerned HOD. Suggestion is then saved in the library system for further processing.

5.1.3.2. Suggestion : Books on Approval Process

Library would receive suggestion for purchasing of new books by different ways as: (in a normal way and not stated in above stated method)

1. Suggestions for procurement
2. Suggestions for direct procurement (Imported Books and society publications)
3. Suggestion received under books on approval process (this method we are going to discuss later in this chapter.)

All the suggestions need approval either from book scrutiny committee or from Head of Department. Library considering suggestions received in above ways are entered in the system and verified by cross checking for duplication. Before going into actual ordering they are sent for approval of competent authorities, along with other details such as availability of funds and information about past purchases history like liability on committed orders placed previously. HOD then receives the suggestions in terms of need of suggested books and their costs, approves suggestions and they are forwarded to library for further processing. If any of the suggestions are rejected then same is stroked off with reasons specified against it. This process can be interfaced to online suggestion process system appropriately.

5.1.4. Allocation of Budget

After taking necessary approvals of the HODs on suggestions, next step would be to actually order the books. However, in the ordering process one needs to first check availability of funds and if budget provisions are made then it would allow to go ahead in the system. Let us therefore look into how budgets are created which could be used in ordering process.

If we consider the functioning of library in its entirety then it needs to create various budget heads and provision of funds in those budget heads. List of budgets would be as under:

- Library's main budget
- Plan budget
  - Library books of non-book material budget
  - Budget for reference books purchase.
  - Budget for books banks collection.
- Library non plan budget
  - Library journals
  - Operating cost budget

Considering all the above budget requirements, the budget system is devised. The funds approved by the parent body are then received in the system. All the received money is put into the main budget head for the respective financial year. Thus the money received in main the budget head is then used to allocate into sub budgets. Once money is made available in sub budgets it can be consumed as and when purchase transactions are taken place. With a view to give weightage to each department depending on its respective courses and faculty strength, it is always convenient to allocate separate budget for each department up to a faculty level so that the analyzing utility of budget could be done rationally.

5.1.5. Ordering

Ordering is the core task in acquisition processing. Ordering assumes that suggestions made by the faculty community have been verified and status is confirmed that :

1. Library does not have books similar to the ones suggested
2. There was no previous suggestion received for it.
3. The book is not available in the library in any way.
4. We have no previous orders of the book similar to the one suggested.

It finally confirms that it is a new book and can be ordered. Now ordering process requires following pre requisites such as:

(A) Vendor code

(B) Type of order sequence
- Procurement order
- Approval order
- Direct order
- Gratis / Donations Processing

(C) List of suggested item which are ready for ordering with the number of copies.

(D) Budget

(E) Respective order template

5.1.5.1. Procurement order

Having these requisite inputs, the order process works like this:

- Respective menu for ordering is opened
- Vendor code is selected by dropdown.
- Order type sequence is also selected by drop down way
- System would assign next serial number of order
- Then list of suggested item is uploaded.
- Required items are selected / marked
- Number of copies are confirmed
- Unit price and total order cost is obtained and confirmed
- Respective Budget is picked up by dropdown way
- Other supply conditions are noted such as:
  — Discount %
  — Delivery charges, if any
  — Time allowance given to vendor
- Finally order is generated respectively.
- Order template is selected. Necessary editing is done
- Order list and order template soft copy both are saved.
- Order is printed with necessary copies.

After the signature of the library authority, order is dispatched physically or by courier and at the same time soft copy order is mailed to the respective vendor.

5.1.5.2. Ordering Decision Making

Taking decision with whom to place the purchase orders may lead into some controversy. It is because identifying genuine vendor (s) is a skilled decision. It depends on their past performance, promptness and understanding. There would be always risk in giving orders to a single party. Another factor which influences the process is who would decide whom to order. Sometimes a single person or librarian's decision might go bias. If it is to be done by a group of members then process gets delayed. Nowadays quotation system get preference over others ways but it does not help in getting quality material or there is risk of not getting books at all. These methods may not help the library. Instead the library can draw a panel of good, sincere and efficient suppliers or have rate contract with them.

In large library, process becomes further critical. In real sense library should consider first publisher and next their distributors. Discount factor should come at last. Having this approach then one can do the sorting and short listing for preparing orders by using a computer. Library may develop database of publishers, distributors, agents, vendors while creating the master data and keys from this database are used while ordering. It becomes easy to sort suggested books based on publishers and then look for distributor / vendor who could supply those books. A care may be taken that library book purchase business is amicably distributed among all distributers and vendors available on library rate contract or panel. Library may insist all to provide maximum flat equal discount so that a competition would be created among them to give prompt service to the library.

5.1.5.3. Ordering conditions

Each order, either procurement, approval or direct, must possess some binding conditions in order to keep rights of both sides i. e. library as well as on vendors intact in order to meet any eventual situation. These conditions may include as:

- Time allowance given to vendor to supply books must be specified, so that library can decide to cancel non fulfilled orders and distribute them to others. This condition is normally built in ordering process and mentioned in order letter/template.
- Discount - as per agreed upon. This also is built-in in the ordering process.
- Conversion rate - Either by bank rate or Good Offices Committee(GOC) as accepted by library and agreed by vendors.
- Handling charges - In case of short discount titles it is normally 15% on landed cost to be paid by the library.
- Freight and forwarding charges as per actuals in case of imported books.

5.1.5.4. Book Approval process

Books are normally purchased by the library in two ways.

- By Procurement process
- By Books on approval process

Procurement method is about obtaining the books as per demand submitted by the teachers, researchers and scientists. Approval process helps library to get books in library as soon they are available from the publisher for the purpose of displaying or for showing them to faculty members. Basically this is the initiative taken by distributors and representatives of publishers or even by efficient book sellers. These people go through publishers announcements and bulletins and make the selection of books in anticipation even well before they are out from publishers. The work is done so efficiently and professionally that selection exactly matches to the interests of teachers, scientists and researchers to a great extent. These books are provided to library as soon as they arrive in the market for approval purpose. Library then organises display of books and invite readers community to browse the books, which helps library in selecting good books. The advantage here is that the readers get opportunity to see the books physically, scan them, ascertain their usefulness and make suggestion to library for buying. Such an opportunity is not available in case of procurement method. However, to make the process more efficient, library needs to handle the approval process meticulously and readers community should also give sincere response by availing the opportunity to select good books.

If the process is handled manually then it is generally observed that it is not attended timely by the library and readers, which fails to respond to booksellers timely and in the entire process newness of book goes in vain and finally the books are returned back to vendor without having much selection done in it.

The process therefore, needs automation to do it effectively. The process can start at distributor's end. If library provides them a data/file structure to enter their books in computer or alternatively library provides vendors facility to input approval books data digitally in the library website online by giving reference to vendor code and approval memo numbers. Thus library could organize subjective wise bibliography of all such books received from number of vendors very quickly. So by the time books are arrived in library, library could circulate subject wise list to all departments and individual faculties. They get a chance to choose good books of their interest, which motivates them to visit library to see and browse the books, if they are convinced of the usefulness of books, they could approve the selection of such books online by clicking the radio button in the online list. Thus, in a very short time, book selection process gets completed. Library can also retrieve the list of selected books and separate rejected books which are returned back to the vendors. In manual process, it is done by filling the suggestion form and submitting them to vendor, which are then submitted to library for further processing. This is the point where vendor may try to manipulate suggested list by adding additional books to it just to promote the sale of books, which is unethical and libraries do not notice such incidences. Automated process in comparison does not give any chance to such acts. Even after books are returned back, if some books are demanded afterwards the library can obtain it as data with vendor detail remains in library archives for some time. The automated approval process has many such advantages and it proves to be one of the effective methods of selecting and buying books in the library.

5.1.5.4.1. Ordering Approval Books

In books approval process, distributors and vendors send recently published books on approval basis to library. They are displayed or shown to faculty members and suggestions to buy them are obtained from them. There would be slight difference in handling this type of ordering. The system in this case works like this.

- Approval memo for selected books received on approval are entered by using codes:
  — Vendor code
- Approval memo No. and Sr. No. (Approval memo entry to be done in advance.)
- Faculty code is used through dropdown menu.
- Order No. for approval sequence to be chosen. The system would assign next Sr. No. of approval order.
- Relevant budget codes are fixed up from dropdown menu.
- Approval order is generated.
- Approval order template is also selected.
- Approval order list and order template to be printed and saved
- After obtaining signatures of authorities, order is dispatched to the vendor.
- Soft copy of approval order can be mailed to vendor/distributor.

5.1.5.5. Direct Order Process

Direct order process refers to procurement of books directly from the publishers or institutions/ organization who do not distribute books through any agent or distributor. Another difference in this type of procurement is that books are not delivered on credit i. e. cost of books is to be paid in advance to receive the books. The process works like this:-

- Vendor or publisher code is to be freshly created as it would not be in master file
- Type of order i. e. direct order sequence is to be selected.
- Order is generated and cost is to be committed.
- Order is to be generated signed and couriered.
- Pro-forma invoice received is to be entered.
- Pro-forma invoice is to be forwarded for payment.
- Payment is to be forwarded
- On receipt of payment, books consignment is to be received
- Books are verified and accessioned and are sent for processing
- Advance payment is to be settled against payments committed.

5.1.5.6. Processing Donations / Gratis

Donation is one more way that library keeps on receiving and adding books to its collection. Although it is not a big source to get books for library but provisions to accept the books and add them in library has to be made. Unless the donation comes from abroad it is likely that local donors may try to dump old and out dated books as donations. In order to avoid this every library need to draw a policy about accepting books as donation only after scrutinizing donation list and only after assessing their usefulness for library, latest and books which are in good condition only should be accepted and rest of books should be returned back else it gets on creating stock of waste material which needs to be disposed off periodically.

The process to accept donation would be as follows.

- Only selected accepted books to be entered by donation list no. and Sr. No.
- Donor may be given a temporary code and acknowledgement may be sent accordingly
- The list is saved for further process of accessioning.

5.1.5.7. Reminders for Overdue Orders

Ordering system must have built-in menu to identify overdue orders or unsupplied items. The program to cross check all orders (procurement and direct orders) and give output periodically listing overdue orders and items. It may have facility to sort them vendor and order wise and list should finally facilitate to send computer generated reminder with pre decided (template) text and further arranged to send by e-mail as well physical copy by post/courier. This process gives opportunity to library to wait for some time and finally to cancel the orders if vendor fails to respond to the reminder.

5.1.5.8. Cancellation of orders

Computerised acquisition system would invariably have menu to cancel all unsupplied orders and record them. It would be done order by order. System would list all the overdue order or orders having unsupplied items. It would seek confirmation from indenter to cancel the order. The next question would be prompted that with whom then it would be reordered. This step onwards it goes on the same line as it is done in ordering process.

5.1.6. E-books Acquisition

5.1.6.0. Introduction

We find a lot of discussion on availability of e-Books and benefits associated with getting e-Books in library. A trend is also seen that libraries have started buying ebooks in their collection. Publishers, aggregators and vendors are trying to convince libraries to get e–books. However, there are many issues relating adoption of e-books in the library and librarians as well as users do not have enough awareness about difficulties and challenges of having e - books in libraries. The issues are as follows:

- Selecting e-books
- Licensing
- Acquisition and
- Management of e-books collection in library

In addition to acquisition issues there are some additional issues like

- Cataloguing of e-books
- Attitude of vendors towards e-book
- Impact of e-books on reading habits of students or faculty
- Restrictions on sharing of e-books

- limits on e-books downloading, printing and sending electronically
- Low probability of availability academic titles in e-book format.

5.1.6.1. Definition of e-book

A common definition of e-books interprets as: e-book is a book like structure having facility to read text on screen of a digital device. Another definition describes e-book as.

Any content that is recognizable 'book like' regardless of size, origin or composition but excluding serial publications, made available electronically for reference reading on any device (handheld - kindle like device or desk bound device - laptop or desk computers) that posses a screen.

It is observed that most students read academic e-book on desktop or laptops rather than iPads, Smartphone or mobile devices.

5.1.6.2. Status of e-books Today

Consumer e-book market is growing steadily and quantitatively. It would be about 5%. The companies which dominate e-book selling are Amazon and Barnes & Noble's and grab almost 85% of e-books sale. However, they are more popular among individual readers than libraries. Libraries prefer to subscribe e-books through publishers and they prefer to buy reference works, text books and specialized subject collections.

There are several factors which impact library's acceptance for e–books such as :

- Publication delay
- Restrictive licensing terms
- Limitations on use of e - books for inter library loan or even restriction or lending them to own users
- No standardization of e - books formats
- Tedious access mechanism.

5.1.6.3. Availability of scholarly titles as e-books

e-Books selection, acquisition and management are found to be complex and expensive due to:-

(i) Comparatively less scholarly titles are available in e-book form.

(ii) Vendor emphasize on promoting popular titles than scholarly titles in e-books

(iii) If library wishes to build e- books collection in various subject then there would not be e-books publishers in several subject areas.

Library may prefer to have books which are heavily and most used text books in e - books form but it is noticed that they are not generally available in new e-books lot.

5.1.6.4. e-book Formats

The e-books are available in various formats. PDF is the most universally accepted file format for e-journals or serials but there is no standard format for e-books. However, e-books are available in almost 16 file formats. With this multiplicity of e-book file format, libraries find it inconvenient to develop e-books collections. Many formats are readable only through a particular publisher's website or devices. The publishers try to bring restrictions on e-books by imposing Digital Right Management (DRM) System. DRM is an access control technology used by copy right holders to limit use of digital contents. DRM may allow or deny the right to transfer content from one device to another. This was the major hurdle faced by libraries in adopting e-books in their collection. For example, kindle e-books can be read only on kindle.

Libraries prefer PDF e-book format. Other format preferred are HTML, e-pub etc. However, there are difficulties is accessing PDF formats due to the way the publisher's conversion software changes display of e-book contents.

5.1.6.5. E - Books Accessing Types

Normally when we buy printed books we own them but in case of e-books they are leased, not purchased or owned. Publishers or vendors lease e-books in the following three ways :

1. Annual access - library pays an annual subscription for one year's access.
2. Perpetual access: Library pays one time fee. However, there would be annual platform fee to be paid.
3. Pay per use - Library need to charge based on the number of users (titles viewed or pages viewed) plus there would be additional platform fee for ebooks usage.

Libraries normally prefer annual access. In order to get continuous access every year payment need to be made else the e - books access would be discontinued. We therefore, see a major shift from ownership to leasing in case of e-books usage.

5.1.6.6. E - Books Licensing

In addition to different ways of accessing e–books, library needs to sign license agreement with the publishers. This licensing process is a bit complex and it imposes a lot many binding and restrictions on libraries, which impacts their efforts to put ebooks into use. It becomes difficult for libraries to handle legal aspect of license agreement. The impact is seen in the following ways :

(a) Single copy of any printed books is bought and is circulated among many readers and further copying is also considered by "fair use" clause of copy right. Whereas e-books circulation cannot be done in the same way. There may be restriction on lending e-books to library patrons liberally

(b) e-book cannot be shared to other library or given on inter library loan. Moreover, fair use clause does not apply while putting e-books in use. Digital millennium copy right act gives more right to put more restriction of e-book usage.

How e-books are marketed

e - books are normally marketed to academic libraries in the following channels.

- Publishers offer e - books directly to libraries. Examples: Elsevier, Oxford University Press, Royal Society Chemistry and Springer.

- SpecialistAggregators – They provide packages of e-book contents in particular subject area. Example: Knives offers engg. titles from 100 publishers.
- Large aggregators : They offer e - books in many disciplines from multiple publishers. Examples: Dawson era, EBL e - library (ProQuest), EBSCO, my library and some nonprofit institutions as J-STOR and project MUSE.
- Library vendors- Who provide print volumes as well as e - book available from aggregators and publishes.

5.1.6.7. E - books Available Offers for Library

Library may go for individual e - books or they can go for e - books package. Various subject wise packages are available for example Springer books

5.1.6.8. E - Books Pricing Issues

There is one more factor making e - books unpopular among libraries, because of their peculiar pricing method. Any academic e - book would cost more than its printed versions only exception is for school books otherwise e - books costs 50% more than printed price. Perpetual access of e - book costs 20 to 100% more than equivalent hardcover price. In every leasing mode libraries need to pay additionally annual platform fee also.

Conclusion : There are various difficulties in acquiring e - books in the library collection. e - book still has not achieved enough sustainability so that their collection in library would grow. Access restrictions, tedious licensing process, harsh copy right laws, publisher's non friendly technology and behavior are making libraries reluctant to go for e – books, although e - book format is becoming popular among the library patrons.

5.1.6.9. Step to acquire e-books in library

Having all the above constrains, libraries still try to make more efforts to facilitate their patrons by acquiring good number of academic e-books. The steps to acquire e - books world be as follows:

(a) To select e-books either individual titles or package of various e - books collection in various subject areas.

(b) Decide type of access i.e. by :
   - Annual access for
   - Perpetual access
   - Use based access

(c) Sign the license agreement with publisher

(d) Pay the subscription

(e) Provide the access as preferred
   - Single user
   - Multiuser

- IP based or through authentication

(f) Provide guidelines about e - books use to readers

(g) Frame lending policy for patrons

(h) Evaluate the usage and take decision to renew or change the e - book titles

Later in this chapter we would discuss about special cataloguing of e - books in para no. 5.2.27

E - Books portals

There are several e - book collections available on Internet. Examples:

Name	Subject Areas
• e – book.org	Engineering, Technology, Medical Economics, Health, Music, Social Sciences, Fashion Design
• Wattpad.com	Allows not only reading e - book but can share e-books and also publish e - books
• Freetechbooks.com	Technology fields
• Googlebookstore.com	Useful to buy e - book download them and read on kindle, ipad, iphone devices.
• Sapnaonline.com	Buying or downloading e - books

E - books Reading Devices

e-book reading devices are : Kindle, iPad and Tab. For android users there are apps available as FBreader- free e - book reader, moon reader - similar to FBreader one can also read e-book using above sources. One can book mark them and whenever needed can open the screen and start reading from the page where he / she stopped previous.

5.1.7. Bill processing

In this system, suppliers supply previously ordered books along with the bills. Acquisition staff would check whether the vendor has supplied exactly the same books as given in respective orders and they have arrived along with the bills in a good condition. Now the processing of bill handling involves the following tasks in the bill process system.

1. Bill entry is made by connecting it with order no.
2. The receipts of books is recorded in the order list by (tick) marking against the item. In case of multiple copy orders how many have been supplied and how many are still pending are recorded in respective boxes. Cost of books is confirmed or updated if there is any change. All the data is saved and output is obtained by adding other details like discount rate, handling and freight charges etc. The output should resemble exactly with the figures given in the bill. Total value of the bill should be cross checked.

The prices charged in the bill needs to be verified with price proofs submitted by the vendor or they are cross checked with prices given in the publisher's catalogues.

5.1.7.1. Accessioning of Books

Books supplied by the vendor along with the bill are taken up for accessioning once order verification, recording receipts and bill entry are done. Accessioning facilitates giving sr. no for each book, volume, part or copy of book. Since this is a valid data used subsequently in all processes of library as a representative codes, a unique number is to be given for each book in the library. There will not be any case where same accession number has been assigned to multiple books. There are various sequences maintained in the library for convenience for collection counting but by giving different prefix letters. Now let us see the process of accessioning.

5.1.7.1.1. Accessioning Process

For accessioning, the following types of books are received in different sequences.

1. Procurement order books
2. Direct procurement books
3. Approval process books
4. Gratis or donation books

Normally, books along with the bill are taken up one by one for accessioning. All the books pending for accessioning would be available in the background. Depending on the type, the list is accessed on the screen by giving the order and bill number, each of them is tick marked. Normally the system should assign accession numbers serially. The last accession number is displayed on top right corner. As a precautionary measure it is verified and accessioning action is invoked. System would go on assigning accession number to each book/copy. As soon as all the books listed in the bill are completely accessioned, output of bill wise accessioning is taken. This output should resemble with the bill. The output should be available along with accession number mentioned against each item. This output is attached with the bill. It signifies that the book is received and accessioned in the library. In partial manual system the accession numbers are manually written on the bill to show that the accessioning of the books has been done. After accessioning the bill, forwarding step is take up for making the payment.

5.1.7.2. Forwarding Bill for Payment

In this step the total amount of each bill is debited to budget either to book budget or department wise budget. The list of bills passed for payment on daily basis is prepared and forwarded to accounts department with librarians endorsement for payment after certifying them by stating that "books in the given bill have been received in good condition and have been accessioned in the library". Such certificate may be signed by acquisitions librarian and the chief librarian.

5.1.8. Advantage of Computerised Acquisition

In comparison with old and manual acquisition procedure we find that there are several advantages in adopting computerised acquisition process. They are as :

- Computerisation of acquisition brings systematization and discipline in acquisition work.

- Since each and every step is built in the process ensures to complete them in all respects which does not leave any loophole or manipulation. No scope to skip any step is left.
- It brings timeliness. One can crosscheck at what stage any suggestion has reached.
- It gives sufficient transparency in the process and if access is given to an indenter one can check to verify action on his / her suggestion.
- It provides to facilitate to obtain instant quantitative report as and when required
- It ensures use of professionalism in the acquisition work.

5.1.9. Transferring Acquisition Data to TPS

In acquisition data entry begins when library attends suggestion received from the faculty community and ends with accession list. The database thus created is continuously refined not only to enrich it but it gets required format (AACR-II) automatically. This happens because data is entered once, which flows further in different steps of acquisitions without entering it repeatedly.

Computerisation expects flow of data in system and no repetitive entry is required to be done and that is the success of it.

Accessioned book data thus created in acquisition process must be passed on to next library activity i. e. classification and cataloguing or to Technical Processing Section (TPS) where it is further refined to present it in the AACR - II format by adding classification number, author mark and subject readings.

5.1.10. E-bidding / E - procurement

It is a well known fact that as per Central Finance Rules, "book" is not treated as a stores item and hence there is no need to follow quotation system for purchase of books and even Auditor General accepts this rule and do not insist to purchase book through quotation system. However, many library managers try to adopt quotation system for purchase of books for various reasons. They are of the opinion that there is a great deal of scope in book pricing and they can save a lot of money if books are bought in competitive bidding, i. e. by inviting quotation.

Handling quotation procedure manually is clumsy and time consuming and in the entire process, purpose is not served i. e. buying book quickly and with competitive quotation system. The solution to this is adopting e - procurement system like other purchase systems.

e - Procurement

e - Procurement is a term used to describe the procurement of product through web enabled tools. This includes the following steps.

- Inviting and receiving quotation online on the website directly
- Execution and analysis
- Award orders via reverse auction

Let us see how it could work for the library.

By using web tools, list of books to be purchased is announced on the library website and quotations are solicited from the vendors.

e - Procurement is a mechanism for buying new books at lowest cost by online. In an online system reverse auction, suppliers have an opportunity to reduce their bids to win the order.

Using web technology suppliers connect to procurement system to bid anonymously against each other.

Benefits of e - procurement -

1. It virtually eliminates paper work and handling
2. Reduces time between inviting prices and getting books.
3. It improves communication within organization and with suppliers.
4. Helps to reduce the errors.
6. It lowers overhead cost of purchase
7. Purchasing needs comparatively less time on processing of purchase order and getting invoices is also done quickly and one can achieve success with value added purchase activity.

How books e - procurement system works? The steps are as below.

1. Library publishes list of books to be purchased on web tool template form and invites prices/ bidding from vendors within a specified time limit.
2. Each supplier registers with their details. They enter their bid price for each book and submit the form online to library.
3. Each supplier is allowed to submit lowest prices anonymously so that no one knows what others have quoted.
4. Library collects data from submissions from different suppliers which are analyzed.
5. Based on the conclusion of analysis, orders are announced to the supplier who wins the bid / quote.
6. Books are received from those suppliers with invoice listing quoted prices.
7. Books are purchased and payments are made.

The entire book procurement process could complete in a shortest possible time and with the lowest bided prices.[1]

5.1.10.1. Online purchasing of books

With advancements of e - commerce online purchasing has become part of our daily life. We prefer to buy things online as it is the most convenient way to browse product details, know the price, select the item, pay online and get product delivered at your doorstep, just by seating across a computer terminal. Individuals like to buy books of their interest through online portals. It almost serves purpose of visiting any book stall. Online books stores provide reviews of books or sometimes a few chapters of books to facilitate to make up readers mind to buy a book. The online purchase process is also very easy to use. If one has internet banking, or credit card, it serves the condition to

1. Supply chain Management -News Letter NC - State University- supply Chain resource cooperative.

buy books online. Vendors also offer service like cash on delivery. The purchaser is also given an opportunity to return the product if he is not satisfied with it in a given time limit and gets his money back.

Libraries are now not exception to adopt this way of book buying. Sometimes online book shops offer discount on some books. They also sell used or second hand books at much reduced prices. The process of online purchase of books is similar to buying any product online. The steps are as :

1. Register on online book store
2. Identify books interested by readers.
3. Select and put them in book cart
4. Finalize the purchase
5. Check out the process by making payment through credit cards or net banking
6. Provide the address of delivery and mode of dispatch
7. Receive books along with delivery challans.
8. Accession the books, process them and make them available to the reader.

As on today there are number of online book stores. It is convenient and cheaper if one chooses online books shop available in our country or otherwise one has to pay additional money for air freight and handling.

There are several online books stores from which a library or a individual can buy book. They are listed as :

- Advanced Books Exchange - ABC books
- Alibris.com
- Amazon.com (also sell e-books)
- Barnes & Noble. com (also sell e-books)
- Booker's shop
- Books a million
- The book depository
- Book finder
- Borders books & music
- Flipkart
- Powell's Books
- Prep books. com

It is better and economical if Indian libraries buy books online in India. The list is as below.

- Flipkart
- NBC India
- Infibeam
- Crossword

- Landmark
- Bookadda
- Simply books
- Amazon India
- Sapna online
- Penguin India
- URead. com

5.1.11. Acquisition Information services

Main objective of acquisition section is to timely procure the reading materials as demanded by the teachers, scientist and researcher communities. As we have seen, books are procured in various ways in the library like procurement (local), procurement (Direct), through book approval process and by adding books received on donation. Naturally indenters always look forward for information services provided by acquisition unit. The main and foremost service from acquisition would be to intimate indenters as soon as suggested books arrive in the library even though they are yet to be processed, as it is the first right of an indenter to know the arrival of a book immediately when library receives it. This is normally an action which is system built in its messaging. As the books are received and accessioned a system generated message needs to be sent to the indenting reader where by one can note the arrival of books and visit the library them process them on priority, if he / she feels so.

Library could incorporate an advanced feature where by a browsing right is given to indenter so that reader can self check the progress and know the status of his suggestion. This way library can provide transparency in acquisition process.

5.2. COMPUTERISATION OF CLASSIFICATION AND CATALOGUING

5.2.0. Introduction

Classification schemes are used in the library to facilitate organizing books on the shelves. Obviously the convenient approach to organize library collections especially from readers point of view in a library is to arrange them subject wise. Classification scheme comes in picture by which books are given subject codes or class numbers depending on the subject of a book. Till recently, library classification was done by an individual classifier by applying his intellectual skills. Although the classification task is a scientific process, it is tedious to carry out. So the work was person or classifier dependent and if there would be change in classifier then it might affect the consistency in classification work. It was therefore, necessary to develop an authority file to note general guideline of classification work done in a specific library by keeping record of newly adopted class numbers. As computer was used in various fields it was thought and questioned whether a computer could play any role in doing and simplifying classification work. This chapter attempts to explore such probabilities. It was thought if authority files could be maintained by using computers it would help to a great deal to maintain the consistency.

Alike classification, computer finds its use in cataloguing work also. It is certainly seen that a computer can be effectively used for cataloguing work. It has been especially found that computerised cataloguing helps to a great deal in typing catalogue cards, which otherwise was very much strenuous by doing it manually. Now let us elaborate these two aspects further.

Computerisation of classification work : Classification of library books was till recently done mostly manually and mostly by skilled person who is an expert in classification. It was recognized as purely an intellectual work. Classification work needs consistency. It was normally handled by a single person having some expertise or a person having fair subject knowledge. Consistency in classification is maintained by considering procedure how the work is done traditionally for years together. Before computers came into library application the work of classification way depending on the memory of the classifier and whenever there was change in classifier, the outgoing staff must pass on the old practice and all the recorded things to the new comer with a view to maintain the consistency. It was then thought whether computer could be used to maintain authority file. It is found now that computer could be used for this work. How it would be done let use discuss it.

5.2.1. Automation in classification

5.2.1.1. Using computer in library classification

Classification work consists of two aspects

1. Assigning class numbers to books depending on the subject (s) dealt in them and providing Call numbers to books
2. Assigning subject heading to facilitate search by subject heading in library catalogue.

As we have seen that classification is done using one of the classification schemes i. e. subject schedules of the scheme. Normally schemes that are commonly in use are DDC, UDC and LC.

Although the schemes are constantly developed and updated, a library would stick to use of a particular scheme and the specific edition as a new class number announced by schemes cannot be straight a way put into use, since it involves reclassification work of previously classified books. Secondly, classification is an intellectual work which involves finding exact subject of book by scanning and reading a bit. Normally this task would be handled by one person for a long time in order to maintain consistency in the classification work. However, it is necessary to take care that it would not become person dependent. The classification section therefore should maintain authority file or guide lines of classification work done since the beginning. The classification authority file would contain guide lines such as:

1. Which edition of classification is in use and since when?
2. Whether detailed classification is done or in a broad way?
3. List of new number coined when class number are not available in that particular edition of the scheme.
4. How subject headings are assigned? Whether controlled vocabulary is used or free language is used? If so, dictionary of subject heading is to be maintained as and when assigned. Authority file thus created helps a lot in classification work to maintain the consistency in library classification. Even if classifier is changed the work should not get affected. Authority file containing all the above information could be maintained using computers, which makes searching contents of authority file easy and to further maintain the same.

5.2.1.2. Using online classification

Classification systems like DDC- Dewey Decimal Classification, UDC- Universal Decimal Classification and LC - Library of Congress classification are continuously updated and revived. For quite sometimes they were publishing printed versions only but due to hard efforts of Classification Research Group (CRG), FID, OCLC, UDC consortium and LC distribution service led to prepare first machine readable forms of schemes, which subsequently resulted in publishing classification schemes in online form. Subject heading tools like LCSH-Library of Congress Subject Headings, which used to publish in printed form is also now publishing in electronic form i. e. online.

The online forms give revised and up-to-date status of classification schemes to facilitate using the latest class numbers in classification. Now let us learn some details about online versions of these schemes.

5.2.1.2.1. Web Dewey 2. 0 (DDC - 23 rd edition)

DDC is the oldest classification scheme which is an enumerated type (which also provides detailed index) and is used in most of the libraries, which is available both in printed and online forms. The DDC scheme was first devised by Melvil Dewey in 1873 and published in 1876, which organized disciplines first in broad field, subfield and then topics. DDC divides 10 main classes from 000 to 999. It has already completed 100 years with 23rd edition published in 2012. From 23rd edition it is available online named as Web Dewey 2. 0. All changes brought out are simultaneously incorporated in printed as well as online editions so it has become the most dynamic, revised, updated and easy to navigate. It is accessed on website at http://oclc. org/dewey/version/ webdewey/ (Accessed on 8th April 2016)

Silent features of Web-Dewey 2-0

- It is simple and easy to handle by the beginners also
- Continuously updated
- Provides tutorials and trials for new users.
- Provides additional searches using bullion operators
- Allows use of truncation and wild card characters.
- Allows users to create notes and to save previous searches.
- Provides ready made number building facility.
- It is interfaced with LCSH (Mapping). It also provides DDC-MESH Mapping without additional cost
- Provides linking facility to library OPAC

5.2.1.2.2. UDC online

Universal Decimal Classification (UDC) scheme is another internationally used classification system mostly used by science and technology libraries. It is slightly different from DDC and is analytico-synthetic type of scheme, which provided freedom to classifier to synthesize class number in dealing interdisciplinary subjects of a book. Secondly, it does not provide enumerated index as classifiers tend to use schedules more than index. The structure of UDC is very simple, as it uses one digit number to indicate a discipline from whole range of universe of knowledge divided into ten main classes by 0 to 9 decimal fractions and Indo Arabic numerals. It is brought out by BS: British Standard (BS. - 1000)

Online version of UDC is available since 2005 (www. udc-hub. com) on internet. It has created an international database (available in multi-lingual mode).

Salient features of UDC online are -

- UDC online is an international database.
- It provides colour combined numbers especially for main tables, common auxiliaries and special auxiliaries.
- Provides powerful searching and browsing facility
- Enables broadening or narrowing the search.
- Easy in locating new numbers.
- Provides search through UDC - dictionary keeps good control on using truncation streaming.
- Number building boxes are available to synthesize complex numbers
- Includes hierarchical subject mapping

5.2.1.2.3. Online Library of Congress Scheme

LCC is the most widely used classification scheme in USA. It has been developed by Library of Congress to organize collection in their library. The schemes is divided into 21 categories labels spreading Universe of knowledge into A to Z numbers (Excluding 1, 0, x and y). Like printed version, it is equally helpful and potential on web which facilitates to make total use for online retrieval of LC class nos. known as "classification web" (http://classificationweb. net). It's salient features are:

- Provides users to browse and search full text schedules of LCC as well as LCC class and their sub divisions.
- User can access correlated interface of LC to LCSH and also to DDC classification.
- Users can create own notes in database
- It provides users with powerful search and navigation tool.
- It facilitates automatic calculation of classification table nos.
- It provides facility of linking to local OPACs for many major vendor system. If we compare up-to-datedness of these classification systems, we find that DDC is the highly updated scheme. See the following table.

	Print	Web
DDC	23rd edition in 2011	Web Dewey 2. 0
UDC	Standard edition BS:1000- 2005	Published on web in 2001
LC	Latest 7th edition 2003	Published on web in 2002 Updated every week.

All these schemes are available in all forms e. g. print, on CD ROM and on web. Except UDC, all are interfaced automatically with LCSH, moreover LCC gives mapping of LCSH to DDC nos. also. Web Dewey additionally facilitates to save previous searches.

5.2.1.3. Subject Heading Tools (LCSH, TEST, MESH, SHE and Sears List)

Normally classification involves two aspects

1. Assigning class no. to a book using classification scheme prevalent in library.
2. Assigning subject headings to the book considering subject content of that book in coder to facilitate key word search.

Assigning subject keywords is normally done by using subject heading tools. Like classification schemes subject heading tools are available in printed volumes if the work of assigning subject key words is done manually. In a computerised library environments the sources are available online so also they could be externally loaded / interfaced with LMS, which could be used both time i. e. while assigning subject key words and in OPAC white searching books by keywords . These tools are listed as :

1. Library of congress subject headings - LCSH
2. Medical Subject Heading - MESH
3. Thesaurus of Engineering and Scientific Terms -TEST
4. Sears List of subject Headings
5. Subject Headings in Engineering(SHE)

LCSH is - The subject heading tool which is widely used in worldwide libraries. It provides subject heading having broader subject perspective.

Sears List of Subject Heading is standard thesaurus of subject terminology, facilitates tool to provide subject key words from small and medium size libraries. It works in agreements with DDC. It is continuously updated to incorporate new heading in growing literature in developmental fields like ecology and environment. It gives special attention to STEM subjects like science, technology, engineering and mathematics. In addition, it also facilitates tagging of key words considering new world events.

SHE or Subject Headings in Engineering was also in use in the library for assigning subject key words. It was contributed by Engineering Index Inc. However, after volume 28 it has not been updated.

MESH is the National Library of Medicines controlled vocabulary thesaurus and is generally used to assign subject heading in medical field, especially in indexing articles published in leading biomedical journals for Medline/ Pub Med databases. It is the most updated source.

TEST - Thesaurus of Engineering and Scientific Terms is another source used by engineering and technology libraries to assign subject key words. It is published by Info-science Today / Engineering joint council USA.

The above tools which are constantly updated are now available to browse online against subscription. The details are as under.

1. LCSH online - www. loc. gov. catdir /cpso /iccu

   www. loc. gov/aba/cataloguing/subject

   It is updated weekly

   It is available with Library of Congress and Dewey Decimal Classification.

   One can go by class no. and find subject headings or vice- a - versa.

2. MESH - www. nlm. nih. gov/mesh

   The latest update 2015 is available

3. Sears List of Subject Headings an essential guide for cataloguers is published online by EBSCO HOST at www. ebscohost. com/public/searslistofsubject headings/

Moreover, it is available free on online. There are other sources for subject headings like NASA Thesaurus and Root Thesaurus.

Updating Library Bibliographic data with classification number and subject headings.

We have seen available classification schemes and tools to choose subject headings while classifying and cataloguing books. At this point of time the book database made available from acquisition section is updated by adding classification nos, author marks, (3 alphabets from author's surname), subject heading and these updated database is made available for further cataloguing.

5.2.1.4. Experts / Intelligent systems for Library Management

Library Management Systems (LMS) are used in the library to convert normally all housekeeping function which were done manually. The LMSs provide library staff with many modules or sub-systems to carry out work by computers. However, they are not called expert or intelligent systems. To device expert or intelligent system requires higher level computing and programming. Need of expert systems is felt to replace the human intellectual task by computer system especially to perform the task of classification and cataloguing, which presently are human intellect dependent.

Several attempts have been made to develop expert systems or ES for library management. They however, remained of importance as experimentation. Considerable amount of literature has been published in LIS area. However, up till now there are no expert systems available for ready to use in the library. While devising these systems, emphasis is being given on developing automated cataloguing and classification work. A few names of ES are given just for the sake of curiosity.

Experts systems for cataloguing- There are nearly 29 systems which have been developed between 1980 and 1990s :

- MacCat
- Mapper
- Nama
- Qualcat
- Synoname etc.

In case of classification also, there were as many as 9 experts system developed for classification: examples:

- CLODx
- Cutt. x Cutter classification etc.

5.2.1.5. Colon Classification of S. R. Ranganathan

We have discussed the different classification schemes which are continuously updated and they are also used by libraries online. As far as quality of classification system is considered we must take a note of Colon Classification developed by S. R. Ranganathan. It was the first ever faceted (Analytico- Synthetic) classification scheme. The use of colon or (:) in classification signifies joining two class nos. to represent multidisciplinary nature of the book. It uses five primary categories of facets to describe different layers to represent subject facets of a book, they are PMEST

Personality : Focus of subject

Matter or properties : Properties of subject

Energy : Process or operation or activity in the subject

Space : Geographic Location

Time : Refers time properties.

Colon has been admired worldwide for its faceted nature. Many organizations including DRTC, Bangalore has attempted to carry out considerable further research on it. It has been recognized as the most structured scheme suitable for computerisation. Unfortunately, the scheme has posed difficulties in library user's point of view. It is not much in use now and it is being eradicated even from Indian libraries from where it was born.

5.2.2. Computerised Cataloguing

In the data flow process of classification point of view class nos. and subjects key words are added to it and it flows further to cataloguing process. We have seen that right from suggestion entries done in acquisition the care needs to be taken to follow AACR - II format. In cataloguing process book data entries are further refined to make them perfect to add the book data to library's main database available for circulation activity and also to OPAC search. The readers may note that the revised version of AACR-II e.g. RDA (Resource Description and Access) is currently being adopted in many libraries (Refer chapter no.7)

5.2.2.1. Refining entries as per AACR - II

Since this is the last chance to refine the database, if the newly added book has any relation with old books then catalogue relations are established accordingly. Any library software, when it is installed it will configure with MARC - 21 data fields. Thus data added in accessioning process all the fields are visualized in MARC-21 format.

5.2.2.1.1. Editing / Converting Book Data into MARC - 21 format

Once the data is uploaded into MARC - 21 formats each field is checked with information physically seen on the book and whenever editing is required it is done and data is saved. Many softwares provide facility to add data of multiple copies in one go. In Koha it is done nicely. When accession no. of first copy in the range of 10 or 20 is invoked it shows its relation with other copies. It needs careful cross checking as one might see data of previous edition also. The accession nos. of exact same edition to be picked up for data editing and edited data is saved. This is the case of editing data to convert it into MARC - 21 when it is an ongoing process.

Some libraries such stage comes when major data is uploaded or imported externally to LMS. Sometimes book data is generated in excel format and then it is converted to MARC format using MARC - editor tool. This essentially requires that the destination data format and imported data format are exactly matching with each other, else data reformation becomes inevitable. At this point it is interesting to see the list of MARC data tags for familiarization with it.

5.2.2.1.1.1. LIST OF IMPORTANT MARC – 21 TAGS

MARC is a machine readable format which enables machine to know meaning of each tag and text entered in it. These data tags are further facilitate to add fields data repeatedly. For example, if the book has number of authors then all authors are entered in a row one after other by inserting data by separating symbol like #. Another example is of data of field imprint. We know the imprint field has definite sequence like place, publisher's name and year of publishing. Thus the field is entered exactly in the same sequence with adding data separating symbols appropriately. There are similar examples of repeatable fields like class nos. and subject headings etc.

Default MARC Tags for Books

000 ?- LEADER

- 00 fixed length control field * Tag editor

020 ? - ISBN

- a International Standard Book Number

041 ? - LANGUAGE CODE

082 ? - DEWEY DECIMAL CLASSIFICATION NUMBER

- a Classification number

100 ? - MAIN ENTRY-PERSONAL AUTHOR

- a Personal name

245 ? - TITLE

- a Title *
- b Remainder of title
- c Statement of responsibility, etc

250 ? - EDITION STATEMENT

- a Edition statement

260 ? - PUBLISHER-PUBLICATION, DISTRIBUTION. ETC. (IMPRINT)

- a Place of publication, distribution, etc *
- b Name of publisher, distributor, etc *
- c Date of copyright, publication, distribution, etc *

300 ? - PHYSICAL DESCRIPTION

- a Extent *
- b Other physical details
- c Dimensions
- d Accompanying material

440 ? - SERIES-TITLE

- a Title
- b Volume number/sequential designation

500 ? - GENERAL NOTE

505 ? - FORMATTED CONTENTS NOTE

541 ? - ACQUISITION INFO-IMMEDIATE SOURCE OF ACQUISITION NOTE

- a Source of acquisition

600 ? - SUBJECT-PERSONAL NAME

650 ? - SUBJECT-TOPIC

- 99 (RLIN)
- a Topical term or geographic name as entry element * Tag editor

651 ?Subject Geographic name
-99(RLIN)

700 ? - ADDED ENTRY-PERSONAL AUTHOR

- a Personal name

856 ? - URL/ELECTRONIC LOCATION AND ACCESS

952

0 Withdrawn status

1 Lost status

2 Source of classification or shelving scheme
3 Materials specified (bound volume or other part)
4 Damaged status
5 Use restrictions
6 Koha normalized classification for sorting
7 Not for loan
8 Collection code
9 Koha item number (auto generated)
a Permanent location
• Current location
c Shelving location
d Date acquired
e Source of acquisition
f Coded location qualifier
g Cost, normal purchase price
h Serial Enumeration / chronology
i Inventory number
j Shelving control number
l Total Checkouts
m Total Renewals
n Total Holds
o Full call number
p Barcode
q Checked out
r Date last seen
s Date last borrowed
t Copy number
u Uniform Resource Identifier
v Cost, replacement price
w Price effective from
x Non-public note
y Koha item type
z Overnight Issue Only

5.2.2.2. Printing catalogue cards

Till then we have discussed data editing in fields as per AACR - II style and we are yet to see catalogue entry of a book in AACR - II format. In AACR - II catalogue entries are rendered differently with different types of books. In order to get exact entry for a particular type of book it is necessary to prepare catalogue templates by programming. To do this, books are grouped as per following types. The list of groups indicates how AARC - II renders significantly with different types of books:

1. Books with authors 1 to 3
2. Books having authors more than 3
3. Edited books
4. Conference proceedings
5. Theses and dissertations
6. Non book materials

Group wise printing program/menu is clicked with giving range of accession numbers. Blank catalogue cards in sheet form having 8 cards in one sheet are fed to the printer and catalogue cards are generated. The catalogue cards for all types of books are generated, arranged in card catalogue or shelf list card cabinets

5.2.2.3. Printing of Barcodes

Barcode technology plays a significant supportive role in library computerization. Use of barcodes brings speed and accuracy in each and every operation. Normally barcode printing facility is built in, in most of LMS, if not, librarian should ask LMS vendor to provide it without additional charges. Many links on internet provide barcode generation facility free, even it is available as one of the fonts of MS windows utility. When the barcode printing is built-in in LMS then one need not type additional prefix and suffix information other than accession no, as it is interfaced with book data base, which may not be available with free barcode printing facilities available on internet.

Generally only accessions no. is considered for bar-coding. One need not generate barcode for entire call number as it would be too long to paste on book. Every book needs minimum two barcode labels for pasting on title page and on the last page. Some libraries prefer to put additional barcode on the book cover. However, it gets worn-out unless it is protected by applying POP on it.

There are various methods to print barcodes i. e. with

1. Thermal Transfer printer (TTP)
2. Laser printer

Barcodes printed on laser printer are found to be more durable than TTP printed barcodes. Barcodes need to be pasted on respective book without any error.

5.2.2.4. F. inting spine labels and book cards

Printing of spine labels and book cards should be offshoot of computerization. Manual input accession number instead of barcode is strenuous task and it might create errors like accession numbers and other book details mismatch which could lead further to create errors in circulation operations. Labels and books card printing requires creating respective templates through programming which could be used successively.

5.2.2.5. Generating online computerised catalogue

Traditional printing of catalogue cards by using print programs and filling them in card cabinet has become an old and outdated method. This is generally done if there is backlog of cataloguing of accessioned books. Logically every accessioned book must be catalogued immediately and made it available to readers.

When library's technical processing section is up to date in cataloguing newly added books then library can very well discontinue generation of printed catalogue cards and every book catalogued is uploaded to computerised online catalogue so that books are promptly available to search in OPAC as well as available for circulation. However, whenever such step is adopted it is the duty of the library to inform about this so that users would search online catalogue than the old card catalogue.

Providing catalogue of library collection is the primary responsibility of any library. Switching to online catalogue is an up gradation to it, which would add values in this service. If any library in the twenty first century fails to provide library catalogue in either of these forms cannot claim to be a library in real sense.

5.2.2.6. Cataloguing e - books and e-Journal

We have understood cataloguing of books in a computerised environment and by using MARC - 21 data tags. We have also gone through list of MARC tags normally used in library to catalogue books.

Cataloguing of journal bound volumes is done in a similar way. As we use AARC - II style for entering data in respective fields, same method is applied in case of journal bound volumes. Data fields in case of journals somewhat differ with that of book data fields. For journal lists of MARC tags are also slightly different than for books. While installing new LMS one has to configure and select required MARC fields to be used for cataloging. Same way respective MARC - 21 tags also need to be configured and selected which would be used while cataloguing of bound volumes. Having taken into account above we would try to understand significance of cataloguing of e - books and e–journals. As a result of proliferation of journal literature publishing journal in both the format i. e. printed and digital forms has emerged as an innovative way to bring up to date-ness and with reader's preference libraries have started subscribing e - journals along with printed journal. This trend is further changed by libraries switching over to e - journals only as it is found economical than preserving printed journals. However, with addition of e - journals to library collection it has posed a new challenge before the libraries of how to handle them or how to bring bibliographic control over this new form of literature.

As we use bibliographic metadata we need to use respective metadata pertaining to journal volumes also. However, here it needs special treatment.

Cataloguing of e-journals we need to do something more than we do for cataloguing of printed journal volumes. We not only catalogue their surrogate data but at the same time we try to justify their electronic format. We give them more prominence so that while browsing catalogue of the journals reader would be facilitated to open the link provided through journal title in HTML form which takes readers to the website of the journals.

e-book collection is not only growing as journal literature which is available online but it is increasing gradually. Library need to take a note of it and give e-books also a special similar treatment by cataloguing them using respective tags to facilitate them to represent in a electronic form. In e-book case also it is necessary to provide book title in HTML form so that readers would be able to click and open e-book directly from catalogue entry. Having considered importance of new change in the cataloguing let us go through special MARC tags used for cataloguing of e-journal and e-books.

5.2.2.6.1. MARC Records Tags for e-books & e-Journals

Default MARC tags for e-books

000 -? Leader

- 00 Fixed length control field* Tag Editor

020 -ISBN

082 -Dewey Decimal classification Number

a classification Number

100 ?-MAIN ENTRY-AUTHOR-PERSONAL NAME

245 ?-TITLE

- a Title *

260 ?-PUBLISHER-PUBLICATION, DISTRIBUTION. ETC. (IMPRINT)

- a Place of publication, distribution, etc
- b Name of publisher, distributor, etc
- c Date of copyright, publication, distribution, release, etc

300 ?-PHYSICAL DESCRIPTION

- a Extent (number of discs followed by format or leave blank for mere web sites) *
- b Accompanying material

440 ?-SERIES-TITLE

- a Title
- Volume number/sequential designation

500 ?-GENERAL NOTE

541 ?-ACQUISITION INFO-IMMEDIATE SOURCE OF ACQUISITION NOTE

- a Source of acquisition

700 ? - ADDED ENTRY-PERSONAL NAME

856 ? - URL/ELECTRONIC LOCATION AND ACCESS

- Link text

Default MARC Tags for e-Journals

000 ? - LEADER

- 00 fixed length control field * Tag editor

022 ? - ISSN

- a International Standard Serial Number

082 ? - DEWEY DECIMAL CLASSIFICATION NUMBER

- a Classification number

100 ? - MAIN ENTRY-PERSONAL EDITOR

- 99 (RLIN)

110 ? - MAIN ENTRY-CORPORATE EDITOR

- 99 (RLIN)

111 ? - MAIN ENTRY-MEETING NAME

- 99 (RLIN)

130 ?- MAIN ENTRY-UNIFORM TITLE

- 99 (RLIN)

245 ? - TITLE

- a Title *
- a Remainder of title

260 ? - PUBLISHER-PUBLICATION, DISTRIBUTION, ETC. (IMPRINT)

- a Place of publication, distribution, etc *
- b Name of publisher, distributor, etc *

300 ? - PHYSICAL DESCRIPTION

- a Extent (v. :) *
- b Other physical details
- c Dimensions
- d Accompanying material

310 ?-CURRENT PUBLICATION FREQUENCY

362 ? - DATES OF PUBLICATION AND/OR SEQUENTIAL DESIGNATION

- a Dates of publication and/or sequential designation *

440 ? - SERIES-TITLE

- 99 (RLIN)

500 ? - GENERAL NOTE

541 ? - ACQUISITION INFO-IMMEDIATE SOURCE OF ACQUISITION NOTE

- a Source of acquisition

650 ? - SUBJECT-TOPIC

- 99 (RLIN)
- a Topical term or geographic name as entry element Tag editor

651 ? - SUBJECT-GEOGRAPHIC NAME

- 99 (RLIN)

653 ? - SUBJECT-UNCONTROLLED

856 ? - URL/ELECTRONIC LOCATION AND ACCESS

- Link text

5.2.3. Generating Computerised Accession Register

Prior to libraries were computerised, library management was bound by sticking to basic library methods like acquisition, classification & cataloguing. Writing accession register manually was also a part of it. Writing accession register made of ledger pages was treated to an auspicious in any library. Possessing and maintaining accession register has gained great importance in almost every library as it was mandatory in auditing and evaluation point of view. In course of time when libraries have fully computerised with all their house keeping functions, libraries do not accept the idea of discontinuing age old method of manually writing and preserving accession registers. They feel scared of auditors whether they would object to preparing accession register by using computer. It is logical that computerisation would facilitate generation of accession register. In spite of all the facts favoring, libraries still try to do a parallel work of writing accession register in administrative or auditing point of view. Many large libraries including IITs have long back stopped maintaining manually generated accession registers.

Most of standard LMSs give provision to generate computerised accession register. It would be the last step in classification and cataloguing activity as by this time bibliographic data is almost complete in all respect. Generating accession register is a kind of report generation in a excel form by specifying required columns in it. May be we can use ledger paper to get a print out of accession register pages, which could be bound and numbered to take a place of traditionally generated manual accession registers and it would be rather a daring step towards modernization of any library.

As accession lists of addition are generated with a frequency of a week or fortnight the same could be published as new list of additions electronically or displayed on website as well are circulated among the faculty and student as a part of Current Awareness Service.

5.2.4. Uploading / Integrating Book Data to Circulation

As new books added are processed in all respect and their digital data is also ready then next step is to transfer or upload book data batch wise, daily weekly or having some definite periodicity, to library main data base which would also be integrated with circulation activity. The books thus presented in library's database would be available for searching in OPAC for physical browsing and also available for circulation. Such books data uploading could be done in two ways that is uploading it in intranet as well uploading it on internet or to web server so that collection can be searched on web OPAC also.

5.2.5. Collection Development of non Book Materials

In library these days we find printed or literature in conventional forms like books, reference books and journals. We also find various non book materials also. Library therefore needs to consider various aspects of collection development of non book materials too. As we consider acquisition steps for conventional forms we need to consider similar steps in case of non book materials also. The steps are as:

- Accepting acquisition policy
- Providing pre - acquisition information service to generate needs
- Accepting suggestions to buy new material
- Check for duplication and availability
- Order them
- Receive material with bills and invoices.
- Accessioning , accounting and bill forwarding for payment
- Classification of providing subject heading / keywords heading
- Cataloging by using MARC - 21 tags
- Processing materials
- Making them available for readers
- Organizing material in separate section (closed access).

In case of acquisition of non book materials, all the conventional way of procurement of books would not be applicable. In case of non book materials we need to tap the sources out of book market.

While cataloging non book material we need to opt for detailed cataloguing by using 2nd or 3rd level of AARC - II in order to provide maximum description in the catalogue for the convenience of readers.

Non book material is generally circulated with closed access and more emphasis is given on their preservation along with making it available for readers in a restricted manner being available only a single copy and of rare value.

5.3. COMPUTERISED CIRCULATION SYSTEM

5.3.0. Tasks covered under circulation system

Circulation is the front end operation of a library. It is a focal point to have contacts of library user's community. Libraries performance relies on new efficient circulation activity, which is performed to the best satisfaction of users. It's attractive ambiance and presentation has lot of importance. In circulation section library, need to perform the following tasks.

Main Tasks

- Issue, return and reissue of books and other reading materials.
- Reservation of books and claims
- Issue of e-books
- Issue of non book material

Other Tasks

- Payment of overdue charges
- Issue of no dues certificates
- Tagging of books
- Reminders and messaging
- Book binding
- Book bank
- Physical verification

5.3.1. Master data in circulation section

Master data is the data which is collected once and used again and again by pulling down the menus. Circulation needs a large amount of master data which eases out the need by picking it out from master data. It needs master data as:

- Names of Institution library which caters the reading needs
- Names of departments available in such institutes.
- Categories of supporting staff
- Categories of readership such as. Faculty, Scientists and Researchers – Professors, AP - Asst . Prof. , Lecturers, TAs, visiting, retired awardees faculties.
- Name and codes of courses taught in the institutes with number of students.
- Category of students UG, PG, Research Scholars, Visiting, Migrated etc.
- Types of degrees awarded by the institutes
- Fine slabs, sealing limits/ rules for waving off fines etc.
- Names of binders
- Names of other libraries having understanding for resource sharing/networking

5.3.1.1. Circulation Rules

Library needs to define circulation rules which need to be incorporated in library computerised system. Such rules include:

- Privileges given to reader and group, for borrowing different types of materials and their loan periods.
  - Faculty
  - Students
  - Researchers
  - Staff
  - others
- Reservation Rules including rules for overdue changes
- Conditions of reissue/online reissue
- Rules Regarding compensation of loss of books by readers

Once master data is collected and circulation rules are entered in the system as above it ensures circulation function to go smoothly. Now let us discuss the computerised operation in the Circulation Section.

In circulation process the main emphasis is given on the core functions i. e. issue and return of library material along with other subsidiary functions such as control on late return of books, reservation and some other administrative tasks. There has been a lot of experimentation on issue and return process in the past. It is always seen how the processes is carried out accurately and without any error. In order to control main circulation process various alternatives have been tried to systematize the process, such as Browne's two card system, borrowers ticket system, or three card systems invented by S. R. Ranganathan and use of punch cards with use of computer for circulation process. It further became accurate and error free. It further simplified the process and also brought accuracy and speed in performing the issue return task.

While switching over to computerise circulation system essential things are, importing book data, patron data and circulation rules. Sometimes old data is converted into new system, by importing in it, if it is compatible or decision is taken to start a fresh by scrapping old system. Since circulation section is the front end section among all other sections proper care needs to be taken in organizing it.

In circulation process patron database and book databases are uploaded through acquisition and technical processing (classification and cataloging) are linked through LMS integration and circulation process is carried out. While computerising this process all redundant old things are dropped and process is simplified and systematized. Care is taken to see how the process works accurately and works continuously without any interruption and breakdown. Emphasis is also given on how reader's community would have faith in the new system. Now let us see how the process actually works.

5.3.2. Circulation Actions

5.3.2.1. Issue / Checkout of library material

The action of Issue / Check out works like this:

- Borrower comes to library checkout terminal with a book and his / her membership card. He/ she takes out book card, writes his member code in designated place and signs it and presents it to circulation staff.
- Staff invokes issue / check out menu, sees curser blinking in input window for membership number (Assuming library has bar-coded library collection and membership cards) staff scans bar code on reader's card, which makes system to popup borrower's account page on the screen. Staff checks genuinity of the borrower by verifying photo and other details
- If the reader is entitled to borrow the book curser will blink in window looking for inputing accession number of the book to be issued. Staff scans barcode of the book to input data.
- If the book details are correct as per physical book presented, then issue is confirmed by enter key.
- If borrower wishes to borrow multiple books then action is repeated by creating loop keeping borrower's details constant on top.
- The entire issue action is confirmed by entering twice.
- Due date slip is stamped and borrowed book are handed over to issuer, which are taken out of library exit point. Issued books are desensitised using designated machine if the collection is covered under 3M security system.
- It is better to have terminal at exit point also to cross check books issued today by once again scanning the barcodes of issued books. This cross checks, if by mistake any of the books taken out were not properly issued at checkout counter and if any discrepancy is found then such books are again brought to the counter. Such check point verification additionally facilitates borrower to bring in previously issued books also for reading in the library.
- Book theft cases are automatically caught by electronic security systems like 3M electromagnetic or RFID Systems. The system may deny issuing of books to borrowers on the following grounds
- Borrower is not entitle to borrow books due to not having free slots in entitled number or due to borrower has crossed his/her sealing limit of overdue charges and thus his account is on hold.
- Book has been already reserved by someone else. If library facilitates to show all these facts in parallel monitor to the borrower one gets chance to see sequence of issue operation as staff executes, so also one can see details of previously issued books and due fine if any on his/ her name
- If library has adopted 3M security system then all the books issued need to be de-sensitized so that no book theft alarm would sound while taking issued books out of library.

5.3.2.2. *Return / Check in*

Return of previously issued books would be very simple. The action would be like this:

- Books to be returned are presented by borrower to return terminal

- Generally return menu / screen is always kept on showing curser blinking looking for accession number input by scanning the book. Pressing key confirms the return action is complete.
- Return counter however checks the condition if return book was reserved by some other person. The enter confirms the activation of claim and mail is sent to respective claimant.
- Book cards for all the returned books are removed from issued card sequence, inserted in book pocket and books are sent for shelving except books which are indicated for reservation, which are separated and kept aside for claimant to have it.
- All the returned books are sensitized by putting it on 3M sensitizing machine showing switch towards shelving.

5.3.2.3. Reservation and claims

Every standard library management system should incorporate reservation module which facilitates readers to reserve books which they are looking for are currently issued out of library. The facility of reservation gives legitimate rights to reserve maximum 3 book. Any book could be reserved by maximum 3-4 readers. Once reserved book is returned to library LMS system should send a system generated message to the claimant stating that the reserved book is available for issue to him / her. Every claim would remain active for 3 to 5 days and after that it is made available to the next claimant existing on the claim list.

There is difference of opinion whether online reservation should be provided to readers. Generally the reservations are accepted and recorded at the return counter against borrower's ID card and with accession number of the book to be reserved and activated claim list could be displayed on notice board for the information of readers.

5.3.2.3.1. Issuing e-Books

In Indian libraries, to have e-books in their collection and issuing e-book to readers is a rare phenomenon up till now. However, in international scenario having ebook and issuing them to reader for home reading is a common practice. We are still curious to know how it is done.

Lending of e-books in libraries in western counties started in 2009 when Sonny brought out e-book reading device and had partnership with New York Public Library. Then onwards it was picked up by many libraries with having reading devices from Sonny, Barnes and Nobel and Kindle from Amazon.

We have seen that e-book format is still available as attached with various ebook reading devices respectively.

In order to avail digital lending process it needs to load over drive e-books lending system. Over drive leading requires Adobe- DRM (Digital Right Management) to ensure protection to downloaded e - books from piracy and manage lending period of library e-book.

e - Books are issued in library like printed book. If library has bought e-book with only one licensed copy then such book would be issued once at a time and it is lent to others when first lending time expires. Secondly, e-books do not get worn out. Publisher normally fix a limit on life of any e-book in library which is normally issued to 26 users, after that library needs to renew the subscription.

Now with the availability of Kindle from Amazon and with 3M cloud, e-book lending has improved. Adopting Overdrive software or similar compatible technology lending of e- books in library has now further become easier. Mobi Pocket, Barnes & Noble, Lendle (for kindle books) and book lending. com are similar other available systems.

Now let us understand how actually reader gets e-books issued from his / her library.

1. Reader to register his device or interface it with his borrowing membership.
2. The device need to have overdrive or similar e-book lending system already loaded in it.
3. One should search availability of e-books and make it sure that it is compatible to one's device.
4. Against membership e-book is issued for a certain period i. e. 5, 10 or 15 days
5. Provide login id. password given by library to download e-book to a reader.
6. The e-book is thus issued is downloaded through ORS Connection from library site to reader's device
7. Reader takes e-book thus issued to his home for reading.
8. Once access date is expired then issued book is disabled to be seen on the reader's device.
9. When lending period of pervious reader is expired then the library can issue it to other reader.
10. Buying e-books works somewhat simpler, only thing is that buyer gets reading access to e-book for a longer period and it continues with him till he renews it.

5.3.2.4. Circulation of Non Book Material

When library is fully Computerised in all respect and is capable to handle all types of library materials including non - book and non print material then there is no need to have separate issuing counters for issue of books and for non book materials like :

- Bound volumes of periodicals,
- Non-book materials - Standards, Patents Theses/Dissertations, Reprints, Reports, Manual etc.

Generally, non book materials are made available with closed access and may not be issued out of library or issued with restriction. Emphasis here is on preserving these materials from losing or from damaging as they are procured only in single copy and replacing them is always difficult. The circulation rules therefore, for non book materials need to be framed separately and incorporated in Library Management System. They need to be bar-coded and also to be protected with some kind of security system (3M).

It is worthwhile not to put digital forms of literature i. e. non print materials like CDs, DVDs, Databases (offline i. e CDs), and Audio books in circulation as chances of damaging them while handling are more. Such materials could be copied on mirror server and provided to users on intranet by interfacing through HTML list on library website.

Circulation Section other menus:

5.3.2.5. Overdue Charges / Fine Collection

While circulating books and other materials library needs to control late return of book and other things with a view to avoid delay in getting books by other members who are waiting for the same. Introducing overdue charges is just to bring some kind of discipline among the borrowers who try to return books deliberately late and charging over dues earning is never been motto behind it.

Circulation system is incorporated with some rational control of the overdue books as an example given below. Such as:

Overdue charges for late return of books for period	Amount to be levied
Up to 15 days	Rs. 0.50 Per day
15 - 30 days	Rs. 1.00 Per day
Over 30 days - two months	Rs. 2.00 Per day
Over two months	Rs 5.00 Per day

Incrementing overdue charges always helps getting materials back to library early. After a certain amount of fine is accumulated, account of borrower to be blocked to make him / her to approach circulation counter say Rs. 50 for students and Rs. 100 for faculty. It is however seen that library should not overcharge more than the cost of books (These rules may differ with library).

5.3.2.6. No Dues Certificate

In academic library a group of students pass out successful. Such students would like to seek no dues certificate while leaving the Institute for further career prospects.

No dues certificates are issued in two ways. i. e.

- GroupWise
- Individual

No dues status is considered mandatory in order to consider student for awarding degrees or course completion certificates. They are sought normally by academic sections of the institute.

Normally work of issuing no due certificates are handled manually. The no due forms generated by academic unit are distributed to all passing-out students who visit library to settle their overdue book and fine charges and get no due certificates which is finally submitted to the academic unit to ensure awarding of degree/ certificates as such it involves lot of paper work and library and academic staff spend considerable time in handling this work.

In computerised library set up it is very easy to convert this manual work in to an electronic mode by providing browsing access to accounts and academic section staff in the library circulation system to check due status of all students which works faster and helps to reduce staff time considerably.

5.3.2.7. Tagging Book Status

Sometimes in open access kind of library books are not found on shelves. Although one reason could be miss shelving or misplacement but there are various reasons for not able to trace them on shelf. Since the frustration is likely to be experienced by readers due to this, care needs to be taken to make the exact facts or status known to readers, which would be reflected in OPAC while Searching books. Let us take into account the reasons for books not traced as :

1. Books lost by readers and cost recovered
2. Books are found untraced / lost
3. Books are damaged
4. Books which are temporarily missing
5. Books were sent for binding

When the books are issued, the status is invariably reflected in books search but books not found due to the above reasons need to be indicated in database which is called 'tagging of books'. In the above cases except for books which are sent for binding and it is definite that they would come back soon, the books may not be traced immediately. It is therefore necessary that above status in data base must be attached by tagging so that respective status is known to reader and staff while searching them in OPAC and they would not waste time. In tagging process respective status is recorded against accession number and saved so the status which remains active until it is changed.

5.3.2.8. Binding Process

Books due to heavy circulation get damaged and become beyond serviceable. Such books need to be removed from circulation till they are repaired. Damaged books need to be sent for binding. The decision regarding type of binding and embossing after binding is governed by the policy of the library which is decided once and followed in certain time period. Decision about selection of good binders need also to be taken once and such panel of binders remains effective in the whole year.

It is the duty of shelf attendant to remove books from shelving or from lot of returned books which need binding. A list of such books is prepared and binders are invited to take up the work of binding. Binding orders are prepared, singed and given to the binder along with physical books as per list. The care needs to be taken while removing books physically out, that such book are issued for binding with probable date by which they would come back so that the status "In Binding" is reflected in books search so also track is kept to obtain books back from the binder in time. When such books are received back they should be returned to system to again change the status as "Available". The books are technically processed by putting due date slips and spine labels so also it is to be ensured that binder has not damaged or removed magnetic tapes of security systems. If magnetic tape is found missing then it is to be reinserted and verified. The same process is applied to restore the tagged status of the books.

5.3.2.9. Reminder and Messaging Systems

As long as reader is borrowing member of library there are several points of time that library needs to communicate to him / her only in the interest of his / her membership, although it is the primary responsibility of member to know his account details such as books issued by him, due dates of return of books, about books he / she has reserved and about liability of payment of overdue charges and also about book lost by him / her. However, on part of library as a courtesy to keep him informed and updated about his account with adding some values to services. Readers also appreciate such service and also try to complain if he / she fails to get an urgent communication from the library. If such communication or messaging are staff dependent then it is likely that it may not be done timely or might be forgotten. In a computerised environment there should be system generated messaging to the users. The list of events/ times the reader is reminded or informed as below.

1. Message when reserved book is received in library (Instantly).
2. Message about due date of return of book on previous day.
3. Message about book is outstanding.
4. Message about payment of overdue charges.
5. Message about indicating his account is on hold due to reaching maximum fine amount sealing.
6. Message about for long time not availing library services.
7. Message about call back of any book required urgently by other reader or by library.

5.3.2.10. Book Bank and study Room Collection

In academic library especially one catering reading need of undergraduate students we find invariably facility of book bank. Under book bank facility students are entitled to get set of text books required for courses taught in a particular semester. These books are issued for a period of one semester. State Government or Universities provide special funds to libraries to develop such collection. The deserving students generally belong to one of the following.

1. Students from SC / ST Specialized Class.
2. Economically Backward Students
3. Other than backward students with parent income limit (EBC).

Such books are procured separately and accessioned separately by individualizing them by prefixing some letters and organized in separate collection. Library may frame circulation rules separately for book bank collection. The opportunity is given to all such students who are entitled by giving them additional privilege or entitlement added to the students library account to borrow books well before they are issued out. All other rules regarding timely return etc are applicable as due in case of normal books. As semester progresses fresh lot of books are issued/borrowed after the students return the previous books.

5.3.2.10.1. Study Room Collection

It could be a rational of librarianship if it would facilitate to give opportunity to students to read essential book pertaining to student's academic needs any time in the library itself. Generally especially academic libraries do provides readers with facility to read books at least one copy in the library which belong to prescribed text book collection, or books which are heavily demanded and reserved by the readers and the reference books having high reference service value. It is necessary to pick one copy each of such books to organize their collection separately under the name "Study Room Reading Collection". These books are meant for reading them only in the library. Availability all such books in the collection is ensured by not issuing them during the library hours. At the most they could be issued as overnight i. e. just before library is closed and returned by the time library is opened next day morning. It is difficult to control this collection manually but in computerised way it can be very well done. As soon as books are separated and marked as "Study Room" the status would be tagged accordingly to prevent them from issuing like other general book. Some circulation rules could be designed and incorporated in the system. Such collection can further be augmented to make it self served. If computer is kept in library near to study room collection student can take a book by scanning barcode of book and member card. In the same way it would be scanned again to mark it as return with toggle menu button (To issue/ to return). This way book movement could be tracked as well as statistics of books used could also be maintained.

5.3.2.11. Reports and Statistics from Circulation Section

Circulation is such a section where library usage could be measured in terms of:

1. Books issued and returned during certain period quarterly/ half yearly /annually
2. Books claimed in a given time
3. Maximum issued / read books
4. Most defaulters of library or paid highest overdue charges.
5. Maximum books read by a user
6. Book lost by users and cost paid
7. No of books untraced, damaged, misplaced etc.

Library Advisory Committee would always demand such statistics regarding usage of library. The reports which are routine type are obtained just by specifying time period. Sometimes queries are asked which cannot be generated through readymade query program on menus. In such cases fresh query script is written in query language like SQL and query is run to get desired output. This is possible with a library system which is based on open source platform like Linux. Else such report is sought from system vendor by paying charges separately.

It is therefore, always advantages if one of the library staff possesses the skill of maintaining and handling LMS so that scripts for new queries could be written and required information could be quickly obtained and provided to library committee. It is therefore advisable that enthusiastic members to acquire such skills which could be additionally utilized in attending small system breakdown problems also or they may be specially trained for the same.

5.3.2.12. Advanced Circulation Automation Features

Librarian should be keen and enthusiastic to provide library users with advanced automation features. It of course needs initiative from librarian to design good features out of his think tank and get them devised with the help of local software expert being an open source software or get it done from LMS system vendor. LMS manufacturers always try to provide generally required things in library softwares. They do not show any innovative features in the beginning while installing the system but in business point of view look towards librarian to think, suggest and get it done against additional charges. However, with open source library softwares librarian have a lot of freedom to provide advanced features. The authors out of his own expertise has attempted to discuss some of such good and probable features while discussing library LMS migration issues in separate chapter which would be useful in the interest of readers.

5.3.2.12.1. Instant Messaging Systems

Web 2. 0 technology have gifted library a tool to post messages to active library users which would provide interactive messaging system under "Instant Messaging" category. The feature works like this :

Assuming that library provides Wi-Fi Connectivity and most of readers are online on website either searching OPAC or reading e-resources, e-book etc, circulation librarian can post announcements and messages to reach one and all available in the library regarding:

- Extension of library timings
- About new services introduced
- To inform calendar events
- Alerting readers that library is getting closed.

Above are the one sided message communication service However, if the librarian remain interactive with users online through chat pop up screen and would like to help users if they have any problem while being in the library and about difficulties they face in using any e - resource, it would be well appreciated. Similar services are provided under "Virtual Reference Services. "

5.3.2.12.2. Self check out and online renewal

Self checkout system would be one of the best and innovative features of the computerised circulation system. With 3M technology such facility can be provided to users by purchasing highly specialized kiosk.

However, 3M equipments required for this feature is very costly. However, this could be devised as offshoot of computerised circulation system. Generally library provides facility to users to access and browse their own library book account page through proper authentication as used on the institute intranet to access internet resources. Such facility can be used to provide self issue facility by incorporating further additional authentication like digital signature or biometric authentication or by providing pin number. Such further additional authentication could be honored by circulation system to provide book issue menu screen to user to issue books and close it by logging out once issue work is done. The issue screen could work with timer so that it gets switched off automatically.

Online renewal is another useful feature which could be provided to users to online renew the books which were previously borrowed by the readers. Same authentication system used to provide users with facility to browse their own account page can be further used to facilitate reader to renew online reissue the book already borrowed by them provided the book which is to be online renewed has not been reserved by anyone else and user has entitlement to issue book online. This facilitates user to have book for further loan period without bringing them physically to library. This helps library to reduce traffic of readers who otherwise have to come to library just to return the books and reissue them, which gives relief for both.

5.3.2.12.3. Use of Biometric or Digital Signature Authentication

Use of barcode technology has brought accuracy and speed in inputting data in library systems which have eventually also increased speed and accuracy of transaction in circulation activity. However, it doesn't provide 100% perfection in the issue work as errors are found in scanning of barcodes. Sometimes exchanging of bar-coded ID cards or misusing them by borrower could create faulty transaction. In order to achieve full proof authentication there are other methods available such as.

- Biometric method
- Digital signature

Modern LMS are still to introduce these new features of such authentication modes. If in circulation activity these methods are used then it would bring perfection in the circulation process. While using these new methods library need to include biometric data of patrons. In issue transaction in addition to bar-coded ID cards, patron's digital thumb impression is also taken and cross checked with the biometric thumb impression of patron in his / her record. If perfect match is found it is accepted for creating issue transaction, similarly digital signatures also could be used as alternative to biometric method. If one of these technique is used then library need not maintain book card backup while issuing the books and the method of maintaining them could also be stopped.

5.3.2.12.4. Providing Collection Location Features in OPAC

Reader search books in library OPAC, which gives them class nos. of books they are looking for. The readers then try to further ascertain where that class nos. are located in library's classified order on shelves. They further try to search where the particular book having that class no. is kept i. e. in which rack it is kept and on which shelf it is placed. Library system does not give readers with exact location like row no, rack no and shelf no. The reader therefore have to spend considerable time in decoding the class nos. of books. This procedure certainly do not provide convenience to library users. However, in computerised environment it is expected that library should logically provide the exact location of books or location data of book shelving in OPAC search.

Author conforms that this could be done by digitizing library shelving map where it provides an aerial view of stacking area. Using Geographic Information Systems (GIS) facilitates linking spatial attributes of books with the bibliographical data. It has been proved that using GIS system, it is possible to give exact location of books that up to a shelf level. This would definitely give great relief and convenience to library users thereby they can straight a way find the exact location of the books. Now with use of augmented reality devices readers can also find out exact location of book on shelves.

5.3.2.12.5. Virtual Browsing systems

Library OPAC till now gives only the surrogate data about books. User is unable to get any more features which gives them some idea of contents of books. Now it has been possible to broaden or widen the scope of OPAC by incorporating the following additional features of every books in the library OPAC:

1. 3D Colour image of book
2. Content pages of book
3. Review
4. Preface
5. Short biography of author-

Readers keep searching books in OPAC when they find the book suitable to their choice is issued to someone else. In this situation if OPAC has above attributes of the required book, then it helps reader to virtually browse and decides whether the book is really required or not and if required he can try to have it using available means. It is not difficult to add these attributes to bibliographic metadata of the book. Virtually browsing the book is an innovative feature to adopt. It would be certainly appreciated by the users widely.

5.3.2.12.6. Library Physical Access Control System

Present day libraries try to provide as much freedom to readers as possible. Open access library system is example of it. This way libraries want to be more liberal towards the readers. However, there are various hazards and risk in this approach. Unauthorized entry to library is one of the concern of today's library security. Controlling unauthorized entries has become a serious issue to library management. Use of 3M electron magnetic security system and RFID help to control problem to some extent. However, if libraries try to adopt better and comprehensive systems and technology they could have better solution to check unauthorized entries. There are several physical access control systems available which can be used in the library such as:

- Turn style and speed style gates and doors.
- Revolving doors / Mechanical gates
- Mantraps
- Smart card access systems
- Biometric and finger print authenticated access control
- Automatic sliding doors

- RFID card access control system.
- Facıal recognition access control systems.

All libraries may not afford to have these highly costing physical access control systems but they can have minimum level of physical access control systems so that it would facilitate smooth entry to library's genuine users at the same time have control on unauthorized entry to the library. Normally libraries maintain registers to record library visitors. Instead it can record visitors by adopting one of the above systems as it would be easy and effective entry system to library. This could also be achieved by the scanning readers barcoded ID cards in a computerised entry system.

5.4. COMPUTERISED JOURNALS / SERIAL MANAGEMENT

Managing journals and serials has been found somewhat difficult, as with subscribing journal monitoring begins and it continues throughout the year. Checking journal issues, receipts and timely reminding non receipts of them is the main task in the journal Section. Libraries have been using manual cardex system for creating records of receipts of issues of subscribed journals and for keeping a track of non receipt of journal issues the work was somehow controlled. However, it becomes really hectic especially in a large library. Computerisation readily helps in streamlining this task. In following paras we would be going into details how it is done in a computerised way.

5.4.0. Tasks Covered

In a broader sense the major tasks which would be handled in journal control are as :

1. Subscription and renewal
2. Monitoring receipts of issues and reminding non receipts.
3. Binding of volumes and processing.
4. Information services from journal management section.

We would discuss how the above major tasks are performed in computerised environment. Let us begin with pre subscription information service.

5.4.1. Pre Subscription Information Services

Like book acquisition possibility of getting frequent suggestions to subscribe new journals is comparatively less. Normally list of journals subscribed every year remains the same with changes here and there. In course of several years journal subscription list is developed and maintained. Journals requirements are generally categorized as core, sharing, interdisciplinary and allied. Efforts are made to keep consistency in procurement. Any journal once subscribed it is liability for the library to continue it every year for long time is very difficult to avoid. Each journal is therefore selected with careful assessment and scrutiny. However, journal subscription list could be trimmed for two reasons i. e.

1. Non availability of adequate funds
2. Due to switching from print to non print (soft copy) to achieve conservation of funds.

In Spite of all these factors it is the responsibility of journals section to keep informed departments and individual subject experts about publishing of new journals. Such information is circulated to all those interested through the following modes.

1. Circulating sample issues physically.
2. By publishing images of (samples issues) contents pages and reviews electronically
3. Forwarding publishers catalogue and announcements. All information about journals is published and updated regularly through following bibliographic tools. They could be purchased yearly or they could be subscribed to get online access. Library staff as well as teachers and scientists can very well consult these tools to get information about newly published journals.

The list of Journal listing tools is as follows :

1. ULRICH's Periodicals Directory-

   It is International Directory of Periodicals. Now it is published on web with name ULRICH'sWeb- www. ulrichsweb. com

   Global Serials Directory-

   It lists over 30000 scholarly journal published worldwide. It is named after its originator Lady - Carolyn Farquhar Ulrich. She was head of periodicals at New York Public Library.
2. Magazines for Libraries - It is brought out by ProQuest which lists 5200 full text magazines. There is journals directory of India also .
3. Directory of Indian Science Periodicals.
4. National Science Library-Directory of Indian Scientific Periodicals, Directory of Indian Science Technology and Medicine Journals http://nsl. niscair. res. in/STM Journals. org
5. Directory - Indian Journals (E - Directory)
   http://www. indianjournals. com
6. Journals Directory of India
   www. connectjournals. com
7. Directory of Periodicals in SAARC
   http://www.sdc.gov.in

   It is published by SAARC Documentation Centre
8. Directory of online journals By National Library, Kolkata.
   www. nationalibrary.gov.in/dirjsoft.pdf

These days joining consortia and subscribing periodicals is found to be economical. There are various consortia in India. Their websites provide list of journals available online.

- INDEST - Consortium - http://paniit.ac.in/indest
- INFONET - INFLIBNET - http:// www.infonet.co.in

5.4.1.1. Master Data Creation

Creation of master data for computerised journals management system is huge but very useful task. It involves pre-recording various data elements relating to periodical literature. The list of such master data would be as :

- Titles of Journals
- ISSN Nos.
- Names of publishers
- Country of Origin
- Language
- Journals websites addresses
- Periodicity - weekly / fort nightly / quarterly/ half yearly / annual or /irregular
- Medium - print / online
- Mode of dispatch - sea mail/airmail/ cargo / airlifted
- International Currency Codes
- Vendor/ agents
- Binding Type
- Binder
- Budget/department budget
- Names of Institutes
- Subjects
- Type - Subscribed
  - — Gratis
  - — Exchange
- Form - Print
  - — E-Journal
  - — Video journal

5.4.1.2. Allocation of Budget

We have considered how budget provision is made while discussing book acquisition system. Similarly we need to allocate budget for subscription of journals in budget master of computerised journals control system, one can go again to budget allocation module and allocate budget for journals as follows :

Library's Main budget
Amount received for the current year

Plan Budget
- Purchase of Books

Non-plan budget
- Budget for journal
- for the division
- Journal Budget
- Print Journal
- E-Journals

The amounts thus allocated are saved which would be further consumed while making subscription payments.

5.4.2. Menus in Journals Management (Serial's Control)

5.4.2.1. Handling Journal Subscription Suggestion

We have seen new journal subscription suggestion is not a frequent thing. Most of the time more or less same list of journals continued with minor changes in it. If library is facing budget crunch then rationally some journals are deleted through process of recirculation of the previous year's list of journals. The list of core or priority journals may be kept untouched and cut is applied to only secondary type of journals. Some times as a conservative step libraries switch only to e - journals mode and simultaneous subscribing of print subscription is discontinued. At this stage some new journals subscription suggestions are entertained. In case of journals if institute decides to allocate subject or department wise budget then budget codes should match with the budget codes considered in allocation done in budget master, or common budget code is considered. Suggestion structure similar to book procurement may be considered to identify journals suggestions. Library would update the suggestions by filling gaps in bibliographic data and suggestions are entered in the system considering AACR - II format.

5.4.2.1.1. Journal Approval Process

If we consider the discussion done in previous para then we would get two lists for approvals.

1. List of previous year's subscription list.
2. List of new journal subscription list.

One can generate list of last year's subscription in an html format having radio buttons for each journal to select and approve. The list is then forwarded for approval, as the library authority would first considering appropriate increase in journal budget, increase in subscription rates and inflation the list is approved and then blanket approval for journal list is given by selecting all or by deleting a few. The newly approved list of current journals is imported in the system indicating it for current years and saved. In case of new journal subscription suggestion, a fresh online approval is taken by making necessary budget provision to take care of newly suggested journal and imported into system indicating the period of current year. Thus newly approved and imported journal entries to system would be further considered for renewal purpose.

5.4.2.1.2. Subscription and Renewal

When we have all the data of the journals which have been approved for subscribing for the current year, next step is to prepare the subscription orders. Subscribing of journals, generally done through publishers, agents or vendors as it is convenient because library can pursue non receipt of journal issues quickly or vendor could be asked for refund if a large number of issues are not received after the subscription is paid.

Subscription orders are generated by picking up order number as assigned by the system. The entire list of journal from approved status is invoked. One may select the vendor code and after sorting journal list agent-wise only tick marked journals are to be ordered to the respective agent or vendor. Before the order is finalized each entry to be verified for completeness by pulling down menus to access respective data fields in master data such as :

1. Title
2. Publisher
3. Frequency
4. ISSN No.
5. Form: Print
6. Dispatch mode
7. Currency code
8. Subscription Amount (to be updated as we get invoice from the publisher)
9. Volume no. (updated for current year). It is always better to subscribe from first volume
10. Year (Updated for current year.)
11. Single subscription by default.

Having verified correctness of entry for each journal the order is saved. List of all titles to be ordered to a vendor is prepared. Respective template for subscription order is selected by incorporating address of vendor and order is generated. Order covering letter and list of journal titles is printed, signed and forwarded. A Soft copy of order is mailed to vendor. Subscription to e-Journals we would discuss at later stage in this chapter.

5.4.2.2. Scheduling

Scheduling computerised journal control is crucial. After subscribing any journal, controlling staff need to deal with structure of scheduled table. Software provides way to create table of issues to be received during subscription year is called scheduling. Each journal title is provided with a separate screen. While subscribing frequency of journal publishing is provided on scheduling page of a journal. When ''create schedule'' button is clicked then the respective schedule for entire year is prepared. Considering dispatch mode for each issue tentative receiving date is fixed giving allowance of days required for an issue to receive in the library as indicated by dispatch mode. For each issue provisions are made to record.

- Date of receipt of issue
- No of copies received
- If received in soiled/damaged condition.

Like this for each journal title separate schedule is generated and kept ready for recording receipt of issues.

5.4.2.2.1. Receiving / Recording Receipts of Issue

When Journal issues are received by Knowing title, receiving /recording menu is opened. Entry of respective issues is recorded at respective point in the table and data is saved. Journal issues are stamped with date and sent for displaying on display stands.

5.4.2.3. Sending Reminders for Non Receipt of Journal Issues

Obtaining details of journal issues in case they are not received or lost in transit is really crucial task, as journal issues go out of print very quickly and timely action of reminding non receipt of issues and obtaining them needs to be done immediately. Doing it manually is difficult and delay results in leaving gaps in journal volumes. In computerised journal management system it is comparatively very easy to do it. It facilitates to generate report of non - receipt of journals periodically and action of preparing reminders and forwarding soft copies to vendor/ publishers is generally built in. If time schedule is prepared then attending the problem timely becomes feasible.

5.4.2.4. Journal Merger, Splitting and Discontinuation

Due to commercial difficulties and adjustment, publishers take decisions about merger, splitting and diseasing of journals. It could happen any time during progress of completing volume of journals. It is however, duty of agents or publishers to keep updated libraries about these developments. As soon as intimations are received necessary modifications in data base are incorporated so post merger or split even supply of journal does not suffer otherwise library would not be aware of these happenings which also results in frustration of readers.

5.4.2.5. Handling of Invoices

When library procures books, it receives books first and payments are done afterwards. However, in case of journals it is the other way round that the subscription payment is done first and issues are received afterwards. Many libraries prefer to make payments to vendors or agents as soon as invoices are raised and wait till library gets the conformation when agents pay to the publishers. Unless vendors do it promptly payment process gets delayed which affects the supply of journal issues to library. Some vendors play mischief by not making payments to publishers at all and keep libraries under ignorance and waiting. Libraries should be careful in handling this issue. They should first ensure that vendor has paid the subscription to the publishers and then arrange to pay to the vendors. Libraries therefore should cross check the proofs of payment made by vendor to the publishers along with invoices and then only arrange the payments of subscription.

As soon as invoices are received from vendors they are entered in the system. The subscription amounts need to be verified. Such payments are debited to journal budget and invoices are passed for payment with certificate from librarian that the subscription payment made to publishers in is verified.

Payments forwarding letters are generated from system and forwarded to accounts for payment.

5.4.2.6. Binding Process

5.4.2.6.1. Preparing Sets for Binding

Subscription work starts with subscription, it continues throughout the year and concludes with binding of volume when all the issues are received by the library. Binding of journals is a step towards adding new volumes to periodicals bound volume collection and also adding new data to holding collection catalogue of the library. Binding of journals has been systematized with computerised journal control systems as year progresses information about issues collection become ready for taking of binding work. Before gathering and verifying all the issues physically it is possible to make sets of volumes from journal issue data.

5.4.2.6.2. Generating Binding Work order

If one goes to binding process of the system the first steps would be to prepare sets and generate work order for binding by selecting binder code and providing list of volumes to be sent for binding could be done very easily and promptly. Having list prepared then staff can go to physical journal display and pick up journal issues listed in work order. Since system provides list of journals of which all the issues have already been received gathering journals physically becomes easy.

5.4.2.6.3. Receiving Bound Volumes

While receiving back bound volumes one has to check whether all sets sent for binding have been received back or not. Next is to check type of binding as agreed in rate contract and thirdly to check correctness of title and volume details embossed on front covers and on spines. Having confirmed receipts of volumes are to be recorded into system for further processing.

5.4.2.6.4. Payments

In binding menu bills received from binders are entered and passed for payments. The expenditure is to be debited to journal operating cost. The bound volumes thus received back and binding process is complete, they are taken up for accessioning.

5.4.2.6.5. Accessioning, Classification and Cataloguing

List of bound volumes which would be in back up is taken up for accessioning by journal title wise, the next acc. no. to previously accession volume is assigned and it is serially assigned to bound volumes waiting for accessioning Entries of accessioned bound volumes are taken up for cataloguing as per AACR–II. The MARC - tag configured at the time of LMS installation pertaining to journal are further invoked and each field data is edited for its correctness. All accessioned bound volumes completed in all respect are taken up for further technical processing i. e. generating barcodes and sticking them on to title pages, preparing book cards, shelf list cards printing and pasting of spine labels. The bound volumes would be now available for circulation.

5.4.2.6.6. Physical Verification of Bound Volumes

Although bound volumes are generally not issued out of library, it is not likely that any bound volumes would be lost. However, if library follows open access system then there is possibility of misplacing or loosing of bound volumes also. In order to check whether all the volumes are on the shelf, periodically physical verification should be carried out. To facilitate this all bound volumes need to be bar-coded so also this collection may be brought under electronic security systems like

RFID System, which takes care of inventory control also. Computerised library system makes provision to carryout physical verification by scanning barcodes and then by comparing this scanned data with that of actual stock that should have been on shelves. If any volumes are lost it could be easily identified. The reason for loosing volumes may be identified and measures are taken to make sure that bound volumes stock remains intact but at the same time it may be seen that they would be used by readers.

5.4.2.6.7. Updating Journal Holding Database

Steps taken to control journal management right from subscribing journal to making bound volumes are recorded and made available for use. The entire process completes only when bound volume data is added to holdings catalogue as successive completed volume of each journal is newly added and is updated to previously considered list of bound volumes of journals. With this now updated holdings catalogue would be available for searching. Thus the life cycle of journal management continues this way.

5.4.3. Subscription to E - Journals

Procedure to subscribe to e-journal is slightly different than subscribing to a printed journal. Once we opt for e-journal format then related specification/ details how e-Journal is obtained and made available are to be provided. We would see these issues in following paras.

5.4.3.1. Selecting E-Journal

Selection process of e-journal resembles with that of print journals. Many journals are published in print as well as in electronic form simultaneously. The journal as physically seen and seen on computer terminal is almost the same. Selecting such journal is easy. Publishers sometimes give some concession if library subscribes to both print and e-journal forms. However, now a days there is trend that libraries are switching to only e-format of journals as it is found economical than to subscribe both.

Some Journals are only published in e-form so their selection needs to be done carefully because once the e-journal is subscribed then it must be used so the spending incurred to subscribe it is well justified.

Another criterion to select a journal is to consider its impact factor. Generally journals with good impact factor are treated as scholarly or peer reviewed journals. Every year impact factor report is published by Institute of Scientific Information (ISI) in the form of journals citation report of Thompson Reuters. Task of selecting e-journal could be handled by special purchase committee which considers all the factors from subscription amount to usage of e-journal.

5.4.3.2. E-Journal Subscribing and Renewal

Set up used to subscribe normal print journal is also used for subscribing e- Journals. Same way master data is created and used by pulling down menus. Once the journal format is opted to e-Journal form then following specifications need to be provided such as:

Availability on IP based or with login and password

(i) Single user or standalone

(ii) Authentication for multi user

Access type

(i) Only browsing

(ii) Browsing and downloading (Unlimited)

Multi- User Mode

No. of users (concurrent access)

- Up to 3 users
- Up to 5 users
- Multiple user or full network access.

In case if journal is available with single user then a few IPs of specific machines are require to be given. If e-journal is obtained and made available in multi user mode then range or dynamic IP for the whole institute is given. Dynamic IP range covers IPs of all most all machines having internet connectivity. All the above details / Specifications are filled online in the subscription from available on publishers web site and printed copy is posted/mailed with payment of subscription amount in the same way as subscription order is prepared in the system.

5.4.3.3. License Agreement for E-Journals

While subscribing to e–journal/ e–book, publisher insist library to sign license agreement considering all specifications of access and availability accepted by the library. It is to be signed both by library authority and publishers. With signing license agreement library remains bound or comply with the use or the way it is made available to the users. Publishers can very well track the usage of e-Journal in a particular library as it is based on IPs of machines and if any violation of conditions specified in agreement is noticed then the library may lose the access.

5.4.3.4. Access Policy user Authentication and handling miss use

Based on the specifications how the e-Journal is obtained in the library comprehensive usage policy and guidelines need to be prepared and circulated among the users. While signing of use, users are made to accept the policy and usage constrains to make user aware of the same.

In intranet misuse of any e-journal could be watched through fire wall and if anybody violets the use conditions then some policy of imposing fine or deterrent could be introduced to prevent violations. Especially, sequential downloading of entire journal issue could cause stopping access of e-Journals.

5.4.3.5. Downloading Journal Papers as per demand

Once e-journals are put into use, reader start accessing the source from several machines It goes very smoothly provided as long as readers try only to browse and read journals online. However, if readers start downloading in addition to browsing then access speed comes down considerably which hampers the use of e-journals. It is therefore, advisable to control the access of e-journal all over by providing only browsing and downloading requirements could be limited only to a few machines available in the library. This helps users to access and browse e journal and put up requirements of downloading papers through library. This helps to make use of e-journal effectively, as downloading multiple copies of same papers can be avoided and at the same time paper once downloaded could be re-used by the others who seek to download the same papers.

5.4.3.6. *E - Journals usage statistics*

Spending considerable amount in subscribing e-journals (subscription cost of e-journals would invariably more than that of print form) would be justified if e-journals are extensively used, as simultaneous use of same source is always possible. Maintaining statistics of use of e-journals within the library or on the campus is manually difficult. Logically usage statistics is available with the publisher and it is their duty to provide it to the subscribing library, whenever asked for. Periodically such statistics is obtained, analyzed to assess whether subscribing e-Journal is justified or not.

5.4.3.7. *Advantages of Participating in Consortium*

It is found always economical to subscribe e-journal collectively through consortium by institutions working in the same field. Publishers themselves now a days provide consortium product to promote journal subscription as due to increase in subscription price and inflation credibility or affordability for libraries is coming down which affects publishers journal business adversely, hence they promote consortium way of subscribing e-journals. In India there are two consortia actively working with libraries i. e. INDEST for AICTE governed institutions and INFONET for UGC based libraries.

5.4.4. Circulation of Journal issues and bound volumes

Bound volumes and loose journal issues are normally not put into circulation. However, it depends on type of readership. If institute is of research nature then library issue policy need to be appropriately liberalized to cater to reading needs of researchers and scientists. Library's circulation rules are framed in such a way that readers would get privilege to issue all types of library material including loose journal issues, bound volumes and non book materials. As far as issuing loose journals is concerned only issues previous to the latest ones are issued only for one day. Bound volumes of journals are also issued one or two at a time and only for 3-5 days. The overdue charges are also fixed in such a way that readers would return issues and bound volumes quickly to avoid paying heavy over dues.

5.4.5. Information Services from Journal Management

There is much scope to provide information services to library users with computerised journal management as compared to manual control of journal management. Predominantly such services would be in an electronic or digital form. We would discuss the services one by one in following paras :

5.4.5.1. Publishing Current list of Subscribed Journal

Normally any library would be keen to provide information services under category "Current Awareness Service. " On the lines as a list of new addition of books the library could also provide list of journal subscribed in the current year. Such lists are forwarded to users (departments and individuals) and they could also be published on the library website. However, the list of journals would be static in nature giving some tips to locate journal issues in Journal Display Section. These days library receives and provides accesses to e-Journals to its users. The access to e-journal would also be available on website through a broad list under name of publishers or resource names. One has to click the resource name then list of journals and to a particular journal html link, which takes user to the website of a particular journal. However, it is possible to provide alphabetical list of e-journals in HTML form separately. Through this list one can locate journal title in the alphabetical way and by clicking it web site of that e-journal could be directly opened. Users find such facility convenient to use the e-journals.

5.4.5.2. Publishing Updated Journal Holding Catalogue

Users would refer current journal list by referring the list of journals subscribed. However, if one wishes to refer or search the available of previous volumes then they need to refer journal holdings catalogue. Considering this requirement library need to publish holdings catalogue also on its website. Off course again it would be in a static text form which is sufficient to give the reader to confirm whether old back volume of a particular journal is available or not. Since holding catalogue provides class no. locating old journal/back volumes on shelf would not be difficult.

5.4.5.3. Publishing weekly receipt of journal issues

This pertains to receipt of issues of printed form of journals. Since receipts of all journal issues is recorded in computerised journal management menu in scheduling table, it is possible to prepare a report giving list of journal issues received in the library at every week end. This report can be mailed to faculty and researches as well could be displayed on library notice board for information of the readers.

5.4.5.4. Content page based SDI Services

Library subscribes to printed as well as e-journals. Issues of printed journals are displayed on stands as soon as they are received. Although in the interest of readers it is expected that they visit library regularly and see/read them. If library in anticipation comes forward to take the scanned copies of journal content pages to readers mail boxes then it would be appreciable gesture on part of library. In the situation when readers prefer soft copies of journal and their visits to library are reducing day by day it is good to invite their attention towards traditional form of literature also.

5.4.5.5. RSS Feed Based Services: SDI Service

Since printed journal number is comparatively manageable to provide SDI service issue by issue, but in case of e-journals it is not so, as their number is in thousands. In such case it is better to be selective. Out of all e-journals readers may be asked if they wish to have content page service for e-journals. If so they could be asked contents pages of which e-journals they would like to see. The readers would certainly overwhelmingly respond to this survey. Once all the responses are collected they may be sorted faculty/reader wise. For all journals interested by each individual are then taken up for registering e-mails of the respective readers for RSS feed posts. Once RSS feeds are set, publisher would post content pages of all journals of interest to a faculty, as soon as they are published to the respective e-mail boxes free of cost. RSS feed is very useful feature gifted us by web 2. 0 technology.

Alternatively content pages of all journals as shown interest by the readers could be obtained in the name of librarian (e - Mail) and could be published on library website. This would facilitate to see content pages of all e-journal in which majority of readers have shown the interest.

5.4.5.6. *Information service on special issues of journals*

Many journals bring out special issues dedicated to a specific subject of journal field. Unless attention of the readers is invited the special issues remain unseen by the readers similarly some time proceedings of conferences are also published in the form of special issues. If library arranges to catalogue these issues separately with a view to cover the issues bibliographically then it is very good initiative on part of library. As a follow up arrangement could be done to issue these issues for home reading. Publishing images of such issue would also help in attracting readers towards them.

5.4.5.7. *Providing Journal Union Catalogues*

No single library can fulfill each and every need of the readers. Similarly all the journals interested by readers may not be available in one library. Depending on the journal collections of other libraries is always worthwhile. Cooperative use of each other's journal collection helps in widening quantum of journal literature. If libraries have some understanding with their neighboring libraries which would honor reader of other library then readers can have access to more number of journals than available with their own library. If group of libraries bring out cumulative list of journals then it would help in fulfilling journal needs of a library very well. If readers find required journal issues in other library then they can very well post a mail request to obtain it on inter library loan. This way good relation among libraries could be developed which could support collective and cooperative use of library literature.

5.4.6. Procuring Photocopies of Journal Papers

Reader's requirement of journal or conference papers always remains very high and it always outscores to libraries' accountability to subscribe all those required journals. Library needs to device a suitable system to attend readers needs relating to this. Library can provide online system to facilitate readers to post their requirements of journal paper to the library. By this document tracking method such requirements could be routed through guides or subject experts to seek their approved. All approved list of journal papers are then scrutinized. Availability of particular issue of journal could be tracked by scanning journal referral tools or catalogues. Once availability of specific issues is ensured inter library loan request could be posted to respective library to get either journal issue on loan or to get photocopies of required articles against payment of photocopying charges and delivery or courier charges. Scanned copies of papers could also be obtained through e-mail. A record of papers thus obtained is created in the form of text file and displayed on library website so that duplication of procurement of same papers could be avoided. Some library networks do provide service to provide photocopies of journals like DELNET, NISCAIR or National Science library. At international level British Library Document Delivery System also provides copies of journal articles and patents but the charges are very high and are beyond the procurement limit of any small libraries. Readers should note that it is possible to obtain photocopies of printed journals but sharing of copies of journal papers from e-Journals subscribed are never allowed by the publishers.

5.4.7. Electronic Document Delivery Systems

In the current digital age scope for electronic document delivery system has very limited scope. It could apply only to movement of scanned copies of paper that too from printed journals. Instead of movement of journal papers physically, papers to be scanned and converted to PDF format and mailed as attachments. It is comparatively faster than physical movement or forwarding of papers and it proves to be economical as it saves courier or delivery charges.

If library has self developed digital source then document delivery system would be operational in real sense. Library has however no freedom to download papers from online source and share them with other libraries or e-mail to any individuals outside the institute premises. Fair use clause of copy right act applied in case of photocopying of printed resources is not applicable in case of digital resources.

5.4.8. Resource sharing of journals

Libraries can come together and form a network to facilitate resource sharing especially of journal literature, applicable only to print from. In such type of resource sharing understanding and arrangement of suitable transport system is operated to facilitate visiting of readers of one library to other library which could also be used for transporting of bound volumes of journals. For handling requirement of visiting other library or requirement of obtaining bound volumes of journals could be operated online and list of people opted to go and visit other library and list of bound volumes to be obtained from other libraries could be done quickly and without time consuming paper work.

5.4.9. Journal Management Reports and Statistics

Using computerised journal management systems various reports could be generated which could be used to analyze cost benefit or cost effective analysis. The reports as given below could be very well generated, circulated and discussed.

- Expenditure on procurement of printed journal.
- Expenditure on subscribing e-journal.
- Expenditure on subscribing to digital form of literature.
- Number of bound volumes added with cumulative figures.
- Use of printed issues of journals
- Use of e-resources

- No. of people visited libraries website and time spent on website by them
- Interlibrary loan / lending statistics
- Journal papers obtained with cost.
- Statistics of library visitors and no. of requirements to visit outside

5.5. VIRTUAL REFERENCE SERVICE

5.5.0. Introduction

Reference service has remained a coherent part of library services. Reference service in its traditional ways did (short and long range services) achieve a great success in the past, as libraries used to develop collection of reference tools and needy readers also used to get reference service through reference librarian. With development of information technology especially due to wide availability of information through internet there was great shift in the basic concept of reference service. Although library services still remained readers centered, readers prefer to receive library service virtually i.e. without their physical foot prints in the library. Libraries too changed their ways of serving readers, now they try to outreach their users as much as possible. The reference service also naturally needed change in mode to provide it to users in and out of library even to users who do not belong to core reader's community.

All together new mode of providing old reference service has emerged i. e. virtual reference service. At international scenario such a service is getting stabilized. Guide lines to provide such service in a modern way have been framed by Reference and User Services Association RUSA. However, in contrast in developing countries such a concept is yet to take off in libraries. In this section we are going to spend time in elaborating it as it is of much relevance to us.

5.5.1. Virtual Reference Service: A Concept

Virtual Reference service is a reference service which is provided through chatting, video conferencing, co browsing, instant messaging (IM), voice over internet protocol or through e–Mail. The reference sources to suit these ways also would be either web based on in digital form with the library. Readers who need information or need consultation of reference libraries choose the facilities provided by libraries on their portals using internet connectively.

Organizing Virtual Reference Service : If library announces virtually reference service then readers would certainly respond to it with rewarding or gifting mood as it is the most convenient for them. However, library point of view it needs proper organization and putting considerable organizing efforts. Organizing virtual reference involves following planning steps:

- Providing VRS need not be limited to location of library it would be mostly outside and for many outside readers.
- Service time is another factor. It could be a few hours during day time, it could be after library is closed or it could be 24/7.
- Human resources required to provide it instantly by some individual or in rotation or organizing by a group of experts or by consortium.

- Individuals or group of people need information skills as well as communication and online interviewing skills.
- Cost involved to compensate efforts of human resources and for technology use. (Hardware and Software)
- Library would need to be equipped with virtual reference tool kits and e-mail Servers.

Instant messaging tools- like Trillion Gain, Fire Blog, Meebo, chat patrol and ask now. These tools have co-browsing capability also. All web browsers to be equipped with pop up facilities to contact reference libraries. It is not just chat and exchange messaging with one to one type communication chat. Technology would be capable to send web links, data sets, files and audio / video clips.

- Organizing Virtual Reference Service involves creation of reference knowledge base (Digital Resources) or knowledge base created by group of libraries or consortium. Use of cloud computing facility as well as readymade interactive digital resources are capable to answer queries of readers automatically without involvement of individuals need to be explored.
- In addition library would need a panel of subject experts to seek help in providing reference service to readers in case library resources fail to give pertinent answers.

5.5.1.1. Software Tools used for virtual Reference Services

Virtual References service looks beyond just chatting or querying through E-mails. There are various Virtual Reference Service softwares and tools such as :

Ask Jives : Claims handling 200, 000 Questions per day.

Web help : A real time information service is live and free with reference assistance on web. Voice over IP and remote control, CISCO, LUCENT, e-gain, Net agent, Human Click, Web agent web line. Among these many are used in call centre environment. For the library relevant softwares are as:

- LSSI - Announced in ALA conf in 2000.
- 24/7 Reference
- Convey Systems
- Question point by OCLC / Library Congress
- DocuTech

Instant Messaging tools are also in use for virtual reference services they are as:

- AOL
- Nordic Track
- Norelco
- Netscape
- Dell and
- Club Med

5.5.2. Virtual Reference Service Through Chat Server Websites

Virtual Reference Service mainly involves use of chat servers. However, it is not just the text message exchanging but it also involves chat along with audio, video, and screen sharing. The chat servers are normally hosted on library website. The significance of use of chat server technology is to make chat or communication live. In virtual Reference Service use of chat server technology is found convenient as it facilitates exchange of communication without interruption.

Chat servers are available to facilitate chatting. The chat server is to be installed and hosted on websites. It has slight difference from instant messaging. Instant messaging is comparatively new technology as it is available as web 2. 0 tool.

Chat server and instant messaging could be used in combination to facilitate in offering virtual reference service to library users even if they are outside the library. As compared all available tools "Google Answer" was listed on top, in usage.

5.5.2.1. *Question Point Software-OCLC*

This is a software available for providing Virtual Reference Service in library. It facilitates patrons to ask question from anywhere any time through cooperative virtual reference service. It provides high quality reference services online and round the clock. Question point provides a complete virtual reference service management system, integrating chat, e-mail, a reference knowledge base, reports and analytics to give reader a complete view of reference activity.

Question point is based on the sharing concept. Library manpower can also participate in addition to global reference service also. In addition to within library system, local consortium etc. questions point offers backup coverage 24 hours and 7 days a week.

Question point expects creation of local knowledge base and also contributes it globally with other member library.

Question point provides knowledge base available with the world cat.

Question point provides membership to libraries at cost. Library can download software and service icon is placed on library websites. Reference librarian and patrons use the tool to operate virtual reference service. www. oclc. org/question point. en. html.

5.6. COMPUTERISATION OF LIBRARY ADMINISTRATIVE TASKS

Up till now we have noted computerisation of routine or housekeeping functions of library. However, there are several other tasks in the library called administrative tasks and there is enough scope to carryout them with the help of computers. Computerisation has been proved in other jobs in bringing accuracy, speed and simplification. In the present day environment most of manually carried out administrative tasks in library are also performed using computers. These tasks include as :

1. Physical verification of library material.
2. Retrospective conversion of library data base
3. Office automation of librarian's work.

4. Handling multimedia CDs, CD collection and accompanied CDs.
5. Digital preservation of library's archival collection.

Now let us discuss them one by one.

5.6.1. Computerised physical verification

With adoption of open access library system, library materials have become more dynamic and mobile. Having freedom, users are free to move anywhere in the library, read whatever they like, they can sit anywhere and are free to move library material as they wish. The result is not only disturbing shelf arrangement but misplacement of reading materials. Over all result of this is seen in finding many books untraced in the library. There is also threat from some (very few) miscreants who try to steal books from the library. Once librarianship accepts the rational of giving freedom to readers to promote use of libraries need to accept risks of loosing or misplacement of library materials.

Secondly, libraries are developed by utilizing huge plan and non plan funds for buying sufficient reading materials to satisfy users. As buying material in an unbiased way is the responsibility of library system, it is also responsible to preserve and safeguard all procured materials. The libraries are always under administrative stress to check whether library stock is intact? Whether there are any losses?

Both the above factors take library on task to carryout physical verification of library material. Libraries have been carrying out physical verifications or stock verification periodically and submitting reports to library authorities. So far they were adopting different methods to take physical stock periodically by using :

1. Accession Registers
2. Shelf list Cards
3. Classified Catalogue
4. Checking inventory by cross marking accession numbers from number tables.

As such the old method to carryout physical stock needs considerable time and manpower. Over and above library needs to be closed during the period of stock verifications.

As computers proliferated in library gradually library routine tasks were computerized. Similarly library's administrative tasks do not remain exception to this. Library systems made it possible to carryout physical verification of library material using computers.

Preparatory Things : To carryout physical verification with the help of computers we need:

1. Bar-coding of library collections
2. File of existing library material
3. Blank file to take head count of library material physically found on the shelves.

Having these things library can very well take up the task of physical verification.

Procedures : In computerised stock verification we need a small program which gives accession number input to blank file to build a excel file. Library material from shelves is moved to computers to scan barcode of each book to input in the blank database. Otherwise computers are taken inside bays of stacking area. Like this entire collection is scanned. Now file of physically scanned book is compared with that of file having records of existing library materials in is possible to get the information about missing books. Book issued out or sent out are considered to get the find missing list.

In library management, system a subsystem is built-in is provided to facilitate to carryout physical verification whenever it is required to be done by making necessary initialization in the system.

There are definite advantages in carrying out physical verification in computerised way such as.

1. It is accurate
2. It is fast done in a short time
3. It is simple
4. No need to keep library closed.

Use of advanced system like REID makes it further simple, faster and accurate. Like books all other library collections are also consider for physical verification.

5.6.2. Retrospective Conversion of Library Database

Every library finds it difficult to manage the time in library computerisation process. The main stumbling block found is large amount of time taken to convert manual catalogue through data entry. Generally in library computerizations planning, priority is given to start circulation section first so that library users can avail the benefits of computerization first. In order to achieve this, database developments is expedited cutting short the method of filling of all fields to entering only a very few fields essential to begin circulation work. With this the data entry work gets over quickly, which facilitates providing computerised circulation facility to users in a short time.

Having completed the first and most essential phase at a later stage refining and updating of data base work is taken up retrospectively. It becomes essential as incomplete database created for circulation activity finds inadequate to carry out other bibliographic tasks like exporting or importing bibliographic database. This conversion and refining work of database at a later stage in computerization is called retrospective conversion. Now there are various methods used to take up retrospective conversion.

In order to undertake retrospective conversion there are some essential things which are necessary to be done:

Library needs to create a comprehensive database structure file considering all the bibliographic elements. It would be beneficial at the beginning stage to convert it into MARC - 21 bibliographic formats by configuring and adopting all essential MARC fields/ tags. Having done this basic requirements, there are various methods to be explored to convert the old data file into newly created comprehensive database structure, which also is MARC - 21 compatible form :

Method One : Data from old database is converted to newly created comprehensive data base using MARC editing tools. Now this database is improved by :

(i) Physically seeing the books and updating the respective entries of new database book by book.

(ii) Library staff can go to shelves and fill the data entry sheets of all books. All such filled data sheets then are used to update and improve the data in the respective entries in the database.

(iii) Instead of using old data viewed in the newly created data base, decision is taken to create parallel fresh database by using newly created comprehensive data file and at appropriate time newly created database is replaced to old database and previous data base is scrapped.

5.6.2.1. Use of Online Tools for Retro Data Conversion

We have seen how all the traditional methods are used to convert library data. These methods require lots of patience, time and additional man power. Every library understands significance of standardization of its bibliographic databases but there are difficulties to go about it. There are several other solutions available to do it by using comprehensive standardized bibliographic databases, which are available externally. Many library networks create comprehensive library database by merging standardized databases of participating library for example database archive or database bank of INFLIBNET.

There are online as well as offline databases available for free. By making use of them library can develop database for example:

Library of Congress library database : Earlier it was available on CDs but now it is available free as open access way i. e. Z39. 50 type, such databases could be used. Method of using them is to search standard data entry for each book available in library by matching ISBN number which is common. If exact match is found then the entry could be downloaded in library database.

OCLC also provides online help in developing library database. In this case library requires to take the membership of world cat of OCLC. Once the library becomes the member library gets facility to match entries corresponding to books with common ISBN number and if exact match is found then entries could be down loaded. This way entire database of library could be developed in a standard way and in a shortest possible time.

5.6.3. Automating Librarian's Office

We have discussed computerisation of most of routine functions. We have also understood how computers could be used to undertake some administrative tasks like physical verification and retrospective conversion of library database. Most of library management systems also try to cover all these aspects in their library computerisation softwares. However, none of them so far have tried to explore automation of librarian's office works. We are now going to discuss it here.

Normally managing library and coordinating all function is overseen by the librarian and his office, although Dy. Librarian and Asst. Librarians do assist the librarian in handling the administrative control but responsibility of implementing decisions remains with librarian only. It is therefore, worthwhile to discuss the issues in detail.

Normally all the admin works carried out from librarian's office is paper based and the records are maintained in files. It is a difficult and tedious job to find required information from files and restore them again to respective files. Years together the situations continues, which leads to complexity and it is necessary to find a solutions to it. It is high times that the work to be systematized and if possible automated. If at all if we plan to automate, we need to consider following tasks handled in librarian's office.

1. Office automation tasks of librarian's office.
2. Planning or control
   (i) Library Budget
   (ii) Handling purchase of machinery, hardware and furniture.
   (iii) Future plans about new library services.
   (iv) Utilization of Human Resources.
   (v) Short term planning
3. Work relating to library committees meetings and decisions taken by the committee.

Advantages of automation of librarians Office work. There are several advantages if library decides to automate librarian's office work. It is significant if we consider large quantum of work and documents handled in librarian's office :

(i) Librarian controls new and coordinates sectional activities and operations.
(ii) He provides necessary guidance and solutions to problems faced by library sections.
(iii) Librarian's office is focal point of functioning of the entire library
(iv) Librarian keeps on receiving information from section as well as from outside world.
(v) It is necessary to consolidate such information and provide it when it is asked for.

If the information technology is used to handle the information work, it would be easy to handle it and provide the services. It has been proved that with the use of computers in various jobs in library can bring quality, speed and accuracy in it.

Office automation generally considers use of information technology tools such as :

Word processing; excel sheets, digitisation, web sites, network tools and telecommunication technology, internet and email. With the use of computers there would be transforming changes in look, feel and ambiance of librarian's office. It would be easy to store information digitally and retrieve it whenever required. No need to have space or furniture to store files and papers. Librarian can communicate electronically with own readers as well as with outside world. He can exchange information with other libraries, with library network and his parent institute would be through internet, where he can use FTP or cloud server for this. He can handle personal records of employees working in library by creating their database. One can create database of dead stock items and barcode them, which facilitates undertaking physical verification of dead stock items in library. Looking into the potential of the computer and information technology it can be effectively used in carrying our library management work with more efficiently than it was handled manually.

With the use of technology, the following major tasks could be handled efficiently

1. Future Planning
2. Handling Library Purchases
3. Budgeting & controlling expenditure
4. Handling and preservation of records and decisions of library committee
5. Handling employee records
6. Handling library networks or consortium issues
7. Infrastructure Development
8. Providing virtual reference service to own readers and outside world
9. Digitizing library (maps) property records
10. Monitoring close circuit surveillance system etc.

5.6.4. Handling Multimedia, CD /DVD Collections of Accompanied CDs

Nowadays libraries especially academic libraries acquire multimedia collections along with traditional forms of literature. Libraries are also procuring publications which are available on standalone CDs or DVDs. Library nowadays also invariably receives CDs along with books as software, support or solutions. Gradually collections of CDs, DVDs and book accompanied CDs keep growing, which becomes uncontrollable and then it required special handling efforts. There would be also in demand from the readers for these multimedia collections. It being fragile medium, there is always risk if we allow users to handle them. In wrong handling they are likely to be damaged and recovering damaged CDs is a very difficult task.

In order to handle this issue library needs to think to copy all such materials to a separate mirror server to protect them and interface is made available to use them on intranet online. In case of multimedia CDs and DVDs they could also be stored on a separate server called video server to facilitate user to access them without any difficulty.

5.6.5. Digital Preservation of Library's Archival Material

Libraries are emphasizing on providing digital resources like e-journals, e - books and e - reference recourses as they are found to be more convenient to the users. However, it is very difficult to maintain their access for years together unless library ensures to have archival or perpetual access to subscribed e – resource. Library can develop its own resources in digital form and store them in digital library.

Preservation of old but valuable library collection, which is paper based form and it is going to perish, unless care is taken to preserve such resource. Logically every library finds classics and rare material in their book collection which is no longer available from anywhere in the world.

Digitizing such material and preserving them for future is the great need for library. Libraries should therefore plan systematically to digitalize, preserve them and make it available to the users forever. However, it needs to handle copy right issues but considering rare value of old collection it is worthwhile to do it legally. The book of which copy right is lapsed could be very well digitalized. Digitization involves, scanning, doing OCR, presenting in a proper shape and saving it like a e-book.

5.6.6. Other Administrative Tasks

Although we have considered computerisation of almost needs to be considered all activities of library there are various other tasks of administrative nature which needs to taken be considered into computerisation fold. For example :

1. Providing bar-coded ID cards to newly admitted students or newly joined faculty and staff.
2. Providing no dues to outgoing students and the institution leaving staff.
3. Collecting fine and cost of lost books and maintain account and their reports.
4. Handling interlibrary lending or borrowing transactions.
5. Controlling entry and access of own users and tracking unauthorized entries.
6. To maintain book bank collection and providing them to needy readers.
7. Maintaining e-mail communication with all groups of library users.

All the above tasks are administrative and ad hoc in nature and need to be tackles separately by devising separate modules in the system.

5.7. ONLINE PUBLIC ACCESS CATALOGUE (OPAC)

Providing Online Public Access Catalogue (OPAC) is an outcome of computerised library system and is the primary responsibility of any library of providing OPAC with quality to its users would be a value added computerised service. There are various studies and research are undergoing to make OPAC more effective. We are going to look into various features of OPAC.

5.7.1. Need and Utility

The final stage of classification and cataloguing tasks is to create a computerised catalogue called Online Public Access Catalogue or in short OPAC. It is a tool to search library collection. Once library provides user with OPAC they prefer to use it than using age old card catalogue, which was finding strenuous as compared to referring to an online catalogue. Search library catalogue using computer is always found to be easy and always appreciated by the users. OPAC enhances level of retrieval and provides searchin many ways.

5.7.2. Types of OPAC

If OPAC provides single window search for all types of library materials (through integration) then it is more useful. Moreover, it should be made like that. Since OPAC is available through computers library should provide enough number of browser PCs to avoid inconvenience to the users. In fact if it is equipped with bigger monitor and of touch screen type then it adds additional attractions to the users.

OPAC in its simplest form is made available within the library premises which is extended to make it available on the entire institute premises through LAN. It then made accessible in hostels, in class room or lounges, which is found more convenient for readers to access it from anywhere but within the premises.

If it is to be made available outside of institute or accessible from any remote corner of the world, then it is uploaded to internet through a dedicated web server. The OPAC uploaded on internet is called web OPAC.

5.7.3. Structure of OPAC

As far as look of OPAC is concern it should be very simple, less clumsy, user friendly and saving reader's time. The background colour and font should be cool for eyes. It should provide pop up messages in an attractive way :

While using OPAC we try to search various types of library material like.

1. Books, theses and dissertations, reference books, proceedings, monographs and corporate books.
2. Serials and journals(periodicals) currently subscribed, of older years and Union Catalogues.
3. Non - book material like standards, patents, specifications, reports, reprints, manuals, pamphlets, booklets, maps and charts.

We can search different types of publications in OPAC such as :

Group-1 : Monographs or books to search with following fields:

- Author(S)
- Title
- Editor for Corporate books
- Accession nos
- Class nos.
- ISBN numbers

We can have simple as well as advanced search with boolean operators like AND. OR and NOT

Group-2 : Publication- serials/journals

- Titles
- ISSN No.
- Publishers
- Subject key words
- Volume No.

For this group also one can use simple as well as advanced search with use of boolean operators AND. OR. NOT the search is narrowed down.

Group-3 : Publication- Non Book material which need following specific fields.

Patents, standards and reports : patent no, standard no. , specification nos. reports No.

Other fields- Title, Organization and Class No.

These materials could be searched by simple method and if required advances search method could be adapted.

Group-4 : Non print material- In this group we find different forms are used to publish materials which are more significant, so form search world help searching these types of materials:

example:

Forms such as:

CDs

Cassettes (Audio and Video)

DVDs

Films etc.

By opting to particular material they could be searched by author, title, class no, subject key words and publisher as they only differ in format from other group publications. Through above paras we considered utility of OPAC. However, there is lot of scope in bringing in more quality in OPAC structure. Let us consider how to improve quality of OPAC and widen its scope such as:

- Integrating search of all types of material through single window.
- Providing additional features of publications: Examples -
  - Image of Publication
  - Content pages
  - Preface
  - Short biography of authors.

The publications may not be searched by the above features but search material can be further elaborated by having additional feature which facilitate virtual browsing of materials in the absence of actual publication.

If we assume that different types of materials are organised on various floors of library then by using Geographic Information System (GIS) mapping of materials and using digital map of library can further facilitates searching exact location of materials e. g. knowing which material is kept where. In case of CDs also one can know which CD is kept where on which shelf of cupboard or rack.

In a very simple way all above referred materials could be searched through single widow by title and subject. However, considering all the relevant fields referred above group publications it is advisable to allow reader first to choose type of material and then provide respective field data to make the search effective.

5.7.4. Types of OPAC Searches

5.7.4.1. Simple Search Method

Let us consider common search points field to search materials in following groups :

Group - I

- Title
- Author
- Call No.
- Accession No.
- Subject Key words

Group - II

If we consider additional specific search points reg. special materials then they would be as:

Theses and Dissertations	• Degree
	• Guide Name
	• Institute or University
Conference Proceeding	• Organiser
	• Year of Conference.
	• Place of Conference.

In general searches are of two types

1. Simple search through single field

2. Advanced search- with combination of different fields.

We have seen simple search as discussed above.

5.7.4.2. Advanced Search Method

Advance search method makes simple search more narrow or minute and more specific.

- Searching multiple-authored books by combination of authors.
- Combination of words of title.
- Searching combined class nos.
- Searching combination of key words.
- Search by specific language
- Searching specific type of book.
- Searching books published in given range of years.
- Searching books published in a specified country.

In order to facilitate search by combination of fields, which is also called Boolean search where operators like AND. OR. NOT are used. Readers may find bit difficult to use the advanced search method. While making data entries of different group of publications cataloguers considers many essential fields. However, all those fields need not be considered in catalogue search. Only for specific types of publications the specific fields other than normal field could be explored: Examples

- Conference Proceedings — Conference Name
  — Place and
  — year of conference
- Dissertations or theses — Name of Guide
- for Monographs — Name of series
- for Multivolume publications — Vol. No
  — Part No
  — Supplement No.

5.7.4.3. Using MARC Tags as Search Tool

We normally consider visually recognizable bibliographic fields like author, title, and publisher etc. as we very well know what it means by author, title or publisher. However, we try to convert bibliographic data into machine readable form i.e. MARC which facilitates communication of bibliographic data (Import or Export of bibliographic data) between two computers. It is therefore also feasible to search material by MARC tags which gives readers still more comprehensive search tool. Searching material by MARC tags has never been explored so far. Since MARC tagging covers all most all major and minute features of all types of materials. Providing MARC tag option in OPAC would be more effective in advanced Search.

However, in order to make readers aware of MARC tags along with normal field table library need to provide corresponding MARC tags and once readers are familiar with them in the OPAC use would be enhanced

5.7.4.4. Facility to save OPAC Search

If searchers are allowed to save the search retrieval in the OPAC itself, it would be a great help to them as they need to perform searches of same topic again and again. They can see previously searched material and improve or refine it further.

All above referred quality features could be augmented in OPAC search structure with little more programming efforts or by using web 2. 0 tools, which can give facility to save the result searched to create one's own profile on OPAC by registering, so that when the reader next time does OPAC search he/she can very well open previous saved search and can continue his/her work.

5.7.5. OPAC for Searching Journals or Serials.

Searching journals and serials should be part of main OPAC and it can have following options like:

1. Search by title
2. Search by publishers
3. Search by ISSN no
4. Search by key words

Simple as well as in combination or advanced search for titles in current journal list or in library journal holdings catalogue can facilitate knowing availability of current as well as previous volumes of journalswhich has also equal importance.

If the searching of current journals and serials plus bound volumes is customized with library's e - resources subscription it would help readers to go to direct publishers website and access particulars e-journal provided library has current and perpetual or archival access of those resources.

5.7.6. OPAC search for non book non print materials

We have already considered necessity of providing search facility in the main OPAC for non book and non print material as in today's library these type of literature is present with considerable quantity. We can group these materials as:

Non - Book Materials

- Patent, standards, reports, specification – documents, specifications etc. by their number search
- Reprints, manuals, booklets, charts - by title, author and company/ organization
- Non - print materials CDs, DVDs, cassettes videos etc. - First by medium and then by author, title, subjects etc.

5.7.7. Other Search Options in OPAC

In addition to above readers should be provided with following options in OPAC.

1. Membership Search
2. Library calendar search to know events in library to know library holidays.

5.7.7.1. Increasing Quality of OPAC Search Retrieval

It is not sufficient to provide search methods and leave it to computer to give search retrieval as it understands. It is necessary to bring in additional quality in retrieval as well as add value to it. Creating search query depends on individual's intellectual skills. It is therefore seen that searches made by different persons for the same topic bound to be different. Let us see how to bring quality in OPAC retrieval. Care may be taken that reader would not get unwanted junk which would frustrate them. Providing on sight help (through instant messaging) would help them to avoid it. If the search retrieval provides following things then the search would be more meaning full, for examples:

- Retrieval to be on the lines of Google search quality i. e. search retrieval to be arranged as per priority of different terms given by the searcher. Moreover one can interface google search method in OPAC search itself. Considering "OR" method won't help the searcher. The retrieval may therefore consider AND & NOT mode which try to connect the search terms with plus sign.
- Clustering copies, editions, volumes and parts, series and monographs would also help to browse whole family of a title.
- Simple search may highlight on top the books which are maximum read by the readers.

- If the reader is not getting expected materials within the library he may be given option to go to the Google search, Google book store or World cat catalogue or Union catalogue of library network consortia.

5.7.8. Use of Z39. 50 Library Catalogue

Z39. 50 is a Client Server Protocol - It is used to retrieve information from the special server which is built on Z39. 50 protocol as per standards published by ANSI (American National Standard Institute) and NISO (National Information Standard Organization). Based on this protocol ISO Z39. 50 library OPACs are published. It has been adopted by Library of Congress. In library and information field it is used by many library catalogues having protocol Z39. 50. The library catalogues published having compliance with Z39.50 are treated as open source catalogues, which can be used to down load entries free of cost. Such catalogues are therefore used for developing library data base.

5.7.9. Collaborative library OPAC

When many libraries are using same LMS then it is possible to create collaborative OPAC which is accessible to all library patrons simultaneously, in which OPACs of different libraries are shown chronologically library by library. Such collaborative catalogues method promote searching availability of material in other library and making use of it through resource sharing understanding.

CONCLUSION

In this chapter we have noted various aspects of library computerisation in a detailed and elaborated manner. In each library function author has touched upon its advanced phase also. One may agree that more or less most of these functions in a broader sense have still remained the same in most of libraries. However, now the new cataloguing standards are emerging with the efforts of Library of Congress including revisions of AACR-II e. g. BIBFRAME and RDA standards, which are being looked as an alternative to MARC-21 format in the light of open linked data environment. These new developments are discussed in chapter-7 of this book.

6

Management of Library Computerisation

6.0. INTRODUCTION

Management of library computerisation depends on the type of library (small, medium and large), size of the library collection and readers strength with it. In a large library, the management needs to be done at various levels or sections. If a library considers all the related managerial aspect, then it may not face any immediate or future problems. Management of library computerisation considers the following points:-

1. Planning and Financial Management
2. Managing human resource needs utilization and organization
3. Preparing draft proposal of library computerisation.
4. Other managerial requirements.

After understanding the necessity of management in library computerization, now let us discuss the related issues as follows :

6.1. COMPUTERISATION : PLANNING & FINANCIAL MANAGEMENT

We are convinced that computerisation brings systemization and discipline in the library functioning. It also brings ease and sophistication. Staff feels vigor and motivation as they like changes in working style. When we think of bringing any technology we must accept that it is a costly affair. There are benefits of using technology, they are not visible but are notional. Once library decides to computerise its activities then it involves steps such as pre-computerisation assessment and planning; from preparations to adopt library system to functioning library without any breakdown; to bring future improvements, requires considerable amount of money. Once availability of funds is ensured one can start planning. It is not possible to evaluate benefits of computerisation in terms of money. It is therefore, necessary to plan properly and by using available funds. It must be seen how the benefits are passed on to users as early as possible. Librarian's responsibility in managing computerisation is challenging and justifying computerisation at each stage is his prime concern.

Considering the requirement of large money required for computerization, management must consider all core, subsidiary and related or even smaller issues of computerisation. However, instead of cost benefit analysis cost effectiveness analysis would be more appropriate. Let us try to understand various costings in the process of computerization.

6.1.1. Infrastructure cost

In a library computerisation, cost on infrastructure would be for:

- Buying computerisation software
- Hardware and related software including to get licensed copy of operating system
- Computer furniture
- Expenditure on UPS

In addition, there would be expenditure overheads like electrical energy, cost of air conditioning of building, changes or civil repairs are to be considered. In addition to above referred costs there would be cost on implementation of system which would also be covered under infrastructure, which further includes costs of:

- Employing human resources
- Payments to be made to contractual workers and
- Incidental expenditure on organising training for staff and readers, and expenses on stationery and consumables.

6.1.2. Recurring Costs

This includes expenditure on maintenance of LMS / system, expenses on hardware, on repairs and trouble shooting , on energy and for maintenance of peripherals.

6.1.3. Library System Development Cost

Under this, expenditure considered cost on system development, on up gradation of hardware and on improvements / changes to be brought in future. Under some special circumstances library is compelled to go for migration to an altogether new system by discarding out older system. In such situation the expenditure on infrastructure has to be done from beginning. At such stage library may have to think of financial management of computerisation freshly with a new perspective.

6.1.4. Financial Provisions: Income Generation

As financial planning needs to be done on various levels, library computerisation also need planning to make adequate provisions of funding, in order to meet entire expenditure on computerization. Library or parent institution need to explore flow of funds for this costly project. Sometimes due to scaring with such financial stress many libraries leave venturing into expenditure on computerisation and just keep quiet. In that case, such libraries lag behind in modernization. However, if the library authorities are firm and positive then they can dare into undertaking computerisation and it is experience that money comes from some or the other corners to support it. Libraries should start computerisation with this hope. We can go through a list of means to raise funds for computerisation as :

1. Utilizing library fees collected from students. Normally such fees are made available to library development.
2. Utilizing overdue charges paid by defaulting readers.
3. Investing library caution money deposit collected from the students and utilizing income from it for computerisation.
4. Many a times considerable budgeted funds remain unspent in the respective budget period. Since budgeted funds are never continued for next year and they get merged with surplus fund. Instead, at the last moment if all such funds are diverted to library computerisation good funding would be available.
5. Institute organizes various new projects and good money is collected at the end, such money could also be used for buying computers of other hardware.
6. Library can device information products and offer them to needy users and institutions at cost. The money/profit earned in such efforts could be available for computerisation.
7. Many funding agencies, foreign universities and foundations or some corporate offices offer to donate funds under their industry-social commitment provision. Government departments and university centers like INFIIBNET also provides funds for library modernization and for removing obsolescence. Such money could be effectively used for library computerisation.

6.2. MANPOWER NEEDS, PLANNING AND UTILIZATION

Library computerisation needs adequate man power at various levels and stages. Proper planning of manpower needs and management is very much necessary. Library needs man power at the following stages:

1. During preparation of computerisation needs of library.
2. During development of systems.
3. At the time of system implementation.
4. For doing ad hoc data entry work
5. In post computerisation management.

It is the duty of the computer expert to prepare systematic plan of computerization by making check list for library. Similarly at the time of system development there would be need of computer experts / programmers. If library chooses to go for commercially available readymade LMS then library may not need computer man power as referred at Sr. No. 2 above. But library certainly needs man power as indicated at Sr. No. 4. i. e. post computerisation situation that too of expert level, especially during handling and maintaining the system in running condition, if there is any breakdown, then trouble shooting and restoring system in running status, experts help is necessary.

The importance of man power therefore, is more at the implementation of system, so we need to concentrate more on it.

If we try to assess overall manpower requirement, we find that much of man power required during implementation of computerisation is of temporary or ad hoc in nature. Once the system is fully implemented then the library may not need the help of temporary staff. If we try to list out such requirement it would be like this :

1. If library's previous data (books, patrons and old issue transactions) was registered in manual way, then in order to convert this data in computerised databases library needs manpower having working knowledge of computers and library functioning plus some secretarial skills.

   Examples : To convert old data relating to cataloguing, acquisition, classification and serials management activities carried out manually.

2. To execute generation and pasting of barcodes on library collections.

3. To feed data sheets of bibliographic information of non book material which did not exist previously with a view to have bibliographic control on this collections.

In order to complete the above tasks in stipulated time the library would need manpower of temporary kind and could be had on hiring basis.

In library point of view, if bibliographic data entry work was done from individuals who know a bit of AACR - II, then it would be better, as there would do less mistakes in data entry work. Any data entry work is done at two levels / stages. One is actual data entry and the second is data validation. Data validation means to verify whether data entry has been done in a proper manner. Library can get this work done from casual employees or a contract could be given to a team, or company where-in such company can provide computers and data entry operators and completes the entire work to the satisfaction of library and finish it well within specified time. Library need to spend money for this appropriately.

Generally one person can complete data entry of 200 books per day and about 5000 books in one month. Depending on collection and expected time to complete the work, library can employ multiple people working on multiple work stations simultaneously. Roughly library need to pay on an average pay of Rs. 10, 000/-. If library employs fresh LIS graduates as trainees then library can get the work done as well as can provide opportunities to fresh graduates to have live training in library.

As far as work of bar-coding is concerned we do not need people of library science background and it could be done by anyone having basic computer knowledge. Normally, any such person could complete barcode generation and pasting of 250 books per day and 5000 to 6000 books per month. Depending on quantum of library collection and time target work could be got done by having multiple persons and on multiple work stations. Similar to data validation, someone needs to check whether bar-coding and pasting work is done properly. Bar-coding work should be done in LMS environment so that the operator need not have to enter the entire data as barcode software could be interfaced with library's online data base of books, which saves the time. As mentioned above, library can undertake data entry work by hiring additional computers and engaging contractual persons or through giving training opportunity to newly graduated individuals for a temporary period.

6.3. PREPARING DRAFT PROPOSAL OF LIBRARY COMPUTERISATION

Proposal for library computerisation could be prepared after proper study of manual operations and after consideration availablity of funds and man power. It would be considered as good a gesture if librarian himself proposes computerisation. In order to highlight contents of such proposal author has given a model proposal as below :

Subject : Drafting Library Computerisation Proposal

Main Points:

1. Background of Library:

   Librarian can give here all details like:

   a. Library collections

   b. Library users

   c. Quantum of daily transactions

   d. Daily visitors to library

   e. Library sections with staff details

   The above information will be useful in convincing authorities to consider the computerization

2. Need of library computerization

   Librarian can specify the activities and priorities of computerization

3. Benefits of library computerization

   Here one can justify library computerization and elaborate on how computerization will impact on functioning of library and its services and further on how it would be helpful to the library users.

4. Time schedule to complete expected tasks

   Here time schedule could be prepared considering activities and their priorities. Logically, top priority should be for commencing circulation activity. Then integrated activities like acquisition and classification & cataloguing could be considered. If funds are not available for automating library in one go then it could be phased out in months and years like:

   1. First Phase covering activities like ... ... Months
   2. Second Phase covering activities like ... ... Months
   3. Third Phase covering remaining tasks like ... ... Months

5. Requirement of Additional (ad hoc) manpower and hardware for computerization.

   a. Additional staff no ..... or ..... man working days for ..... months.

   b. Additional ..... PCs for ..... months.

6. Estimated Expenditure on computerization

   i. Expenditure on Phase I Rs .... (In Lakhs)

ii. Expenditure on Phase II Rs .... (In Lakhs)

iii. Expenditure on Phase III Rs .... (In Lakhs)

While estimating expenditure on library computerization the following things are to be considered:

a. Cost of Library Management System Rs .... Say 'X'

In case if the library chooses to have an open source software like Koha then there would not need cost of new LMS provided the librarian has the adequate expertise to install O. S. and software and commission it. However, if the library need to go for installing of O. S. and software through a service provider then there would be need of cost of system installation and data porting.

b. Cost of licensed copies of operating systems if windows is used or cost of royalty paid in adopting open source software Rs .... Assume as Rs. 'Y'.

c. Cost on additional man power required Rs .... Assume as 'R'. Mainly it is required to complete data entry, execution of bar-coding etc.

d. Cost on the purchase of computer hardware, software, peripherals, consumables and equipments and other things like networking, printers and UPS etc. Rs .... Assume it as 'L'

e. Cost on hiring additional computers Rs .... Say Rs. 'H'

f. Expenditure on other points as:

1. Consultancy charges to be paid on the planning of computerisation

2. Cost on training of staff and users in using software

3. Expenditure on meetings of action plan and task force committees meetings assumed it as 'I'

Considering all the above account heads, the basic total cost of computerization could be estimated as:

Total Basic estimated cost say Rs. 'Z' = Cost Rs. X + Y + R + L + H + I

Recurring Cost on Library Computerisation

Once the basic computerization is completed then there would be certain recurring (annual) expenditure on the maintenance of computeried system .

They include as:

i. Cost on LMS maintenance, improvements and major changes, normally it would be 8-10% of cost of LMS adopted. = S Librarian need to present a review report in justifying selection of the LMS

ii. Cost on up-gradation of hardware and software 'T'

Total Recurring cost would = M = S + T

List of documents to be attached with the proposal as:

- Quotations for hardware
- Cost of LMS + installation charges
- Information brochures
- Charts
- Plans
- Information collected from other libraries and the most important
- Consents from library staff for their cooperation in computerization

6.4. LIBRARY COMPUTERISATION : OTHER ADMINISTRATIVE TASKS

We considered up till now the main points about management of library computerisation. However, there are still other tasks left out which we would discuss now. They are

1. Designing layout of computer network in the institute (in and outside library)
2. Prepare records of computer hardware, software and peripherals.
3. Security of computers, providing stabilized power supply to the system and /or online UPS supply.

Now let us elaborate on the above points.

6.4.1. Designing computer network (LAN) layout

While implementing library computerisation project, it could start with minimum number of computers which includes servers, client machines and browser (OPAC) machines facilitating readers to search library materials. Initially, there could be one or two servers but strength of client machines could gradually increase step by step as the need arises. When we consider servers and client/ staff machines or machines for OPAC, it is necessary to prepare the layout or structure diagram to indicate where the servers and other machines would be located. Such a plan should have provision to add additional machines with their definite locations. It would be better if the layout is prepared with current and future expectations in mind. One should consider decisions on the following points :

i. Should every library section have independent or cluster of computers or all sections would have common computing facility?

ii. Is there need to provide independent computers to the librarian and other officers / section in-charges?

iii. How many computers to be provided to users / readers?

iv. Whether library computer network (LAN) is limited to the premises of library only or connectivity is to be provided round the institutions i. e. departments / divisions and sections? Whether LAN would be connected to hostels and residences of academics?

v. If it has been decided to increase the computer numbers phase wise then whether LAN cabling is done has provision to accommodate further increased number of computers.

If LAN network is decided or layout is prepared considering all the above points then there would be fewer problems in the future and there would be systemization in organizing the locations of servers and computers etc.

After systematically designing LAN layout design then task of LAN cabling and wiring is taken up and completed. Having done this, there would be requirement of network of electrical fixtures and fittings to provide power supply to PCs and other related equipments (light points and power points). This would also ensure uninterrupted power supply to all hardware and equipments. One should be careful in selecting data cable which should be of high standard and capacity. The work of cabling must be executed by an expert and knowledgeable person in LAN cabling. Network cabling need hubs, ports, and switches; it is therefore necessary to provide them where ever required considering present and future needs so that expansion of network could be taken up without any difficulty. While laying LAN cabling it should be ensured that the speed of signal transmission within the LAN would be adequate so that it would not result delay in communication between server, library clients and between all the networked computers. There should not be loss of any data in LAN communication.

6.4.2. Creating Inventory of Computer Hardware, Software and Peripherals

Once library starts functioning in a computerised environment, it would create large collection of servers, computers, equipments and peripherals, which would keep on adding more and more hardware items in it. Such collection adds risk as well as responsibility of providing security to it. Library therefore must prepare records of all the computers and related hardware and peripherals and see that library would not lose them in the course of time. Many a times computers are moved out of library for repairs and up-gradation. Such movements must be tracked properly with security and ensured that things taken out of library are returned back in reasonable time or else responsibility be fixed on concerned individuals or contractors for non return of computers and other equipments. All the gate passes relating to computer movements must be screened by responsible security staff at exit gate. Cost of servers and other hardware is very high and library cannot afford to lose them due to lack of security checks.

6.4.3. System's Security and Need of Uninterrupted Power Supply (UPS)

As the strength of computers, servers, equipment and other peripherals increases during library computerisation process, the security of all these equipments becomes a matter of concern to the library management. Computer technology is very much fragile and due to some faults in power supply, like tripping, fluctuation of voltage or due to short circuits can lead to damage of computers and crashing of systems. It becomes, therefore essential to have stabilized and uninterrupted power supply to the systems. Moreover, keeping fragile equipments along with highly inflammable paper based library material adds to the risks of library security. It becomes therefore necessary to handle security issues of library equipment very carefully. It is always better to go for insurance while stocking the computers and other costly equipments so that in a eventual situation of major accidents like fire, natural calamity, losses of materials and equipment could be partially recovered.

6.5. USE OF HARDWARE AND SOFTWARE

Up till now we have understood that the library softwares used to computerise library are of two or three types.

1. Software developed in-house.
2. Readymade commercial softwares available in the market.
3. Open source softwares

Library software, if it is developed with participation or association of librarian then it is better for use. One should cross check these facts while buying library software. Once library software is available and computerisation is in progress it is the responsibility of the librarian and staff that it is fully utilized, it should justify its use in all the tasks. It is also the responsibility of the librarian and library management team to maintain the software carefully, upgrade it time to time and to bring improvements in it. It is, therefore necessary for the librarian to have enough awareness of handling issues relating to management of library computerisation. With this background let us understand what care needs to be taken while handling library softwares :

6.5.1. Handling and use of Library Software

(In-house and commercial LMSs)

In the process of use of computers in library functioning there is significance of use of library softwares. We have already reviewed how library software is developed. The steps involved are systems study, systems analysis, and system development, designing systems and implementing it, testing and maintaining the same. The system thus goes into this life cycle and passes the tests. The software which once adopted a close and constant watch on its operation is kept. As users handle the system then system administrator starts getting feedback, suggestions and complains. The bugs in the system, if any are found and reported, which are repaired quickly online. Necessary trouble shooting is done to attend minor errors. In this process of implementation and further improvements, the system should become more and more efficient, it should also become more user friendly. In case if it becomes difficult and unwieldy to repair or set right all the complaints then it is always advisable to scrap the system and design all together a new system.

While using the new system, reporting of all the difficulties needs to be documented. This reporting helps to take further decision whether to continue using the system or scrap it and design a new one.

It is better if the issues relating to implementing and handling is done by a senior person who has adequate knowledge of use of system in different activities of library especially sectional activities. Such person only could maintain dialogs with the programmers in overcoming the system problems. It is also essential and necessary for a programmer to visit library and over see computerised library operations frequently. All this discussion was pertaining to use of library software which is developed in house within the institute.

In case, if library adopts, software which is commercially available in the market then the main responsibility of software maintenance lies on the system manufacturer.

In such case, library has to depend totally on the software company on each and every aspect of system use and handling. Such library software is maintained through the same vendor by giving an AMC (Annual Maintenance Contract). It is obvious that cost of software maintaining is more in this case than software developed in house. However, there is no alternative but to depend on the system vendor; comparatively it is easy and economical to maintain in-house software. There are difficulties in maintaining in house developed system due to high mobility of programmers and system administrators.

In case if the adoptable system works on open source platforms then the software maintenance could be easy to handle by the IT expert of the institute or the task could be given to a library person who is having the adequate expertise to handle system trouble shooting.

We have considered two options of library computerisation in relation to handling and maintenance of library systems i. e. 1. By using in-house developed software and 2. by adopting commercially available LMS. However, we have already noted the third option of library computerisation i. e. computurising library by using open source software. Now let us discuss the third option. In case of using open source type software there could be two possibilities.

6.5.1.1. Handling Open Source LMS

Possibility No. 1 : When library adopts for O. S. type internationally available free downloadable software then it becomes absolutely necessary to have service providers who undertakes adoption of O. S. software and maintain it against certain fees. Although we need not have to pay any cost of software while downloading and adopting it. This becomes necessary where librarian does not have such expertise with him / herself. Spending on service provider's work becomes mandatory in this situation even in adopting free software as system server remains in possession of service provider.

Possibility No. 2 : In this case, it is assumed that librarian by him / herself have the necessary expertise and knowledge of adopting O. S. type software and maintain it. Librarian can install the software, customize it and maintain it through a local server which is in the possession of institute / library. In this case library need not have to spend almost anything on maintaining the system. Moreover, it is easy to improve the system and to upgrade the version with the convenience of library. The computerised operation in this case goes very smoothly and without any interruption or breakdown.

6.5.1.2. Re-engineering Library Software

Software development is a continuous process. It proceeds from development , design, implementation to maintenance and further re-development. Computer field is constantly progressive in nature. Progresses in software always prompts up-gradation of systems. Computer hardware also keeps on changing and upgrading. In this scenario, things become older and obsolete very quickly. At the same time, new and more efficient technologies emerge. Operating systems too keep on changing and new ones look for replacing the old platforms.

It is naturally true that with development of library softwares, while using old system if there are considerable complains and inconveniences in use, then situation demands redevelopment of new software. It equally applies to any kind of software whether it is developed in house or commercial software or even open source software. In case of in-house software, redevelopment could be taken up from the beginning. In case of readymade or open source software version up-gradation becomes necessary.

In case of in-house software, the old system structure is available in redevelopment of system, existing outgoing system provides a lot of advantages and time saving features.

The redevelopment process of software is termed as "system re-engineering." In the process, first a report considering all possible expectations is prepared, which is called, "feasibility report". In feasibility reports the following issues are touched upon:

- System Development
- System Design
- Estimated expenditure on system redevelopment

Advantages over old system : Preparing feasibility report through consultancy, system design and development, system implementation requires considerable cost. However, the process gives a lot of feedback which gives significant vision for system development. System revision, up-gradation or redevelopment brings user friendliness in the system use. New system platform becomes available and which becomes compatible to web technology. Considering all these advantages, it is always worthwhile to redevelop or upgrade the library systems, provided support of adequate fund is available. Considering difficulties in maintaining in-house developed library software there is a trend in libraries of adopting either commercially available softwares or open source type of softwares.

It would be a bit diversion to current discussion to talk about general scenario about library software development in country like ours but it would be worth to touch upon the issues. Rationally or ideally it would be always good and convenient if all the libraries, at least of same type use same kind of software, developed by a research oriented national institute as promoted by national library software development policy, which could be a part of National policy on library and information. Up-gradation and revision of library software in such situation is very easy as versions of library software could be made available either free or at a nominal cost. Having one kind of software in most of libraries, which are well connected to each others in a network, creates condusive atmosphere to promote library co-operation and resource sharing among libraries, as data format remains the same and providing union catalogues , consortium on regional group OPAC becomes feasible and also bibliographic data communication is easily available. However, unfortunately such situation may not come in reality in India, due to libraries adopting variety of softwares which create a lot of hurdles in library co-operation. Moreover, upgrading these variety of software is waste of time and money. INFLIBNET did undertake the task to create a situation by developing SOUL software, but since there is no national policy supporting to the adoption of this software at national level their efforts may not be adequate in bringing uniformity in use of SOUL in India. As such they may not be successful in a large scale SOUL adoption but whatever efforts undertaken by

INFLIBNET have certainly resulted in promoting LIS professionalism but they may be negligible as compared to the vast demand.*

6.5.2. Management of Computer Hardware in Library

As library computerisation begins to settle in library, there would be tremendous flow of computer hardware items into the library. Library would need additional terminals, printers etc. In such situation, handling of library computer hardware becomes a matter of concern. It requires proper organisation to handle the hardware equipment which includes tasks such as recording equipments, machines and related items in dead stock records. Bar-coding them would facilitate their stock verification, controlling movement of equipments taken out for repairs and maintain them all the time in working condition. It is desirable to handover responsibility to an individual or team of persons who have adequate knowledge of computer hardware. Generally library would posses computer hardware as listed here. **The author is of the opinion that it is high time to** avail the facility of cloud computing instead of bothering too much about hardware **maintenance.** Amazon(AWS) has special pricing for use of their cloud for library computerization. When library opts for open source type of software and operating system, it is most convenient to use cloud computing facility.

The list of Hardware

1. C. P. U. (with different configurations)
2. Monitors
3. Keyboards
4. CD/DVD Drives and CD writers etc. (By now this technology has become obsolete)
5. Sound Blasters / Speakers
6. Various types of electronic printers
7. Scanners (for scanning documents)
8. Laser scanners for barcode readers
9. Barcode printers and scanners
10. Library fine payment receipt machines
11. Electronic security systems:
    - 3M electromagnetic system
    - RFID systems
    - CC-TVs

Various types of servers

- LMS Server
- Web OPAC Server

---

* INFLIBNET : A UGC Centre at Ahmedabad

- Digital Library Server
- Multimedia Server
- Sip-2 Server (in case of RFID systems)

If Library has LAN

1. above hardware
2. LAN server
3. Hub, port and switches
4. Computer network with software

Equipments to maintain uninterrupted power supply

1. U. P. S
2. Voltage stabilizers & regulators
3. Air conditioning equipments

Parts of computer

- Hard Disc
- Mother board
- SMPS
- RAM
- Processors

Stationary and consumables

- Printer cartridges
- Bar-coding stationary
- Paper
- Bar-coding & labeling stations
- Book cards
- Catalogue cards(not relevant now with everything is online)

The task of handling above hardware is really a major one and it requires adequate skills and knowledge.

6.5.2.1. Use of computer hardware in library

Library computerisation functions with a suitable LMS and computer hardware equipments. However, to let functions of library systems smoothly, it is necessary to maintain all the machinery in working condition. It needs to be done with sufficient care and precaution. Breakdown equipments need to be repaired quickly. It so happens that due to nonfunctioning of minor part of hardware the entire library systems comes to stand still. In computerised environment library wholly depends on computers. It is therefore necessary to take utmost care in handling hardware. Handling work of computer hardware is done in the following ways :

Taking external care of hardware

- To provide stabilized and UPS supply and keep stand by battery backup.
- To Protect equipments from dust, dampness and heat.
- To provide air conditioned facility to protect the servers.
- To maintain cleanliness of computers and other equipments.
- Provide necessary instructions relating to proper handling of computers etc.
- To have proper electrical connections so that chances of short circuits could be avoided

Taking internal care of computers

- To protect systems from infecting them by virus (antivirus softwares).
- Maintain IMPS and FANS continuously functioning
- Maintain equipments protected from dust and heat.

Taking care of other items

- Taking care of various printers
- Replacing exhausted printer cartridges
- Carefully using CD / DVD Drives and CD/DVD writers
- Verifying the intactness of cables and connections

Computer Furniture

Computerisation adds computers and other equipments into the library. The use of systems also need appropriate furniture facilitating use of computers comfortably. Selecting ergonomically designed furniture adds ease and comfort in use.

Upgrading Computer Hardwares

As computerisation progresses and use of computer increases in course of time, speed and capacity of computer functioning comes down, which prompts enhancing speed and capacity of computing.

There would be need to increase storage capacity. Erstwhile storage in KB and megabytes needs to be converted into terabytes. Sometimes it becomes necessary to replace the old systems with new ones.

Care in buying new computers also needs to be done carefully. There would be faulty and duplicate items available in the market. It is therefore necessary to buy computers; equipments and peripherals form authorized vendor or rate contractors who supply standardized products. The person who handles purchase should be aware of proper terminology of hardware and working measures such as

- Hard disk capacity - MB / GB / TB
- Processor speed - MHZ
- RAM in GB

A typical computer system would have minimum configuration as:

- High configured Processor
- 32 GB RAM
- 40 GB / 1 TB HD
- i7 processors with adequate speed
- CGA / VGA card
- Suitable wide monitor
- 105 keyboard
- Mouse CD / DVD Drive
- Stabilizer

Security of systems

We have considered things in order to secure security of computers and systems such as:

- Stabilized UPS power supply
- Air conditioned environment
- Dust and dampness free air supply and ventilation
- Sufficient protection towards infecting from virus
- Protecting equipments from natural calamities like fire, earthquakes and floods etc.

Finally to protect valuable computer equipments, it is always worthwhile to protect them from losing or damaging, by insuring the values of the same.

*INFLIBNET: A UGC Centre at Ahmedabad.

7

Introduction to BIBFRAME : The Future Cataloguing Standard

7.0. INTRODUCTION

Libraries have progressed through different walks of professional phases e. g. from traditional to non-computerised to computerised and now they are in digital age. Bibliographic data of the materials they hold in their collection has also gone through various revolutions. Initially they created registers/list of books to handwritten catalogues cards which subsequently changed to computerised catalogue. In one of the phases of generating catalogue cards and computerised cards the emphasis was on style e. g. AACR or AACR – II cataloguing rules. When libraries started converting their catalogue data it was done in various ways e. g. through formats like Access, Excel, FoxPro, dbase, CDS ISIS and C- programming language platforms. Need of bibliographic communication prompted libraries further to adopt communication formats like MARC, UK, US-MARC, UNIMARC, CCF etc. These formats were further rationalised in one format named MARC-21 or advanced Z39. 2 / MARC. Most of libraries now insist to have data in their LMS only in MARC 21 Format. However, in the semantic and linked data age, MARC - 21 format has become obsolete. The main reason for advancement of libraries from their local and non-web invisible status was to have web visible libraries by adopting linked data design. The project based on linked data and semantic web technology initiated by Library of Congress (LOC) known as BIBFRAME is about bringing the revolution in library bibliographic data assets. In this chapter, we are going to understand about the concept behind the BIBFRAME.

7.1. HISTORICAL BACKGROUND OF BIBFRAME

Up till now libraries were working for standardisation of bibliographic data structure much needed while creating the library database in respectively adopted library management systems (LMS). In the process, each librarian has common bibliographic standard structure format in mind e. g. MARC or to be specific MARC - 21 format. This is because MARC facilitated exchange of bibliographic data among the libraries and it also helped smooth conversion of library bibliographic data while migrating from one LMS to another. However, these developments were okay in the pre-web environment. When there was a revolution in the use of information technology in libraries and about use of semantic web and related linked data model librarians started envisaging future possibilities for libraries and cultural heritage institutions. Although MARC facilitated libraries to exchange bibliographic data among the libraries and related communities the data remained invisible for the web world. MARC or so called technically Z39.2/MARC served libraries for almost forty years but now it looks like older technique for data management, as it has become obsolete in the programming style of today. Looking into this situation Working Group of Future Bibliographic Control recommended Library of Congress to take action in devising a new format for bibliographic control, which would suit in the current web development and would work with the library and other interested communities to specify and implement a new carrier for bibliographic information, which could be capable for representing the range of data of interest to libraries and to facilitate the exchange of such data both within the library community and also to open it for communities through the web platforms. In US, National Agriculture Library, the National Library of Medicine and Library of Congress conducted a survey-cum test on 26 participating library community which also revealed the same opinion that the MARC format used for several years is now showing limitations/ shortcomings and for having full capabilities of RDA (Resource Description and Access) a new bibliographic framework is necessary. Readers to note that RDA is the revised guidelines or up-gradation of our old AACR–II rules. With strong recommendations from Working Group of Future Bibliographic Control and result of RDA test, Library of Congress initiated the project "Bibliographic Framework (BIBFRAME)" in collaboration with libraries, bibliographic standard experts and IT technologists, expecting that it will serve the library community in a better way in the future to come.

It is worthwhile to remember the benefits of MARC standard at this juncture. The MARC has been responsible for the creation of millions of bibliographic records around the globe. The MARC was created in the late 1960 and early 1970. Librarians along with computer experts decided to take a revolutionary step to share bibliographic data. This resulted for an individual library to become a node in the larger network of libraries for adoption of MARC which yielded in reducing cost of cataloguing. On this backdrop, it is expected that the newly thought bibliographic framework will certainly broaden library participation in the network of resources, at the same time librarians would also be able to link their patrons to bibliographic resources of all kinds (from library and also from many other resources) at the affordable cost.

7.2. WHAT IS BIBFRAME PROJECT ?

Bibliographic Framework or BIBFRAME : This project is the initiative launched by Library of Congress(LC) which intends to provide new means for capturing and sharing of bibliographic data. The initiative further expects replacement of the age-old MARC format used for exchanging bibliographic data among the libraries. The BIBFRAME project is based on the recommendations of 2008 report of LC's Working Group of the Future of Bibliographic Control, which has been the outcome of discussion undergone in librarian's community. The new format, would reinforce the data infrastructure, developing information technology and would comply with changing patterns of resource description, which has suggested a transition to a more current and futuristic data creation and interchange environment. The developments of semantic web and its related Linked Open Data (LOP) model has provided many future possibilities for libraries and cultural heritage institutions.

The MARC series based data infrastructure has been extensive and flexible to a limited extent with changing technology. However, a quantum effort is needed to create a competitive data exchange instrument which would be based on the current set up and expected to give future shape of data interchange. In order to ensure a new environment which will allow the reuse of valuable data and remain supportive to current one, in-addition to innovating it, there are certain requirements which could provide a basis for this work. These requirements have been discussed in the library community, which have been considered while beginning the transition to a new bibliographic framework. The initiative of bibliographic framework indicates an environment rather than a format. The requirements are as:

1. Broad Accommodation of Contents : Rules and Data Models – Libraries use different cataloguing rules. Different rules are used by various communities for different aspects of data description. Various guidelines have been created in different eras, and some metadata are not rule based. The BIBFAME initiative expects to have rational to accommodate all these variations. The accommodation of RDA (Resource Description and Access) will be a key factor in the development of data elements as other mainstream library archive and cultural community rules i. e. AACR - II and its predecessors as well as DACS (Describing Archives a Content Standards) VRA(Visual Resource Association) core, CCO (Cataloguing Cultural Objects) have been doing.

2. Provision for the types of data that logically accompany or support bibliographic description : The types of data here include such as holdings, authority, classification, preservation, technical rights and archival metadata. All these types could be accommodated through linking technological components in a modular way with standard extensions and other techniques.

3. Accommodation of textual data in linked data with URIs instead of text and both.

4. Consideration of the relationship between and recommendations for communications format tagging record input conversions and system storage manipulation.

Up till now the bibliography data management was seen in library cataloguing point of view. However, future bibliographic framework would be handled less by cataloguers than the current MARC Format. Internal storage, display of communicated data and the input screens are unlikely to have the close relationship to a communication format which was visualized in the past.

5. Consideration of the needs of all sizes and types of libraries from a small public to the large research library.

Although the MARC format became a key factor in the development of systems and services of different types and sizes of libraries, which have tried to implement services according to the local needs of their patrons and with their resources. The new bibliographic framework would continue to support simpler needs in addition to those of large research libraries too.

6. Continuation of Maintenance of MARC data no longer necessary.

It is expected that during migration in the near future of a large segment of library community from AACR-II to RDA will be needed to have RDA adapted MARC format. So, the changes required in old MARC format in new RDA point of view are only necessary and thus there is no need to maintain the entire MARC data which would save the time and energy of library community.

7. Compatibility with MARC based records

8. Provision of Transformation from MARC - 21 to a new bibliographic environment

It would require a software which could transform data from MARC - 21 to the new bibliographic framework and back to old which would facilitate experimentation, testing or other activities.

It is important that library of congress (LC) and its partners e. g. Zepheira and others are interested in bringing change in bibliographic environment which will further facilitate library community to progress into the future form with a more robust, open and extensible handler for our rich bibliographic data. It would further accommodate the library community's new cataloguing rules i. e. RDA. Efforts would also be on both i. e. evolving new system and maintenance of MARC - 21 systems while testing of new model. It is expected to happen in a cost saving manner.

7.2.1. Think-tank behind BIBFRAME Concept

Think-tank of web inventor, Tim Burners Lee and his revolutionary concept i. e. web of all things, is now greatly influencing the new way of representing the data e. g. linked open data. Lee argues that web should use the basic principles of the web more directly to data (contents of our traditional data bases) and that we should not be shy about making links to non-computer resources such as people, tangible and abstract things, places and so on to our data. In his view this expansive linking is called "the web of data", which forms the basis of linked data.

In the Lee's point of view the BIBFRAME draft is to provide framework for modeling future resources and bibliographic assets also which traditionally are encoded in MARC-21. This pattern will shape as common descriptive framework which would achieve the following objectives.

1. To integrate the existing bibliographic resources and
2. To provide a road map for moving forward towards further refinement.

Library community has been doing pioneering work of creating bibliographic assets, its management, organisation and collaborative utilization of the data of works of our culture. All these efforts has led to evolution of library data interchange format i. e. MARC -21. This data asset is proving now as specialised market for bibliographic modelers. The enormous amount of high quality data available with library community has been successfully utilized in providing library services to their patrons. Now this same data has become valuable assets to take it beyond the traditional library boundaries. By restructuring MARC-21 format to linked data model it is expected to expand the utility and value of the data as well the community which would be served. In remodeling the MARC-21 format as a Web of Data it is important to deconstruct and then reconstruct the information assets. In doing so the following primary functions of MARC-21 are the most important for its evolution to the new framework.

1. Data relating to the intellectual essence of work
2. Data relating to the actual instance of the work, which you hold in your hand retrieved from an electronic source network.
3. Record metadata such as control numbers, record handling codes and other annotations.

The deconstructing of the data elements corresponding to these functions, one can begin to materialize the concept embedded in these data element sets as linkable information resources. These MARC based data resources then to be resembled into a coherent architecture which provides the basis of new bibliographic framework and allow for cooperative cataloguing as it was done in shared cataloguing in the OCLC model. However, now the co-operative cataloguing would be of more granular level (persons, places, subjects, organisations). Then whenever updates to these MARC resources would occur (as someone adds new information about the existing person, new mapping relating to subject etc.) notification could be sent to system to automatically update the resources. Having these innovations these information assets can now be more effectively utilized at a granular level to provide a richer substrate to local collection, special collections and third party data can be easily annotated with library contents to be utilized co-operatively.

BIBFRAME : Library of Congress along with its partner institutions are working to create a new cataloguing standard to replace the existing standard i. e. MARC-21. The new standard named BIBFRAME would facilitate linked data model to enable library collection bibliographic data to integrate with web. The following paras would cover the details of the newly evolving standard BIBFRAME.

7.2.2. New Approach of BIBFRAME Project

The new BIBFRAME project has focused on web environment, linked data principles/ mechanism and the RDF (Resource Description Framework) as basic model. The idea behind linked data is to open the scope for bibliographic data from a library to web as it would have association with substantial related resources even beyond the cultural heritage sector. It is expected that with the use of RDF model and with other W3C (Worldwide Web Consortium) developments bibliographic data which was otherwise locked in library system would enable integration of library data and other cultural heritage data existing on web there by providing wider user access to the information.

With availability RDF model as recommended and emphasised in W3C recommended method, it has facilitated conceptual description or modeling of information. Now RDF data could be serialized or written out in various syntax formats, such as XML (Extensible Mark-up Language). RDF data can also be used in relational database manner as most library data exists in the computerised systems in the form of MARC–21. RDF would also facilitate triple stores mechanism which would be readily available in the new model which would further facilitate library community with more options about how to store and retrieve its data in the future. It is further expected that the common exchange technique (web and linked data) and broadly adopted data model i. e. RDF/ XML will transform the current library technological environment away from being a closed market into itself to the one more readily understandable by the current and future data creators, data modelers and software developers. It is anticipated that all these considerations taken together, will result in greater cost saving for libraries.

7.2.3. Need of BIBFRAME

Before we discuss BIBFRAME we need to know why new standard is needed. In-order to find this we should look into past development of standardising bibliographic data held by library community.

Libraries since their inception have been maintaining structured information about their collections. The purpose was to help library patrons to find information they needed. It was done by providing them access to key information about the collection i. e. title, author and the subjects. The very first method of recording these bibliographic details was to record them serially in a book catalogue. Then card catalogue emerged. The card catalogue with its dictionary and classified form could establish relation between the information provided in the catalogue cards, so also it is used to help readers to find interested document on the shelf. The card catalogue method of describing data of library holding worked for quite some time.

However, as library collection grew it was necessary to improve efficiency of catalogue card production (as they were manually written or typed on typewriters). In the late 1960 Henriette Avram at Library of Congress developed a new method of encoding bibliographic information. This facilitated to create data which was readable by machines (Machine Readable catalogues) and the same further facilitated to print catalogue cards by automating the process. It is seen that during the last half of 20th century and first half of the 21st century libraries were rushing to computerise their functions and they used stable foundation of MARC records. Most of world wide LMSs have adopted the MARC - 21 format in building their databases.

7.2.4. BIBFRAME - "The project Review"

Before we elaborate further on BIBFRAME let us try to review about BIBFRAME initiative and about some important points and terms associated with it as appended below:

- Library of Congress contracted with Zepheira (2012 through early 2014)
  - To develop the model and the model description that kick started the BIBFRAME project
  - Produced a model for profiles and use cases
  - Opted to pursue active hands on experiments
- Involvement of Library of Congress, National Library of Medicine, George Washington University, British National Library, Princeton University, the National Bibliotheca, OCLC, Zepheira.
- All parties continue to experiment and move forward the evolution.
- Working Group of Future of Bibliographic Control and Resource Description and Access (RDA) test / survey outcome (RDA would be new style of MARC) Recommended to go for

new / future bibliographic structure i. e. BIBFRAME

- **RDF (Resource Description Framework)**

  It is a common model for creating web data

- **Linked Data** a term used to describe recommended best practice for exposing, sharing and connecting pieces of data information and knowledge and the semantic web using URIs and RDF (http://en. wikipedia. org/wiki/linked_data)

7.2.5. Aim of BIBFRAME Project

The aim here is to take library bibliographic data from its invisible status to linked data platform on web through RDF and restructured it through RDA, (reformatted from AARC-II), which would be visible to web world and open to harvester to use it for fruitful purpose.

7.3. REPLACING OLD MARC WITH LINKED DATA

Libraries were depending on MARC based data systems for bibliographic communication storage and demonstration of their bibliographic data. The MARC era worked for quite some time. However, in course of time when web technology is evolving speedily MARC based systems started showing their limitations. There is no doubt it helped to automate the catalogue card production in libraries and the MARC was so structured that it helped libraries to create reliable and stable data. However, on the other side libraries started realizing that the MARC based data is only with library and not visible to world at large especially in the web world, as MARC cannot integrate or link with world wide web. It was so happening that on oneside libraries were investing their time, efforts and money into building computerised data based on MARC but on the other side web technology was born and was further progressing very speedily which changed the concept completely how we express and share information. Web was conceptualized one time as web of documents but now has evolved to form a new concept of data on the web or "web of data". Now with the common Internet standards we are in position to use the web to share, reference and store data. The new innovative form of web/Internet is known as linked data which is everywhere on the web. At this juncture libraries also started feeling that they need to replace old styled MARC with linked data so that library data could be integrated and engage with wider information seeker community i. e. on the web.

Libraries built all their systems, processes and work flows around the MARC. No doubt it served them very well but it had only quality of machine readability but it did not possess machine actionability. The old web was a fun technology but now we realise that it was a dumb. It contained a lot of unstructured and unorganised data in terms of documents. However, in the new and modern form of Internet i. e. in semantic web, the web understands data and can make connections and links, if the things are encoded correctly to express relationships. Semantic web facilitates relationship between things through structured data which expresses explicit relationship so that machines and humans can understand them in the same way.

The bibliographic assets of world literature are available with the library community but it is invisible to web world and it just cannot remain isolated with libraries. Thus, the bibliographic data with library community encoded in age old MARC structure badly seeks its visibility in the web which would be looking further for integration and for expression relationship with machines & humans. So, the next objective of library should be to replace MARC with linked data and facilitate its integration with web environment and link library data with wider information community to make MARC machine actionable than only to be machine readable. So, the replacement of MARC with linked data was essential in modern web technology.

7.3.1. Visualizing Bibliographic Data in Semantic web

We have understood in early chapters of this book how Internet has evolved from its first generation to third generation i. e. semantic web. We also had introduction to semantic web. Now let us try to revisit our MARC based bibliographic data in semantic web and let us know benefits of it.

Now we say Web of Things rather than just Internet. Semantic web is the real web as Tim Burners Lee visualized. Semantic web brought new way of structuring data called "Linked Data". (As lectured by Lee in- Ted talks http:// www. ted. com/ talks/Tim-Burners Lee on the next web language-en) Now there is new method/ tool available to encode data in RDF / XML. There are four rules to represent data in linked data format as:

1. Use URIs to indicate things
2. Use HTTP URIs so that the things can be referred to and looked up on web (Re-referenced)
3. Provide other useful information about things when it's URI is re-referenced using standards like RDF (Resource Description Framework) and SPARQL (Sparql Protocol and RDF Query Language) RDF entry relationship model is the foundation of linked data.

   [RDF is a model for encoding semantic relationship between items of data so that their relationships can be interpreted computationally. SPARQL is an RDF Query Language means a semantic query language for databases which is able to retrieve and manipulate data stored in RDF format]
4. Include links to other related things (Using their URIs) when data is published on web.

We can imagine if linked data pattern is also used to structure bibliographic data then local library holdings would be displayed in search engine results like it happens in Google search. Linked data emphasises all about building and encoding relationship between things so that computers can make sense of data and relationship in it. The same would be with bibliographic data if linked data encoding is also applied for building of bibliographic data held by libraries.

Now let as visualize an example of Google search for well known personality: Paul Outlet - in normal Google search and the linked data form displayed on your right side on the monitor, (see Plate 7.1).

7.3.2. Significance of Linked Data in BIBFRAME

If the library integrates its catalogue in linked data format the google search would also display additional information about your local library holding. Finally, we understand that linked data tells us about building and encoding relationship between things making computers to sense the data and its relationship.

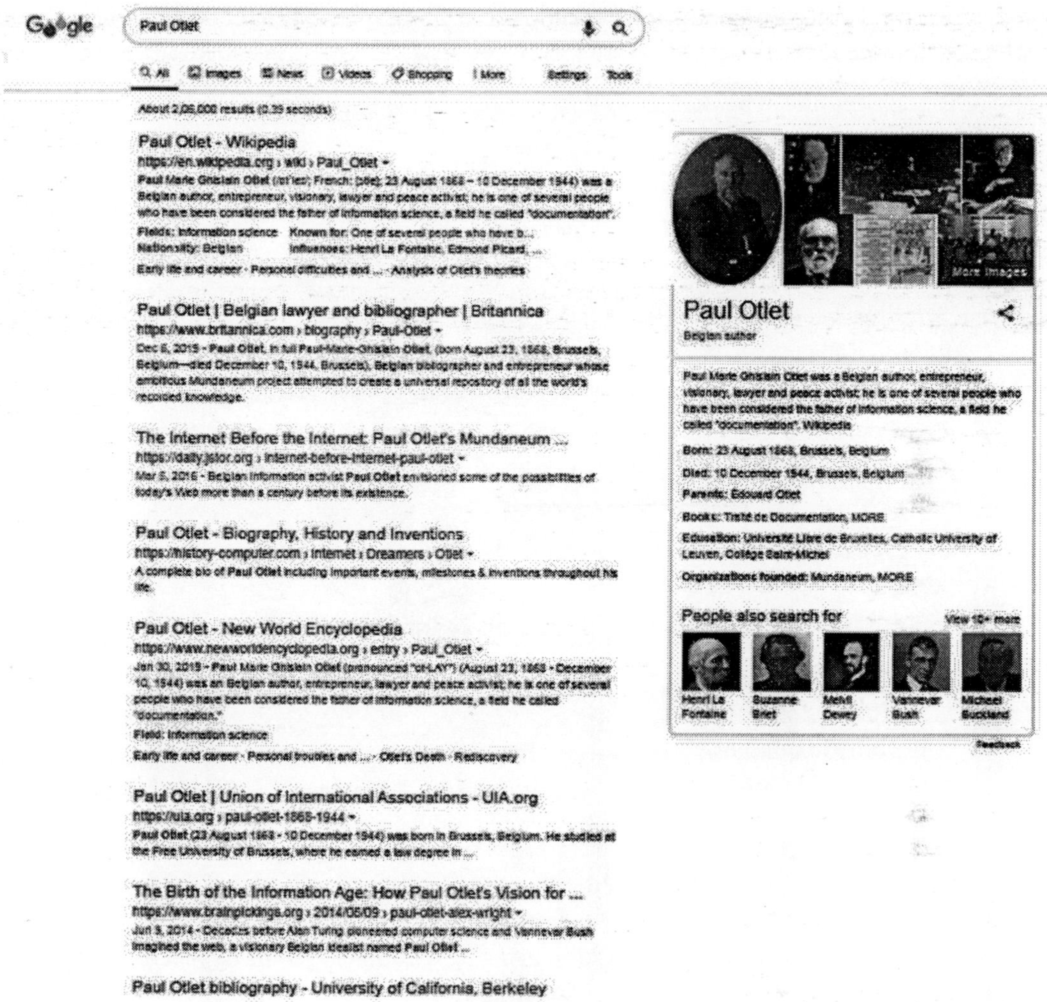

Plate 7.1

Let us now explore the concept further as:

7.3.2.1. RDF Foundation

Thus, RDF is the foundation of linked data as:

1. Data is encoded in RDF structure
2. RDF is a standard model used for data inter linking on the web.
3. It facilitates creating the relationships between things on the web.

Now let us try to know more about RDF. RDF expresses relationship through a structure called "triple" of things i.e. Subject + Predicate + Object. We can very well compare this method with the way we interpret library data e.g.

An author is the creator of work} = subject

so, it is the }

The subject/title of book is the = object

We express their relationship = Predicate

So, the relation can be shown as

Subject —— Predicate ——— Object

Now if we take an actual example of one book and its bibliographic details we can see how the triples could be represented, see Fig. 7.1.

Author : Ranganthan, Shiyals Ramamrita

Title : Five laws of library science

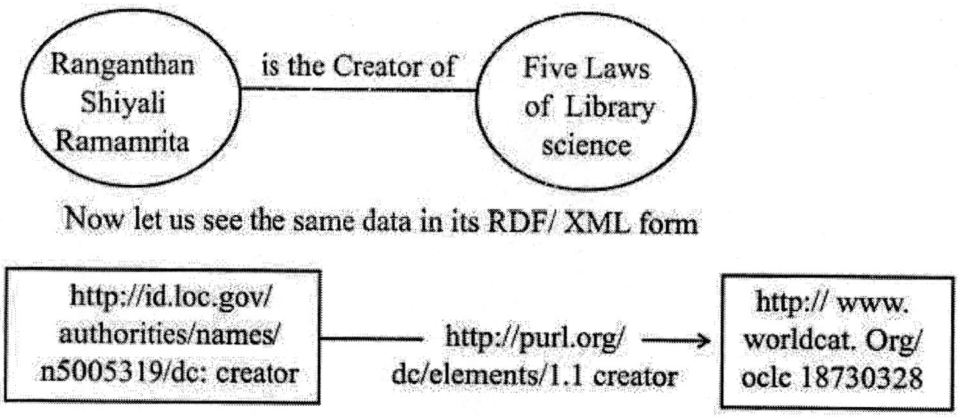

Fig. 7. 1

Advantage here is, if bibliographic contents instead of structured in just text form if it is described in RDF form then web understands it and if any one searches or enquires with SPARQL it could be retrieved on the web also. In structuring RDF form we get the help of its ontology and vocabulary. We can take another example of bibliographic data of a book and see how it is structured in RDF / XML form:

Bibliography in Catalogue Entry Form

Example : The Budha walks into the office: A guide to livelihood for a new generation by LodroRiazler. Boston; Shambhala Publications: 2014

This bibliographic data when we see it in RDF / XML form it looks like as below:

<rdf: RDF Xmlns: rdf= “http://www. w3. org/1999/02/22-rdf

Xmlns: dc” http://purl. org/dc/elements-rdf-syntax#ns>

<rdf: Description rdf : about = “http://www. worldcat. org/oclc /8636325305>

<dc: titles >The Buddha walks in the office: a guide to livelihood for a new generation / dc:title>

<dc: Creator> http:// id. loc. gov / authorities / name/ n2011023258. html </dc creator>

<dc: publisher > Boston: Shambhala< dc/: publisher>

<dc: data > 2014 </dc: data >/rdf : RDF

The above example is an example per say and it is not complete in all respect.

7.3.3. Inter linking Bibliographic Data

There is another advocacy behind recommending linked data/rdf structure for bibliographic data is that, libraries have been considering relational databases keeping OPAC point of view and hierarchical data bases while thinking thesauri in mind however they have never thought about Graph form of bibliographic data bases. In Graph Databases, arbitrary object relationship is considered which is the most flexible in describing relationship among bibliographic contents i. e. among objects or nodes not only of one object but different objects also could be linked in graph data structures. This is however achieved with the help of linked data structure.

Let us try to understand the above graph data structure concept by considering following example Fig. 7.2 as below :

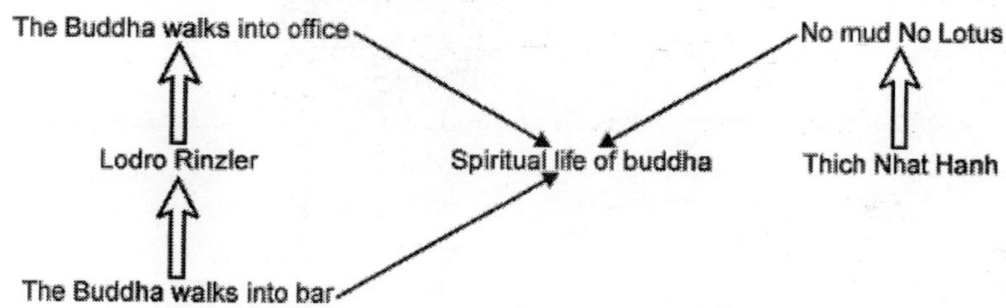

Fig. 7.2. Showing linking two objects with a graph data structure

One more supporting evidence put forth towards new bibliographic framework model is-

With linked data, we would be able to take Rules of Dictionary Catalogue as Outlined by CharlesAmmi Cutter to the next level. Recording relationship between bibliographic entities to organise resources and promote enquiry has been core of the cataloguing work but we are still striving to achieve objectives of dictionary catalogue, even today.

It is strongly expected that it would be achieved in adopting linked data framework. It is also expected and argued that linked data or new BIBFRAME framework will help libraries to follow Cutter's dictionary catalogue rules better than catalogue cards or MARC format. BIBFRAME is essentially a framework or structural standard for expressing bibliographic meta data and the relationship between bibliographic entities. BIBFRAME is developed primary to replace MARC. The main objective of linked data technology is to express and expose relationship between bibliographic entities within library environment and beyond. The advantage in converting framework from MARC to BIBFRAME is that linked data and library meta data can integrate with and could reach to wider information community than before. It is envisaged that new method of describing library data, libraries could return to age of Cutter's dictionary catalogue. This relationship within bibliographic entities somehow was lost in the course of library automation and during data conversion/ uploading it to LMS in the MARC form.

7.3.3.1. Interlinking Data : Graphical Mode

Now let us take further and see how different bibliographic objects could be inter linked with first in text from then in triple structure method, then graphical mode and finally in script of machine readable forms as shown in table 7.1 and Fig. 7.4.

Subject	Relation	Object	Field
Paul Outlet	Creator of	Traite de Documentation	Library Sc.
S R. Ranganathan	Creator of	Five laws of library science	Library Science

Table 7.1

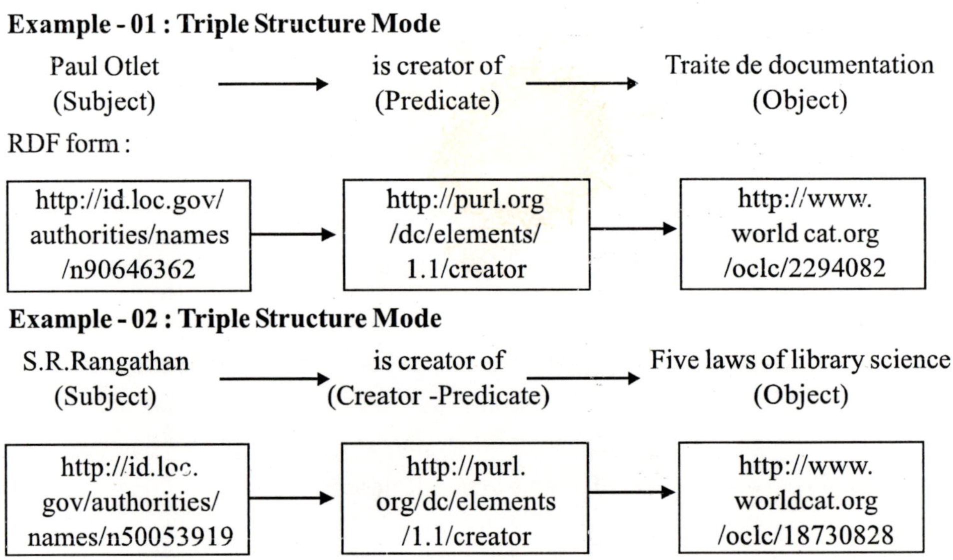

Fig. 7.4. Linked Data Expression Relationship in Graph form

Showing bibliographic contents in graph mode has been facilitated in using linked data expression which was not possible in our traditional cataloguing method see the following Fig. 7.5.

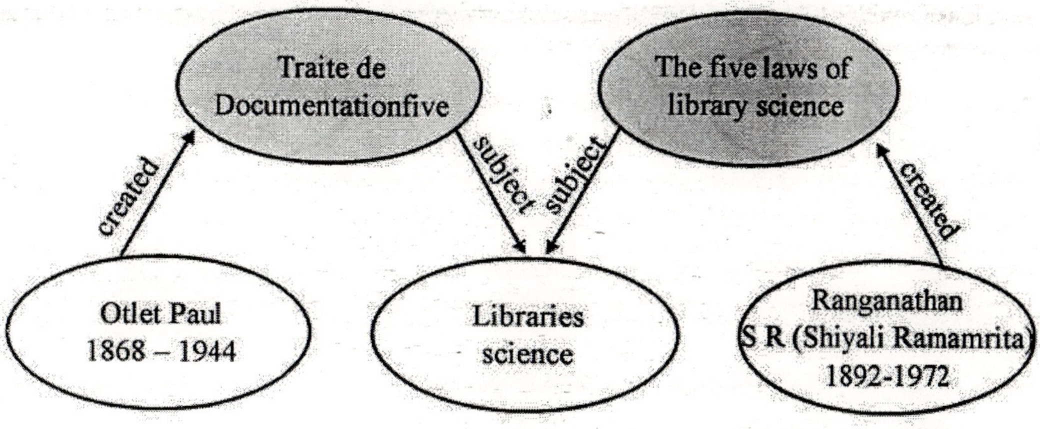

Fig. 7.4

Linked Data Expresses Relationships in Machine readable format as shown in Fig. 7.5.

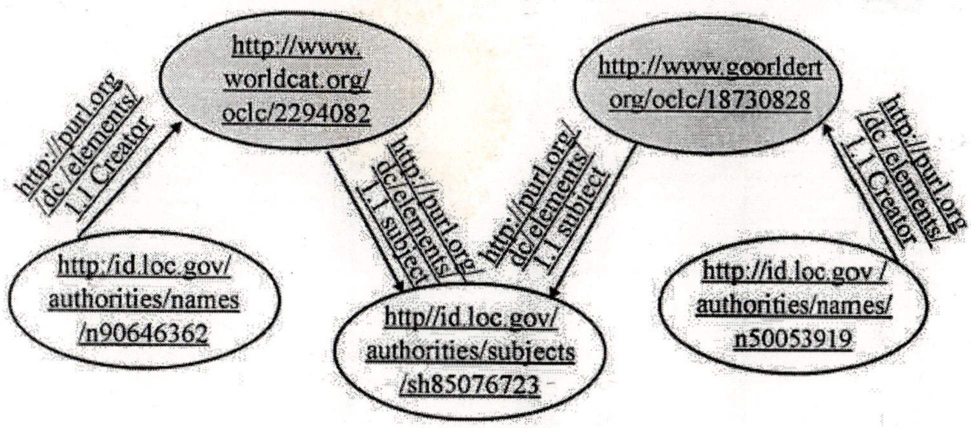

Fig. 7.5

Linked data always facilitates more relationship in various bibliographic objects considering some common attributes among them. Let us see a graphical view of such relationship in the following Fig. 7.6.

With reference to the above figures it is differentiated as :-

In our Library bibliographic environment or in library science section two bibliographic entries could be seen. However, while describing same objects in linked data environment it gets additional textual information. The potential of such relationship can go far more in linked data which we could never imagine.

After knowing the significance of linked data and its constituting elements i.e. **Universal Resource Identifier (UDI)** which represent every smallest content of bibliographic data and finally shows data structure used to encode the contents i.e. RDF / XML. Let us see how the entire data relationship discussed in previous example is represented in RDF / XML which computer can understand in the following script.

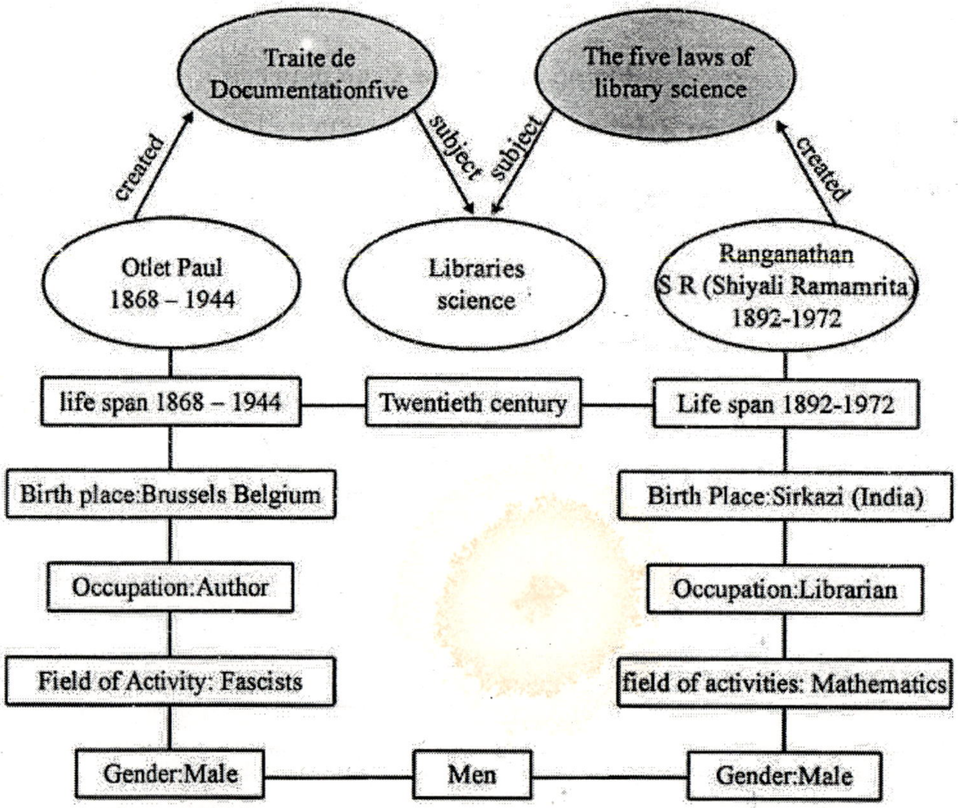

Fig. 7.6. Comprehensive Relationships in Bibliographic Objects.
Courtesy : **(Fig. 7.4 - Fig. 7.6) BIBFRAME Basics by Amber Billey, Columbia University Libraries You Tube Presentation on 12-08-2015**

RDF Triple in XML

```
<? xml version = '1.0'?>
<! Doctype rdf: RDF Public
        "-//DUBLIN CORE//DCMES DTD 2002/07/31//EN"
        "http://dublincore.org/documents/2000/07/31/dcmes - xml/dcmes-xmldtd.dtd">
<rdf:RDFxmlns: rdf = "http://www.w3.org/ 1999/02/22 - rdf - syntax-ns#" xmlns:dc =
        http:// purl.org / dc / elements 1.1/">
<rdf: Description rdf: about =
        "http://www.worldcat.org / oclc / 2294082">
<dc: title>Traite de documentation: le lure surlelivre, theorie et practique</dc:title>
<dc: creator> http://id.loc.gov /authorities/names n90646362 < /dc: creator>
<dc: publisher>EditionesMundaneum<dc : publisher>
```

```
<dc: data > 1934 </dc: date>
<dc: subject> http://id. worldcat.org / fast /997916 < /dc: subject>
        <rdf: description>
<rdf: description rdf: about = "http:/ www. world cat.org/ oclc / 18730828">
<dc: title> the five laws of library science </dc. title>
<dc: creator> http: //id. loc.gov/authorities /names/n50053919 </dc : creator>
<dc: Publisher>Asia pub. House </dc: publisher>
<dc: data>1963</ dc: date >
</dc: date>
<dc: subject> http://id.worldcat.org /fast/997916 </dc: subject>
        <rdf: description>
        </rdf:RDF>(1)
```

As linked data is encoded using RDF / XML structure there are other RDF like encoding languages such as RDFJ and JSON and Turtle. When we see the above script written in RDF/ XML we might feel it is very laborious task but it is not so. For most of subjects, objects etc. there are readily available URIs which could be picked and incorporated in the script. Secondly, for the common nouns like, "subject" or predicates like "creator" their URIs are available in the vocabulary/ dictionary. These tools can very well be used to create RDF / XML script for any item in the content of bibliography. RDF validator is used to create the graph. (http://www.w3.org/RDF/validator)

Another speciality of linked data method is that, one can also structure each and every content of data and it can be described with a Unique Resource Identifier URI which is structured in RDF. Linked Data technology also further facilitates to encode the relationships among the unique URIs and it can utilize external metadata available in open data domain i.e. web, thereby enhancing bibliographic relationship beyond cataloguing limits, as seen in the Table 7.4 with unique URI of each attributed.

Table 7.4

Subject	Otlet, Paul http://id.loc.gov/authorities/ names/n9064362	Rangnathan,Shiyali Ramamrita http://id.loc.gov/ authorities/names/n50053919
Predicate	Creator of http://purl.org/dc/ elements/1.1 creator	Creator of http://purl.org/dc/ elements/1.1 creator
Object	Traite de documentation http://www.oclc.2294082	Five laws of library science http://www/worldcat.org/ oclc/18730828

Table 7.4. Contd...

1. Courtesy : BIBFRAME Basics by Amber Billey , Columbia University Libraries You Tube Presentation on 12-08-2015

Authorities subject predicate	http://purl.org/dc/elements/ 1.1/subject	http://purl.org/dc/elements/ 1.1/subject
Authorities object Library Science	http://id.worldcat.org/fast/997916	http://id.worldcat.org/fast/ 997916
Life Span	1898-1944	1892-1972
Birth Place	Brussels (Belgium)http/id.loc.gov/ authorities/names/n79013830	Sirkazhi (India) http/id.loc. gov/authorities/names/ n80672712
Occupation	Author http://id.worldcat.org/fast/ 821688	Librarian http://id.worldcat. org/fast/997301
Field of activity	Pacifists http://id.worldcat.org/fast/ 1050133	Mathematics http://id.world cat.org/fast/101212163
Gender	Male http://rdaregistry/ins/termlist/ gender/1002	Male http://rdaregistry/ins termlist/gener/1002
Men	http://id.worldcat/fast/1015978	Common

As mentioned above RDF linked data can be expressed/ serialized/ marked up in a variety of syntaxes / languages such as :RDF / XML (http://www/w3.org / TR / rdf - syntax grammar RDFS - https://en.wikipedia.org/rdf schema. http://www.w3.org/2001/ sw / wiki / RDFS)

When we try to mark RDF to be functional and useful, it must adhere to the standards(agreed upon) vocabularies and ontologies. Linked data vocabularies are used to outline various elements (classes and properties) used to describe things. Author hopes that with this understanding of linked data methods to encode and describe the relations among various bibliography contents gets clearer to the readers. Now we would try to understand BIBFRAME model and what it is in the following paras.

7.4. BIBFRAME MODEL

The main objective behind development of BIBFRAME is to replace the MARC with new data structure to provide bibliographic relationship model. RDF / XML structure or standard is used to encode bibliographic data to convert our MARC based data to web or computer actionable format i.e. linked data format. So, the constituting parts of BIBFRAME model are:

1. Structural standard - BIBFRAME. It is upgradation of old MARC format and similar to ISBD,FRBR, Dublin Core, EAD, MODS, VRA-Core, CIDOC etc.
2. Content standard = RDA (Resource Description and Assess). It is a revised standard of AACR- II and similar to CCO and DACS
3. Encoding standard = RDF / XML. It is an upgradation of MARC, CVS, XML and JSON or similar to our old 3x5 catalogue card.

4. Value standard = RDA Vocabularies and is similar to LCSH, NAF, LCGFT, RBMS Thesaurus.

BIBFRAME vocabulary contains classes and properties. The classes are type of things (subject or objects). The properties connect or relate resources to each other called predicates.

Now let us look into what BIBFRAMEorganisation is :

7.4.1. BIBFRAME Organisation

The Organisation of BIBFRAME has 4 main classes:

1. works
2. Instances
3. Authorities
4. Annotations

Creative work : A source reflecting a conceptual essence of the cataloguing item. So, it would be subject and object. In case of book it would be creator and created item or title of the book.

Instance : A resource reflecting an individual material embodiment of the work

Authority : A resource reflecting key authority concepts that have refined relationships reflected in the work of instance. This includes people, places, topic, organisations etc.

Annotation : A resources that decorates the BIBFRAME resources with additional information example of annotation include library holding information, cover art and review.

So, there is creative work and instance, authority and annotation are the other resources key authorities and additional supplementing information resources.

Now let us see the graphical representation of the BIBFRAME model and the relationship among main BIBFRAME classes in the following diagram. Fig 7.7.

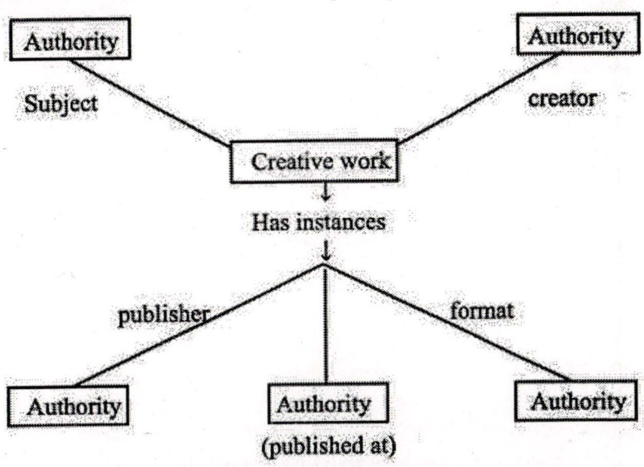

Fig. 7.7. BIBFRAME model in graphical from

***Courtesy* : BIBFRAME Basics by Amber Billey, Columbia University Libraries You Tube Presentation on 12-08-2015**

After seeing the core BIBFRAME model now let us see the model with a definite illustration in mind in Fig. 7.8.

Modern fairy Tale

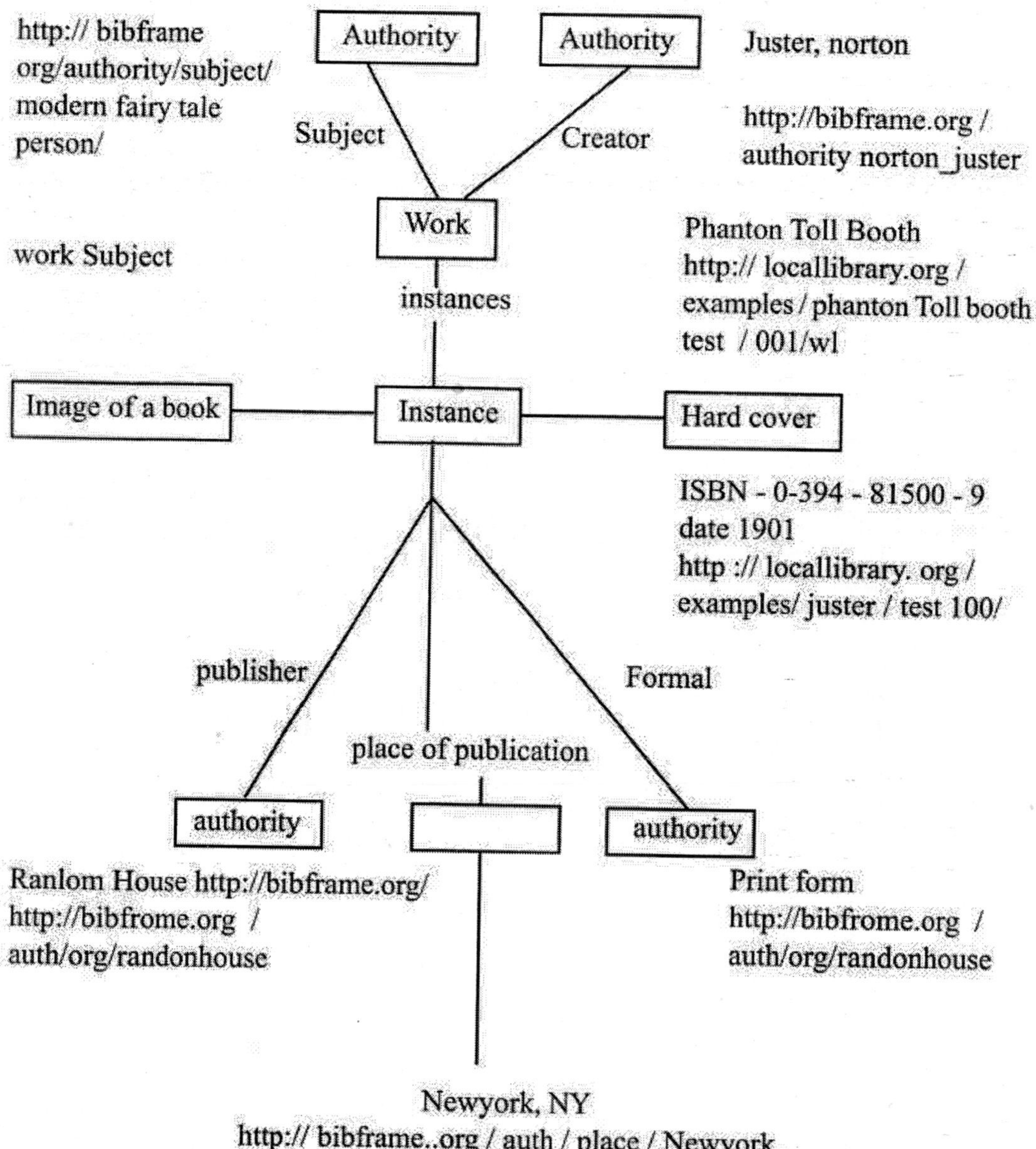

Fig. 7.8. BIBFRAME Model

Courtesy : **BIBFRAME Basics by Amber Billey, Columbia University Libraries You Tube Presentation on 12-08-2015**

Above graphical model (Fig 7.8) explains the relationships among the main BIBFRAME classes and it is displayed just for our understanding. Inorder to convert the contents of a relationship to a machine identifiable presentation it needs following actions:

1. A system of machine processable identifiers to identify BIBFRAME classes (OR A system of identifiers which can be processed by machine) to identify BIBFRAME classes.
2. A machine processable presentation of the model.

In linked data environment, it provides form of identifier called the Uniform Resources Identifier (URI) for each bibliographic content. The process involves creating BIBFRAME primer document to XML serialisation of the RDF data model. In XML sterilization, the particular work is encoded in its corresponding instances and associated authority information. With this background let us visualize another work in terms of BIBFRAME structure as given below.

The document name is: Functional Requirement of Bibliographic Record - A final report.

The work has three instances (one physical print, one PDF and one HTML website). It possesses authority information as (subject, author, publishes etc.) The links in this example would appropriately/ actually encoded in RDF / XML structure, which is not appended but we would again see it in the graphical example as Fig. 7.9.

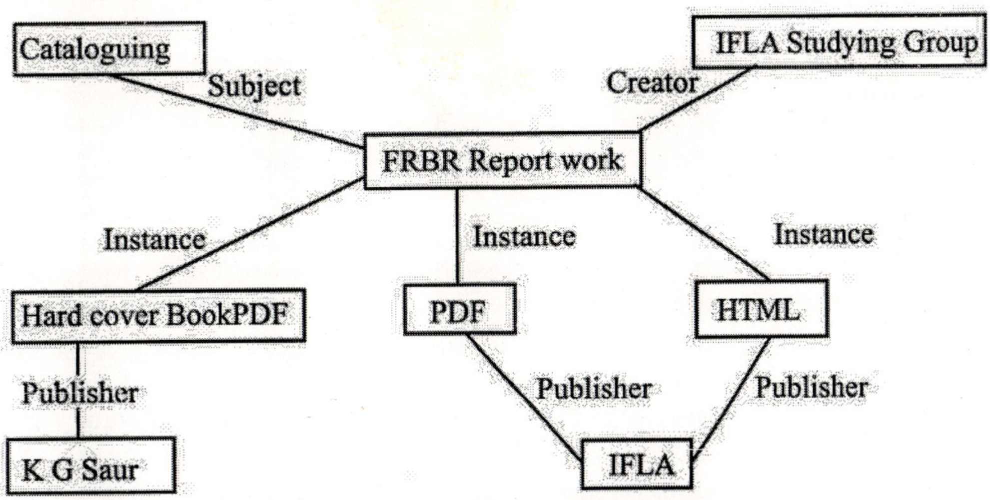

Fig. 7.9. Shows RDF model associated with XML serialization
***Courtesy* : BIBFRAME Basics by Amber Billey, Columbia University Libraries You Tube Presentation on 12-08-2015**

The report in question possesses 4 authorities and 3 instances associated with 2 publishers.

Subject or creator.

Formats - Hard cover, PDF or HTML

Publishers - K.G. Saur and IFLA

7.5. HOW TO BIBFRAME?

After having understood the BIBFRAME project, its framework and about the BIBFRAME model, now let us try to know how library MARC data could be converted in to open linked data and then incorporated in BIBFRAME structure, which would be searchable with the web search tools. Logically the MARC to BIBFRAME conversion involves procedure of gradually converting library bibliographic data into a final BIBFRAME format. The purpose is to use the existing MARC data assets and try to convert them into a new format.

There are various ways available for libraries. Some expert say that we need to follow four building blocks for cataloguing systems to work i.e. content standards (RDA like AACR – II), schema, serialization and exchange systems.

The BIBFRAME has been designed to replace MARC (our current schema) by breaking the information which currently comprises of our bibliographic records into atomic units which can then be reconfigured using RDF / XML structure into various URIs.

As presentation given by Amber Billey in her speech "BIBFRAME Basics" she has mentioned the following steps to achieve the conversion as:

- code
- scribe
- customise
- transform
- Store and
- Deliver

The above steps she expects to work as:

1. Code : Create hand codes of existing information data units of existing MARC data into BIBFRAME compatible RDF / XML structure

2. Scribe : For this there is editing tool available provided by Zepheira as per contract given to them by LOC to design BIBFRAME model 1.0. This tool works as a native link data editor tool to create bibliographic description as endorsed by BIBFRAME. There is test site or sandbox of zepheira scribe process.

3. Customize : Then create a custom profile for editors to meet cataloguing experience or needs say one only wants to see the classes and properties associated with book data.BIBFRAME profiles allow for custom editor interface presently locally hosted installs can be customised.

4. Transform : To use LC- MARC to BIBFRAME Transformation tool to convert data into BIBFRAME (BIBFRAME Editor). BIBFRME editor is an open source tool for creating BIBFRAME metadata. Available to test data on web and can be downloaded at http://bibframe.org/ /tools. In transformation of MARC to BIBFRAME services, one need to supply URI to MARC data or one can paste MARC / XML data in BIBFRAME editing tool (http://bibframe.org/tools/ transform/start).

5. Store : Store BIBFRAME -RDF data in a triple store (Similarly as we do with any RDF linked data). Open linked Data can be stored in nosql database in triplestore. Zepheira is stills working on it.

6. Deliver : To deliver BIBFRAME RDF linked data using linked data publishing software and by using Library of Congress demonstration data sets (http:// www.loc.gov/bibframe/implementation)

While the task of chapter writing was in progress, the author had e-mail conversation with Amber Billey. Amber Billey is the Metadata Librarian at Columbia University Libraries and posses 10 years experience of cataloguing and digitization. She is Zepheira Alumna. The author found her presentation (webinars). 1 : Essentials of BIBFRAME and 2.BIBFRAME BASICS were very informative. Author felt that if the e-mail communication with Amber Billey is incorporated in the form of Questions and Answers it would help the readers to understand the topic and would help in refining their idea about the theme.

Q. How to BIBFRAME? – 28 Feb 2017 —*Amber Billey wrote on 1st March 2017*

A. In : How to BIBFRAME I have described steps as:

Core : To hand code BIBFRAME data.

Scribe : This is the tool developed by Zepheira. It is a native link data editor tool to create bibliographic descriptions using BIBFRAME RDF data...

She explains further BIBFRAME steps as:

Customise : To create custom profiles for editors (scribe) to tailor one's cataloguing needs.

Transform : To use LC-MARC to BIBFRAME transformation tool to convert data into BIBFRAME.

Store : To store BIBFRAME data in triple store.

Deliver : To deliver BIBFRAME linked data using linked data publishing software or use LC's demonstration data sets.... Amber Billey

Q. The significance of BIBFRAME Initiative of LC is to provide vision for future of library cataloguing. The main theme of BIBFRAME is to bring library catalogue in the middle of the web search domain, so if one googles a title/author then one would know the entire open linked data about it and one would also know availability of item in nearby library. Is it not so? 28th Feb2017

A. Being able to find bibliographic information through an internet search engine is just one main theme of BIBFRAME. Perhaps the most important purpose of BIBFRAME is to migrate bibliographic data into a (new) standard syntax that is primarily used and governed by the web and W3C. The first step is bibliographic data in BIBFRAME, and then we will need to figure out the functional and transaction work flow (Acquisition, holdings and circulation) in the linked data environment. In an ideal situation (I agree that) one would be able to know availability of a book in a nearby library based on bibliographic linked data. Moreover having bibliographic data freely available on web makes you question the necessity of proprietary platform like worldcat. Many American Libraries view BIBFRAME and library linked data efforts as a possible solution to being locked -into a single vendor a handful of vendors.

Amber Billey.. Wrote on 20th March, 2017.

Q. What has been done at Columbia University Libraries about the implementation of BIBFRAME? Have your patrons been benefited by it? ..... 2nd March 2017

A. Columbia is currently testing BIBFRAME. We have not implemented it into ILS or OPAC. So our patrons have not experienced any BIBFRAME data yet. We do use linked data technology for our digital collections and our patrons are benefiting from the linked data infrastructure through that interface..... Amber Billay...20th March2017.

Q. Do you know any LMS which has already incorporated BIBFRAME data structure in it facilitating development oı new database in library in IBIFRAME format directly? ...... 2nd March 2017

A. The only ILS/LMS that I know of that is incorporating BIBFRAME is Casalini's Share Catalog. It is in experimental development stage. They have version available to test out http://share.vde.org/sharevde/clusters... Amber Billey......

Q. Finally in your view how do LIS professionals in US look towards BIBFRAME developments?

A. Introduction of Linked Data concept and BIBFRAME to LIS professionals in US and third world countries has equal importance. To make real world wide web of linked data and therefore the semantic web, we will need the entire world to participate in creating linked data using standard ontologies like BIBFRAME-even third world countries. BIBFRAME is where IT and LIS colloid. Our experience in US has shown that introducing these concepts to LIS professionals (at all levels) increases their understanding and enthusiasm for linked data...Amber Billey.......22nd March 2017

7.6. BIBFRAME DEVELOPMENTS (IMPORTANT MILESTONES)

7.6.1. BIBFRAME-Pilot

At the stage when the BIBFRAME development reached to a saturation level it was tough time to take-up BIBFRAME Pilot (BIBFRAME 1.0). It was organised from 8th September 2015 to 31st March 2016. A network development of MARC standard office (NDMSO) and Co-operative Instruction Programmes Division (COIN) of the Acquisition of Bibliographic Access Directorate planned and developed a pilot to test the efficacy of BIBFRAME. The pilot was organised by Library of Congress. The pilot actually begun in October 2015, by this time it was yet to see the full functionality of BIBFRAME but BIBFRAME model and vocabulary was fully developed. The next phase of pilot was named as BIBFRAME - 2.0

Around 40 staff as mixed of cataloguers and services specialists were chosen as the participants for the pilot. The participants were responsible for processing monographs, serials, cartographic materials, music (annotated), sound recording, movie images and two dimensional artifacts (prints and photographs). They were also told to process the materials as they do normally in library. They were told to catalogue materials in MARC - 21 first and then in BIBFRAME format.

Training Programme : At the beginning participants were given exhaustive training of semantic web, linked data and use of BIBFRAME editor. The participants then began using the BIBFRAME editor. They entered data both in LC-LIS (voyager) and BIBFRAME editor. They created MARC - 21 records in voyager first and then in BIBFRAME. The experience of trainees and suggestions were used to refine and upgrade the BIBFRAME editing tools.

While training was in progress searching was available to primary datasets on the LC linked data service. Authorities vocabulary web site (http://id.loc.gov). There were LC / NACO Authority file and LCSH. In BIBFRAME both these datasets were accessible. The enhancements were made to the searching mechanism to improve the retrieval.

The outcome of training Requirements was found as:

1. Good understanding of RDA is essential for working in the BIBFRAME editing environment. So, the emphasis must be on RDA terminology than MARC coding.
2. Participants were seen curious about RDF sterilization. They found seeing and analysing BIBFRAME RDF sterilization in the pilot as it was first time live experience about using linked open data.

7.6.2. BIBFRAME Vocabulary

In MARC exchange environment one identify data elements with content designation. It is like:

- Tags to group and identity
- Subfields to identify
- Serialized with ISO - 2709 and further with XML, whereas, in BIBFRAME we use RDF conventions such as:
- Classes to group and identity
- Properties to identify and relate. They are with initial in lower case (Names have first letter in capital case.)
- Serialized with use of RDF triple.The list of classes properties and their attributes are the BIBFRAME Vocabulary. It is comprised of the RDF properties, classes and relationship among them.

BIBFRAME vocabulary is the key to the description of resources like MARC formats has a defined set of elements and attributes, where in classes identify type of BIBFRAME resource and properties serve to further describe the resource.

Version 2.0 of the vocabulary for BIBFRAME was released in April 2016.BIBFRAME vocabulary is available at home website http://bibframe.org/vocab. In this home page, there are three different views as :

- Model view
- Category view
- List view

Class is defined as a "type of things" while properties represents relationship between entities. Any term i.e. class will be the subject or object of RDF triple, whereas any term that is the property be the predicate of triple. In BIBFRAME model "Resource" is the top most class. Every other class is a subclass of resource. Domain and range terms are provided for properties which are reflected in terms of RDF triple. Domain is the subject; the property is the predicate and the range is the object. An easy way to decide whether a term is class or properties then remember that class always begins with caps and properties always begins with a lower-case letter. In a consolidated manner BIBFRAME model is described as shown in Fig. 7.10.

BIBFRAME model -

Four Main Classes
- Creative work
- Instance
- Authority
- Annotations

Fig. 7.10

There are total 53 classes and 289 properties. There is no need to actually enter the data in RDF templet but data is readily available and from other vocabularies like LOC, Worldcat, OCLC and Dublin Core can be searched and incorporated directly.

7.6.3. Zepheira

Zepheira has played a significant role in designing BIBFRAME a new bibliographic standard. Zepheira was technological partner in developing BIBFRAME model as it has been contracted by Library of Congress to bear this task.

Zepheira is a leading provider of software and services designed to help clients across industries to make information available more prominently on web. Founded in 2007, Zepheira has extensive experience of creating products and solutions focused on the modernisation of library information systems. Zepheira linked data readiness assessment has provided guidance and concrete steps for libraries to adopt open linked data and semantic web technologies in converting MARC to web actionable bibliographic format i.e. BIBFRAME. Zepheira was responsible to develop BIBFRAME 1.0 model and created linked data vocabularies for addressing the web visibility of library and similar organisations. It launched a new Linked Data Readiness Assessment (RA) product. In 2012, US Library of Congress selected Zepheira to architect BIBFRAME a new web friendly linked data format for library data to replace MARC-21. Zepheira has also facilitated to provide training to librarians in adopting BIBFRAME model for their catalogue data.

website : http://Zepheira.com. Its website on linked data library solution is as -

http://Zepheira.com/solution/library26.6.3.1 http://zepheira.com solution library

7.6.3.1. Zepheira's Training Program

Zepheira has designed a programme for academic library people who intend to go for early adoption programme and who wish to accelerate their team's education around the BIBFRAME standard and to participate in LIBHUB initiative by converting, contributing, linking and publishing up to 1000000 of their MARC records.

Zepheira is providing these training services to Academic Library teams since December 2015. They are delivering following services on an agreed upon schedule as:

- Zepheira's Practicals consists of linked data and BIBFRAME essentials. Training series is generally for 1-10 participants with conversion of 100 MARC record samples.
- Linked Data Readiness Assessment and converting up to 1000000 MARC record.
- Finally, conversion of up to 1000000 MARC records
- Transforming and connecting BIBFRAME contents publishing on the web.
- Collaborating in making additions and deletions to the web.

The libraries who purchase early adopter programme would get status of LIBHUB initiative as "Early Adopter" on the libhub.org website. LIBHUB initiative aims to raise the visibility of libraries on the web by actively exploring the promise of BIBFRAME and linked data. The following shows the list of libraries who are early adopter of LIBHUB initiatives.

- Denver public
- Dallas public
- Arapahoe library district
- Edmonton public
- Sno - Isle public
- Douglas county
- phoenix public
- Calgary public
- Anthric
- Worthington public
- Multnomah county
- Hamilton public

7.6.4. LIB-HUB

On 2nd September 2014 at Columbus, Ohio USA founding sponsor Zepheira introduced LIBHUB initiative to create an industry wide focus on giving collective visibility of libraries and their resources on web. Before BIBFRAME development was under taken by Zepheira the situation was that libraries had rich bibliographic contents resources that the web cannot see or use. The LIBHUB initiative aims to find common ground for libraries, providers and partners to publish and use bibliographic data with non-proprietary web standards. The libraries therefore could communicate in a way web application understand and web users can see them using enabling technology like linked data and share vocabularies such as schema.org and BIBFRAME.

The LIBHUB initiative emphasised on linking of these newly exposed library resources to each other and to other resources across the web.

Denver Public Library took the first lead in taking LIBHUB concept further by purchasing Zepheira's solution for libraries. They implemented the BIBFRAME model to convert their bibliographic data to linked open data.

Michelle Jeske, Director of Collections, Technology Innovation Centre at Denver Public Library expressed his feelings about this innovative library initiative as:

> "Libraries need to find new ways of reaching out and demonstrate that they truly are where their people need them, which includes Google and other search engines. When they would be able to showcase their rich collection and fabulous Western History and Genealogy resources more readily on the web, it is really an exciting."

About LIBHUB initiative Vailey Oehike, Director of Libraries for Multnomoh County Library and the President, Public Library Association on early LIBHUB initiative supporter said that:

> "Libraries have long been the greatest free source of information in each country. However, as people increasingly turn to Google and other search engines for their information needs we see that libraries' role is diminishing That is because our data is largely dark to the Internet and held in proprietary cataloguing systems which creates barriers in discovery. The LIBHUB initiative offers the possibilities for making library holdings discoverable directly through search engines like Google"

> Zepheira helps libraries to tell their stories on their web as News Break Information Today. http://newsbreak.infotoday.com.newsbreak.

> http://zepheira.com

7.6.5. Linked data for Libraries (LD4L)

It is a project designed to explore how libraries can use linked data and the semantic web to improve discovery / search and access to scholarly information. In 2014 Stanford University, the Harvard library- innovation lab and Cornell University were awarded a Mellon foundation grant to create Scholarly Resource of semantic information store model. The project has been named as Linked Data for Libraries (LD4L) with website : http://wiki.duraspace.org/pages/viewpage.action?page id=41354028/.

In this project, it has been attempted to link three large resources of data about scholarly resources, bibliographic data, person data and usage data and to connect library resources with institutional and other data on the web. LD4L also intends to provide a transparent mapping from the MARC records which currently housed much of this information to source via BIBFRAME. It is also expected that the project would produce an open source LD4L ontology compatible with BIBFRAME and other OLD efforts. An open source LD4L semantic editing ,display and search system and a project Hydra has compatible interface to LD4L.

7.6.6. BIBFLOW

It is a development to set a roadmap for migrating essential library work efforts to a

BIBFRAME/ linked open data ecosystem. It is believed that libraries on their own cannot adopt the modern technologie; in their current work flow constrains being the complexity and dependencies on a large ecosystem of data software and service provider. It is a two years' project funded by IMLS of the UC Davis University Library and Zepheira. It's official title is, "Reinventing Cataloguing"- Model for the future of library operations. The University is investing the future of library technical services (cataloguing and related work flow) in the light of modern technology infrastructure, such as the web and new data models and formats such as Resource Description and Access (RDA) and BIBFRAME, the new encoding and exchanging format in development by the Library of Congress. The university hypothesis behind starting BIBFLOW project is that while these new standards and technologies are essentially needed to help the libraries community to avail the benefits and efficiencies that the libraries cannot remain far from modem developments of open linked data. However due to complexity of this technology and the constrains of libraries due to their current library standards i.e. AACR - II and MARC the research is therefore needed on how research libraries should adapt new pra_tice, workflow software systems and partnership to support evolution of new standards and technologies.

BIBFLOW is expected to take up this agenda and set these activities to modernise library community understanding of the resource description landscape the current and desire future state. This university world begins to develop a roadmap that the library community can be ready for planning investing and changing over the coming years.

The BIBFLOW project would focus on Academic Library technical services/ processes, including acquisition, licensing, cataloguing, technical processing, digitization etc. in the light of new bibliographic standard BIBFRAME. Ref Blog: - http://www.lib.ucdavis.edu/bibflow.

7.7. LIBRARY SOFTWARES READY WITH BIBFRAME STRUCTURE

As Amber Billey has mentioned in her mail correspondence that then software named - casalini is available now. Let us see what it is.

7.7.1. What is Casalini's Share VDE (Virtual Discovery Environment) project?

Casalini's share VDE project is a prototype of a virtual discovery environment where BIBFRME's three layer architecture (person/work, instance, and item) has been established through the individual process of analysis, enrichment, conversion and publication of data from MARC-21 to RDF. It is expected to work with the context of libraries with different systems.

Share virtual discovery in linked data is a platform which allows the browsing of library collection organized as per BIBFRAME standard. The portal (www.shar-vde.org) to share VDE project is equipped with navigational tools with three layers of BIBFRAME as :

Person/Works : This level facilitates to enrich to get data from external resources with a view to extend the research potential.

Instances : At this level it tries to aggregate the resources of various editions, works with different languages of one creator and try to connect them with the overlaying person/work.

Item : With this instance the publication is linked to the information contained in a data set of the local library OPAC.

Now let us visualize how search in Virtual Discovery Environment seen in linked data. Share VDE is a experimental platform for searching and accessing bibliographic resources according to BIBFRAME data model which is available in some important libraries like:

Stanford University, University of California, Berkeley, Yale University, LC University of Chicago, University of Michigan, An Arbor, Harvard University, MIT, Cornel University, Columbia University Library, University of Pennsylvania, Texas A & M University and University of Toronto.

The search page looks like this: Fig. 7.11.

The search has the further options as :

- Refining search
- Advanced search
- Browsing the Index and
- Finally where to access the resource, where one can export bibliographic records with choice of desired format. One can alternatively access the OPAC of the library where the resource is held.

Ref. Share Virtual Discovery Environment in linked data : Brief user guide

Courtesy: www.shar-vde.org (Share VDE is a CasaliniLibri and@ Cult partnership)

7.8. HOW TO GET INVOLVED IN BIBFRAME MOVEMENT

Now it is the question how world libraries, librarians and LIS professionals would get themselves involved in this modern development. It could be done by:

- Following BIBFRAME related projects and experiments.
- By exploring BIBFRAME tools
- By participating in BIBFRAME discussion LISTSERVE groups
- By attending sessions at ALA

  One can also attend live session like as:

  1. MARC Transition Interest group sessions: Saturday between 3.00 to 4.00 with focus on BIBFRAME tools
  2. BIBFRAME updates Sunday at 10.00
- Zepheira offers a Linked Data/BIBFRAME training class with access to ongoing alumni group http://zepheira.com/solutions/library/training.

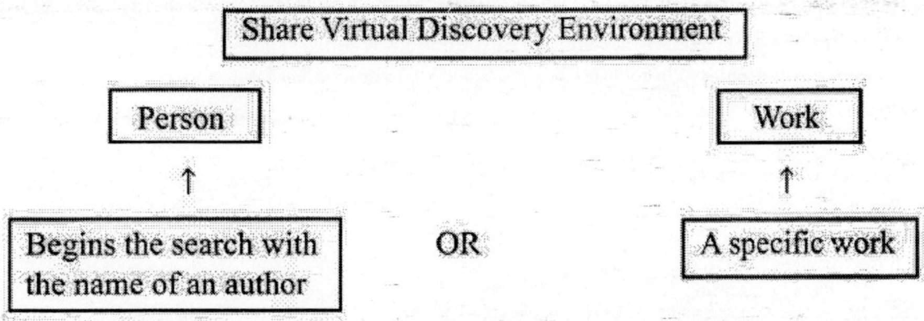

The result page of person will show the following information.

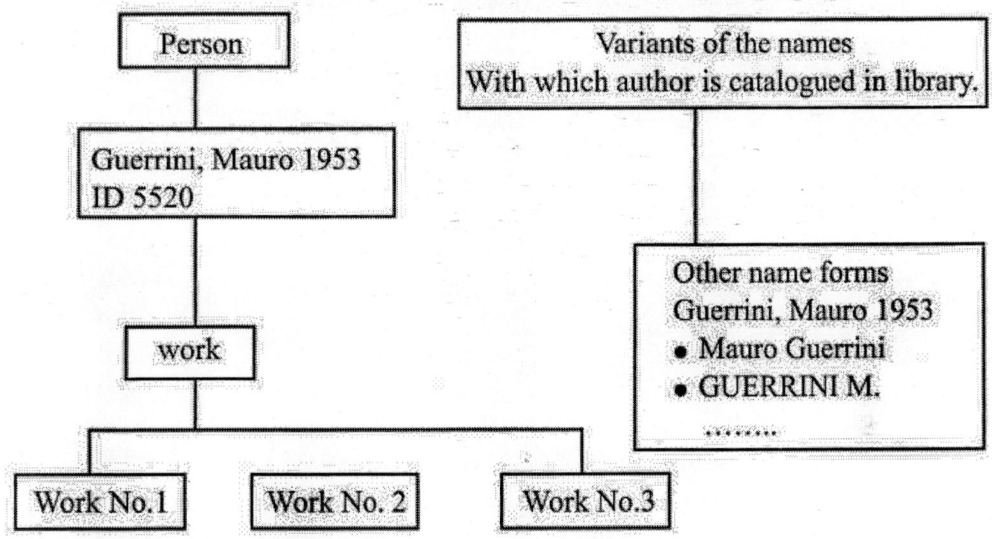

(List of work in a alphabetical order)

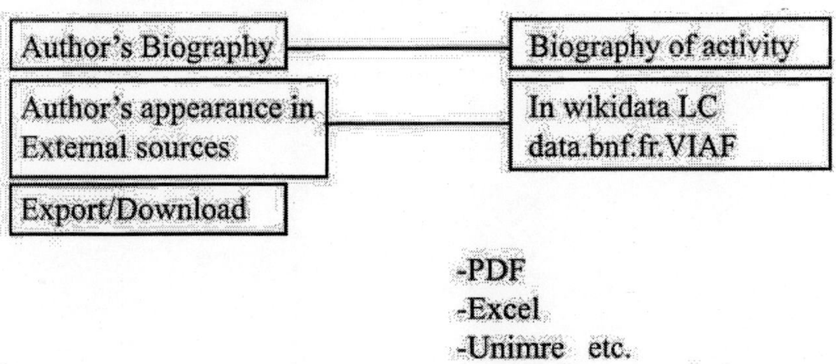

Fig. 7.11. Casalini -Share video project design

REFERENCES

1. ALA: From MARC to BIBFRAME: An Introduction: Webinar: Carolyn Hansen http://www.ala.org/alcts / confevents/upcomingwebinars/051315. (accessed in February 2017)
2. BIBFRAME bibliographic framework initiative (Library of Congress) http://www.loc.gov.bibframe. (accessed in February 2017)
3. Over view of BIBFRAME 2.0 modelhttp:// www.loc.gov/bibframe/docs/bibframe2.model html.
4. http://bibframe.org
5. Zepheira :http://zepheira.com.
6. Linked Data for Libraries (LD4L) :http://www.ld41.org
7. Libhub :www.libhub.org/join/
8. Bibflow :http://www.lib.ucdavis.edu/bibflow
9. Amber Billey(Metadata Librarian) :Essentials of BIBFRAME; Columbia University Libraries http:// www.youtube.com/
10. Amber Billey : BIBFRAME Basics Academic commons Columbia University Libraries 12/08/2015
11. Amber Billay about your Presentation on BIBFRAME : E-mail response date 01.03.2017 amber.billey @columbia.edu

8
Migration of Library Management System-LMS Migration

8.0. INTRODUCTION

While writing on library computerisation in subject literature, while discussing it with various librarians and having long experience of dealing with computerisation at his own institution the author has noticed that the process of library computerisation especially in developing countries proceeds through various stages in different libraries. The stages could be categorized as below :

Stage 1 : Convinced for library automation but due to lack of adequate fund no decision on computerization is taken.

Stage 2 : Only a few selected library activities are computerised : say only circulation due to shortage of funds.

Stage 3 : Library computerisation process is on since long time.

Stage 4 : Computerisation process has been completed in all respect.

Stage 5 : Upgradation of present LMS is going on

Stage 6 : Library has decided to migrate to a new LMS

Considering the above scenario, it is observed in the discussions and feedback from the researchers that strength of libraries having first three stages is more. However, it is also noticed that the number of libraries having last three stages is also quite good. Then the question arises, what would be the future probabilities as well as main issues of library computerization? The answer to the question obviously would be problem of migration from old software to a new alternative one. Today many large libraries are facing inconveniences with the old LMS and are thinking to migrate to new alternative LMS. The main reason behind the problem has been seen in the fact that, library had never imagined that in future they would need to change or migrate to a new LMS.

The author feels that library LMS problems and migration experience must be shared among the libraries. However, very rarely librarians write on it or share with others. There are no case studies written on this topic, so the experience of LMS migrations is generally not shared.

With this background, the author felt that it would be good if the issue is discussed at length, hence this chapter. It is expected that the discussion would help librarians to know the difficulties and problems that libraries could face and consider some probable solutions. It would be more significant for the libraries which are actually going through the process of LMS migration.

8.0.1. Migration of Library Management System: Concept and Nature

Before we actually start the discussion and know the concept of LMS migration, it would be worth to know meaning of and terminologies used:

LMS : It is an abbreviation of Library Management System. This term indicates that it is a software used to computerise library's day to day (routine) functions. Moreover, it covers entire functioning of a library. The software is a current one and is prepared using some standards.

ILMS : It is Integrated Library Management System. Normally, there are various modules or subsystems pertaining to different library activities. Further, all these modules or subsystems are inter connected to link the related activities which are dependent on each other. There are certain advantages in integrating them; hence the word integrated.

With this initial background, let us try to know the concept of LMS migration. The concept of LMS migration could be spelled out as - A library leaves the currently used software and goes for all together new library software. Old and new library softwares are type of LMS or ILMS. Here one can assume a situation where previously used LMS was properly installed and implemented, databases required were developed. It was used to computerise all the housekeeping functions of the library and after a gap of time due to some serious problems it was felt necessary to leave it and explore a new LMS. The ideal situation of LMS migration also assumes that in old LMS which ever databases were developed are available for exporting and importing into a new LMS, and with the help of old database the computerisation of library is once again completed. The migrated LMS is thus available for use by all library sections in a shortest possible time.

There could be another situation where the previous LMS was installed and new databases were developed fully. However, due to some technical hurdles it was not possible to make LMS operational and hence, there was no alternative but to switch to a new LMS.

If we consider the above situations it makes us clear that there are two issues concerned with LMS migration i. e.

1. Developing necessary databases is a significant and important library activity.
2. With the help of library databases and LMS structure the library computerisation is completed and made operational.

The author feels that in LMS migration process the first issue e. g. database development is the most important where as completing computerisation with LMS is the secondary issue.

Generally it is noticed that librarians are not serious about development of relevant databases. In fact they hardly understand how the databases are developed in library computerisation. The LMS vendors do this task independently without much of involvement of librarian and finally claim a copy right or ownership of library databases and try to trap library authority on the database ownership issue.

The author is of the opinion that library should take its own efforts to create standardised library database using available bibliographic tools and should own the copyright of it and make it available to LMS vendor. Having this situation, it would not be difficult to migrate to any new LMS if felt necessary at a later stage. However, generally it does not happen as librarians do not have full control over library computerisation process of their own library and they finally land into problem when LMS migration time comes. Sometimes the problems become so severe that it becomes too difficult for the library to come out of the situation. In such status there would not remain any alternative but to start from scratch, which is a huge task.

8.1. LMS MIGRATION: PROBLEM EXAMPLES

If we try to review computerisation situations in various libraries we would find that many of them, somehow or the other, are found stuck into some problems of library computerisation process. There is still quite some time to reach the stage of LMS migration. Let us review some of the examples of probable problem situations faced by libraries in computerisation process in western region of India. This discussion would help readers to have clarity of LMS migration stage in the library.

8.1.1. Examples of Problems in Library Computerisation

1. Library has accepted software and work of developing databases of library books and periodical is in process. This continues for years together. Library is not in a position to make circulation module operational. It is not benefitting readers or library staff.
2. Library has accepted software. Most of activities are now operational. Computerised working and old manual working continues in parallel due to lack of confidence in software and it continues for years. Readers might be benefitted but staff needs to do work in duplicate.
3. Library has accepted ordinary software at nominal cost. Book database is ready, circulation continues as manual and transactions are entered in system in a batch mode. However, library is not in a position to do acquisition, cataloguing or journal control. Every time entries are done repeatedly. There is no OPAC search available for readers to the library search materials. Circulation status of any book is not possible to check.
4. Similar to the above case library has bought substandard software. Initially, with book and patron master circulation work started. However, later some problem in software was developed. Subsequently, as software vendor has closed his activity, as such there was no one available to maintain the system. Computerised operation comes to a standstill.
5. Some librarians with the help of window's access or excel tools create library book collection data file. Circulation transactions are done manually and then are entered in the computer in a batch mode, no OPAC search facility is available for readers. The database created cannot be exported / imported to a new software.
6. Library computerisation was made operational with a software. Library did not keep the backup and server / server hard disc is scratched, it has become almost impossible to retrieve or recover the old data. As such computerised working of library has come to hold.

7. Library has computerised its activities with the help of software. It is made operational from cutoff date. Whereas old transactions are handled manually.

8. The library has taken up data entry work. However, with date wise accessioning, barcode generation is not possible. Library functioning would be only possible when the entire data entry gets over. It is taking unlimited time to resolve the issue.

9. The data in software is not secured from unauthorized manipulation. The transactions are not safe.

10. Readers do not have faith in computerised library functioning. They are not ready to accept procedure as set in the computerised working. Library has also lost records of old manuals transactions. As a result readers are not returning old books. Library is losing a considerable number of books in the process. Librarian is taken on task and compelled to compensate the loss.

There could be many more examples of failures in the computerisation of library like above. However, all the above cases do not come under LMS migration as in most of these cases computerisation needs to be started from the beginning. Although it is not relevant to provide solution to these problems but author would like to draw some conclusion from these examples which are representatives of situations in many libraries show in the examples of improper attention of librarians towards the library computerisation resulting :

(a) Libraries remain many years in the same state of art.

(b) Library staff does not understand capability, short coming or even benefits of the software.

(c) Librarian is not in a position to extend benefits of computerisation to the users.

(d) Librarian do not explore to test the capability of software fully.

These situations are suitable for switching over to new standardized software as there would be serious problems of data porting as the previous softwares are not of standard nature. After reviewing situations in a group of libraries and knowing the problems in library computerisation now let us come back to the discussion of our topic viz. library LMS migration.

Leaving all the above situation, in some libraries there is the favorable situations to migrate to a new software as technically it is feasible. Based on a survey report it could be stated that in the western (India) region 10-15 % of large libraries are on the verge of LMS migration in the next 3-5 years and the percent may grow up to 50 to 60.[1] This could be because libraries find it difficult to maintain the software by paying huge maintenance cost and on other side availability of open source software which is an economical and easy way of computerisation available to the libraries.

In this case also we can consider group representative cases or situation in the libraries in examples as below, these would help readers to understand relevance to library LMS migration status:

---

1. Ojaswini Upasani : Study on LMS Migration in the Libraries in India (Western region) Thesis submitted for Ph. D. to YCMOU, Nasik, 2017 (Author happened to be the guide in this research)

8.2. EXAMPLES OF LMS MIGRATIONS

1. Library has accepted a standard LMS for computerisation. LMS vendor is working on customization of LMS. The work continues for 3-4 years. Except one activity, all others have been made operational. After passing of considerable time, vendor is refusing to maintain the software and is not ready to take up work of computerizing remaining major activity. Moreover, they have leased the old version of LMS. They are demanding almost same cost of new LMS for providing next version and for further software maintenance work. In this situation it is worthwhile for library to migrate to a new LMS.
2. In this example there is a similar situation as described in the above case and difference is that the vendor who provided LMS does not exist due to dispute among the partnership. As a result there is nobody to provide the next version of LMS neither there is vendor available to maintain the software although the library is ready to pay for both the things. With the help of local IT expert library functioning is continued not sure how long the situation could be continued further.
3. Library has taken up computerization some time back, it would be complete the soon. However, library professionals and users are not happy about the performance of software in terms of:
   (a) LMS technology is outdated and it gives slow response.
   (b) Programming language used is not web based and there are difficulties in interacting on internet platforms.
   (c) Database is not developed as per AACR-II or not done in MARC format. It needs to go for retrospective data conversion which requires long time to complete. It does not allow online editing of database. Readers are not happy with the search facility.
   (d) LMS is not meeting expectations of system uses and readers. This situation demands LMS migration.
4. Library had adopted a LMS to computerise library operation, which continued to work smoothly for some years. Library now wishes to adopt RFID system to introduce self check in / checkout and also use for its inventory control, but old LMS is not compatible to adopt RFID technology. The situation needs migration to a new capable system.
5. Library successfully computerised its functioning. After some time they felt to adopt RFID system to provide security to collection and have inventory control. However, existing LMS vendor is demanding huge amount almost equal to cost of LMS for making provision of necessary SIP-2 server required for RFID adoption. Without co-operation of vendor they cannot proceed further. The library is not convinced to bear the cost of creating SIP-2 server.
6. Library enthusiastically adopted a LMS and computerisation was made operational. First year went off very well. However, subsequently they realized that they need to spend good amount on maintenance of system. In the absence of provision of funds LMS vendor refused to maintain the system. As such library computerisation is likly to suffer a setback. They need to look for LMS migration.

7. A library wishes to introduce revisions and improvements with the co-operation of LMS vendor but they are not ready to co-operate or not ready to accept the task.
8. LMS adopted in a library breaks down frequently. It takes long time to repair the problem. The LMS technicians do not report timely or demand considerable charges including air fare. As such library computerised functioning gets disturbed.
9. LMS vendor claims the copy rights of library bibliographic database, does not allow library to export the data to alternative LMS.
10. There are some serious problems with vendors on payment account. The relations between them are strained, which is impacting maintenance of library software and as such library functioning was suffering.

All the above situations are representative. In each situation there is some valid reason making library to think for LMS migration. Considering all the above situations and other probable problems one can prepare a list of reason behind the LMS migration as :

8.3. REASONS BEHIND LMS MIGRATION

1. LMS vendor declares the old LMS version as ceased and compels library to go for next version for considerable cost.
2. LMS vendor stops their service and does not attend software maintenance work.
3. LMS vendor refuses to undertake improvements and revisions in LMS as per library expectations.
4. Performance of LMS is not good in giving information retrieval and in satisfying users.
5. Library is not in a position to afford the recurring heavy expenditure on LMS maintenance after the warranty period.
6. Library wishes to change software platform from windows to Linux and LMS is not compatible to work on it.
7. Library need to adopt RFID security system but LMS is not compatible to RFID or LMS vendor refuses to co-operates on the matter or they demand heavy charges.
8. LMS vendor locks library data base, does not allow exporting data to a new LMS since they claim the ownership. They may also refuse to give data backup.
9. Open source software service provider stops serving and maintaining LMS server or demands heavy charges or library wishes to maintain LMS server by itself and wishes to come out of service provider's contract.
10. Library wishes to bring innovative features in LMS, provide more LMS based library services to its users and wishes to make LMS up-to-date and of international standard.

8.4. DATA CONVERSION ISSUES IN LMS MIGRATION

While studying the theme author observes that there are several issues relating to LMS migration process, but data convertibility was found the prominent issue among all. The data convertibility here means data of the old LMS to be ported to a new LMS or it is export and import of data from old to new LMS. It is also noticed that many a times LMS migration process in library goes into trouble. The main reason behind this is the data structure and format of old LMS, which is not convenient for migration. There are various types of data formats and libraries face problems in converting to a new LMS. This happens because of database incompatibility. In LMS migration process handling the library bibliographic database or data about related transaction are difficult to convert into the new LMS.

In view of the above, let us try to take an overall view of library databases considering their various formats available. We could find various types of data formats in library softwares such as:

1. dbase - 2 / - 3 / - 4 or FoxPro
2. Windows utilities - Ms Access, Excel or word / text
3. CDS-ISIS
4. PDF file format
5. Software's own format
6. Unicode form.

If LMS considers compatibility or it is of latest type then the formats should be based on the following standards :

1. MARC - 21
2. ISO - 2709
3. XML or MARC - XML
4. Database developed as per web based languages VB++, Perl etc.

Readers may note that AARC-II is data style and not the data format RDA is next version of AACR, II. The success of data convertibility depends on what format data is in the old LMS. If the old data base fields are not matching with that of new LMS data fields then a fresh data conversion program needs to be written and then only data conversion is done. Some times converted data is found flat type. In such case hurdles are faced in database management task. In the latest type of LMS, software has data base management systems and generally it is relational database management system. As such all DBMS works as an intermediary tool between database and the software. Normally these days LMS adopts standard database format i. e. as per ISO- 2709: 2008 standard, which facilitates export and import of database across the LMSs. This issue is of bit technical and complicated to understand but it is worthwhile that librarians and library professional to understand it. There are various ways and means to convert data of old LMS to new ones, which are normally adopted by LMS vendors to convert the data.

8.4.1. Data conversion case study in LMS Migration

At this juncture it would be interesting to discuss one case study published in a literature, which will help us in understanding inside issues and difficulties faced in LMS migration. Here purposely name of old LMS is presented as anonymous.

Reason for LMS migration : Reason for library to go for LMS migration is, that library cannot afford to meet recurring cost of LMS maintenance and it prefers to go for free or open source type of software.

Scope : It considered data conversion from commercially available proprietary software to a free software.

Problems in Data Conversion

1. Library had collection of 18000 monographs, manuals and standards but old LMS had bibliographic data of 13000 library collection.
2. Since old LMS was of commercial type or proprietary type the source codes of software were not available. It was therefore impossible to get the data from LMS back end.
3. In the old LMS version DBMS was not in use therefore the data structure was of flat type. The LMS data was developed in machine readable form i. e. MARC by using MARC tags and field record separator.
4. Although old LMS had inbuilt data exporting facility but it was not giving data in a suitable format to import it in the new LMS. Moreover, old LMS vendor does not allow data to be exported out especially backup data about circulation and acquisition transactions. The challenging task was to get data in back end in the following format.
    - Own LMS format
    - MARC format
    - ISO-2709 format
    - Text format (fixed / variable length)

Background of New LMS

1. New LMS was not of open source type but was available free of cost.
2. New LMS was working on windows platform and stores data in MS-SQL server and data format was MS-Access, which is available at back end.
3. New LMS has a provision to export database as per will of the library.

How Data Porting was done finally: Solutions to problem.

After considering the background of both old and new LMS, constrains / limits of old LMS and considering over all the data porting problems the following steps were under taken to overcome the problems.

1. Considered machine readable data of old LMS
2. Retrieved data in text form with fields as title, author, edition, editor, corporate author, place, publication, year, registration, series notes, ISBN, report / standard no., class no. , book no., key word and acc. nos.

3. Reformatting of above text form data was done, by using Global replace utility of windows and data was transferred to MS-Access by writing small utility programs in Visual Basic 6.0. Entire MS-Access data was then imported into MS-SQL server. After data porting it was tested in new LMS. After the test was successful new LMS was brought into operation.

4. In the above process there was cost involvement for data conversion but it was considerably less than maintenance of old LMS and there was no cost for new LMS. The cost of installation was negligible.[1]

We can see, in spite of limitations created by old LMS vendor the problem of data conversion was done skillfully. Off course every case may not be like the above, however, it proves that after studying the situation and problems, the solutions could be found out.

The example certainly tells librarians some lesson that: Librarians need to keep in mind while purchasing software that library might have to decide to migrate to a new LMS in future. They must have answer to the following questions in mind while adopting new LMS in library that:

a. What is data standard format of LMS? Is it convenient to export the data?

b. What about copy right of database? Whether LMS is convenient for data exporting? or there would be any difficulty?

Now let us consider about some software tools used for data conversion to make it suitable for import it in LMS having MARC standard.

8.4.2. Use of UNESCO / ISIS data conversion tools

Many librarians having pressure either from management or as a part of fulfilling NAAC requirements for accreditation try to do something to show as evidence of library computerisation. They try to create database in a very crude way by using utilities of windows i. e. MS-Access or MS-Excel or Dbase (old package) or Foxpro etc. This is treated equivalent of data entry work, which has no future or utilization possibility for computerisation. This action in real sense does not lead to database creation. Moreover, they do not have any kind of awareness or expertise that for converting such data one needs to follow the standards like ISO 2709 or in MARC format; although it is possible to do it. Unless the data created is not reflected in library OPAC, such work has no meaning. There are ways and means to convert various types of raw data into a standard data with MARC - 21 or as per ISO-2709, which could facilitate importing it into a new LMS. Logically if data is convertible to ISO-2709 format then it can be converted into any LMS based database. Now let us try to understand how the available tools could be used to convert the library data. The list of software tools used to convert raw data into standard library data is as below :

1. **DB-2-ISO / DB32150 :** With this software tool one can convert old data available in DBase or fox pro to ISO-2709

---

1. Matoria, Ram Kumar and Upadhya P. K. : Migration of data from one library management system to another : A case study in India. **Program:** Electronic library and informatics information systems vol. 39 No. 2, 2005 Emerald Group Publishing Ltd. pp 160-166

2. **TXT-2-ISO :** With this data available text file format can be converted to ISO-2709
3. **XML-2-ISIS :** Normally any data based on RDBMS if it is in MS-Access or in SQL server then it can be converted first to XML format then to XML-ISIS and then to ISO-2709 by using above tool. Data in MS-Excel could also be converted to MS-Access then to DBF file to ISO-2709 by using internal drives.
4. **GENISIS :** By using this UNESCO tool library can prepare an OPAC from data available in ISIS format. It is possible to prepare data in CDS-ISIS form or library can use its old data in CDS-ISIS which could be published as OPAC by using GENISIS

8.4.3. MARC-21 Editor

If a library has prepared the database in excel sheet it can be converted to MARC-21 format by reformatting excel shit to make it compatible to MARC structure. Data prepared in excel sheet can be uploaded to Koha open source software by making it compatible by using MARC - Editor Tool.

IIIT & M at Trivandrum provides training for using GENISIS software to prepare and publish library OPAC.

The use of the above tools is found very much useful in data conversion. The librarian who have prepared raw library data should go ahead to convert their data which could be used in modern LMS by making use of the above software tools.

8.4.4. Care and Precautions to be taken for data conversion

Having understood the problems and solution referred in former case study librarians should take the following care and necessary precautions while adopting commercial software.

1. They should avoid purchasing LMS from vendors who claim copyright or ownership of library data.
2. Such LMS may be selected which is compatible to ISO-2709 data environment to handle the data conversion.
3. If exchange format of XML type is used then it becomes easy to handle in RDBMS environment.
4. Whenever data is converted from one XML to another format then it needs a middle stage or buffer like phase. A small utility program is written to create such phase. If the required changes are carried out in this phase then it becomes convenient to port data to a new XML. Generally, Visual Basic is used for this purpose.

In data conversion, it is necessary to see that the former and latter LMS data base has similar data structure or same number of fields; otherwise there is risk of losing some data fields if data structures are not matching with each other. If these requirements are verified while purchasing a new LMS then it helps in avoiding future difficulties.

Now let us consider the overall problems in LMS migration and probable solutions to them:

8.5. CARE AND PRECAUTIONS TO AVOID LMS MIGRATION PROBLEMS

LMS migration is not an easy task, there are difficulties in it. It would be difficult to provide case to case solutions. However, on broader sense considering common or general type of difficulties occurring during LMS migration problems, it is possible to provide some suggestion and precautions while buying first LMS so the problems in LMS migration at a later stage are reduced.

1. If in the beginning of adoption of first LMS, sufficient care and precaution is taken then there would not be necessity to go for LMS migration in future at all.
2. **Technology standardization :** One should verify standard of LMS whether, the software is developed as per standard. Technology of LMS should be latest one and suitable to current technology environment, specially programming language should be the latest and compatible to web technology. There should be flexibility to accommodate change in operating system or it should have versions to switch over open source platforms like LINUX.
3. **Software database structure and database management system :** The database of LMS & its structure should be of international standard and it must have quality of markup format. The MARC format, should be of latest one i. e. MARC-21 or MARC-SGML. The database management system which works as co-ordination between database and LMS should be of current one.
4. **LMS should incorporate innovative features :** This is normally done as a later stage or in future. The LMS should be accommodative to have revisions and addition of new features.
5. **Capability to interface new technology :** In the future if the library decides to adopt RFID technology facilitating or self check out and check in system then LMS should have provision to interface with RFID without any additional cost. It requires SIP-2 server to make it possible to interface RFID and the LMS database. Librarian must verify this capability before adopting basic LMS.
6. **LMS source code sharing policy :** As far as possible library should insist vendor to provide LINUX based software, so that program source codes are transferrable to the local IT person. Such situation helps library to arrange minor trouble shooting with the help of local IT expert which makes maintaining software smoothly without any interruptions 24 X 7.
7. **LMS Maintenance cost :** The maintenance cost of LMS should be affordable to the library. While purchasing LMS, library should go for contract agreement with vendor to maintain system at least for 3-5 years from the first purchase by negotiating the recurring expenditure, so that the library functioning goes smoothly for next 3 years and it need not bother for maintenance cost. The maintenance period should start after installation process is completed in all respect and all the modules should be fully operational. Librarian should insist vendor to give the latest version of LMS and they should not ask for any additional money for version upgradation up to next five years.
8. **Cost on future improvements :** once LMS is accepted then the improvements and changes suggested by users for the next one year's period should be provided without any additional cost as it is a warming up or the honeymoon period.

9. **Post purchase service :** In case after adoption of LMS if vendor stops receiving complaints or discontinues its maintenance service then as per provision made in the legal agreement, while buying software, library should have right or option to fine the vendor or recover such expenditure from the vendor by filling suit in the court. Library should sign legal agreement considering all such future problem with proper clauses in it.
10. **Availability or right to have future versions of LMS :** Library should secure provision in legal agreement with vendor while purchasing LMS that vendor must provide next or upgraded versions in future without paying any additional payment and it should be treated as right of library.
11. **Library must reserve its right to have copy right of library database** when it is ported to LMS and it should never be given to LMS vendor. Secondly, vendor should be bound to allow export of database and basic library data if the library wishes so at any time in future.

All the above points suggest that how library should be careful in purchasing LMS and about making necessary provisions in the legal agreement to be signed with vendor, so that library would not unnecessarily suffer or involve any undue problem or should not meet a situation impacting functioning of LMS and ultimately functioning of computerised library systems.

It is suggested that librarian must have full control on all the above aspects of computerisation, he should be alert and enough aware about library software developments globally. He should also have knowledge about capabilities of local and international kind of softwares and of innovative features available with them. Process of LMS improvements never ends and he should think in bringing in as many innovations in LMS in serving readers better way.

He can have further plans and priorities to adopt the innovations and improvements with the co-operation of LMS vendor. Librarian should have broad or modem perspective of LMS database, technology, and metadata standard. He must evaluate LMS thoroughly at the beginning of LMS purchase process.

If library acquires an expertise to first develop library database with available software tool and then think of migrating to new LMS, then things work smoothly.

8.6. INNOVATIVE FEATURES OF LMS – A FUTURISTIC VIEW

In the above discussion we have considered the future of LMS or their "**Innovative features**." However, it is experience that software vendors never think to provide any innovative features while providing the particular version of LMS. They would provide LMS having lowest profile and try to keep an inbuilt provision or scope for future business with library and for additional earning. It is therefore, the duty of librarian to have innovative vision about the library LMS and should see that right from beginning how the graph of innovation goes up. One can learn about innovations of LMS from LIS literature where LMS evaluations and comparative analysis cases are discussed.

The author has made an attempt to list out all new and innovative features that the future library software should have. The list is as below :

New LMS Features

1. **Transparency of information in LMS :** Normally librarian answers all the question put by readers. However, normally teacher community do not have access to information relating to progress and status of new suggestions given by them or information regarding budget required by HODs and others who approve library requirements at department end. Author feels that all of them should have access to get the required information on their own without asking to librarians, such transparency would be appreciated by user if provided in the LMS.
2. Teachers or scientist should get first hand report about their new suggestions. If such report is sent is anticipation it would be of great help to the indenters.
3. Concerned teachers and guides can be provided with feedback about what material is read or referred in library by their students.
4. **Online suggestion systems :** Normally a suggestion to purchase new reading materials is forwarded on paper which is attended by library to enter the details into LMS database. Instead, if LMS has provision to submit suggestion online by indenters it would save paper work and time. As the suggestions could be submitted in data base format it could be received by library in data entry format and could reduce the burden on library staff. The online suggestion could be further automated by creating document movement and delivery system, e. g. the suggestion could be routed through the approving authority like HODs. The next approval stage can also be completed and suggestion with status as approval would be received in library, which would help to avoid unnecessary paper work and delay in handling papers at various points.
5. There may be provision in LMS to facilitate forwarding information about new announcement and about publication of books by publishers, distributor, and agents or even by authors to library, which can be repacked and forwarded to teachers & department as a library information service. Such facility could have provision to inform library about books available for approval by vendors and distributors. The information can be further made available to concern faculty and exhibition of such books could be organized to facilitate teacher's community to browse and see books physically and recommend for purchase.
6. If there is provision in LMS, library could forward the soft copies of book purchase orders to concern book sellers and vendors.
7. Library can introduce e-bidding method through online facility of LMS to get books at a competitive pricing from the book trade. This could be useful and economical while buying costly reference books.
8. Library LMS could provide interface/connectivity to online resources of classification schemes and of subject heading tools as such a service would be very much required by the classifiers in classification of books.
9. LMS can incorporate new feature to widen the scope of library's OPAC by including additional information in OPAC like :

— Image of a book
— Contents page
— Author's brief biography
— Sharing exact location of a book on shelf in a digital map of library shelving layout
— Users can see virtual position of reading material in digital picture up to a shelf level.
— provision of connectivity to catalogue of other libraries
— Worldcat OPAC Links
— Gate way to Google scholar
— Connectivity to web sites of online book stores.

10. Readers take a lot of efforts in searching library materials in OPAC and finally they get list of desired material. However, no LMS gives facility to save the searches made by readers for their future reference. This facility if given can help to built a reader's virtual library in OPAC, if successive search saving facility is given to users.

11. Readers should have facility to tag their choices of material searched in OPAC and assign their own subject headings and sort the list as per their tagging. Such facility could be useful for researchers. They could also give suggestions and feedback to classifier to improve classification.

12. Normally any LMS have provision to store only surrogate data about library collection. There should be provision to store full text digital documents within the OPAC and provide direct connectivity to browse through and read such digital collection. Such material includes types like photos and images, paintings, animation films, digital video and audio films, material in languages other than English, talking books/podcasts etc.

13. LMS to have provision to catalogue multimedia materials like e-books, e-journals, databases and other digital forms by using respective MARC tags and with provision of links to access such materials directly through OPAC.

14. LMS should have provision to incorporate accompanied soft documents like CDs and videos along with catalogue entry of original work and it should be available online to access on intranet while reading the respective original books. This can be done by copying all such material on mirror server and linking it through an interface to catalogue entry or acc. nos. of original material.

15. OPAC to have provision to show search list in order of material accessed maximum by the readers so that they can see entries in the list which are many times referred by other reader, which could also help readers to know about usefulness of material known by others.

16. Normally the barcodes printed on books by publishers are not useful in library LMS and library has separate barcodes of its materials, which are used in LMS operations. It is possible to synchronize library barcodes to that of ISBN or ISSN barcodes printed on back cover of the book and journal issue especially if library is able use barcodes of journal issues to make their receipts entered in LMS journals scheduling input page, it would save a lot of time.

17. Till then we have not seen any LMS providing QR codes facilitating for quickly reaching various web pages of library home page. If there is provision it would help readers to directly open the desired web page by scanning the QR codes in mobile and using it to access the web pages.

18. Each LMS to give mobile version of library web site to facilitate users especially youngsters to search library catalogue on their smart phones or etc. Library can also create library apps for users.

19. LMS should provide menus to facilitate self checkout of library material without involving library staff with proper security checks incorporated in the system. This would be an alternative for purchasing costly 3M type work stations, so that readers can avail issue facility 24 * 7 all the time as long as library is open. Similarly borrowers should also get self renewal facility through their own authenticated account page without bringing books to library only for renewal purpose.

20. Library circulation system should have facility to issue e- books to readers through kindle.

21. Library should provide facility to readers to make use of web 2.O tools.

Such a list of innovative features is very rarely found in LIS literature by the readers. If we see the features of every LMS critically we hardly, find the above features built-in in them. It is expected that the above list of features would be challenging for LMS manufactures and it is also expected that librarians community would be assertive to have above features in their LMS by insisting LMS vendors to consider them.

9

Library Website Development : Techniques and Tools (HTML, CSS, Java Script, Ajax & PHP)

9.0. INTRODUCTION

In iibrary automation, developing library website has a great significance. It could be termed as the highest point in any library automation. Library web site should work as a showcase to represent all the facilities and services provided by a library. In reader's point of view it is the key or mirror of a library. Nowadays most of the libraries possess their own library websites and non availability of website could reflect backwardness of a library.

Developing library website is a skilled task and it requires adequate programming knowledge and expertise. Nowadays there is a new trend that librarians try to acquire such skill or library professionals feel it is necessary to do so while entering into the profession. However, it is not always true and many librarians especially working old librarians find it difficult to acquire web developing expertise. It is not necessary that a librarian should be a programmer as he could get such technical work done from an expert IT person. However, it is advisable that at least one should be aware of some basic knowledge of website development. With this need in mind let us try to know the details about the various techniques and tools used in library website development. Generally, the following tools are used in development of websites, if one wishes to understand them with the relevant programming tools:

1. HTML or XHTML (Extensible HTML)
2. Cascading Style Sheets (CSS)
3. Java Script
4. AJAX
5. V. B. Script
6. PHP

7. RSS Feeds etc.

By using the above tools and by having some working knowledge one can start a website development task. In the above list most of them are programming languages and they are called fundamental programming languages in web development. Developing website by using these tools is one of the ways of web development. However there are readymade structures available today for creating website and one does not need programming language but needs some training and practices. These structures are called Content Management Systems (CMS)

The Examples of CMSs are:

Joomla

Drupal

World Force etc.

Developing websites using CMS does not require big efforts like using formal programming tools. So we have now understood that library website development can also be done by the above two ways. We are going to study the use of CMS for web site development in the following chapter. In this chapter however we are going to know about some essential programming tools used for website development.

9.1. HTML : BASIC PROGRAMMING TOOL FOR WEBSITE DEVELOPMENT

Actually website development is an enjoyable task and any beginner with some knowledge of web tools could take up the task with efforts. HTML or Hypertext Markup Language is the basic programming tool used generally by beginners. There are of course various advanced tools available for higher level work. Now let us begin to know how website is developed using HTML. In HTML one need to write a script or set of codes by using HTML instructions which is saved in the file and when we run it we can see how it looks like. We have seen that HTML is a markup language used to write internet web pages. This requires HTML text editor. The text editor in this case is nothing but notepad utility available in windows. One can invoke note pad by going to start button and clicking the link in the list seen there. On note pad one can write simple script as shown below:

<html >

<head>

<title> My first website // </title>

</head >

<body>

<h> This is my first website </h>

</body>

</html>

Now one needs to save this file by giving suitable name and with HTML extension. Now to see the created web site one can go to the browser and record the file name to open the file, the following things would be displayed. The outcome would be seen as below:

"My first website"

Now let us see another similar HTML script:

```
<html>
<head>
<title> my second website </ title>
</head>
</body>
<h1> This is my second website </h1>
<P> This is paragraph </P>
</ body>
</ html>
```

After saving, the final output displayed will be,

"This is my second website"

Now let us understand the different HTML tags and their meanings.

Types of tag start	Tags, Meaning	End tag
<html>	This is a root tag and program begins with it	</html>
<head>	In this pair of tag program name is written which is not reflected in program display	</ head>
<body>	Normally it comes after head	</body>
<h1>	Under this tag we can write text in six types with different display characteristics	</h1>
<p>	This tag is for paragraph. Text can be entered in it	</P>
</>	Forward hyphen used to close the tag as we see at your right.	

HTML is the basic and simple language used to write web pages. It is also called core language of World Wide Web in which a combination of the above tags are used. It has so much significance that probably without HTML Web pages would not have been written at all. For the beginners of web designing it is the most easy language to understand and use. HTML is also called as hypertext markup language and we know that the internet technology is also based on creation of hyper texted words. This facilitates the creation of different web pages and linking them through hyper texted words so we get home page and WebPages are included in the home page.

However there are limitations on developing web pages using HTML as with it one can create static web pages. Static web page means it does not update automatically. We see dynamic page is refreshed after a gap of few seconds; secondly, in HTML created website we cannot include moving text or images or to include moving objects which gives liveness to the web page, which gives it a dynamic quality. One can bring such dynamic features with the help of higher level web language called Java script, V. B. script or PHP. They are called advanced web languages. However they are a bit difficult to understand and acquire. Any web developers however always begins his web development with HTML and gradually goes to learn higher level web languages like Java, V. B. or PHP. The basic web page is written in HTML and to bring decorative features in it different styles are used. To bring styles in web page utilities like CSS are used known as Cascading Style Sheets. Now we would try to understand about bringing various styles by using CSS.

9.2. CASCADING STYLE SHEET (CSS)

Cascading style sheet or in short CSS is a web development utility consisting of collection of tools used to incorporate different decorative styles in web pages. Once the basic web page is created using HTML further decorative features are brought with CSS. CSS facilitates bringing layout design style as well as gives expected appearance to the website.

In the following paragraphs we would understand the stages of web page development i. e. how to create different style sheets and how to relate them with basic HTML structure, to give background colour, and leave margin, padding and streaming media materials in web pages etc.

9.2.1. What is CSS?

CSS or cascading style sheet is an utility to enrich web pages by incorporating various styles, layout, colours and the look. This is an advanced web developing tool or language. This enables giving better appearance, its internal designing, inserting images, giving internal links and connectivity as over all presenting facts in the web page. The activity here involves configuring CSS related tags in HTMl script. The CSS is therefore called as an advanced version of HTML. This application of CSS styles in HTML started in its 4. 0 version, when it was first tried. Earlier there have been attempts to use CSS along with HTML but it got momentum when Netscape and Internet Explorer brought out new and innovative tags for HTML. The process got further standardized as it got acceptance of W3C consortium. Then onward using CSS in HTML script became very common. In addition to the above features CSS also brings the following features through HTML script as :

1. Background Colour- Colour combinations in charts, Elements and Paragraphs.
2. For a particular tag or for a group of tags assign particular colour or font such as tags <42><P> give Blue colour and bold font.
3. To select space between lines so also to decide about top and bottom margins.
4. Giving look to page internal links
5. To create styles for multiple web pages by defining once so that it would not be necessary to do it again and also highlighting links given in web pages by blue or pink colour.

All these procedures are defined only once and utilize at different pages to bring those changes. Now after understanding the usefulness of CSS let us try to know a bit of each style as:

9.2.2. Types of style sheets in CSS

Normally there are three types of style sheets:

1. Internet style sheets direct for WebPages
2. External style sheets for external incorporation
3. In line style sheets for putting styles within HTML tags

Now let us understand more about them.

9.2.2.1. Making internal style sheet in CSS

In this style the script or tag would be like :

<Style type = "text/CSS">

Style goes here

</style >

After putting this style HTML tag would look like this :

<html >

<head >

<Style Type =" Text/CSS">

P (Colour green)

</Style >

</head>

< body >

< P> The text in this para would be green < /P >

< P > This para too

</body>

</p><html>

When we view this, it would look like :

"The text in this para would be green.

This para too

They would be seen in green colour"

9.2.2.2. Making External Style Sheet in CSS

When one particular style sheet is to be used in many web pages then one can prepare a tag, give code no to it and use it whenever it is required. For such tag CSS extension is necessary and specific link is to be used to achieve this and wherever required effect is seen and used as :

Set in this value of external Style – "Style Sheet"

Type - in this value of specific text is considered

HREF - In this location of external style is consider

Now having the above meaning see the example of external style tag is as :

Style. CSS= P {Colour Green}

Now when we incorporate about style tag in the original HTML tag then it looks like :

```
<html>
<Head>
<link rel. = "Style sheet . " Type = "Text . CSS"
href= "Style . CSS "
</ head >
< body >
< P > the text in this would be blue < /P>
< body >
< html >
```

The result of this tag would be as, "the text in this para would be blue" (in blue colour)

9.2.2.3. *Inline style sheet*

In this type of style the tag looks like :

< P style= "Colour: gray" this text would be gray </P >

In this style we tried to use colour command. Wherein we can define style which can be used on multiple pages and also with defining styles with different properties they can be used in a sequence as defined. In such case inline style sheet get priority than internal and external style sheet. In case if your browser does not support, such sequence by using built in sequence the style is used.

Example of multiple style sheets

```
< html >
< Head >
< Link relf - "Style sheet type = text / CSS"
< / Head >
<href = "Style. 2. CSS"
< body >
< P Style = "Colour= yellow"
"The text in this para will be yellow. ">
< / P >
< / body>
< / html >
```

The result of this tag would be as:

"The test in this para will be yellow" (in yellow colour)

9.2.3. CSS Syntax

In CSS there are three parts of syntax sector {Properties: Value}

1. Sector is used for <P>< Body > and < h>
2. Properties used to set background colour.
3. Value for selection of particular colour, Specific Character etc.

Example: body {background-colour:grey}

If for values, if there are more than one texts, then one should write it in inverted commas

h2 { font- family: "Trebrecbe MS"}

like this one can note multiple values

body { background- colour: gray, colour: yellow. }

See one improved example as:

body {background- colour= gray, colour= yellow, margin- top:0;}

This style is considered in group

P, h1, h2, h3, h4

{Colour: blue ; Font family: courier} the meaning here is that under h1 h2 h3 and h4 text would be in blue and with font as courier.

9.2.4. Classes and ID's in CSS

CSS Classes

In CSS classes we can use different colours in different paras such as:

P. green {Colour: green}

P. blue {colour: blue}

We register tag and the above class command can be used as.

< P class= "Green "> This text is in Green < / P >

< P Class= "blue"> this text is blue < / P >

We can indicate class- the extension. text and further name of the class. Here we can use both for internal as well as external purpose.

< Style Type = text/ CSS">. text

Font Family : Tahoma

Font size = 16 Px

Font Weight : bold

Colour green}

In the above script the style text font is of Tahoma, font size is 16 pixels and it is in green colour

CSS IDs

In CSS, IDs are noted with sign# style < Style > Type = "Text / CSS"

Text {font family: Georgia, font size : 18 Pixels font weight: bold, colour: blue

</ Style

In above way IDs are prepared and inserted in HTML program to see the respective properties.

< P id = text > This text will be blue , bold, Georgia and have fort size 18 Pixels < / P >

One can see the results as expected.

9.2.5. CSS Comments

In order to understand HTML codes comments are used. Comments command starts with / *and ends with */

Example :

```
<html>
<head>
< Style type = "Text / CSS>
/*This is a comment and this is another comment*/ The tag of this script is created as :
P {Colour : Green /* the colour of the text in Paragraph will be green*/
Font family : Courier;
Margin top:0
Margin left:0; */ the left margin of the paragraph/}
</ Style >
</ head >
< body >
<P>
The text in this paragraph will be green
</P>
</ head >
</ body >
</ html >
```

Result: "The text in this paragraph will be green"

9.2.6. Setting Background Properties in CSS

By using this style sheet one can achieve two things :

1. Background colour- Colours in parts of web page such as : table, text boxes and links etc.
2. To install Background Images : In order to set Images and also to set URL externally in web

page this utility is used. While setting background colour one need to give RGB Value or hexadecimal value such as :

```
<html>
<head>
< title > background properties </ title >
< style type = "txt/CSS">
< body { Background colour : # sds FF:}
h1 {background colour: light blue }
P {background colour: rgb (220, 220, 220)}
a { background colour :# e6dcbe;}
</Style >
</ head >
< body >
< h1> some text < /hl >
< P > A paragraph < /P >
< a href=" http // www. iitblibrary. com >
IITB Library main web page
< /a >
</ body >
</ html >
```

See the result as :

"Some text" (In Blue Colour)

"A paragraph"

"www. iitblibrary. com"

9.2.7. Setting Background Image using CSS

One can use CSS to set the images on the website. See the features of this tag.

```
< html >
< head >
< title > Setting Background Image < title >
< Style Type = "text /CSS">
body {background Image : url < Image / obo20 jpg:>
table {background images url <Image / apple. jpg. >
</ Style>
```

```
< head >
< body >
< table border = "2" >
< tr >
< td > cell1 </ td >
< td> cell2</ td >
< /tr >
<tr>
<td>cell3</td>
<td>cell4</td>
</ table >
</ head >
</ body >
</ html >
```

One can see the effect in following Fig. 9.1

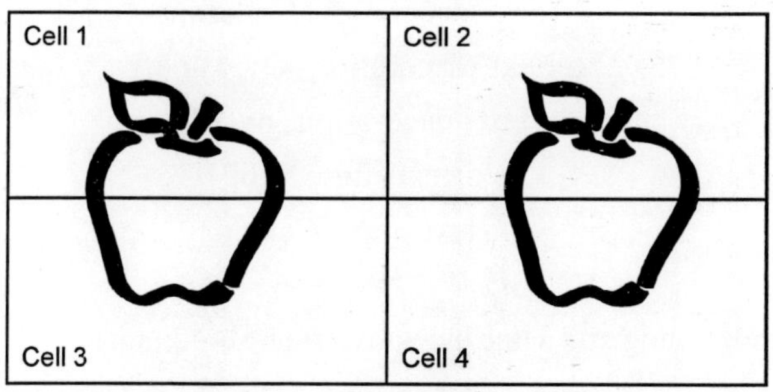

Fig. 9.1. Example of Setting Background Image

9.2.8. CSS Setting

In this type of styles one can set the following things.

Example : Text colour
Text Alignment
Text Decoration
Letter spacing setting

Now let us see them in detail.

9.2.8.1. Setting color properties in CSS

See the colour setting style as:

```
< Style Type = "text/CSS">
```

```
hl {Colour : # 00008b;}
P. text {Color : rgb (47, 48, 49)
</Style >
```

In this hl would be seen in green colour

P - in dark blue

P1 - In dark gray colour

9.2.8.2. Text Alignment Setting in CSS

```
< Style Type = Tex CSS" >
h1 { text. Align: relf;}
h2 { Text align: right;}
P {text align: Center;}
</ Style>
```

9.2.8.3. Text Decorating Style

```
< Style type = ''Text /CSS''
P {text - decoration: Underline ;}
a {text - decoration : Over line;}
h1 {text - decoration : over line;}
h2 {text align: right;}
p {text align : Center;}
</ Style >
```

In this first underlining and a line in text would be blinking.

9.2.8.4. Letter spacing setting in CSS

```
< Style type = "text / CSS" >
P {letter - Spacing: Normal}
P2 {letter - Spacing: 5 Px;}
P3 {letter - Spacing: 10 Px;}
P4 {letter - Spacing: 15 Px};
</ Style >
```

9.2.9. Font of Letter Size Setting in CSS

In CSS these styles are used to set letter fonts & their sizes. The style tag is as:

```
< Style Type = "text CSS" >
h1 {font family: helvetica georgia;}
```

P {font family: tahoma, trebuhet;}

</ Style>

After Letter font Setting let us see setting of letter size.

Under this, for letter font size setting the following style tag is used.

< Style type : "text / CSS">

h1 {Font Size = 40px;}

P {Font Size = large;}

</ Style>

With this the letter sizes set would be visible in the web page.

9.2.10. Setting list Properties in CSS

Under this style one can set the following properties of tables:

1. List Marker setting
2. To locate the list and confirm it. This style is used to select bullet type for tables.

Now let us see some examples.

< Style = list. style. Type- square" >

See the result as :

Green

Yellow

Blue

Black

{ul style : list. style. type- upper alpha;}

see the result

A. Green

B. Yellow

C. Blue

D. Black

{ul style : list. style. type- lower alpha}

see the result as

a. Green

b. Yellow

c. Blue

d. Black

To fix the location of list

{ul style = "list- position: outside;}'

< Green

< Yellow

< Blue

< Black

{ul style list = list. style. position- In side}

1. Green
2. Yellow
3. Blue
4. Black

9.2.11. Setting Border Properties in CSS

This is about setting borders of the tables seen on the Webpage.

Example: Border Thickness, Colour etc.

Example:

< style type = "text CSS" >
h1 {border style : dashed}
h2 {border - Style : double}
P {border - Style : dotted}
a {border - style : grove:}
</ Style >

Now the properties set would be visible

Similarly one can set border thickness and border colour.

9.2.12. Setting margin properties in CSS

One can work for setting of margins on all four sides:

To set left Margin

<p style : Margin - Left : 20 px" >

To set right margin

< p style = Margin right : 25 px>

To set top margin

<p style = Margin top: 45 px>

To set bottom margin.

< p style = Margin Bottom : 35 px>

This way bottom margin is set as:

It is possible to set border properties as:

1 Width of the border

2 colour of the border

9.2.13. Setting padding in CSS

Padding means to decide spacing among the contents e. g. how much distance it should be from the border. All such setting is considered in this style. Let us see one by one.

- Setting Padding from left

  text align; left Padding left : 20 px
- Setting Padding from right

  text align ; Right : Padding right: 34 px
- Setting Padding from top

  text align; top :padding top = 35 px
- Setting Padding from bottom

  <Padding - bottom - 35 px>

  We can see the result on web as per respective padding setting.

9.2.14. Setting outline Properties in CSS

This style is used for setting text outside the border. Here also there are various types.

1. To set outline style
2. To set outline width
3. To set colour of outline

9.2.15. Setting Table Properties in CSS

This style can be used to set table columns and rows and it has the following different styles.

1. Setting table border
2. Setting distance of cells from border
3. Setting table caption
4. To set visibility of vacant cells
5. Set cell, rows and columns.

9.2.16. Setting Dimension in CSS

Under this style following settings are done :

1. Letter light
2. Letter width
3. Line Spacing

9.2.17. Setting Classification Properties in CSS

Examples

1. How the element would look like
2. Display visibility of element
3. How one element will look like in another element.
4. Setting cursor position.

9.2.18. Setting Positioning Properties in CSS

This style is meant to set positioning of various elements, which includes.

1. Element Positioning Properties.
   — Static
   — Relative
   — Obsolete
   — Fixed
2. Element Positioning
   — To left
   — To right
   — To top
   — To bottom
3. Element stocking properties. Under this, index setting is considered

9.2.19. Setting Pseudo Class in CSS

On web page some element are needed to be given special effects such as

Find out - Local weather

Today's breaking news

Similarly there are some other styles in CSS like

Pseudo Elements

Short Cuts of

Media type

In the above paras we have understood the use of CSS in structure of HTML programs by using different CSS styles.

9.3. JAVA SCRIPT

We have seen in previous section that in website development the web page codes are first written then they are inserted in HTML or XHTML. Now after knowing easy method of web page writing we are going to see how to bring interactiveness in them by using other available tools and techniques. One such tool called Java script is nowadays widely used, like cascading style sheets. Codes written in Java scripts are also to be incorporated in HTML program. Now we are going to understand about Java script.

9.3.1. What is Java script?

It is one of the scripting languages which have originated from Netscape web browser technology. With Java script we can bring inter-activeness in web pages, which makes them alive or dynamic. For example, features like self activating/ refreshing of web pages or moving objects or scrolling text messages etc. are possible with the use of Java script. The Java script is the first invented scripting language. Presently available all the browsers can adopt and work with Java script Ex. Netscape, Firefox, Opera as well as MSN internet explorer.

9.3.2. Difference between Java and Java script

People always get confused in Java and Java script. Many feel that Java and Java script both are the same. However, it is not. Java script enables web developer to bring a liveness or inter activities in web pages; whereas Java is another web based language tool which enables programmers to write program in application software. Now let us see the various features of Java script.

9.3.3. What can be done with Java script?

Following things are possible with Java Script :

1. It provides inter-activeness on the web pages liked by the users. Whatever questions the user prompts on screen the system very well responds it. Such as when user writes his name Datta the system would respond as Hello Datta!
2. It receives and validates data filled in online digital form, such as getting form details filled from the user.
3. It helps in recognizing type of browser of the user. When an user uses Firefox or MSN, the browsers validates it.
4. To write cookies and read them. Cooky is a small script which is indirectly written by the system and preserved them on hard disk. These cookies keep opening on browser through pop up screens and prompt user his / her preference of web use. It remembers user ids and passwords if user allows cookie to do it or always provide users preferred background colour and when ever user logs in it provides users with all his / her preferred setups.
5. Prompting quick messages to users. Suppose if a user unknowingly clicks a different button than the expected one, the Java script would ask user as, "If you really want these features or like to continue or not?" And further action takes place as user answers it as Yes or No.

9.3.4. Introduction to Java script

Now let us understand how Java script tags are written and used in the web programming. Java scripts are to be written separately and put them into HTML programs, for which (script) tags are used and it is indicated which scripting language is used as:

<script - type - "text / Java script"> Java scripts are written within head or body sections of HTML and whenever body or head sections are used the script gets activated. It also indicated where Java script is included either in the head or body section as :

<html>

<head>

<title> Java script in the head section <title>

or

<script>

<script type = "text / Java script goes here </script>

Java script is incorporated in the head or body section and it gets activated while using respective ones. Sometime Java script is used in both the head and body of the same HTML programs or as many places and they are activated in the order as they appear in the respective sections. This was about direct inclusion of Java scripts in HTML programming. Some time Java scripts are written in files outside the program and the files are then inserted in programs. Such files are given extension as . js indicating it is the Java script. While calling such files word src is recorded to run those files. Example :

<html>

<head>

<title> external Java script file </title>

<script type = "text / Java script" src = "script. 1. js" >

</script>

</head>

<body>

</body>

</html>

Java scripts are used in other various forms and with different purposes as : to print text on web page

Document write ("text to print") this command is used.

At the place "text-to-print" required text string is incorporated. Whenever scripts are incorporated in the source codes of program then the necessary comments are written to make programmer to understand about them, however these comments are not visible on web pages; they are seen by programmers only. The comments could be in single or many lines and they are written in two quotes.

/ comments / for one line

/ * comments for many line * /

Java script is a recent utility and old web browsers do not respond them. In that case the HTML program is used by dropping the Java script. In order to facilitate this, comments are indicated by the symbol<? //->

In some programs Java scripts are purposely disabled. Like Java script, there is another scripting language prepared by MSN explorer which is known as V. B. script. Naturally it is owned by Microsoft, which is proprietary type so it is rarely used by getting license of it. The V. B. script serves same purpose as Java script does; which can also bring inter-activeness in web pages.

9.4. AJAX

AJAX is a web programming tool. It's extended form is Asynchronous Java script and XML. This is an advanced web programming technology available today. In 2005 Google first published this tool and used in its search engines. It provides additional interactive features while browsing web pages; as it remembers URL the page already obtained and it does not require to load the web page again. AJAX is brought out as combination of Java script and query tool of HTML.

9.4.1. How AJAX works?

We have already seen that AJAX is an extended version of Java Script. Now let us understand how it actually works, by taking example of Google search. When we enter the search term(s) in Google search window, we get the search list corresponding to words as we enter in the search box. Suppose we change some words in the search string the system (with AJAX) sends the fresh word string and updated search link list without even clicking enter key. This brings speed in internet search and response becomes user friendly, giving the user relief and satisfaction.

AJAX is not only a web language tool but it is an advanced web technology which brings more inter-activeness and ease in internet search. AJAX provides additional support system to all types of browsers and with Internet explorer active or object technology, whereas in normal browsers XML, HTML request systems is used.

Now let us try to see where AJAX is used. As we have seen the most use of AJAX is experienced in Google search, so Google is the prominent user of AJAX. However, we can see its impact more in Google suggest search.

Del.icio.us web 2. O tool is one of the well known bookmarking sites available today. As we go on entering words in bookmarking tag we are prompted with relevant websites to be bookmarked. The similar experience one can see while purchasing things from online stores, as we go on selecting and putting item to be purchased in the shopping cart the shopping cart list gets automatically updated without doing anything. Every browser experiences different and admirable impact in internet search which is the characteristics of the AJAX. AJAX is also used as search facility of Digital Library.

9.5. P.H.P (PHP)

Php is another scripting language used in web development to bring interactive and dynamic quality in the web pages. With the use of php it facilitates things such as text printing use of variables loops, arrays and in obtaining data from users, and updating databases are possible in this programming language.

9.5.1. What is php?

Php is a scripting language like Java but comparatively more advanced than Java. It's full form is Hypertext Pre-Processor. php is useful as content management tool to bring more inter-activeness in WebPages and in making it a dynamic website.

This scripting language works with open source server APACHE. It can also work with IIS (International Information Services) web server of Microsoft.

Codes of php do not work independently and they need to be incorporated in the main program tag to decode them. However, there is no need to compile php codes. php is a web development language. It only works with php server and not through client machines. The php codes are therefore not visible on client machines. Its process is done in server and not in browser. Once the programming task is accomplished all the files are sent to php server. This is an object oriented type of web programming language. In php re-definable data structure are called object tags. In the same way properties of objects are also defined, which invokes the methods. In php we see relationship between various objects and their respective data structures. Another important quality of php is that it is on open source type web language, where program source codes are easily seen by any one. While writing php the extension like php, php3 or phtml are necessary to be attached to programs.

9.5.2. What we can do with php?

One can do the following things with php.

1. To interact with users, to get data form filled. It helps to incorporate certain data element like e-mail ID and include it in mailing list.
2. To write cookies - when user works of web page again and again then it creates cookies and saves them to help users in following visits. Cookies facilitates inter-activeness and creates user friendly environment for the users. Such cookies as created are saved on hard disk.
3. Recognize data filled by user and add it to database or to get a guest data filled.
4. Recognize the type of browser the user is using and accordingly adjust the response.
5. To edit and update database. By using php, program scripts are written and they are inserted in basic HTML programme. Let us see the syntax of php as:

```
<?php
   Content?
```

Means php script begins with ? mark and also ends with ? mark. Normally all the things achieved in other programming languages can also be achieved in php. Moreover, php is an advance scripting language among all. The special utilities of php are as below :

1. Write php scripts as required in HTML program.
2. Write php script externally and add the files as tags.

3. To print required text as webpage.
4. To incorporate HTML commands in php script.
5. To create comments in script to describe type of a script.

Like php an open source scripting language, there is another independent scripting language meant for Microsoft browser called ASP. ASP means Active Server Pages, which is created by Microsoft and it works like any other scripting tool. In case of ASP tag command starts with <% and ends with %> symbol. The files created under ASP bears extension as . asp.

In above paras we have studied various web development tools and technique, which includes HTML, CSS, Java script Ajax and php. These are webpage development languages. After having introduction to various web development tools, the author hopes that readers would read more details about these tools and would start writing their web pages themselves. They can visit the site www. landofcodes. com or W3C to get more knowledge and guidance and to use it in developing their own web sites. Author appeals to readers to take interest in learning and acquiring these skills. Interested readers can avail full-fledged training in web page development using above tools by attending training programmes organized by many institutions and announcements on LISFORUM and on INFOLIBRARIAN or similar sites. If they keep a habit of visiting such websites of specialized courses on library information technology regularly they can get ample opportunities to learn and update themselves.

10
Content Management Systems (Joomla and Drupal)

10.0. INTRODUCTION

In the previous chapter we have taken a short review on how websites are developed using useful basic language tool like HTML and some other scripting language tools. Designing full fledged website with the help of formal programming tools is a challenging task. It does require detail knowledge and skills of website development and it is not so easy to acquire them by a normal person having just basic computer knowledge. People these days have a lot of interest in developing websites as they are important for library computerisation and for one's career development. However, due to lack of appropriate knowledge it is not always possible in reality. Due to advances in ICT now there are solutions available to design websites in a short cut way by the individuals who do not have complete knowledge and skill of website development. For the people who do not have web programming skill there are Content Management System tools which can very well be used by normal person to fulfill their interest of web site development. In order to understand how it is achieved one should know the concept of Content Management System.

10.1. WHAT IS A CONTENT MANAGEMENT SYSTEM (CMS)?

In a simple way if CMS is to be described then it could be as :

The content management system is a program tool or package by using which one can publish contents on web, to make changes in them, edit it and further to maintain contents in a website. Now most of the available content management systems provide necessary procedures and by using them it becomes possible to handle work flow relating to web contents and to manage them becomes feasible and in an easy way. Content management systems are used on a large scale for developing and managing blogs, news as well as shopping related contents on the network websites.

In short, content management system or in short CMS could be defined as, "the content management system is used to manage contents on website. The main function of CMS is to upload files relating to contents on website, to organise them, to provide access to the contents and also control the versions of CMS".

An ordinary CMS could be called as a show case of handful features but when it is used to corporate fields CMS works with high grade and could handle complicated tasks of web development as required by the field. CMS works like a centralised repository which helps in gathering documents, pictures or contact details as contents required for website development. CMS stores these types of data contents, controls them, helps to revise or improve them and helps publishing them on internet. There are two distinct features in CMS in users and systems development point of new:

1. Content Management Application (CMA) is available as a front end interface for the user who by using his/her little skills can keep publishing contents on the website constantly.

2. Content Delivery Application (CDA) By which developed websites are updated. In the workflow of content management developer handles contents like text, images, graphics, video, audio or animations. All these contents are in digital form and they are handled by digital content management ways.

There is a specific CMS rules to store these contents.

CMS is such a tool which is handled by technical as well as non technical people. one can create web sites using available CMS tools and make changes in them subsequently and publish them on web. Now let us understand certain characteristics of contents management system.

10.2. CHARACTERISTICS OF CONTENT MANAGEMENT SYSTEM (CMS)

The CMS is useful for the following features:

1. Maintenance is done in a decentralized way.
2. An individuals can use CMS tool with their IT knowledge skills.
3. One can configure access to websites managed by CMS.
4. It provides consistency in website development and provides a reliable storage place for web contents.
5. Navigation is adjusted automatically.
6. All the contents are saved in database of the developer's login.
7. One can develop website with dynamic style.
8. Web contents are kept secured.
9. There is always co-operation available from CMS managers.
10. CMS is available as an open source platform.

The current website development statistics show that 30% of website in the world are developed using CMS. In which 16. 8% by using World Press, 2. 8% by using Joomla and 2. 2% by using Drupal. Well known sites like e-bay, City Bank, MTV, Wikipedia and Amazon are developed by using one or the other CMSs. With this initial background now let us try to know little more about CMS.

10.3. LIST OF AVAILABLE CONTENT MANAGEMENT SYSTEM

As on today the list of available CMS looks like as follows :

1. WorldPress
2. Joomla
3. Drupal
4. Silverstripe
5. Umbraco
6. From CMS
7. MODX
8. CONTAO (Typolight)
9. Dot CMS
10. Expression Engine
11. Radiant CMS
12. Concrete-S
13. CSS-J Trick (learn to built your own CMS with php)

However, out of this long list of CMS we are going to understand the following two CMSs which are the prevailing ones as on today :

Joomla

Drupal

10.4. JOOMLA

Joomla is one of the preferred CMS which provides sound platform for website development. This CMS makes website development easy. This CMS makes use of php as web language and SQL as an open source data server. A group of open source developers designed the CMS in 2005. As on today this system has been adopted by as many as two lakh customers all over the world. This is an open source type CMS and available to anyone for free downloading. People make use of it for extending their website and also it is well known due to its readymade template collection. One can visit its website http://www. Joomla/download. html to download its current version.

Out of the list of CMSs we have referred in the previous para there are three topmost CMSs as Joomla, Drupal and World press. Among all these, Joomla seems to be the most easy one to learn and adopt. The collection of templates of Joomla is its most attractive features. It is also known to be most user friendly CMS. However, there is one constrain in using Joomla i. e. time taken to install it and as such some people find difficulties in creating sub categories architecture. Except these constrains Joomla is one of the best CMSs available today. Now onwards in the following paragraphs we are going to understand the structure of Joomla and about how to install it; how to configure it and how to create one's own website with Joomla. In order to be acquainted with Joomla CMS, one can visit a common website called, makeuse.com. One can find, complete beginners guide to Joomla created by Taty Sena. We are also referring this guide while understanding Joomla. It would be easy for readers to understand Joomla if they also keep this site open on their desktops.

10.4.1. Joomla Installation

There are two ways to install Joomla as:

(i) Manual Method

(ii) C-panel way

In both the methods, the system requirements are almost the same. In C-panel method one needs to host server's fantastico or C-panel on your computer first. Now let us try to know about the manual way of installing Joomla. In this particular way of installing Joomla we need to install database FTP program and Joomla installation files. One should be ready with the following details as :

Database Name

Database ID

Database Password

Database Path

and whenever the system prompts the need, these details should be entered in it. So having the above details Joomla files are to be downloaded by visiting Joomla website. The files are available in zip and they need to be extracted and saved in website folder http://mysite/joomla. Having done this the Joomla files are to be uploaded on your host server by using FTP program. By using server manager now Joomla set is to be run by going to its root folder. http://mysite. com/index. php or sub folder.

http://yoursite. com/joomla folder/index. php

- For installing Joomla, corresponding wizard instructions need to be followed.

The steps for the same are as:

1. Language : select language as English (US)
2. Then to complete basic permission formalities
3. License : GNU (General Public License)
4. Next database configuration Database type : MY SQL

Host Name : Name of your computer (Path and Address)

User Name : Name of your system administrator

Password : To be recorded.

Database Name : As named by its host name one can give local user host. If the local host is WAMP or XAMPP based and user name is root then password would be nothing / (Blank).

Continue this process

By clicking the finish button, installation would be complete and a message as

"Congratulation" is seen. After this, to use Joomla one needs to go to FTP where the installation directory is to be deleted. Next step in installation is to do the configuration settings. By using previously recorded ID and password, system admin should login the system. At this place system manager can create new users. Now you need to set your Joomla site to offline mode. Then one should go to global configuration settings and required details are to be filled in the form on screen. Now having done this successfully, we would see how to publish the contents.

10.4.2. Joomla contents - Articles

In Joomla content management systems contents are recognised as articles. Each content has a relation with its section and its category. Section and category are pre-created and articles are connected by getting particular related section and category by pulling it down and selecting. One should have the first names of sections pre-decided and then the names of articles to be kept ready. To understand we may consider example of our normal filling system - as

Section	-	filling cabinet
Category	-	folder in the filing cabinet
Article	-	An article / content is a document in the folder

About section and category one can consider as menus and within that different pulled down menus. Suppose you wish to record your company details - then click - menu - about my co. by pulling down submenus under this where you can add details such as staff team and address

For staff team you can create text and save under the staff team and for address write address details and save it under address.

10.4.3. Creating sections in Joomla

For creating sections in Joomla one should click section button and select various options or as prompted on screen among those "title" and "description" are the important things. By selecting title and giving description completes section creation task.

10.4.4. Creating Categories in Joomla

As it is mentioned sections and categories are created before contents are created and while creating contents already created sections and categories are selected from pulled down menu. Creating sections and categories has broader perspectives of contents. Creating categories one should click contents menu and as we did in case of sections names and descriptions of categories are filled and saved. Now let us visualize how the structure of sections, categories and contents looks in the following tree structure:

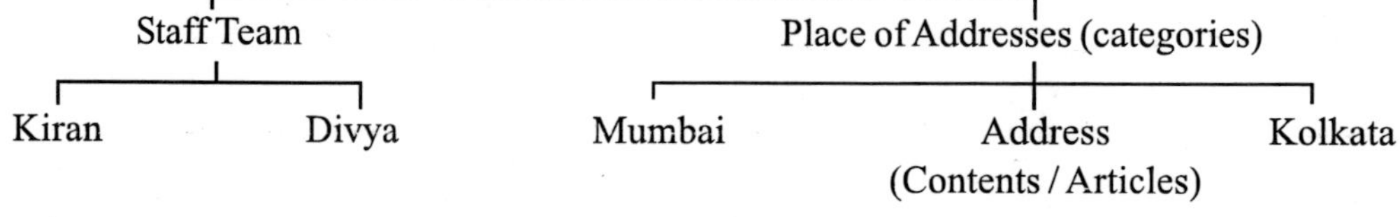

Now so far we have created sections and categories as shown in the above structure. After this, we are going to understand how the last level i. e. how articles or contents are created in Joomla.

In order to create articles one should click article menu. In that select "new" we would get world processing screen. First name the article then selects the corresponding section and category by pulling down menu. In this process on screen relevant text may be entered. If there is already created text file in computer, same can be uploaded by copy paste method. One can provide read more facility like available for blog by giving link, which can take reader to designated file located on web. Somehow, Joomla has advanced apps in this part, which could be seen and understood for using them.

Till now we have created sections, categories and contents articles. Now let us see how to create menus to facilitate searching contents.

Media Manager : In this, there is a facility to manage content images means which image is placed where. We can manage to put images taken into respective contents.

10.4.5. Joomla Front Page Manager

In this section one can see first how contents prepared would look into website. Such facility could be given in buttons for menus like "About this site" or "Welcome. " After this more menus are to be prepared. In which main menu and subsequent menus are created. For this one should go to menu and click menu Manager. In this one can select menu item type. Normally the main menu is created first. In the menu creation step we can get the main menu by default.

10.4.6. How to Design and customize your website in Joomla

In order to bring innovative features in the website designing various styles are incorporated. By using style sheets like CSS one bring features like Book marks, modules, mailing list, calendars, photo albums as well as other similar contents to give web pages a dynamic status and they are the main constituents of websites. However, for those who does not have adequate knowledge content management systems like Joomla are used. CMS provides you 5000 plug-in, modules and templates. From Joomla one can download required features and install them on Joomla based websites. Then one can use menu like extension manager. Normally the file contents are in zipped form and we need to extract them. We can get various components modules, plug-in and templates. Now let us understand about modules, components & pamphlets.

10.4.7. Plug-in, Modules and Templates in Joomla

Plug-in : Plug-ins are provided with the contents in Joomla or plug-ins are interfaced with them. The plug-ins facilitate browser to handle contents such as : to bookmark the useful articles, this gives user facility to share contents with others. This provision makes it easy for user to use articles. This is done easily with plug-ins than doing it manually. Once the plug-ins are interfaced and enabled then each articles can be provided with links to use them in social networking.

Modules : Modules means leaving text matter as centre of page. There are boxes on right; left or bottom like links in blogs. There is a provision to download files relating to basic literature or links to login new letters. These modules are pre-created and placed them around main page at left, right and bottom. It is done with, "Extension Manager" link. HTML script is used to create modules. Modules give a liveliness to the website.

Components : Like plug-ins and modules, one can create high level apps in Joomla called components. In these components, social networking features can be brought in. One can also buy such readymade components and adopt them in Joomla. The extension manager is used for this.

Templates : Whenever we try to open Joomla based website we can understand the significance of templates as they are prominently visible in front. The developer who has good knowledge of HTML or CSS can design web pages with good feel and look. But for those who do not have such expertise there are ready made templates in Joomla template collection. These templates are adopted for developed websites very quickly. Just add the logo of your institution to give it a look of your customized website. Otherwise templates are adopted as it is having their self designed logos. There are sources to down load readymade temples, from out-side sources like site BEEZ

10.5. DRUPAL

Drupal is another CMS platform used to develop websites. Drupal named project was undertaken in Belgium by a student Dries Buytaert in 2000. He first prepared codes for site drop and opened source codes of it with name Drupal. Readers can visit site http://drupal. org/node/org to know more about Drupal. Up till now the following versions of Drupal have been brought out:

Drupal 4. 7 May 2006

Drupal 5. 0 15th Jan 2007

Drupal 6. 0 13th Feb 2008 and

Drupal 7. 0 9 Jan 2011

By now there must be further versions available.

10.5.1. What we can do with Drupal?

Drupal is one of the flexible Content Management Systems, which provides excellent web development activity and with it variety of websites are created such as:

1. Websites of static contents
2. Websites of dynamic contents
3. Creating of blogs of one/many authors.
4. To develop community websites

Being an open source tool one can import data from Drupal tables and save it. Similarly charts, graphs and data fields can also be imported. Drupal is famous for creating facilities like private messaging, user relationship, content rating and content forwarding. The characteristics of Drupal could be listed as:

Characteristics of Drupal

1. Development from simple to comprehensive. In the beginning one can create blog of a single author, then extend it for multiple authors and finally end with development of community website. This way web development activity grows and it does not require changing the platform.
2. Provides multiple facilities with web development technology. With Drupal one can do everything needed to be done to develop good websites. Drupal can be interfaced with Google Analysis. It can also be integrated with antispan services like Aksmet or Mollon to bring security with WebPages.
3. With Drupal one can develop community website with wide range of individuals.

10.5.2. Technical Features of Drupal. Following are the technical features of Drupal

1. In order to use Drupal one should have web hosting account for developing website under Drupal.
2. In order to create a database, to configure and to store contents for Drupal one should use, respective open source tools.
3. One can use php codes in Drupal structure, which also needs php software.
4. It is required to look for FTP facility.

Content management systems are constantly developing. This principle is also applicable to Drupal. It is also growing with time and it can give all progressive features to web developers.

10.5.3. Useful Available Sources for Drupal

There are various information sources which are useful in using Drupal from installation to application as:

1. One can find Drupal : Own web site at http://drupal. org/forum.
2. There is Drupal hand book which is useful for Drupal's static document based source guide for web development at http://drupal. org/handbook.
3. There is video cast about Drupal at http://drupal. org/handbook/customisation/ casts. There are various e-books about use of Drupal. In addition there are various websites, style share sources; Drupal community, Drupal groups and associations where one can get guidance and solutions to problems.
4. **Parts of Drupal :** Drupal is one of the open source type content publishing platform. Drupal has its own terminology.

10.5.4. Nodes and Taxonomy in Drupal

1. Drupal Nodes : Nodes in drupal are its building blocks. Each content which is added in Drupal structure are Drupal nodes. They are like contents posted to blogs.

Drupal has the facility of content construction kit (CCK) which is used to different types of nodes. Like other CMS they have titles and descriptions but Drupal has in addition attributes like address, web links, mail addresses , file uploads etc. System provides facility to attach additional contents. Custom contents creates flow in Drupal. Forms are created so that user can submit their contents. Due to view module facility, one can see CCK Nodes from anywhere, plus one can search Drupal nodes on site: Drupal . org.

2. Taxonomy in Drupal : Drupal has built-in taxonomy. Taxonomy means dictionary of key words or headings. Due to taxonomy it becomes easy to create categories of system nodes. One can define new words in Drupal vocabulary / taxonomy, vocabulary contents synonymous terms. Taxonomy help to create keyword groups like thesaurus. There is no limit for the number of terms. One can tag in vocabulary as per his /her choice, therefore one can use tag in place of terms. While posting contents the respective terms are automatically added to taxonomy.

10.5.5. Experience of using Drupal

Drupal is today's widely known and used open source type CMS. One can use Drupal to create website of complex in nature. There is wide Drupal users community which helps to develop website with some knowledge of it with Drupal modules. Now let us know something more about Drupal in the following paras.

10.5.6. Advantages and Disadvantages in using Drupal

Characteristics of Drupal

- Drupal is an open source software tool.
- Drupal is much flexible, where contents are prominent. This software is created with collaboration of users. This has many modules; It's further characteristics are : one can fix the bugs; provision of core updates, reliable support and excellent documentation as well as enough tutorials for user training.
- Due to modules it gives strength to website created with Drupal.
- It is a user friendly tool for website creation, in which developer can get many opportunities to use his/her own skills of web development.
- Drupal has built in catching system, which gives facility to interface various Web pages on the same platform, which does not add load to the server and search process is completed without any problems.
- Drupal has an excellent search facility as compared to other CMSs.
- Drupal is a comparatively higher level system and it could be difficult to handle developers without having adequate knowledge of it.
- The list of various well know websites developed using Drupal is as :

  Mozilla

  Firefox

  Spread FireFox

UBUNTU etc.

These websites reflect the capabilities of Drupal.

10.5.7. Drupal installation Procedure

First of all, user have to visit Drupal site- http://drupal. org/drupal. 7.9 to download the same in their system. Drupal can be installed on their local host or it can be installed on XAMPP or WAMP platforms. The procedure is like this :

- Copy drupal files in XAMPP directory and extract them. Use XAMPP\htdocs\drupal\sites\default folder for installation.
- Next step is doing settings in php. Make files default setting and save it with the new name.
- Install it in setting. php. However, do not delete the default settings.
- Next is to install My SQL database for Drupal, as Drupal uses this type of database management system. For this first set the php my admin i. e. browser based my SQL, with administration. This facilitates to write, read and editing of data. This facility is always available along with XAMPP. While doing this, one should create dedicated user who can give permission to other authorized system users, which needs to be created in dedicated user group. In my SQL one should give all the facilities and privileges to users in local host i. e. select, insert, update, delete, file creation, alter, index-drop creating temporary log files and having done all this one can start installation of Drupal. (http://local hot/drupal. S

In installing Drupal it changes file as new name Drupal in ad doc folder. So that process can be completed faster. One can follow process done and input as prompted on installation screen for which one can see Drupal back-end screen. You would get the message of installation completed successfully.

10.5.7.1. Drupal Modules

Modules of Drupal are the extensions which gives it an additional strength. There are various preinstalled modules in Drupal. In addition there is Drupals official repository of modules and one can download useful modules from the collection.

In Drupal\sites\all modules one may not get readymade folder for nodes which are to be created. Keep Drupal\sites\all\modules separately

Drupal modules. One can add on modules by using CCK kit and install them. The procedure is as :

- To create Drupal administrator page.
- Install Administration menu module.
- To set home page
- To set menu on home page
- To set input format
- Carryout html filtering

- Set comments
- Set authorizing information.
- To publish contents
- To check front page of Drupal

Now let us know about creating Drupal nodes.

10.5.7.2. Drupal Nodes

Drupal nodes are significant parts of Drupal structure. They are the building bricks of Drupal based website. In Drupal each content is called nodes i. e. comments, single page or forum post etc. Only admin and user profile of back-end pages are not called nodes. We can recognise node with file extension as node.

Now let us see how Drupal is actually installed:

- To create custom contents, which help customising Drupal contents and one can visualize how the contents are visualized.
- In creating community so also due to custom contents it is easy to customize. One can control how each content is presented While creating community website there is job board facility to publish individual's job vacancy with contents as:

  Job title

  Job Description

  Department (With dropdown)

  User Experience - A text file.

  Salary - Text File

  <Administrator>Content type> add content type

With the help of CCK kit one can type contents and also can customize them. The procedure for this is as:

- Submitting form setting
- Work flow setting
- Create job content type
- Customize contents with CCK kit
- Enable adding some form fields in CCK
- Add the form fields
- Create job posting
- Display setting

10.5.7.3. Drupal Themes

We have seen templates in CMS like Joomla. Similarly we have readymade screens in Drupal known as Drupal themes. One can select and adopt suitable theme from the collection and upload it in website. It can be done from site: drupal/sites/all/themes/directory to install them in website.

10.5.8. Demos Available for Drupal

Once Drupal is installed one can host account with login-in. This process gives response message "Welcome to my web site. " To add new contents in it click link "add contents". This is a page of administrator, which has the following things :

- Articles
- Basic page

Articles are used for blogs where as basic page to create static webpage. Next there is a screen for Content Management. In this structure there are headings like: block, content types and taxonomy. The meaning here is that: block of contents seen on site or any other place, which pulled down and installed.

Content Types	:	Default status Front page promotion, Comments setting etc.
Menus	:	There is a facility to add menus or improve previously created menus. One can add menu links
Taxonomy	:	One can tag or classify by using terms in dictionary.

It is expected that developing websites using various content management system is easier than going for higher level programming. Nowadays there are various online free tutorials available for quick learning and designing the websites. However, in spite of having firsthand information about using the tools through self learning way, one needs some kind of hands on training. Such training could be possible by attending a short term training programmes, which can certainly help in achieving the expertise required for developing websites independently.

11

Development of Library Mobile Website : An Introduction

11.0. INTRODUCTION

In the previous two chapters we have studied the website designing techniques and tools. We are now aware about the use of web languages to develop website like HTML and use of supporting tools like :

- CSS - cascading style sheets :
- Java script
- PHP etc.

Also we have seen use of CMS content management systems i. e. bit simpler way of designing websites like Joomla and Drupal in a detailed way. By using all the above tools and techniques we can develop library website, which are most suitable to browse on desktops, client machines or on laptop. Nowadays there is a trend among youngsters to use internet on mobiles and on smart phones or tabs. As such the current mobile and smart phone technology makes it possible to do so. Having this usage trend in mind a large no. of libraries are thinking that, as young readers are so accustomed to this technology then why not provide library websites on smart phones, so that they can make maximum use of the library facilities. Considering the fact that the current generation is techno savvy, the libraries are providing library website on smart phone so that they can make maximum use of it. While just playing on it, it is expected that they would also try to browse through the library services and facilities. However, for librarians and system developers to develop website suitable for mobile phones is certainly a challenging task. How technically it could be done is the theme of this chapter.

11.1. LIBRARY MOBILE WEBSITE CONCEPTS :

There are two things in the issue.

1. Capability of mobile phones to access internet websites on them
2. Designing website only for mobile phones.

Generally whenever websites are developed it is assumed that they are meant only for using them on desktops or laptops, which have bigger screens. However, many a times efforts also seen that corresponding concise website edition for mobile phone are also designed and made available separately, so that as per situation users can opt to have either full website or concise website. Moreover, whenever user try to access any internet page on mobile/smart phone technology itself understands that user is accessing the site on mobile phone then automatically only mobile compatible website is made available. For example if you try to access Times of India website on smart phone you are directed to see mobile edition of Times of India website. So it is so promptly done. Now let us understand what care is to be taken in designing mobile editions of websites. However, before taking up this issue let us learn something more about the mobile phone technology.

11.1.1. Development of progress of mobile phone technology

We saw the real innovation in mobile technology when Apple brought out its first I-phone in 2007 in the market. Till then mobile browsers were not at all capable to handle advanced internet use. The browsers developed by Apple (Steve Jobs) for iPhone are well competent to web languages like HTML, CSS and CSS animation. The Google, in the meantime, developed android software for mobile phones and produced mobile phones based on it. Today we see the latest version of Android used in mobiles is 10.0, whereas iOS of Apple has recently released its upgraded version of 13.5.1. There R & D efforts really brought a revolution in mobile technology. Now they are working on using Augmented Reality (IR) technology in mobile phone. Today we see sandwich, lollypop like other softwares are used in mobiles so also windows platform is used such as in Nokia phones. In short we can conclude that these developments made mobile competent for internet use.

The issue was about making library websites compatible to mobile phones. Now let us explore if there are technological frameworks available to do it. The list of such frameworks is as follows:

- Zep to js
- Dynamic-X
- Secha
- J-Query Mobile
- J-Q Touch
- IOS Mobile
- wink Toolkit
- LUI
- iwebkit
- Webapp net
- Android frame work
- PMob. com

Literature supports that by using the above available frameworks, it is possible to design websites for mobile phones.

11.2. DEVELOPMENT OF LIBRARY MOBILE WEBSITES

Issues to take up in this section : Let us have a look at the list of contents of library mobile websites as seen in some well known library mobile websites:

University Library Mobile Website Contents

- Library Hours
- OPAC

- Library skills
- My Book A/c
- News and Events
- Feedback
- Link for full site
- Contacts

We see nowadays that the use of mobile phone has increased tremendously. Currently we see a trend of switching from simple mobile phones to smart phones. It is also seen that surfing internet on mobile phone has become a hobby, especially among young users. In 2009 the number of mobile users globally was 530 lakhs and it is estimated that in India it would touch 420 millions users by June 2017 and it would reach 1 billion soon. If we see the statistics, the sale of mobile (smart) phones has left well behind comparative statistics of sales of desktops. To have and use a smart phone is the dream of every young individual. Librarians hope that this trend of mobile use would also be applicable for surfing library websites on mobile phones. The developers of library mobile websites are seen busy in getting related answers to questions from the library users :

- Which are the top five things used by users in browsing library websites? Probably it would be difficult to answer this question. Another question could be :
- Would you like to get all the services of the library available on mobile phones? The users would be positive in answering this question and they would like to share their suggestions. Considering this now let us look at the services normally provided by advanced libraries on their website as:
    - Social Media
    - SMS / Email Messaging
    - Event calendar
    - OPAC
    - Audio Library Tour
    - Library Instructions
    - Location Guide
    - Floor Map
    - Classification Mapping
    - Image collection (Digital library)
    - Research Guide
    - Open Access Repositions
    - Mobile Apps
    - Databases
    - Virtual Reference service

There could be many more web based library services which could be added in the above list. If one plans to design mobile library website then suggestions from the readers should be invited. A library mobile website development unit formed in library could consider the readers feedback and finalise the list of services to be provided on library mobile website. Library need to organise technical provision to provide access to reader for accessing library mobile website published by it. This provision includes creating WIFI or WIMAX zone in University or Institute campus. It is important that the library web services which are available on main library site cannot be provided on mobile websites due to screen and processor constrains. It is therefore necessary to arrive at some feasible design of library web services adequate for mobile phones accordingly a list of services could be prepared.

In addition to provide the suitable design and providing internet connectivity provision it is also necessary to create a separate capable server to take care of reader's traffic within the campus, as it is expected that it would be accessed by the readers to an optimum level being innovative mobile app. The mobile website server could be interfaced to library main website server, so that accessibility of main website server would not be affected due to traffic jam. Normally while designing mobile sites the images or animated or images displayed on main website need to be dropped and only textual material is considered for mobile websites. It is also found that reading a full text paper or e-book on mobile could be cumbersome , unless it is a tab, it is therefore seen that e-resources are made available to the extent feasible to include and to the extent it is possible to read on mobile device.

11.3. TIPS FOR DESIGNING MOBILE LIBRARY WEBSITES

With the following preparation it would be possible to develop mobile version of library website.

1. To bring web applicability by using mobile application tools.
2. Java frame could be used for this purpose and by using readymade tools like :
   — i-query mobile
   — i-UI
   — J-QTouch

   There is guide available at 'Chad Haefele's mobile site generator.
3. One can consider following points relating to website designing and its functionality such as :
   — style sheet (CSS) or by selecting available frame work
   — RSS feed APPS
4. While deciding website content parts for mobile site, contents should be as minimum as possible
5. To use QR codes to market mobile websites
6. Devising frequently asked questions (FAQs) to guide users in browsing mobile web sites.

11.4. EXAMPLES OF CONTENTS DISPLAYED ON A WELL KNOWN LIBRARY MOBILE WEBSITE

- Visit library site
- Search
- Current exhibition
- Help
- Library catalogue
- Self Account login
- Library Hours
- Holidays

- Feedback
- Link to full website

List of other similar contents

- FAQ
- Library Instructions
- Media centre
- Ask a librarian
- Downloads
- Off campus access
- Reservations
- Reference work
- OPAC
- Contact us

Other connectivities to main library resources

- Media Centre
- UH Libraries
- Mobile version of Digital Library
- YouTube
- Library Flicker site

10.5. GUIDELINES FOR DEVELOPMENTS OF LIBRARY MOBILE WEBSITE (PLANNING)

Considering the limitations of mobile devices the mobile version of the website has to be a supportive web service. One can browse through the examples of library mobile websites available on internet to prepare list of contents. Some guidelines are listed below which would be useful to developers in the task :

1. Library may take a survey from readers whether they need mobile apps of library web services or they are looking for special mobile website.
2. Beginning may be made with simple mobile style sheet.
3. It is not advisable to encourage readers to access full website on mobile as there would be difficulties in accessing it. Learning data bases, e-resources and images / animations could be omitted in preparing mobile version of the main website
4. It is better to select and provide minimum contents with high capability and quality access so that readers would enjoy surfing rather than frustrating in the beginning.
5. It would be a good gesture to mix with the readers to judge responses and feedbacks of readers.
6. Specific contents which have high demand and for which readers would frequently visit the site may be provided.
7. Finally the library mobile website should create a feel of library environment among the user and it should not be for entertainment.

REFERENCES

1. The anywhere library: A premier for the mobile web.
   Courtney, Green, Missy Roser and Elizabeth Truant, ACRL 2010
2. M-Library: Haefele's library success wiki
3. Chad Mobile site generation

4. Google Mobile site generation

5. Library Mobile web design: Tips and Tricks and Resources by Rachel Vachel, University of Houston Library. Berika Willams. Victoria College / University of Houston library Victoria slide share (Accessed on 17th June 2016)

12
Use of Barcode and Scanning Technology in Library

12.1. BARCODE TECHNOLOGY

12.1.1. Introduction

In the present age of information technology, speedy progress in computer technology has given the momentum to bring computerisation in all the fields including our day to day affairs. While doing things with the help of computers, we notice use of several related tools and equipment. Examples : credit cards, ATM cards or smart cards, which have made the financial transactions easy and quicker than before, we also see use of various supportive technologies associated with the use of computers. Use of bar-coding is widely seen in many day to day activities such as departmental stores, malls, in office automation, or even in document movement tracking systems, in courier and speed post, in hospital in identifying patients, in industry warehouses for identifying spare parts or in taking inventory of dead stock items in offices. In a computerised library functioning also we see use of bar-coding in putting data about documents while transacting and handling them efficiently. We also see wide use of scanners in office automation. There may be rare case where library is yet to use barcoding in its operations.

Knowing the importance of use of barcode technology, readers may be curious to know more about these supportive technologies. In the present chapter, we are going to discuss about the barcode and scanning technology at length.

12.1.1.1. Barcode Technology : Background and concept

If we want to understand the barcode technology in a very simple way it would be as , "Barcode" means a technology which facilitates reading representative form of "data". Normally barcode represents numerical number in the form of line code or group of vertical lines. The lines in barcode are not similar; they vary in width as well as spacing in between lines. The structure of barcode is according to a specific standard. Arrangement of lines, their width as well as spacing has specific meaning. In the early state of evolution of barcode technology, it comprised of lines but was in one dimension. The form of barcode got changed subsequently and we now see them in different geometrical forms of triangular, point hexagonal, or even three dimensional forms.

For reading barcodes, optical scanners are used which are called barcode readers/ scanners. In order to generate barcodes of data or for coding, specific programmes are used and while inputting this representative data or for decoding same programs are used in the application software, which helps in reading as well as interpreting data and carry further action in the software.

In the very first instance, use of barcodes has been seen in labeling rail road cars. However, that time it was not found so successful. The use of barcode technology was successfully seen in super markets in selling packaged things. The use of barcode then got real momentum and wide use. The concept of bar-coding data and reading them by scanners while using software is called as "Auto ID Data Capture. " In the history there are evidences of preparing universal barcodes and using them in all the countries in marketing products globally. We see along with barcode technology, evolution of several technologies for similar purposes have emerged such as RFID means Radio Frequency Identification Systems.

However, barcode technology found today is the cheapest comparative technology than any other technology. This is due to its ease in use, wide use and due to its availability in minimum cost, which has put barcode technology on top of all other alternatives.

12.1.1.2. Barcode Technology : Historical Background

If we look into the history of the development of barcode technology, we find that the need of bar-coding was first felt in 1948 at Philadelphia by the researches of Drexel Institute of Technology. It was needed to have control in food malls for handling and selling products in local demand chain network. Two scientists, Sever and Woodland were the first to take lead in the development of barcode technology who did a lot of research in inventing this technology. Initially it saw the use of ultra violet ink and Morse code. Woodland attempted to read / scan lines in sand surface with high power cameras. Subsequently printed barcodes came into picture. In 1949 successful invention of barcode led to filling patent application by Sever and Woodland and USA awarded patent of bar-coding to these scientists in 1952 as US Patent No. 2672994. This original patent was bought by several companies to make further research in the technology. IBM undertook further research.

Subsequently, Collins, another researcher did further research in developing barcode technology in 1961 needed for his rail-road project at Pennsylvania. The system developed by him was well known as "Car track system." He used blue and yellow coloured reflective strips for pasting on vehicles. The barcode designed this way included 10 digit company code and four digit vehicle no. The experimentation done in the project although was not so successful but the idea was used to track the movement of vehicle on a bridge at New Jersey for collecting toll. The idea was also used by US Post Office in tracing and recording movements of postal vans.

After 1967 Collins offered his technology to many industries at a cost as he needed funds to develop black and white barcodes. However, he did not get much response from the industry. Finally he left the railway project and formed his own company named, "Computer Identic Corporation" and took lot of efforts to make further research. He further attempted to develop optical scanning technology much needed for reading the barcodes. With his successful efforts finally helped in developing easy and reliable barcode technology. In 1969, Collins' company provided barcode technology solutions to track movement of spare parts on conveyer belt in vehicle assembly workshop of General Motors. It was useful that it could track the inventory of spare parts right from beginning to loading totally assembled vehicles on to ships.

In the process of barcode development, this technology was effectively used as universal product codes in selling and billing work. It could be stated that barcode technology was stabilized in 1970s in the form of simple and reliable bar-coding solutions.

12.1.2. Types of Barcodes Symbologies

Description of different types of barcodes and their respective codes is called "Barcode Symbologies. " Barcode specification explains symbologies of respective barcodes. The specification are things like the way how character or digit represented (to code) and how it is read (decode) description of symbologies comprises of rules starting and end of barcode, spacing in lines and existence of quiet zones at the beginning and end of the barcode.

Symbologies are of two types:

1. Linear (one dimension) or
2. Two dimensional

There are further two types under linear type of symbologies :

1. Continuous v/s Discrete
2. Two widths v/s of many width

In continuous type of barcode sequence is as - one character or digit then space then digit / character/ and space. While scanning/reading such barcode, space is considered where as in discrete type of barcode which begins with bar and ends with bar, where space is not considered while reading the barcode.

In comparison to above two width type of barcode symbologies bars or spaces are thin or wide. In many width type of symbologies, bar or space width is in ratio of 1 : 2 : 3 or 4. In this type of symbologies, white bars are mixed or interleaved in black bars. Example: For first character black bar and for next white bar of varying width. In this there are bars for dual characters also.

There are barcode symbologies where there are layers of linear barcodes placed one above another. Two dimensional or 2D type barcode symbologies consists of matrix type of codes. Where there are symbols with x and y axis. Example point, rectangle or circle etc.

Laser type of scanner can read a horizontal line or even a slice of barcode. However, for reading layered barcode, laser scanner needs to be moved from bottom to top.

In 1990, Charged Coupled Device (CCD) type of barcode reader came into market. For reading two dimensional (2D) barcodes CCD type of scanners are used. It contains a band of rays.

Barcode type is characterized by symbology number, whether it is continuous or discrete and also on what is width of bars and spaces.

Barcodes which we generally come across are of linear type and mostly of code-39 (discrete) and two width type or code 128 (continuous and with many widths type). In liner type, there are 33 different types of barcodes having the above characteristics. Where as in 2D or matrix type of barcodes, there are 48 different types as per above rules, which gives an idea of having large variety in barcode symbology. Normally a particular type of code for a particular barcode requires specific scanner to read it, having capability of reading that a code or device need to be set to do the particular task.

12.1.3. Different Uses of Barcodes

Bar-coding is prominently used in departmental stores, super markets or mall where most of the products (in packets) available for selling are pre-bar-coded which is synchronized with the billing system at the counter. Customers gather things of their choice and take them to the counter. The counter assistant scans barcodes of each and every product and bill is prepared gi ing the product name, quantity, measure and cost. Thus selling / billing become easy and accurate. Barcodes are also mostly used in packing and forwarding or in courier transactions in tracking movements of documents and things. Barcodes technology helped in globalization of marketing management by bringing uniformity in these businesses.

There are other uses of barcodes as listed below:

1. In selling products having multiple demands, in grocery shop and departmental stores where barcodes find major use.
2. In industry where manufacturing is done on shop floor or conveyer belt having computerised control.
3. In retail customer chain where the consolidated billing of things purchased is given, barcodes finds its use.
4. In big hospitals each patients have barcodes on their wrist giving detailed history of the patient such as existing treatment and drug allergy and which could be easily know at various points wherever patient is moved.
5. Barcodes are effectively used for tracking movement of documents or files in various departments of an office.
6. Barcodes are also used in movement of equipments, tracking movement of vehicles or also in handling language of travelers at airports.
7. In sorting of mail in post, in courier movements, in delivery of speed posts barcodes are used.
8. Since 2005 various airlines provides bar-coded boarding passes to their travelers.
9. Migration of small insects or wild animals could also be tracked by using barcodes.
10. Barcodes are also used in cinema hall entry passes, for tracking movements of visitors in stadiums, which helps curbing use of bogus tickets.
11. Now days many advertisements or websites bears particular 2D(QR) barcodes which

facilitates scanned of those barcodes in finding those websites on internet.

12. In programming also source codes are printed in barcode to maintain their confidentiality.
13. Barcodes are used to maintain statistics of computer games played by people.
14. We see each published book or journal issue bear publisher's barcode on it.

If we consider above uses of barcodes we find that barcode system is widely used in several fields. Nowadays barcodes are effectively used in library computerization. We are going to discuss use of barcodes in computerised library functioning in detail in further paras.

12.1.4. Standardization in Barcode Technology

Normally institution or organisation where barcode technology is in use there should be barcode testing and verifying system to check correctness of barcodes. Under any circumstances barcode readability is the success of this technology. Then there would hardly be any errors found. The vendors of supply chain would invariably verify or test the quality of barcodes. Moreover, there are barcode verifiers to give grades to barcodes according to their quality. Instead of just decoding, barcodes verifiers undertakes nearly eight quality tests of barcodes and give them grades from 0. 0 to 4. 0. Normally a standard barcode should be of grade 1. 5.

Barcode verifier standards : For linear type barcode the verifier would be of ISO standard ISO/IEC - 15426-1 and for 2D type of barcodes verifier would be as per ISO /IEC - 15416-2. Present specification of international standard of barcode is ISO/IEC-15416 (linear) and ISO/IEC - 15415 for 2D type of bar-coding.

Up till now we have covered the conceptual and technical side of barcode technology now we are going to look into how barcode technology would be useful in library management.

12.1.5. Use of Barcode Technology in Library Management

Barcode is a collection of bars which represents particular number or alphanumeric data to be inputted in a application software. It could be a product number or a customer ID or in library it can be accession number of a book. Data coded in a barcode establishes relationship with a record of a book which is linked through its key data field i. e. accession no. Book record in addition to acc. no. contains bibliographical details of the book. Normally, in library for bar-coding, accession number is considered to be the most, as this number is used several times in computerised library function as the representative of document record. In manual system the acc. no. is entered manually in issue, return & other processes with barcode of document or ID number of borrower is scanned and inputted. As each book has unique acc. no. and each copy also has particular acc. no. same way a book or copy of a book possesses unique barcode.

Once entire library collection is bar-coded library collection establishes relation with library database then it facilitates issue, return transaction at counter. In doing so in data input window of circulation module accession number of book or customer ID in the form of bar-code is scanned and entered in window at cursor point instead of manually entering these numbers. Data inputting through barcodes is always fast and accurate. In manually entry errors may occur which will not be the case of barcodes. In library as collections are bar-coded all borrowers IDs are also bar-coded, to make it convenient in computerised operations, which makes circulation transactions full proof.

12.1.5.1. Advantages of Use of Bar-coding in Library

Use of barcodes is always advantageous in many ways, such as :

(i) It helps in reducing burden on counter staff.

(ii) It helps in bringing accuracy in work and in avoiding possible errors which occurs in manual input.

(iii) It helps to issue return and reissue of library materials without much efforts.

(iv) It brings speed in counter operations and in also reducing queue of readers at counter thus saving their time.

(v) Returning or checking- in books is very easy.

(vi) It improves performance of computerised circulation.

In short, computerisation associated with barcode technology facilitates ease, speed and accuracy in operations. In addition to circulation, barcode technology is advantageous in library management in many ways such as :

Management of Library Collection : With use of barcode management & control of various collections like books, back volumes, music records, CDs or video become easy. Instead of bar-coding of only acc. no. is possible to include other data fields of books like copy number, vol. number, which helps in increasing utility of barcodes in library management.

Organising Library collection and inventory control : Bar-coding of library collection further helps in organising library collection on shelves, withdrawing library material and having inventory control on the entire library collection especially it helps to undertake computerised physical verification of library books and other materials. If library provides smart barcodes then it is possible to even know the exact location of books in shelf arrangement, and it could also navigate and trace misplaced material in the library.

Inventory control of dead stock items : We have considered how library collection bar-coding helps in having inventory controls on library materials. It is also possible to have inventory control over collection of furniture, fixtures, computers, peripherals, equipment and stores item by using barcoding. In this case, database of all such items needs to be created and bar-coding of all the items also needs to be done with pasting barcodes on all these dead stock items. Having such preparations library can easily handle movement, handling, repairing of dead stock, and it would also be easy to conduct physical verification of the same.

12.1.5.1.1. Significance of Types of Barcode Symbologies for Library usage

In normal way of using bar-coding we see use of one dimensional barcodes. In other variety of barcodes there are two prominent types like Code-A-Bar and code 39 (code 3 of 9) and the contain chain of 14 bars / digits. In case of library usage of barcode technology is concerned, there are various options available; to include only acc. no. is the simplest way of using barcode technology in library.

With such option, having return transactions becomes possible with ease. However, such mode restricts the use of barcode in only the respective library. Barcodes applied on books are different from barcodes applied on patron cards. Combined bar-coding of these two things is possible with higher level of technology. It is also possible to have one type of barcoding in campus group libraries. Now let us understand the structure of the above types of barcodes - through the following examples:

1. Code - A - Bar : It contains collection of 14 bars or digits. Where digit - 1 is combination of barcodes of patron or books. The digit - 2 indicates that barcode of patron is being read. Digit - 3 indicates that it is reading the barcode of library materials. Further 4 digits from 2 to 5 indicate the code of library. For this we can consider 4 digits of either pin code no. or last 4 numbers of phone numbers. Next eight digits pertain to either book acc. no. or patron ID No. The last digit indicates that the entire barcode was correctly read. In printed barcodes, it is necessary to print actual nos. in the same sequence either on top or bottom, which helps to actually read that number and paste the barcode on book accordingly.

2. Code 39 (code 3 of 9) : In this type of barcode there are less digits than 14 as we saw in case of code- A Bar and contains 10 digits in which first digit is either for patron or books, next two digits are for library code No. and next 7 digits for book acc. no. This type does not need check digit. This type of bar-coding can be used in an individual library or in library group, which facilitates inter library loan (ILL) transfer of materials from one library to another.

12.1.5.2. Smart and Dumb Types of Barcodes

When we look for higher level bar-coding for library use we find two examples e. g. smart and dumb types of barcodes. Each of them has certain advantages or problems.

Dumb Type of Barcode : Characteristics

- Economical
- Ordinary staff can apply them on books
- This is of generic form
- Each barcodes gives details of respective book.
- If there is change in book data then no need to change the barcode.
- Very useful for library issue and return functions.

Problem : With dumb type barcodes, one cannot use it for inventory control.

Smart Barcodes : Characteristics

- In this type of barcode label reflects additional attributes like call no. Part no. or copy no. along with accession number.
- With smart barcodes library can conduct physical verification very well, and it can also be used to locate book on shelf or to navigate misplaced books.

Problems : There are difficulties in pasting barcodes on books as the person involved needs good knowledge about the book retails.

Considering the above problems we may feel whether library should adopt using smart barcodes or otherwise. It is recommended to consider the following things:

- For books which have single copy should have dumb or ordinary barcodes.
- In special, research type or large libraries where there is need of additional attributes of books with acc. no., smart bar-coding can be adopted and also if library wishes to do higher level inventory control tasks can use smart barcodes for its collections.
- If library collection is of few thousands it may use simple barcodes. Higher level barcodes could be complex and it may exceed length of barcodes. One more important thing of library bar-coding is that one should remember that bar-coding should not be done independently of library LMS. Library should first install the LMS and then do the bar-coding as byproduct of LMS else barcode reading compatibility may come in trouble.

12.1.5.3. Where to paste barcodes on books in the library

There are various prevailing practices in library about how many barcodes for a books to be prepared and at which places barcodes are to be pasted and whether they could be put on book covers or not? Normally in most of libraries barcodes are 'pasted on title page and on the last page respectively, as these barcodes remains in tact in covered book and thus can last for long time. Multiple barcodes provide alternative if one of them is lost or damaged. Some libraries prefer to put additional barcode on top cover, which may help in speedy issue return transaction. Sometimes in some libraries barcode scanning is combined with desensitizing action of 3M electromagnetic security system. In such case, it is preferred to put barcode on left bottom square / quarter of the page/cover to facilitate scanning and sensitizing actions together. However, there are chances that barcodes put on book cover may deteriorate or damage faster due to friction among the books, unless barcodes are protected by applying POP on them.

12.1.5.4. Ways of Barcode Printing in Library

Generally barcodes are printed in the following three ways in library :

1. Photo Composition Method
2. Laser Printer
3. Thermal Transfer Printer (TTP)

Let us understand these methods of printing of barcodes.

Photo Composition Method : In this type, barcode labels are printed in photographic way. The paper used in this type is of special quality. While printing labels a protective layer is applied. Such barcodes can be pasted on book covers as they are durable but cost of printing becomes high and probably unaffordable for library use.

Laser Printing : In laser type of barcode, printing resolution of 600 DPI is used. These barcode labels need POP in order to protect them from damaging. If barcodes printed on laser printer are pasted inside book i. e. on title and last page they remain intact fairly for longer period. These barcodes last longer than TTP type barcodes.

Thermal Transfer Printer (TTP) : In Thermal Transfer Printer or TTP type of barcode printing requires consumables such as carbon ribbon and label role. As print signal from computer is received at printer carbon particles from ribbon gets heated and exact image of barcode is doped on label. Since the barcode is generated out of carbon particles it does not last long. Secondly, if such barcodes are pasted on book top covers then they deteriorate due to friction among books. It therefore, needs POP cover to protect it from damaging. In this type of barcode printing requires costly consumables so also cost of TTP printer is very high.

In printing barcodes, instead of paper labels which are found durable, anti-tearable anti scratch labels of special material made of polyester are also used. Naturally the cost of such barcode labels is considerably high.

12.1.6. Barcode Readers / Scanners

There are softwares to generate barcodes of library materials. Most of the times such software are built-in in library management system (LMS) and such LMS have built-in modules to print the barcodes. This way generated barcodes are printed using one of the above printing methods, and barcodes labels prepared this way are pasted on designated places on the book. When the readers bring the bar-coded books at the circulation counter for issuing, staff at counter first inputs borrowers ID number from bar-coded ID cards into a window for inputting member ID by scanning the barcodes, then the barcodes of books to be issued are also inputted one by one by scanning their barcodes from the book title page or behind cover and thus process the issuing of books is completed in a very short time. When the barcodes are read by laser scanner a line laser ray is beamed on the barcode by pressing the scanner trigger for a few seconds and the barcode is read within that short time and entered acc. no. in software window meant to input the data.

In barcode scanner the task of barcode reading is done by two devices within the scanner i. e. the input device and the decoder. Decoder is a software or intelligent agent where as input device is an eye to read the barcode. The scanning involves three things i. e. reading, decoding and inputting. Nowadays for scanning or reading and inputting barcodes there are various equipments available in the markets such as :-

1. Laser scanners
2. C. C. D. scanners
3. Cordless Barcodes Scanners

Laser scanners or generally used to read barcodes. The speciality of scanning is that it does not need to touch the barcode as it is read through a distance by laser rays. The scanning by laser scanner is quick, accurate, and error free, naturally they are more costly than other type of devices. It costs on an average Rs. 8, 000.00-10, 000.00. Other devices used to scan or read the barcodes are of CCD type (i. e. Charged Couple Devices). In case of laser scanner, it emits thin layer of laser rays, where as in case of CCD scanner a band of rays is emitted. CCD type of scanner needs more time to read the barcodes and one has to take scanner close to barcodes. In case of laser even from a distance also barcodes are read. The cost of CCD type scanner is between Rs. 4,000.00-6,000.00

Among various types of scanners available, cordless type of scanner are of advanced nature. Cordless scanners are used to scan the barcodes and store the data in its memory. The data of barcodes stored in memory is then transferred into the computer without actually connecting it to a computer. Scanning with cordless scanners one doesn't need to take a computer near to book collection.

There are stands available to mount the scanners on it, so the barcode is scanned just by placing bar-coded book under it without handling the scanner. The reading is so synchronized that when there is barcode below the scanner it is put on and it is put off as the book is taken out. Cost of cord less scanner is around Rs. 15,000/-.

12.1.7. Examples of Different Types of Barcodes

If we try to look at any linear type of barcode with necked eyes we find all the bars in barcode are alike. It is also difficult to understand various specifications by which different barcodes are generated and what is the difference among them. We may make out the difference between linear and 2D type of barcodes. With a view to understand the different types of barcode and gain some knowledge about them here is the list of barcodes samples with their images as tabulated in table No. 12.1

Symbology Type	Characteristics	Sample Images
1. Code-39	Simplest type of barcode in which alpha numeric data is coded.	1 2 3 4 5
2. Extended Code-39	It could contain 128 characters data. ISO-646 is extension of Code – 39	
3. Code-128	In this type of barcode One can include data like Upper and lower case Letters, numbers, punctuation Marks and all special Characters.	CODE 128
4. Code a bar	In this type of barcode It contains 0-9 numbers, alphabetical characters and other symbols.	AB12345678910
B. 2D Type of Barcodes		
1. Databar Extended	Barcodes as per GS-1	
2. Databar Extended and Stacked	Barcodes as per GS-1 but placed one above the other	

Symbology Type	Characteristics	Sample Images
3. PDF 417	These are two dimensional type of barcodes which Includes large size of Text data.	
4. Data Matrix	It is 2D/Matrix or Grid type of Barcode	
5. Maxicode	2D/Matrix type of barcode	
6. Aztec	2D type, consisting of all characters, symbols and Text data	
7. QR Codes Quick Reference code	Same as above, used for picking from add/ websites by copying them one can reach to particular website.	

Table 12.1. Examples of Different types of Barcodes with their Images

12.2. SCANNING TECHNOLOGY

12.2.1. What is scanning?

Prior to the time when scanning technology was invented the only technique to copy printed text or image was photocopying. So copy of printed paper was produced on another paper. There was a real need to convert the printed paper image to an alternative medium other than the paper as it has limited life. With the invention of scanning technology it was possible to preserve copy of printed page in a computer, which has unlimited life. In office automation scanning plays a vital role. It is difficult to preserve paper based documents in files and folders as paper gets deteriorated with its age and makes it difficult to handle. Converting paper based documents in digital form was very much needed. Scanning technology has fulfilled this need. Nowadays scanning technology is widely used in various fields.

The simple principle of scanning technology is, to create a digital image of textual document and preserve it in a computer in the form of a file. Scanning is the first stage of digitizing a printed page. We can further carryout different processes on the scanned image to digitize it. Next to scanning is to use Optical Character Recognition (OCR) process to convert it into fully digitized page. Preserved image of the page of digital form can be used to print further copies of it. Normally scanned copies are saved in PDF (Portable Document file), which can be sent through e-mail from one place to other, from one computer to another or to many computers. Scanning technology nowadays finds use in our day to day life. Not only black and white printed images are scanned and preserved but it is possible to scan colour images of photo, picture or text and preserved them like original. We are going to know about this important technology in the following paragraphs :

12.2.1.1. Layout / Design of a Scanner

In scanning technology the scanner is the most important equipment. Normally it contains the following things :

1. CCD (Charged Coupled Device) which picks the image / photo of documents.
2. Mirrors - series of angled mirrors to carry the image.
3. Scanning Head
4. Glass Plate
5. Lamps
6. Lens
7. Cover
8. Filter
9. Stepper Motor
10. Stabilizer bar
11. Belt to move scanning head
12. Power supply unit.
13. Interface port
14. Control circuit

12.2.2. Scanning Process

We are all aware about scanning operation. A paper bearing text, to be scanned is kept on the glass of a scanner upside down and then upper shutter is closed. One then clicks 'scan' radio button and in a short time image of text on the paper is captured and shown on the screen. The image is saved in a file and preserved in the hard disk of the computer. This is a simple processes of scanning.

Inside scanning cover mostly we find flat type of scanner, which is white in colour only, exceptionally we find them in black colour. White cover gives the back ground behind the text bearing paper to understand scanner the size of document. Once the scanning process is on, the text side paper gets illuminated by the high power light beam. The recent type of scanners contain cathode florescent light. Once paper is illuminated the scanning head moves across the paper with a belt drive. This happens with stepper motor.

With stabilizer bar, it confirms that scanning process is complete. The image of text on paper is transferred through lens with the help of series of two or three mirrors. The mirrors are fixed in such a way that the image of the paper is seen in every mirror angled to each other. Lens is focused with filters on CCD array and the text on the paper is then converted to image by software built in the scanner, which is then sent to computer. In some old scanners the images used to travel with series of two mirrors or in some with three mirrors. However, now a days it is done with just one mirror. In advanced type of scanners the contact image is formed with sensors, in which CCD arrays are not used, where along with filters, lens, red, blue and green coloured light emitting diodes (LED) used to illuminate paper to capture the image. In scanning process resolution and interpolation of scanner are the significant features.

12.2.3. Scanning Resolution and Interpolation

We find that various types of scanners are depending on their resolution as well sharpness of their scanned images. As resolution and sharpness increases it gives incremental quality of the scanner. Resolution is measured in dots per inch (DPI). The minimum resolution of scanner should be from 300 X 300 DPI. The resolution of scanner indicates the requirement of number of CCD scanners in line. For example for scanner having resolution of 300x300 DPI then there would be 2500 sensors in line where as for 600 X 300 DPI resolutions there would be 5100 sensors in line. If the scanner is of single pass then it would have sensors 3 times more. The sharpness of scanner depends on optical quality of lens and intensity of light beam. With bright Zenon beams and with high quality lens one can get clear image and sharpness is also better. In addition to resolution of a scanner we also need to know about its interpolation. Under interpolation resolution is inbuilt adjusted or increased through software. In scanning for increasing quality of scanning additional pixels are added into the images. For example if the resolution is 300 X 300 and if it is necessary it is increased up to 500 X 300 DPI to maintain quality of resolution. Interpolation of each image varies with the angle by which image is scanned. In addition to Interpolation and resolution there is one more term called Bit Depth. Bit depth has relation with colour scanning and for different colours have specific bit depth. Normally with 24 bit depth scanner becomes capable to scan all types of colours images. With Bit depth of 30 or 36 is considered to be high quality scanners.

12.2.4. Image Transfer Process

In scanning process the first step is to capture the image of the document to be scanned. The next step in this process is about sending image to the computer to store. For this the process needs the following types of connectivity of the computer.

1. Parallel port
2. Small Computer System Interface (SCSI)
3. Universal BUS interface

Out of these if the process is done through parallel port then the scanning process works slow. However, for SCSI interface we need some special support. Moreover, computer in this case needs SCSI card then only we can connect scanner to computer with USB connectivity, such task is done quickly and with less cost. In case of large computers for scanning task, we need connectivity of higher capacity.

So we have now understood that with the above accessories we can connect scanners to the computers. Having the above connectivity accessories we need to install specific drivers available for the drivers. The installation process is called TWIN. With this, communication between computer and scanner becomes easy. In fact TWIN is a special instruction language of scanners, which is accepted by the computer. Once the TWIN installation is done in computer then one can connect any type of scanner to the computer and scan the documents and transfer images to the computer.

In some, high grade scanners without having drivers are installed. It is possible to transfer document image to a computer and also do editing on it. With optical character recognisation software image captured with scanner can be converted to a digital document. Readers should understand that scanner captures is just an image of document. It cannot be called as digital page. All images taken by scanners are just photo images. However, scanning is the first initial stage in the process of digitization. We can get normal type of scanners with a cost of Rs. 8,000.00-10,000.00 and higher grade scanners are available with a cost of around Rs. 50,000.

12.2.5. What is a Colour Scanner?

Colour scanner means a scanner which can take copy of colour document in the same colours like original. Each scanner normally has capability of scanning colour documents. However, we do not use this capability and they are used only to capture images in gray or black or white. In technical details the resolution measured in its bit depth of scanner are the important things of colour scanners. Normal flat bed scanners have resolution of 300 X 300 DPI. The sharpness of image depends on optical quality of the lens and its power of light beam (brightness). Bit depth or colour depth means capacity of scanner to create image in colour. In colour scanning for each pixel approximately 24 bit depth is required and each colour scanners bears this capacity.

12.2.6. Types of scanners

Normally we find four types of scanners as :

(i) Flatbed Scanner : They are called desktop scanners.

(ii) Sheet-fed-Scanner : They are like flatbed scanners. The only difference is that in this type scanning beams is stationary and documentary moves across it. They are similar to small portable printers.

(iii) Handheld Scanner : In this case the basic technology remains same as flatbed type scanner, in which motor belt is not available and one need to move scanner manually.

(iv) Drum Scanner : These types of scanners are used in publishing industry, where fast and immediate scanning is undertaken. These scanners are called multiplier tube scanners. The documents of large size are mounted on glass cylinders. The sensors are at the centre of cylinder which makes the light beam to reflect in different rays. Each light beam passes through a filter which is converted into scanning signals. This technique helps in creating good images. The actual images of the scanner could be seen on the website www.images.google.com.

CONCLUSION

In this chapter we had detailed information about the barcoding and scanning technologies. This technology can be effectively used in library management. Barcoding is used for faster inputting codes of numbers whereas scanning technology can also be used in office automation of librarian's office. One may not be able to create paper less librarian's office but it can be used to maximum extent for digitizing office correspondence which is important step towards office automation.

Considering the usefulness of barcoding and scanning technologies librarians and library professionals should understand what these technologies and are and think to acquire skills to use them effectively in day to day functioning of library.

REFERENCES

1. Haberman, Alan : Who ushered in the barcode, dies at 81, The New York Times 15. 6. 2011.
2. Fishman, Charles : Killer app-bar nonce American way, 18 Aug. 2001.
3. Sideman, Tony : Barcodes Sweep the world, wonders of Modern Technology.
4. 150 website (http://www. iso. org) (accessed on 13th June, 2016.)
5. Barcode-Wikipedia the free Encyclopedia (Accessed on 11th June 2016).
6. How stuffworks, How Scanners work. http://www. howstuffworks. com/scanners.html (accessed on 15/7/2011)

LIST OF SOME OTHER USEFUL REFERENCES

1. Burke, Harry E. : Automating Management Information Systems : Barcode Engineering and Implementation. Thomson Learning. ISBN 0-442-20667-4.
2. Burke, Harry E : Automating Management Information Systems : Principles of barcode applications. Thomson Learning.
3. Burke, Harry E. : Handbook of Barcode System, Van Nostrand Reinhold Co. ISBN - 978-0-442-21430-2.
4. Bingham, Eugene F. : The Barcode Manual, Thomson Learning, ISBN 0-0-3-016-173-8.
5. Harmon, Craig K:Lines of Communication, Helmers publishing, ISBN- 0-911-261-07-9.
6. Nelson, Benjamin : Punched Cards to Barcodes, Helmers Publishing ISBN - 0-911-261-12-5.
7. Brown, Stephen A. : Revolution at Check Out Counter : The explosion of the barcode, Harvard University Press ISBN - 0. 674-767-20-9.

8. Harmon, Craig K. Rusofs, Adams : Reading between the Lines, Helmers Publishing ISBN -0-911261-00-1.

9. Palmer, Roger C : Barcode Book, Helmers Publishing ISBN. 0-911261-09-5.

10. Russ, Adams & Lana Joyce : Black and White Solution : Barcode and the IBM PC. , Helmers Publishing ISBN 0-911201-01-X.

11. Russ, Adams: Sourcebook of Automatic identification and Data Collection : Van Nostrand Reinhold, ISBN - 0-442-31850-2.

13
Networking Technology : Applications in Library Management

13.0. INTRODUCTION

In the modern age we are generally familiar with the concept of network. Moreover we are already using networking knowingly or unknowingly. As such we avail network services some or other way while dealing with things in our daily life, for example, we get a water connection from a civic body, we get an electrical connection, cable connection, we use bank network, ATM or we make online reservations and travel by rail, roadways, waterways or airways. We make use of all such networks in fulfilling our daily needs. Other than these we also use networks which are meant for information flow and telecommunication and are equally important for us like radio, television, telegraph, telephone, fax or even communication through satellite. We make use of special networks to search and obtain information in our daily or professional life, wherein we use internet or library network. In using information networks telecommunication based network technologies play a very significant role in our life.

While using any network services as a customer we are the end user. We never think while making use of any network about its development or about the concept behind it, or try to know how it works or how it is managed. Rather we never feel it is necessary to know about them but we just use them.

However, as librarians and library professionals when we think of information technology or when we try to understand in library and information point of view we are certainly curious to know the concept, technology, working, management and application of network. Considering these need in mind the author has planned the present chapter on networking technology and its application in library management.

13.1. NETWORK - CONCEPT & OBJECTIVES

Network Concept : Network means two or more nodes or points connected with each other by a telecommunication medium, which works for one integrated system or program or it can be described as systems and program area when all the nodes are connected with each other to form a communication mesh. For example : When two computers are connected through cable, they can communicate with each other. It happens with the combination of computer and telecommunication technologies. Such network is called computer network. Telecommunication technology consists of several technical parts such as telephone, satellite, radio, optical fiber, digital data lines, etc. Network could be small, local or big.

When we think of network structure, we think about every participating part and its technical hardware which needs to be compatible and competent. It needs to possess mechanism and intellect or software to collaborate and give expected response with each point. When all the parts of a network function with equal speed and capacity then only networking works successfully. If we describe this in technical terminology, it would be as - in a network there would be compatibility in the hardware and software parts, there need to have network connectivity, flexibility, modularity, reliability and protocol based networking communication and the platform for signal communication, then the network design must be as per specific networking standard so that there would not be difficulty in understanding, handling and if necessary repairing and upgrading it.

Objectives of Networks : The main objectives of networking are to propagate task of communicating useful information with the collaboration of network participating nodes or with the help of network participating node carry out task of communication in multiplied way. In network there could be nodes which are locally, regionally, internationally connected. Now with the help of the following examples let us try to understand the concept and objectives of network more clearly:

1. In a multi-storied office to provide intercom facility to all the departments situated at various floors.
2. In a small village to connect all the telephone subscribers through a telephone exchange to provide telephone facility.
3. At one place establish infrastructural set up to receive program of different channels of television and provide facility to view channels to nearby customers via cable network
4. To connect all railway reservation counters through microwave systems. Provide computerised railway reservation facility throughout the country even at any remote place.
5. With the help of computer, internet and either through cable and telephone the system provides internet connectivity to needy customers to search information on web.

After going through the above examples we understand how networks work at local, regional or national level and also understand their various objectives. It makes it possible due to communication medium technology established while setting any network. In networking we never face geographic barrier. Moreover at international level even if network nodes are not directly or physically connected their network works very smoothly and this is the specialty of networking technology. Only it is necessary that every networking node needs to possess fast and competent machinery to provide speedy communication among them. Secondly, network environment must provide more facilities and benefits than pre-networking situation and it is the main objective of any network.

13.2. TELECOMMUNICATION TECHNOLOGY

When we study about network technology we consider how information is exchanged or how it flows through electronic medium between two points irrespective of the distance between them. In a network how participating nodes are connected to each other and how communication takes place among them is a very curious thing to know. In the following paragraphs we are going to understand specifically about information networks.

In information network the important medium is telecommunication; hence let us try to know about telecommunication first. Network is possible with the following two things :

1. Connecting Medium
2. Transmission and control mechanism

We reviewed the various networks connected with our daily life. We know how our brain communicates with our sense organs and how it instructs them. We know how blood flows in our body as controlled by the heart. These things work like a network. Another example is, how goods are transported from one station to another. In this case the railway yard controls the traffic. This mechanism is called "switching system". The switching system is the core technology in telecommunication technology. So now let us try to understand about switching system.

In all the networks which were referred so far, the main objective is to allow something to travel from one point to other which is controlled by a switching centre. Telephones or computers also work with some switching mechanism. Secondly, computers have information sources and the information seekers try to access them, thus information flows from source to client. This communication is controlled by switching system which works on certain rules called protocols.

From ancient times humans searched for communication tools, they formed communication protocols and also invented communication medium for it. Telegram, telephone, radio, television technology have been invented out of their efforts, which are now available for our use.

Telecommunication has now become easy, powerful and more competent than before. Now we see a lot of improvements in storing and transmitting information from one end to other. Now fiber optics and microprocessors are used in communication systems. It has become possible to transmit voice or video signals along with information (data). General objective of communication system is signal transmission or exchange the information without considering whether information is in the library or anywhere else. Whenever geographic distance increases technology appropriates itself, even complications increase, it never changes the quality of signal transmission. We experience this when we talk on the phone with a person in UK or USA. We feel the voice so clear as if the person in next door is speaking with you, and also we experience the same thing when a live cricket match played anywhere in the world is viewed by people by sitting at home at any remote location. This is the success of today's communication technology.

13.2.1. Telecommunication and Networking

In tele type of communication system, there are various types such as telegraph, telephone, telex information transmission. They are categorized based on mode of transmission and type of signals. Generally telephone subscriber are connected with telephone exchange or so called single switching system through the copper wire, whereas if they are connected with two switching system the connectivity is through coaxial wire or through microwave communication system. Signals of tele-printer are quite different than telephone or other signals. Considering this we can say that any network is characterised by type of signal, for example telephone network, telex network or telegraph network.

13.2.1.1. Telephone network or Telephony

Generally telephone networks are of public switched type of networks (PSTN). The specialty of this type of network is that even if many companies are manufacturing the parts, they are compatible with each other. Other type of telephone network is Electronic Private Automatic Branch Exchanges (EPABX). In both the above types of network they carry our voice is an analogue voice signals. Voice communication is of same type in them. Leaving pauses in between words, we cannot notice any small mistake, leakage or drop out of singles.

13.2.1.2. Telegraph Network

Telegraph or telegram were sent from post or telegraph offices all over. There was also existing network of telegraph called telegraph network. Telegraphic signals were carried through wires. Invention of telegraph transmission is the base of today's modern message communication.

13.2.1.3. Telex Network

With the use of telex network technology one can send message in typed form to all over the world.

Teleprinter : It is an electro-mechanical typewriter which can be used to send and receive typed message from point to point and point to multipoint over various types of communications channels. In tele-printing technology variety of different communication media are used which includes a simple pair of wires, dedicated non switched telephone circuit, switched network which operates like public telephone network (Telex) and radio or microwave links (Telex or radio or TOR). Teleprinter attached to modem could also communicate through a standard switched public telephone lines. Now teleprinters have largely been replaced by electronic computer terminals which use a computer terminal instead of printers. Teleprinters are still widely used in the aviation industry (AFTN) and airline teletype systems. Devices having brail key board are also used by the hearing impaired.

13.2.2. Telephone : Technical Background

Since telecommunication or telephone is the basic platform for networking concept, now let us try to understand the technical side of telephony.

If we try to look backward in the history of telecommunication we find that its beginning was made in ancient times when people used to communicate the signal through drum beating or by sending messages through predefined symbols, knots or through code words. Subsequently, we find that humans improved the communication through their skills, now we have media like radio, electro or electro optical equipments and microwave devices. We can quote several inventions in the field of telecommunication devices and mass media as listed below, which have greatly contributed to development of modern communication system:

- Telegram: Samuel Morse USA 1837
- Radio(wireless) - Gugliemo Marconi - 1895
  (Wireless Telegraphy)
- Telephone: Alexander Graham Bell 1847 - 1922
  - — Elisha Gray
  - — Antonio Mencci
- Telex - Sir John Robinson - 1981
- Television - Philo Taylor and Farnsworth 1927
- Fax - Alexander Bain 1846
- Wireless Telephone : Nathan B. Subject field 1908
- **Cell/mobile phone :**

1 G Mobile	:	Martin Cooper 1973
2 G mobile	:	1991
SMS text	:	Neil Popworth 1992
3G CDMA & GSM	:	Japan 2001
LTE / 4G	:	2009
5G	:	2013 Samsung

Sending telegraphic message was the first event in modern telecommunication field. Alexander Graham Bell presented the first hand set of his telephone which made dream of human kind to carry human's voice over a long distance come true, when two persons located at any remote places in the world could speak with each other. It was the land mark development in telephone technology which made it possible to establish telephone connection anywhere in the world. In the current modern technology voice signals are carried by laser rays through optical fibers.

13.2.2.1. Switching systems

In telephone network one telephone subscriber connects with other subscriber through telephone exchange. It is not possible to have straight connections among all the subscribers, who wish to talk to each other. One single line is used to connect as many subscribers and allow them to talk to each other. Switching system does this work. Whenever two people talk on phone at that time only they are linked with each other through a common wire and once the telephone talk is over they are delinked. Several types of switching systems have been developed in the course of development such as:

1. Manual switching system : In this type a telephone operator does the job of switching by connecting and disconnecting people

2. Automatic switching : Under this there are two further types such as:

1. Electromechanical switching systems
2. Electronic switching system

In electromagnetic switching also there are sub parts like :

- Strowger switching systems
- Cross bar switching systems

These systems work with speed 1-10 m/s and they are found robust.

3. **Electronic switching system :** In this case switching is done by a computer or processor. In electronic switching also there are further types like

- Time division switching
- Digital time division switching
- Space switching
- Time switching and
- Analogue time division switching

13.2.2.1.1. Switching Techniques

Generally there are two switching techniques e. g.

- Circuit switching
- Store and forward switching

In circuit switching methodology especially in telecommunication network two network nodes establish a dedicated communication channel (Circuit) and remain connected with each other. The circuit guarantees the full bandwidth of the channel during the communication session. The example of circuit switching network is the early analogue telephone network. Whereas as in case of store and forward type switching there are two sub-techniques such as:

- Message switching
- Packet switching

In store and forward switching network node has the facility to store and when the network is available stored message travels from one node / connection to other. The processor works to create buffer storage. In this type sender and receiver need to be connected before the message / signal is sent. In store and forward system, the system is responsible to deliver the signal in the network. The signal or message is stored at a nearby node and it is delivered at the right time when there is connectivity.

13.2.2.1.1.1. MESSAGE SWITCHING NETWORK

In this type the entire message is forwarded at one time. In case if the length of message is more, then difficulties are faced in delivering the messages. It becomes necessary to verify whether the respective node has sufficient space to store the signal/message, which is complicated thing.

In packet switching network these difficulties are overcome.

13. 2. 2.1.1.2. PACKET SWITCHING NETWORK

In this type message is broken in small segments or packets. These packets then allowed to travel through a shortest route available. When a packet travels, they are independent. They could travel through different lines. Care is taken so that two packet do not get mixed, as each packet bears beginning code, code of destination, identity of message number and identity code of each packet. Due to such arrangement all the packets travelled in different line and finally come together at the destination. With different sequence of packet they are rearranged in the same sequence as it was sent so the right message is delivered at the other end without any leakage or mismatching. In packet switching type it is possible to use the communication medium to its optimum capacity. The packet switching is the latest, safe and reliable technology available today.

13.3. NETWORK

In network fundamental, basic technology is the telephony. We have seen the progress and development in telephone technology especially about innovations in switching system. In this section we are going to understand the network technology in detail. If we broadly try to look into the network then we may consider that two computer are connected. In order to establish any network it needs to have high capacity and high speed transmission facility. Computers in the network are interlinked through microwaves, satellite, fiber optic and cables. Sometimes instead of connecting computers face to face they get the connectivity from a centralized minicomputer. These minicomputer works as a host of network. It performs functions such as :

1. Process the message/ signal and send / forward
2. Analyse the faults in communication
3. Adjust with communication protocol.
4. Decode the received message and forward them to next respective destination
5. Direct the communication in the network

Centralised minicomputer or hosts depending on its size of network, as the network expands the task becomes complicated and main systems works appropriately, where two computers in a network avail connectivity they are abide by the same protocol. In other words the entire network works with a common protocol. The hardware of each participating computer need to be compatible with such common protocol through a telecommunication medium then it creates a simple network which facilitates computer to dialog with each other. They can even share the common software or they can send/ export or received/import the data. Such computers can also share their intelligence if required. In networking along with computers hardware and equipments are also used. For example radio waves, satellite, telephone connectivity and optical fiber, digital data lines and tools and equipment relating to it. We know that in telephone networking signals pertaining to digital data stored in computer is transmitted through communication medium in analogue mode and at the end of network part of it is again converted into digital data at receiving computer. This was the beginning when networking concept emerged and it progressed further by bringing innovations in it. In order to make network function smoothly related protocols and appropriate network architecture have also been invented and used. Now let us try to understand first the bit about computer and data network and look into its advanced technology.

13.3.1. Networks Types

13.3.1.1. Computer Networks

The network in which computers participate is called a computer network. In establishing a computer network the main purpose is to utilize the capacity of participating computers to an optimum extent. In computer networks, computers communication medium and network connecting equipment are invariably used. The telephone connectivity forms the basis of computer networks. The latest and best switching system is used such as circuit, message and packet switching systems. In addition to switching systems, network broadcast system is also used. However, multiple switching systems are not used whereas signal transmission line equipped with all stations participate in the network. In such systems we can take radio and satellite network as the examples.

Main parts of Networks : There are two main components of network such as :

1. Communication participation system
2. System which carry out network operations

Parts of Network : Considering the above type of network it contains the parts as below :

1. Computers and software require for establishing the network
2. Network interface hardware
3. Communication medium and equipments
4. Network controlling software
5. Computers and equipments of network nodes along with interface

Following is the Fig. 13.1 showing network software connectivity and computers participating in the network :

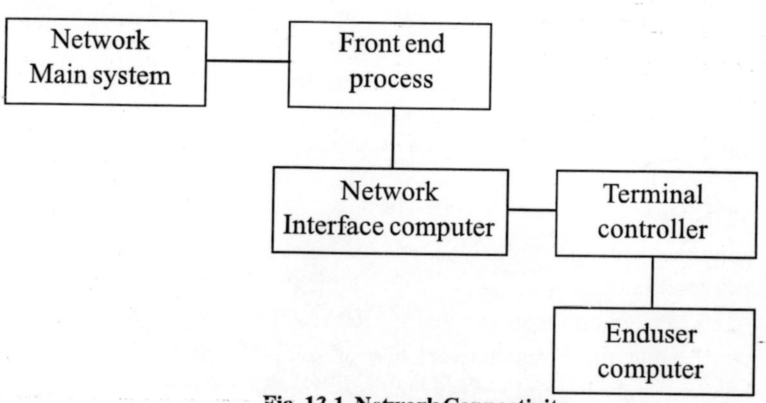

Fig. 13.1. Network Connectivity

13.3.1.2. Data Networks

Combination of computer and telecommunication technology has emerged to form network technology. This technology is called data transmission or data network. If the computers in such networks are nearer then they could be connected through local cable network. However, if they are far away from each other then they communicate with each other through telephone network. Earlier such communication was through telex or fax. Nowadays latest telephone technology like Public Switched Telephone Network (PSTN) systems are used, which facilitates faster communication in the network.

Our emphasis is on information network. In information network different types of signals are carried such as voice, radio, video and binary type of signals, there are thus three types of signals such as :

1. Audio signals - Radio Broadcast
2. Video signals - Television Broadcast
3. Binary or digital signals - Handled by computers

Communication between two computers depends on how individual computer works as well as on the speed of communication. When the message/signal is necessary to be sent the communication system should send it at once. This means data transmission medium is 80 to 90% which remains standby i. e. in working condition but actually it is not utilized. This results in availability of comparatively less speed than it is required so the data transfer is not effective. The data transmission therefore needs less bandwidth but need more speed. Secondly in audio voice signal transmission any mistake or loss of signal is tolerable. However, in data transmission any mistake or loss of data in not acceptable.

When two auto-controlled computers dialog with each other such communication happen as per real time sharing. Now let us understand what real time sharing systems is? When a main computer or server is connected to several client machines and people carry out their tasks through communication between client and the server they share the central processor at central machine or server. An individual seating across a client machine feels that virtually entire central server is solely working for him. However in reality central server simultaneously works with many client machines as it provides time to every client as required. It happens so quickly that people do not realize time shifting which is in microseconds. This make it possible that time of central processing machine is optimally utilized. This is called real time sharing system.

13.3.2. Network Historical Background

The first network was originated at US Dept. of Defence in 1960 called as ARPANET. It was proved that network facilitates various types of communication. ARPANET was finally converted into today's internet. The basic concept emerged at ARPANET was like - when a computer at remote location contacts with a machine in the network, it tries to look for the main machine or the host of that network and thus user gets the required information. Looking into reliability of communication in a network environment the technology first was explored for exchanging military related confidential information especially during the warfare. After this basic invention of network at ARPANET many small and big networks emerged like academic, private etc.

13.3.2.1. Network Categories

Networks are classified into the following categories :

1. Networks based on usage
2. Networks based on types of users
3. Types of users
4. Networks depending on composition and protocols
5. Network depending on geographical design
6. Network depending on mode of transmission.

13.3.2.1.1. Network Based on Usage

Normally network is used for the following purposes.

1. To utilize or share the computing facility
2. The exchange or share the data
3. To establish the communication

In case of the first purpose expects to utilize capacity of available computer by sharing it. For example, if an institute has powerful central computer then departments can collaboratively utilize the strength of the computing or a smaller computer located at distance uses capacity of powerful computer.

Computer network with second purpose is to share the data by participating computers in a network. In this type a database held centrally is used by computers located at a distance. The example could be use of stock exchange data or hotel, airline or railway reservation data sharing etc. In the third type of data network it expects, for example people from world over communicate with each other using the network and exchange figures, documents and information. In all these cases there is no limit of geographic distance. Electronic mail or bulletin board are the example of this type of communication.

13.3.2.1.2. Network Based on type of users

In this type, classification would be as follows :

1. Private Network
2. Public Network
3. Cooperative Network

The private networks are owned by a company which is used by various divisions or department whereas public network is established by an institute or organisation and used by other institutions or individuals. Cooperative network is jointly established and used by the member, institutions participating in the network. Designing a communication is a complicated process. It is therefore necessary to make department wise division of network activity. This is called a structural approach out of which design of network is kept at a manageable department and process of communication is described in the form of architecture. Network architecture coordinates network services and its functions, which is done on the basis of common interface and on network protocol.

13.3.2.1.3. Network Based on Topology (Geometric Design)

In the context of network communication, topology means in what way last two nodes are connected to each other forming some geometric form or design of network. Topology in other words describes how communication links and switching elements to form a geographic figure. Topology here is used to show the direction of communication path within the network nodes. Considering different communication paths we get different geometric figures or topologies, which give the particular topology name to the network. There are various topologies considered in naming the network where points, nodes and network control points are taken into account.

13.3.2.1.3.1. SIMPLE TOPOLOGY

A simple topology as shown below indicates the communication path

Normally network node is indicated by the symbol ○ or □ whereas ○ symbol is for indicating one node whereas □ symbol indicates a node which performs controlling task also.

Any particular topology figure of network depends on how controlling in network is done, whether it is done from single node or from central node or from outside or by all the participating nodes.

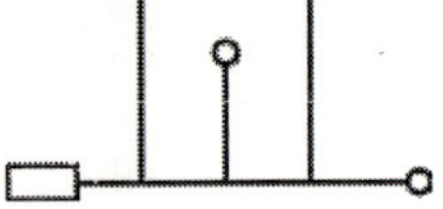

The above topology figure shows how the nodes are connected with each other in a network. Now let us try to understand the various topological figures, as :

13.3.2.1.3.2. STAR TOPOLOGY

In this type, network topology indicates that the network is controlled from the central node. See the Fig. 13.1 which looks like a star hence the name, star topology.

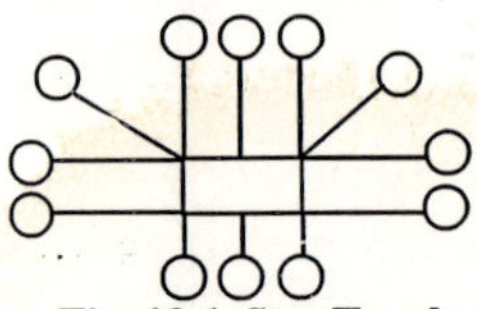

Fig. 13.1. Star Topology

The communication flow to all nodes is controlled from the central node. The problem in this topology is if the central node stops functioning the entire network goes into trouble.

13.3.2.1.3.3. RING TOPOLOGY

In this topology all the nodes are linked to form a ring like structure, hence the name ring topology. In a ring topology network, the communication flows in one direction and each node participates is controlling the network. In this topology, the disadvantage is that if one of the nodes in the network stops functioning, the entire network stops functioning (Fig. 13.2).

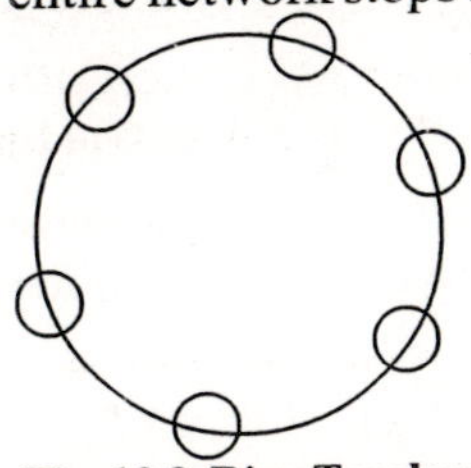

Fig. 13.2. Ring Topology

13.3.2.1.3.4. DISTRIBUTED BUS TOPOLOGY

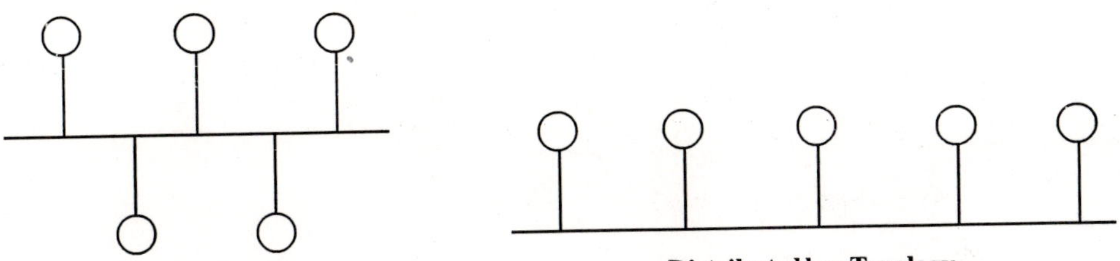

Simple Bus Topology **Distributed bus Topology**

Fig. 13.3. Distributed Bus Topology

The specialty of this topology is that it is an open ended network which provides scope to expand the network. Since it contains multi access links making communication between two nodes possible through nearest available path and it is from both sides. In this topology, however, needs powerful communication technology (Fig. 13.3).

13.3.2.1.3.5. LOOP TOPOLOGY

In this case, ring topology and star topology combines to form a loop topology. Since it looks like a loop hence the name loop topology. Its figure is shown as below (Fig. 13.4).

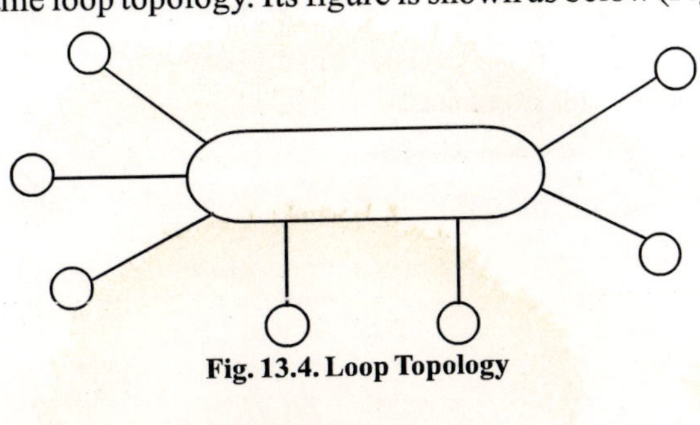

Fig. 13.4. Loop Topology

13.3.2.1.3.6. TREE TOPOLOGY

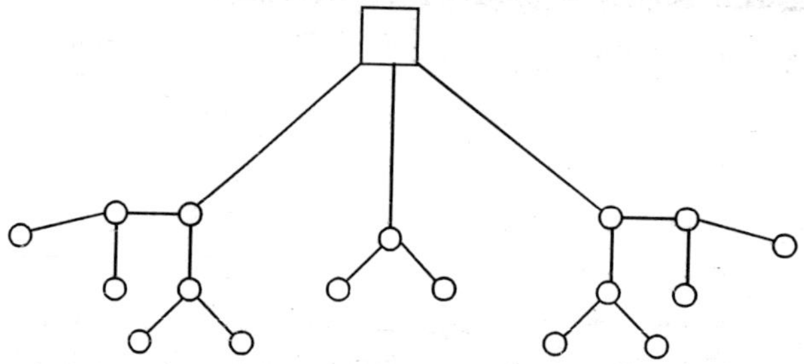

Fig. 13.5. Tree Topology

This topology looks like an inverted tree hence named as tree topology. In this topology special type of distributed bus system is used for communication. In this case where there is more communication between two nodes they are technologically brought closer to each other. In such topology, expansion of network is difficult (Fig. 13.5).

13.3.2.1.3.7. HYBRID TOPOLOGY

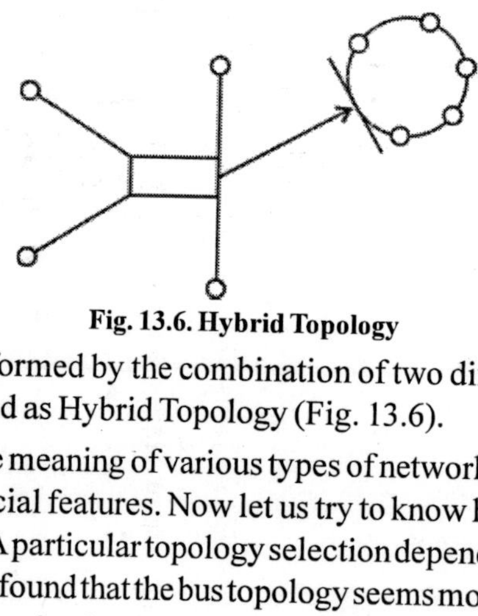

Fig. 13.6. Hybrid Topology

Since this topology is formed by the combination of two different topologies like bus and ring topology hence it is named as Hybrid Topology (Fig. 13.6).

We have understood the meaning of various types of network topologies in terms of figures as well as in terms of their special features. Now let us try to know how a particular topology for a network is selected and fixed. A particular topology selection depends on dependability, expansion capacity and performance. It is found that the bus topology seems more flexible than others in which information collection/ communication is done with different speeds and it has the capability of handling more number of nodal devices. The ring topology provides maximum productivity, faster linking so combination of two different topologies is certainly advantageous. In star type of topology it involves minimum synthesis. Topology also depends on communication flow direction and in such case topology could be classified as:

1. Topology not having particular direction
2. Topology having definite direction
3. Network with combination of two different communication and flow directions.

13.3.2.2. Network Based on Geographical Area

As far as geographic area or scope is concerned, there are two broad categories of network such as:

- LAN = Local Area Networks
- WAN = Wide Area Networks
- MAN = Metropolitan Area Network

In LAN type, network works in limited geographic area. For an institute data communication with computerised network, it is the most suitable one. In such network with all computers are interconnected with cable network. Transfer of information happens promptly and speedily, where client machines, data servers, sensors, light pens, printers etc. form the peripheral.

LANs are also effective in a city or at company campus. It can also be used in multi-storied office or university campus which could be effective up to 10 kilometers. In all the above scenarios LAN type of network can efficiently work.

A company for its divisions or for its sister companies can think of establishing LAN network. Since LAN covers limited geographic distance and communication distances are lesser, data communication takes place faster and mistakes and data losses are as minimum as possible. Another advantage with LAN is computers can share the computing capacity of central machine. As central processor is used jointly other accessories like printer and scanners can also be used collaboratively since the data is processed centrally, many users through their machine can very well share it. In case of a library, a central Online Public Access Catalogue(OPAC) can be used by all other institutes participating in the network.

At university place online catalogue of main library can be used by all the department libraries in searching their respective materials. In public library network, the central library remain at the top level and branch libraries are connected to it. In case if branch libraries are located at long distance then the network can opt for star topology. LAN can facilitate the following things:

- Efficient central control
- Multi way communication system
- Can accommodate interdisciplinary component.
- It can use total communicating capacity.

Wide Area Network (WAN) : Wide Area Network (WAN) is used when the network is spread in wider geographic area. It can cover a region, nation or can spread even at international levels. Such network would naturally need higher level of hardware and software plus the competent and powerful communication link. Its establishment, management and maintenance need higher level of organising skills. It could adopt appropriate topology like tree or hybrid form.

13.3.2.3. Network Based on Mode of Transmission

Based on the type of communication or mode of transmission category of network we find examples like cable television, videotex, teletext, e-mail, telex / fax and teleconferencing. Now let us know them in details.

1. Cable Television : Normally combination of television technology and broadband television network comes into existence. Television broadcast entertainment programs as well as educational or social information. It is available in various channels or stations. Nowadays television broadcast in digital form and DTH (Direct to Home) mode is available via satellite.

2. Videotex : Videotex (or Interactive Videotex) was one of the earliest implementation of an end user information system. From the end of 70s to early 2010s, it was used to deliver information (usually pages of text) to an user in computer like format, typically displayed on a television or a dumb terminal. Videotex is defined as an electronic information transmission and retrieved technology enabling interactive communication.

3. Teletext : In teletext the broadcast can be seen on sets like television which was used in U. K. in 1970s. It was one way or non interactive system of transmission of text and graphics via broadcasting or cable for display on television sets. It comes frame by frame and viewer can choose the interested frames out of whole and read.

4. e-mail : We use e - mail communication facility with the help of computer modem and telephone broadband connectivity. It is a bi-product of internet technology. One needs to have internet license and registration with a mail box of choice.

5. Telex : Telex facility is available with telephone connection with telex type writer. Earlier it was used for communicating short messages like telegrams.

6. Tele-facsimile Transmission : It is called facsimile or tele-facsimile transmission or in short known as fax. In this system of transmission a photocopy of document is transmitted over telephone network. It is very useful for sending copy of a document to any remote place. This technology is used for electronic document delivery services among the libraries.

7. Electronic Journals : Through electronic communication systems soft copy of journal i. e. e - journal issues are made available to the subscribers. The e - journal can be accessed and browsed on the computer screens. In this way one can get issues of e - journals the moment they are published.

8. Video conferencing : With the combination of electronic communication system and video technology one can establish contact via video conferencing with any one located at geographically far distance. In addition to voice, one can also see live face to face, while talking. This facility is used for conference talks by many people at the same time even if they are geographically located at different locations. Now a days people use systems like Skype or face time for conference calling.

13.4. INFORMATION NETWORKS

We have so far taken a review of network from its concept to their various types and categories. We have also seen technical background of network and networks based on different transmission modes. We are now going to know about information networks. Knowing value of information and importance of information transmission, information networks came into existence. The origin of information networks is traced in library's catalogue or index where only bibliographic information of library literature was gathered and displayed on network with a view to help readers in searching library material and at the same time to have bibliographic control on the collection housed in the library. In post Gutenberg's printing invention many literary forms other than book were evolved like scholarly journals and reference books. In order to help readers of scholarly journals literature a secondary information form came into existence which was the indexing journals which contained bibliographic information plus the abstract. Until soft copies of journal or e - journals started publishing indexing journals were dominated in libraries. However, subsequently as e - journals started publishing indexing and abstracting journals also started in electronic form. Initially, they correspond journal to journal but subsequently subject wise databases started dominating in commercial publishing so we have seen how the bibliographic information concept originated or emerged in library, which is now evolved outside libraries in the form of commercial information sources and data bases networks. As far as information networks are concerned we see different types such as:

1. Information Network:
   (a) Bibliographic information networks
   (b) Full text information network
2. Library Networks

Now let us try to know more about them.

13.4.1. Bibliographic Information Network : Developmental Aspect

As libraries started making bibliographic catalogues, commercial publishers also started creating databases of bibliographic information on a large scale. Databases came into existence in order to sell them in a comprehensive way, so the need of forming their network was also felt.

Bibliographic databases in machine readable form started emerging which could be read in and outside libraries. There was a sort of competition in making machine readable bibliographies at libraries and at information centers, commercial publishers, research institutes. The bibliographies data bases thus formed were available on networks.

The process of bibliographic information network generation was nearly same everywhere, however, it had a different context. The information was publishing in a spontaneous manner. The information generated in various fields and in various languages was huge. It was therefore a problem of how to bring bibliographic control on the published information up to a minute or on narrow subject field. With this purpose in mind information networks were formed. The main purpose was to gather and consolidate bibliographic information on network on different subjects and publish and make them available to everyone who is in need through a computer. The emphasis in the process was on collecting, storing, processing and making it available to everyone. Users of such information were people at local, regional as well as at international levels.

However, subsequently the entire process of generation of bibliographic information, forming network and making it available worldwide was grabbed largely by the commercial publishers, leaving basic purpose of information to all somehow side tracked. The exception to this was generating bibliographic databases at international level on a few areas like unclear, agricultural and environmental fields etc.

Collecting information or creating database was done in two ways such as :

- Full text information source
- Bibliographic information source with abstracts

For some time these sources were available online as well as offline (i. e. in CD format) however, since CD form is almost vanishing leaving its availability only in online form.

13.4.1.1. Development of International Databases

In the course of development of information sources, many international information systems in various fields were established. This resulted in creation of databases based on research projects in a number of fields like agriculture, nuclear science, environmental science, developmental studies, road construction, mechanical eng. standards, food technology, oceanography, information science and technology. In order to develop data bases at international level, many organisations were established in various fields. As international database organisations were formed corresponding institutes at national levels in developed and developing countries also emerged. This facilitated exchange of bibliographic data bases based on research output from international organisations to national institutes and vice a versa. Govt. of India permitted local institutes to form a part of international exchange for those who are engaged in undertaking comprehensive research in different fields. This has really benefited in making comprehensive information systems in various fields at national and international levels and it further helped in saving time of the researcher to a great extend. Now let us see the list of international information systems and their corresponding centers at national levels :

International Information systems

1. AGRIS : International System for Agricultural Science and Technology www. agris. fao. org
2. ASTINFO : Regional Network for the Exchange of Information and Experience in Science and Technology in Asia and Asia Pacific
3. BIOSIS : Bioscience Information Service
4. INIS : International Nuclear Information Systems International Atomic Energy (http://www.iaea.org)
5. MEDLINE : Medical Literature Analysis and Retrieval System Online or MEDLARS online. Bibliographic Database of life sciences and biomedical information - U.S. National Library of Medicine.
6. IOC: International Oceanographic Data and Information Exchange (www.iode.org)

Above are the major international information systems. However there are examples of international database creation systems in the following fields also:

- Medicine or Health
- Demography
- Transfer of Technology

- Rural Development
- Social Science Information System

As the above information systems developed the responsibility of data collection in the respective fields, it was given to the concerned libraries which were associated with the organizations working in those respective fields. In support of database collection centers at international level corresponding data exchange centers were also developed in different nations. There were centers affiliated to international information systems in India also. Now let us try to know about them.

13.4.1.1.1. INIS Center in India

India is the first country to use international nuclear information systems and its input center is at BARC Trombay. INIS came into existence in 1970 at Vienna. INIS provides comprehensive information service in nuclear science in the form of Atom Index. INIS used to provide database in magnetic tapes to BARC's Library & Information Division where it was decoded and stored. BARC in response used to provide data on nuclear research undertaken in India to INIS. The libraries used to carry out the following documentation on the information as :

1. Follow up the literature produced on nuclear research and obtain the same
2. Prepare, publish bibliography of research outputs with abstract
3. Share the information handling skills from international centers and provide data received from them for the benefits of Indian scientists. The system has dual benefits of getting information about research conducted at international level and promotes progress done by Indian scientists at International level. Presently such data exchange takes place online / electronically, which saves the time in exchanging data and in providing international data instantaneously to our scientists.

13.4.1.1.2. AGRIS center in India

AGRIS is another information system working in the field of Agricultural Science and Technology. AGRIS was established under Food and Agriculture Organisation of the United Nations in 1970. Since 1975 it is publishing Agrindex in the form of computer tapes for the benefits of worldwide countries. It provides data on research undertaken at international level in the field of agriculture and related fields. Such as:

- Geographic Information System
- Plant science and preservation
- Forestry and Animal Husbandry
- Fishers
- Natural Resources
- Human food
- Pollution and Environment

The main objectives of AGRIS are:

1. Develop database of agriculture field at international level, by which creating awareness about food production, rural development and about updating research undertaken in the field among the world wide countries at the same time to promote the importance of research in agriculture in removing difficulties and in becoming self reliance in food production by providing information at global level.
2. To provide information services like current awareness and selective dissemination of information services to the scientists and researchers working worldwide.
3. To increase the performance in information system and at the same time work to avoid the duplication of research efforts at national and international level and save their time.

AGRIS is more relevant to India because 70% of our population lives in rural India and agriculture is our prime business. AGIRIS information system can help us in becoming self reliance in food production and to promote export of excess food production to other countries and earn foreign exchange. Efforts are on to recognise agriculture as an industry. AGRIS information services are useful to promote fruitful research in agriculture science and technology, promote increase in food production, to modernise agriculture techniques and in replacing old and outdated agricultural systems with new modern agro-tech techniques, which can help us in preventing and grabbing of our patentable research by the scientists in foreign countries, there by claiming and getting intellectual property rights to our farmers and scientists. With these objectives in mind Agriculture Research Information Centre (ARIC) was given responsibility of exchanging information at international level and making arrangement to get information services to our researchers and farmers, engineers, which would help in recognising their research output at international level. ARIC works with the following objectives

1. To provide CAS and SDI information service to our scientists by documenting international data locally.
2. To prepare and publish bibliography of research undertaken by agricultural scientists in India and providing data to international organisation and help in giving international status to our research. ICAR has published bibliography know as, "Indian National Agriculture Bibliography" since 1975 to 1984 out of their interaction with AGRIS

13.4.1.1.3. Other International Information Networks

ASTINFO : ASTINFO is a regional network for the exchange of information and experience in Asia and Pacific. It was established under UNESCO. The objectives of ASTINFO were to keep bibliographic control over experimental research in the area, creating bibliographic databases on subject which are important to region specific. ASTINFO was also responsible for sharing local research data to the respective international database system. NISSAT-National Information System in Science and Technology under DSIR provided necessary support to it.

ISDS (UNISIST) : UNISIST formed under United Nations Organisation established an information system named International Serial Data System (ISDS). The objective of the system was to assign unique code to world wide published periodicals known as ISSN. This number will represent the bibliographic data of that specific periodicals & it would help in exchanging bibliographic information/data at international level correspondingly under ISDN. The task of assigning ISSN to periodicals published in India was fixed with INSDOC New Delhi (NowNISCAIR)

OBIS (Ocean Biogeographic Information System) : Inter Governmental Oceanographic Commission established an information system named International Oceanographic Data Exchange. The purpose was to develop bibliographic data-base on oceanographic means ocean science. In India, the task of data base coordination was given to NIO - National Institute of Oceanography in Goa.

13.4.1.2. Information Service Networks in India

In India, to promote communication and to provide information services a few networks have been planned. However, only few of them have become operational up till now. Let us try to know about them:

NICNET : It was thought that computer networks through collaboration of hardware, software and human resources, it could be possible to provide information services in terms of network. With this possibility in mind Department of Electronics and Department of Telecommunication jointly decided to establish a network called NICNET. The purpose of this network was to facilitate in sharing government information with people at large. National Information Centre became the host of this network. It was planned that in this network all the government departments would be connected to each other, which would help government to take timely decisions. First of all the ministries and department would be inter-connected with the help of a computer at Ahmedabad. All the state capitals would be connected and brought in network via satellite. It is thought that with effective communication between central government and state government, developmental works would be promptly completed. NICNET presently provides information services to all states and to public through mass media channels.

INDONET : It has been decided that CMC System Maintenance Corporation would plan and establish INDONET. The objective of the network is to interconnect all and computer networks existing in metros. This is a private network and it would be used for commercial purpose.

VIKRAM : This would be a public network. It would be established and controlled by department of telecommunication. It is expected that it would attain status in terms of technology. Right from the common man to business like banks, railways, airways would make use of it.

Indian Railway Reservation Network : Reserved travel by Indian Railway is facilitated by Passenger Reservation System (PRS). Presently PRS provides reservation service to 1.5 to 2.2 million passengers per day on over 2500 trains running throughout the country. The PRS Application CONCERT (Country Wide Network of Computerised Enhanced Reservation and Tracking) is the world's largest online reservation application developed by CRIS (Centre for Railway information Systems). The system currently operates from 5 data centers. The server clusters are connected together by a core network that enables universal terminals across the country through which the people can reserve berths on any train between any pair of station for any date and class. On the above lines, several networks have been planned. Some of them are in pipeline. It would be difficult to say when they would be operational. There are some field specific networks like :

ERNET **:** Educational and Research computer network (DOT) mainly used as e - mail network.

Banknet **:** Most of the bank have core banking systems where all branches are networked to provide any where banking. Most of ATM machine facilitate inter banking withdrawal service. However inter banking network is yet to be seen.

ONGC **:** Network of all ONGC offices

SAILNET **:** Steel Authority of India have networked their offices

LIC **:** LIC works with networking of all their branches. Air India and Indian Airlines Network

13.4.1.3. Integrated Services Digital Network

Integrated Services for Digital Network (ISDN) is a set of communication standard for simultaneous digital transmission voice, video and other network services over the traditional circuit of the public switched telephone network. It first came into existence in 1988 in the CCITT red book. The key features of ISDN is that it integrates speech and data on the same lines, which were not available in old telephone system, ISDN defines several kinds of access interface such as Basic Rate Interface (BRI), Primary Rate Interface, Narrowband ISDN (N - ISDN) and Broadband ISDN (B - ISDN)

ISDN is a circuit switched telephone network system, which at the same time provides access to packet switch networks designed to allow digital transmission of voice and data over ordinary telephone copper wires which results in better potential, better voice quality than an analogue phone is provided. It offers circuit switched connections for either voice or data where as packet switched connection (of data) in increments of 64 Kbps which can be increased up to 128 kbps or more, making internet accessibility faster. ISDN is said to be an intelligent system and with the help of ISDN network tasks of management, repairs and services are becoming easy. ISDN provides communication of several things like :

1. Videotext
2. Electronic Mail
3. Fax
4. Teletex
5. Money transactions
6. Networking Databases
7. Transfer of image and graphics
8. Storing data & information
9. Security purpose communication

10. Audio & video conferencing

13.5. LIBRARY NETWORKS

Before we look into the library networks development, its activities and the objectives, it would be worthwhile to know the concept, definition and need.

13.5.1. Library Network – Concept

Library's main objective is to organise information carriers i. e. collection, assist users in getting required information. With these objective libraries' participation in development of networking is always found useful. Computer and telecommunication technologies and their progresses have opened many opportunities for libraries. This made it possible to computerise their routine functions and innovate their information services to readers. In library science point of view, concern of network considers from inter library cooperation to form computerised library network. The broad objectives of library network are as:

1. To cooperate interlibrary sharing of technical services such as shared cataloguing.
2. To give general and specific service and control them from one point.
3. Establish connections with librarian of each library

Library networks are prompted on the background of budget crunch with diversity in currency conversion rates of developed and developing countries, inflation, and devaluation of currencies. At the same times increase in prices and subscriptions rates of periodicals. These situations are compelling libraries to go for library co-operation. Library co-operation makes it possible only after libraries are computerised and automated.

Converting computerised libraries into network was the next step. In establishing library and information networks the following objectives are considered :

1. Collaboration of collection, information and human resources
2. Cooperation in inter library exchange in centralised acquisition and bring bibliographic control and also actual lending and borrowing of literature and exchanging catalogues of library collections.

Need of library network and the objectives of information network through libraries can be listed as under :

Equal opportunity to all to get information : Library network facilitate creation of comprehensive and wider information sources which gives equal opportunity to all to get the information.

Interdependency : No library can be self sufficient as it cannot house all the published literature on any one subject in it and there is no alternative to any library but to depend on others. With this, it may happen that the ownership of information may not remain with any one library as it needs to share the ownership to other collaborative libraries.

Widening Horizons of Information sources : As network facilitates consolidation of library resources it helps in widening horizons of information resources for one library.

Improve quality and standardization of library services : Establishing network naturally helps in improving quality of bibliographic data and also in bringing standardization in them. This helps exchange of information tools among the libraries effectively.

Loosing ownership : Networking process obviates in losing ownership of library's own collection.

Collective Decision process : With mutual consultancy it becomes easy to take decisions which would be beneficial for every single library. It becomes possible to expand information services scope further by which all libraries can avail the benefits.

Integration and coordination : Networking makes it feasible to integrate efforts, collection, funds, and human resources and infra structure which provides benefits to all.

Centralized control : Network is normally controlled by a central headquarter which ensures centralization of collection and bibliographic control.

Increase in value and productivity : In networking process expenditure of exchange of information and collection becomes affordable, which leads in increasing productivity.

Research : In networking environment data becomes available in many ways and also in online way. This gives many new opportunities for research.

Multination status : Network allows sharing of data and resources even at international level and libraries could get a chance to obtain data from international level. Now let us look into the various definitions of library network.

13.5.1.1. Library Networks : Definitions

National Commission on Libraries and Information Science (NCLIS) has defined the library network as : "Two or more libraries coming together with the objective of information sharing, exchange and connecting them by telecommunication media is called library network. " Having this concept in mind, libraries are bound together with the same format arrangement so that the available collection and services would be available to all the potential users of network. Although the functioning of one library has limited scope but in networking environment providing services and treatment to outside readers at par with own users would be binding on all libraries. Computers and communication infrastructure would also be shared by all participating libraries, which help in widening the scope of library services otherwise not available to any library before it becomes part of network".

The above definition and discussion on the theme so far suggest the following points to consider for any library network.

1. Library computerisation must be completed and library has adequate computer technology and communication infrastructure which would facilitate provision of needed networking infrastructure of technology.
2. Libraries intend to participate in network should have signed joint declaration or network rules and regulations under MOU.

3. Libraries would not differentiate between own user and other network library users and they would provide library services equal and uniform to all network library users without any discrimination.

Reynard Coe Swank defined library network as:

"Library network is a concept that includes the development of cooperative system of libraries on geographical, subject and other lines, each with some kind of centre that not only coordinates the internal activities of the system but also serve as the systems outlets to and inlet from the centre of other systems".

Alphonse F. Trezza define it as : Library network is a formal organisation among libraries for cooperation and sharing of resources in which the group as a whole is organised into subgroups with the exception that most of the needs of library will be satisfied with in the subgroup of which it is a member.

With the above definition we get more classification about library networking concept that - Libraries participate in network on geographic ground.[1]

On similar working field or on other reasons they would extend cooperation among libraries. A library at the centre of network would control the network in addition libraries would also extend communication and computer infrastructure.

Main components of library network

1. Information resources or collections and exchanging of tools and technology. Mainly it involves bibliographic databases, physical collection of all types of reading materials, information services and human resources involved in providing services.
2. Networking Technology - Public and private communication networks, network softwares etc.
3. Network users - Libraries and all library users.

13.5.2. Library Networks: Background

In the introduction we have understood that the library networks did not come into existence immediately. There was no alternative left for libraries but to establish cooperative understanding in the situation when the information was pouring in with tremendous quantity and when it was impossible to collect all published material on all subject in any one library, prices of books especially subscription amounts of journals has gone beyond affordability of libraries, at one side there is divide on currency conversion rates in developed and developing countries where as on other side library budgets are shrinking. All these developments encourage co - operation among the libraries, promoting library cooperation and with the objectives to help readers at various backgrounds library groups started forming networks . All the libraries working in the similar field came together and joined as local library network. It was felt that simply having co-operation understanding among the libraries was not enough and libraries to come forward to accept network

1. Library and information science (blog) http://dhyrachmaa.word press.com

bindings. This resulted in first forming library cooperatives or the library consortia, the memorandum of understanding (MOU) to that effect were framed to give it a format shape and with the signing by all participating officials library cooperative first came into existence. Converting these cooperatives or consortia into library network was the next step. Progress of computer and communication technology and with their inter cooperation innovative project of joining libraries into network started coming into reality.

At international level with the help of computer technology attempts of bringing libraries together and form their network have been taken quite early. The first such attempt was taken when California, Harvard and Yale university came together to form a network named COHAYA, but it was not so successful. However, immediately after that OHIO college library centre or in short OCLC (Now Online Computer Library Centre) network was successfully established. The main objective was to create library catalogue through library cooperation the concept was popularised by name shared cataloguing. This helped in hosting centralised or union catalogue automatically. In short the concept was like, if any participant purchase a new book then for creating its catalogue entry it would search in union catalogue whether any other library has generated the catalogue entry for the book, if so library would download the entry into its catalogue data without freshly creating it again. This was found time, effort and stationary saving for participating library.

13.5.2.1. History of Library Network Developments in India

During the last 40-50 years there have been progressive developments of establishing library networks in India. The mile stones of the developments could be listed as :

1. India's First Prime Minister Pandit Jawaharlal Nehru envisaged that results of scientific research should reach to grass root of society which led to accept science policy resolution in 1958.
2. To follow up this policy, several educations commissions were appointed.

   These committees gave their recommendation in support of the idea.

   (a) Sinha committee Report

   (b) Dr. Ranganathan committee presented it report to UGC

   (c) Dr. Peter Lazer report

   (d) Dr. M. V. Kamat committee report 1972

   It is seen that the actual work towards planning library network started some time in 1980. It was emphasised to collect information and provide it to the researchers.
3. In 1983 technology policy commission working group was established under chairmanship of Dr Sheshadri and recommendations were submitted to the then government.
4. In 7th five years plan had thought of automating libraries services and extend the benefits of information technology in inter connecting libraries.
5. Then onward three important events took place such as:

   (i) National Policy on Education was announced in which guidelines were suggested to improve all the libraries in the country and their services.

(ii) A committee under the chairmanship of Prof. Chottopadhyay 1988 was asked to prepare feasibility in this direction in National policy on library and information systems in India.

(iii) In 1986 NISSAT (National Information System in Science And Technology) summoned a meeting under the chairmanship of Head, CSIR laboratories in Kolkata. The committee considered the recommendations of Dr. M. U. Kamat and exploration plan of establishing network of science and technology libraries in Kolkata was approved. It was also decided to give the task of network formation to CMC (Computer Maintenance Corporation). CMC submitted it feasibility report in 1989 to NISSAT and Calcutta Library Network (CALIBNET) name was suggested to the network.

6. In 1988 India International Centre (IIC), committee was organised to decide establishment of Delhi Library Network (DELNET). The committee was asked to submit a network feasibility report. NISSAT had agreed to provide necessary support and assistance in forming the DELNET.

13.5.3. Need and Objectives of Library Network

What is the need of library network? is the natural question which comes to any body's mind. There are several advantages of library network. It has been already proved that libraries avail the benefits of networks and extend them to their users. The benefits of library networking and its objectives are listed as below.

1. Without much efforts one can get referral information about the availability of book among network libraries.
2. One can very well ascertain about which library contains books on which subject.
3. Network facilitates speedy lending and borrowing of books among the libraries.
4. Comparatively smaller libraries can get access to collections of large libraries
5. Networking encourages to bring improvements in library functioning and its services.
6. Since the required books are found in some of the networked library, it avoids unnecessary duplicate purchase of books which results in saving of funds
7. Library gets confidence and support in following copy right restrictions
8. It is possible to prepare subject bibliographies out of total books available in all networked libraries.
9. It promotes effective exchange of information at local or regional level.
10. With the availability of latest and up to date information it helps in social and economic progress of the region.

The great advantage in forming library network is the interlibrary lending and borrowing of books. In order to make this facility easier and faster network libraries should pay attention to the following things :

1. To prepare union catalogue of collections of all libraries
2. Libraries should be equipped with facilities like e - mail, fax, telex and photocopying facility
3. Lending and borrowing of books on interlibrary should be allowed free of cost.
4. To keep network functioning away from red tapism , which brings hurdles in the flow of information
5. Network to establish a reliable courier or pilot services.

13.5.4. Library networks Types

Considering network size and geographical area it covers, there are different types of network such as:

LAN : Local area Network Examples: CALIBNET, DELNET

WAN : Wide Area Network Example: INFLIBNET

MAN : Metropolitan Area Network Limited to a metropolis BONET, MALIBNET and AADINET etc

We have DELNET, CALIBNET and INFLIBNET which are somewhat settled and functioning to a considerable extent. There are other networks which are in the process of establishment which are yet to take off or yet to be fully operational such as: MALIBNET (Chennai), AADINET (Ahmadabad), PUNENET (Pune), BONET (Mumbai). Mysore library network (MYLIBNET), West Bengal Public Library Network (WEBPUBLIBNET). Now let us try to know about the existing library networks in India.

13.5.4.1. Local Library Networks

13.5.4.1.1. DELNET (Developing Library Network)

The major Digital Library Resources in south Asia. Web Address: www.delnet.nic.in

About

DELNET was started in January 1988 at India International Centre Library, New Delhi, which was registered as a society in 1992. Initially it got the support from NISSAT, DSIR , Govt. of India. Subsequently it had support from National Information Centre(NIC). DELNET was established with the main objective of promoting resource sharing among the libraries through the development of network of libraries. DELNET aims to collect, store and dissemination of information along with computerised information services to users through coordinating network collection development and to help libraries to reduce unnecessary duplication in buying materials. DELNET has compiled various union catalogues available with network libraries such as union catalogue of books, union list of periodicals, and union catalogue of CD-ROM resources. Databases of Indian specialists, list of video recordings, Urdu manuscripts, database of Theses and Dissertations. All the DELNET Databases are residing on DELSIS (an in-house LMS developed by BASIS Plus an RDBMS the product of Information Dimensions-Inc.)

DELNET since in operation has promoted resource sharing which has been proved most effective. It has also contributed towards modernisation of network of participating libraries in India. It is controlled by a Governing Body.

Objectives

1. To promote resource sharing among the network libraries
2. To undertake scientific research in the field of information science.
3. To provide technology guidelines to member libraries regarding collection, storing, sharing of information and documents.
4. To coordinate collection development among member libraries with a view to reduce unnecessary duplications.
5. To establish referral centers and to maintain central union catalogue of books, non book materials, periodical and CD resources and keep then up to date
6. To facilitate interlibrary lending and borrowing manually as well as mechanically / electronically
7. To generate specialized bibliographies of books, serials and non book not - print materials
8. To prepare bibliographic list of specialists and projects for member institutions.
9. To equip and maintain facility electronic document delivery system.
10. To coordinate and act as liaison with regional, national and international network of major libraries for exchange of information and documents.

Membership

One need not be in Delhi to get DELNET Membership. Any institution or library in India and from SAARC Countries can apply for membership.

As in 2016 April, DELNET has 5488 members out of which 260 are libraries from Delhi 5203 libraries out of Delhi from different states and from 25 overseas countries

Membership fees

For India of SARRC Counties

- Admission Fee - Rs 5,000/-
- Annual Fees and Renewal Membership - Rs 11,500/-

13.5.4.1.2. CALIBNET

It was first planned and started by NISSAT in 1986. NISSAT Supported CALIBNET, NISSAT also supported to develop MAITRAYEE LMS for CALIBNET based on INGRESS 5. 2 which was developed by CMC Ltd.

Objectives

1. To facilitate remote online access to the holding data of Calcutta Libraries to help resource sharing among the member libraries in Kolkata.
2. To provide electronic access to globally available information.

Present status

Efforts are on to develop databases and to activate services of CALIBNET.

13.5.4.2. Regional Library Networks

13.5.4.2.1. INFLIBNET

INFLIBNET or Information and Library Network Centre is an Autonomous Inter University Centre (IUC) of University Grants Commission was established with broad objective of creating infrastructure for sharing of library and information resources and services among Academic and Research Institutions. The project was established as project of IUC in 1991 and UGC formally established INFLIBNET in 1996. The major activity and services of the centre include automation of academic libraries, promote resource sharing among academic libraries, facilitate information access and transfer, support scholarship learning and academic pursuits. The centre acts as nodal agency for networking of libraries and information centers in universities of higher learning and R & D Institutions in India with an aim to promote scholarly communication.

UGC has taken up this major initiative for the benefit of academic community in universities under the purview. The initiative is known as UGC Infonet Digital Library Consortium which intends to provide access to selected scholarly journals in electronic form and to databases in different discipline. INFLIBNET is responsible for executions and monitoring of this initiative. It also extends access to e - resources to all govt aided colleges under a project named "National Library and information infrastructure" for scholarly content (N - List) funded by MHRD under the national mission of education through ICT.

INFLIBNET has taken up a number of new initiatives for the benefit of academic community which includes:

(i) Shodhganga - a repository of Indian theses and dissertations

(ii) Shodhgangotri - another repository of synopsis submitted to universities for registration under PhD Programmes.

(iii) Ojas @ inflibnet - an open access journal publishing platform

(vi) Shibboleth - based access management system

(v) Open source software R & D

(vi) Info portal - A comprehensive gate way to all Indian electronic scholarly content

(vii) E - PG pathshala

(viii) E - content for PG courses

(ix) Measuring Research output of Indian Universities

INFLIBNET : Aims and objectives : INFLIBNET Functions with aims and objectives as:

1. To establish and promote communication facilities, to improve capabilities information transfer and access which would provide support to scholarship, learning, research, academic pursuits through cooperation and involvement of concern agencies.

2. To establish information and library network, a computer communication network for connecting libraries and information centers in universities, deemed universities, colleges, institutions of national importance and R of D institutes etc. with a view to avoid duplication of efforts.
3. To facilitate academic communication amongst scientists, engineers, social scientists, academicians, faculty, researcher and students through electronic mail, file transfer, computer/ audio/ video conferencing
4. To undertake system design and studies in the field of communications, computer networking, information handling and data management.
5. To establish appropriate control and monitoring system for the communication network and organise maintenance.
6. To collaborate with institutions, libraries, information centers and other organisations in India and abroad in the field relevant to the objectives of the centre.
7. To promote R & D and develop necessary facilities to create technical positions for realizing the objectives of the centre.
8. To generate revenue by providing consultancies and information services.
9. To do all other such things as may be necessary, incidental or conducive to the attainment of all or any of the above mentioned objectives.

Development of library management system i. e. SOUL (Software for **University Libraries)** was the major contribution from INFLIBNET toward computerisation of libraries, university and college at large in India.

SOUL Version 2. 0 was released in 2009. As far as pricing of this software is concern the details are as below/.

- SOUL 2.0 Full Edition = Rs. 80,000.00 (First copy)
- Additional Copies = Rs. 50,000.00 of SOUL 2. 0 Full edition
- SOUL 2.0 limited edition Rs. 30,000.00 (For 50000 records)

There are additional charges for SOUL membership, training charges, on site instillation and for data conversion etc.

One can download demo version of SOUL 2.0 with installation guide from INFLIBNET Site: www.inflibnet.ac.in[1]

13.5.4.3. Library Network Services

Library Network renders various types of services depending on the purpose such as :

(a) Bibliographic Information Networks : This type includes generating bibliographies, keeping them up to date and database generating in this way are made available to libraries as the master data base which is used to create bibliographic database of the library. OCLC and western

1. Courtesy = INFLIBNET, Ahmadabad www.inflibnet.ac.in

library network are the examples of this type of network. In the past OCLC and some western library network are the examples of this type of network. In the past OCLC network was mainly like LOC are used for shared cataloguing.

(b) Resources sharing network : Generally any resource sharing network services depend on the following things :

- Type of library
- Subject field of library
- Type of collection
- Level of computerisation
- Usage

(c) Retrospective conversion networks : Based on international bibliographic cataloguing standard MARC, MARC - 2 and CCF and UNIMARC are some networks which provides assistance to libraries to carry out retrospective conversion of their catalogue database. OCLC is one of the important examples to quote.

13.5.4.4. International Library Networks

As compared to developing country like India concept of library networking at international level came into existence quite early and benefits of it has been availed by their libraries as well as their readers. We find good and ideal type of networks in UK and USA. When we think of library networks at international level, we certainly remember one network e. g. OCLC , which was established in 1967 in USA at OHIO, where college and university libraries of OHIO state were connected to each other to form college library centre. The prime objective of this network was to first computerise all the network libraries and share resources of each other. Fredrick G Kilgore became the first founder president of OCLC. The network which started only with OHIO state colleges and universities in 1977, it was also adopted by outside country libraries. In 1988 the name was changed to "Online Library Computer Centre". As on today there are over 50, 000 US libraries and 84000 libraries from other countries, which are member and are availing the benefits. The objectives OCLC which were set at the beginning are still continues today.

In those days when libraries were finding it difficult to catalogue newly purchased books, OCLC inspired them with the wonderful idea of shared cataloguing. Each new book purchased by any networked library and prepared its catalogue entry which was shared with all. As such it helped in avoiding duplication of cataloguing work. Now the situation is changed, everything has become online, no library prepares catalogue cards and now they share the catalogue record and adopt in their database. This was possible as OCLC adopted information technology as it was found appropriate in library management. Now it provides information services and consultancy to needy libraries of the world such as:

1. Online cataloguing and meta data creation : OCLC provides online cataloguing services to libraries in the network based on international standard and format like MARC. The libraries who avail the OCLC services need to pay annual fees.

2. Collection management : OCLC also provides collection development consultancy to library. It provides guideline on teller maid collection development plans as per objectives of library and the parent institutions wherever discrepancies of collection development of library are identified and solutions are suggested.

3. Digital Collection Development and Preservation : OCLC network provides consultancy to libraries on digitization of rare materials, developing digital collection, microfilming and preservation of library's valuable assets. In addition it also helps libraries on how to preserve old collection and offers training on this aspect to library staff.

4. E-Contents : Under OCLC's net library services it provide guidelines on how to provide e - journal contents to library users and developing online reference collection as a support to reference service, and also on downloading audio books and add them in library collection.

5. Reference service : One of the prominent reference services in OCLC services is the first search service under this with the support of OCLC library provides full text documents online. In collection of these services resources available at library of congress library has been made available.

6. Resource sharing : OCLC provides inter library lending and borrowing facilities to all OCLC member libraries. The system has been established to handle ILL requests to search the availability in other libraries and deliver the needed documents and obtain them back for lending library.

13.5.5. Management of library network

We have understood so far the concept and mechanism of library network. We have also considered parts of networks, needed technologies, and hardware required in establishing the library network. Once the network is established it needs to maintain its functioning to continue without any interruption. The responsibility of managing and maintaining network rests with its apex body. Management body keeps a watch on all the aspects of a network. The following things are generally considered :

1. To attend difficulties and problems of hardware and software of the network.
2. To attend complains of members
3. To provide adequate funding
4. To prepare budget and assess the expenditure
5. To maintain flow of services without any break
6. To take important policy decision
7. To Adhere to standardisation
8. To keep improvement process
9. To Increase quality in functioning and services of network
10. To maintain the security of information within the network.
11. Security of hardware and software equipments and security of data

12. Expansion of network
13. To implement network plans phase by phase.
14. To maintain liaison with other similar networks
15. To decide policy on exchange of information

The above related aspects are looked into in the management of any library network which makes network the function smoothly and beneficiary libraries and readers would continue to get the benefits from it.

13.5.5.1. Networks management : Need of human resources

In order to develop network and to keep it progressing, management need specialized human resources. There is also the need to have expertise and networking skills to provide necessary training to the people who are engaged in the task. Otherwise difficulties are faced in network functioning. If the participating libraries do not get expected services then member may lose faith in network creditability. In order to maintain consistency in network functioning the need of permanent technicians is always felt.

There is also the need to make adequate arrangement for manpower development for networking task. Only library computerisation or automation of libraries would not be sufficient. In fact for the individuals along with library automation it is also necessary to have advanced engineering training in establishing and managing network so that the management team can depend on such people.

13.5.5.2. Adopting Network Topology

We have gone through the different types of topologies used in network formation. A particular topology depends on :

1. Area of network coverage
2. How the participating institutes are located and whether network needs centralized or distributed approach
3. Need of communication flow
4. Quantum of networking tasks, quantum of demand and expectations from network
5. Need of expansion of network
6. Policy of information exchange.
7. Flexibility in coordinating with other similar network

It is interesting to see what types of topologies have been adopted by the existing library network in India which is given in Table 13.3 :

Name of Network	Topology / Network Architecture
1. DELNET	Star Topology 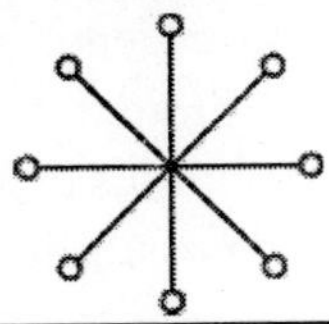
2. CALIBNET	Distributed Bus Topology 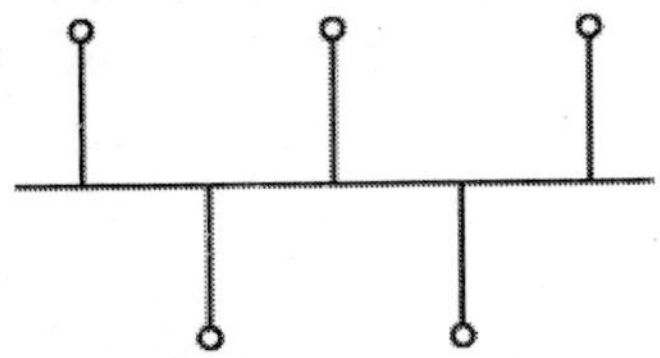
3. INFLIBNET	Hierarchies Type of Network Architecture or somewhat like tree Topology 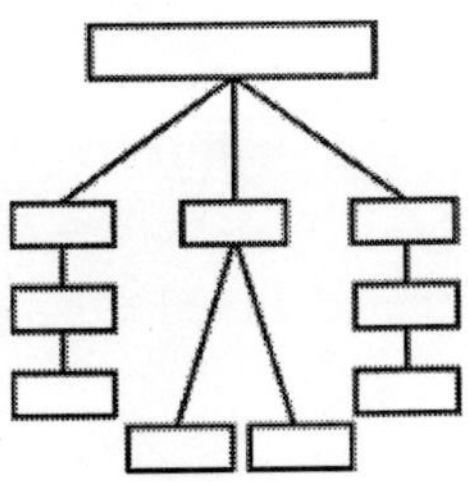

Table 13.3. Topology of Indian Library Networks

13.6. COLLECTIVE USE OF LIBRARY RESOURCES THROUGH LIBRARY NETWORKING

Use of collections and other reading material among the libraries through cooperative understanding is called resource sharing. Resource sharing helps libraries to provide effective and able services to their users. The reasons for Indian libraries going for resource sharing are as below:

1. Information explosion which has led to publish material with a great speed.
2. Devaluation of Indian currency and inflation
3. Increase in the cost of publications
4. Limited financial resources with libraries and budget crunch
5. Increase in the demand of readers
6. Developments and research in various fields, emergence of new field
7. Need of bibliographic control at national level and sharing it internationally

8. Developments and advances in computer and telecommunication technology resulting availability of newer IT tools for library management
9. Possibility of connecting libraries through computer networking

Due to shift in library functioning from custodian to readers centered services; due to addition of non book and non print materials in library collection, limitation and inability of making all the published materials in any one library have prompted libraries to think seriously in cooperative sharing of library resources. There are many ways and possibilities while going for sharing of resources among the libraries such as:

1. By making library services available to readers of other libraries.
2. Exploring to find out availability of information in nearby other library to obtain it on loan and making it available to library user.
3. Exchanging library materials among the group of libraries.

Success of inter library lending and borrowing depends on following things:

1. Preparedness of the library
2. Type of library
3. Level of readership in libraries
4. Responsibility of collective use of library materials
5. Availability of library networking and courier facilities.

When there is desperate need of any article or a few pages from a book either a photocopy of required material is sent or scanned copies are mailed. In order to make resource sharing feasible libraries need following tools as:

1. Union catalogue of books
2. Union catalogue of journals
3. Union catalogue of non book and non print materials.
4. Availability of e - mail
5. Referral information about availability of needed materials in the libraries.

13.6.1. Library Resource sharing :Activities to consider

In library resource sharing following function and services are considered

1. Acquisition and Technical Processing
2. Exchanges and sharing human resources
3. Database development and information services
4. Translation service
5. Developing special collection
6. Cooperative warehousing
7. Inter library lending and borrowing.

13.6.1.1. Resource Sharing in Acquisition and Cataloguing

In these days of information technology, library acquisition considers online ordering of books and other reading materials. In acquiring these materials generally emphasis is on acquiring materials in shortest possible time. Libraries also try to keep necessary budget provision and expenditure up to date for this.

In developed countries publishers and book distributors also participate in library networking, naturally it benefits to all in knowing newly published books. This helps libraries in selecting quality materials. The purchase process also could be carried out in cooperative manner such as collective buying and distributing. Centralized book purchasing promotes acquisition in a large scale, which helps in saving on efforts and money. It becomes very easy to know which books have been bought by which library. This referral kind of information is useful in inter library lending and borrowing. This process recommends instead of buying multiple numbers of copies of one book, libraries can buy number of books with minimum number of copies. This helps finally to readers in getting variety of materials. In subscribing journals also such centralized and cooperative buying process can be used very effectively. Due to limited funds increase in subscription rates due to inflation, number of journals subscribed in library is decreasing day by day. Solution to this problem is that if all the libraries come together select the journals in library group and pay the subscription together. This method is called consortium way of subscribing journals. Arrangement is made to generate union catalogue of journals subscribed by a group of libraries together then even if one library is not subscribing to a journal the journal would be available in another library of group which is easily accessible. This method is always advantages for publishers also as their business does not get affected. The advantages of subscribing journals in consortium way are as below :

Journal Subscription	Advantages
1. If consortium Subscribes a single journal	The journal would be minimum one copy of available online to each such consortium libraries
2. If libraries in consortium subscribe a journal in duplicate	The first library get online access free plus next multiple subscription consortium get 20% discount
3. If three or more libraries in a consortium subscribes a journal.	First library get online access and each library further subscribing get discount of 10%

Now in the process, consortium as a whole gets considerable discount which could be equally distributed to all in saving funds for all libraries participating in the consortium. If this process is to be implemented successfully then consortium need to have good facilities like inter library exchange of materials through digital document delivery system so also system of exchanging contents pages of journal issues. Then cooperative cataloguing and generating union catalogue for the consortium becomes easy which can provide referral kind of information on journals subscribed in the consortium.

13.6.1.2. Exchange of Human Resources

The human resources and expertise available in the network libraries can also be effectively shared by the entire network in which temporary exchange of people to share the best practices among library can also be explored. Experts available in network can be used in organising training programmes for the benefit of all libraries which would result in improving quality of library services as a whole.

13.6.1.3. Information Services & Database development

Libraries participating in the network can avail benefits because of availability collective information. They can very well generate union catalogue of books and journals and other non book materials , which helps in providing referral information about availability of library materials. They can also develop databases of books and other materials based on international stands and formats. They can adopt a common communication format for easy bibliographic data communication. Libraries can even exchange bibliographic data and databases with institutions held internationally. Libraries can also share the translation expertise available in network to carry out translation of foreign language materials.

13.6.1.4. Developing Specialized book collection

If one of the libraries of network happens to be special library in a particular field or subject then such library can be provided with external funding and support to strengthen the collection in that subject and further making it a sectoral center. Such a resourceful library can provide material to other libraries on the subject effectively.

13.6.1.5. Developing cooperative warehouse facility for network

Now a days many libraries face space problem while preserving physical printed materials. It becomes difficult to build additional space for the want of funds. As libraries grow, this problem becomes acute day by day which brings a lot of inconvenience to the reader. The solution to this is to develop central warehouse facility for the entire network. A library can weed out or discard unused or unnecessary material available on shelves to the central warehouse. If all libraries shift such material to warehouse, that can help in developing good collection in different fields. As the materials found unserviceable in one library could be useful to other library. Such warehouse could provide facility of lending materials and in providing library services to a limited extent.

13.6.1.6. Inter library lending & borrowing

Inter library lending among the libraries is done many ways:

1. Reader of one library goes with an authority letter to get a photo copy of journal article or of a part of book and other library responds to it positively.
2. Under inter library lending facility request letter is sent by post and the other library sends required book by post.
3. Library staff finds out availability of a required book or periodicals by referring union

catalogue of books journals and library sends a request letter for lending the same to the nearest library where the same is available.

4. Interlibrary loan request is sent by e-mail and the other library responds to it positively by doing the needful.
5. If the required document is available in digital form, then it is forwarded to needy library. The receiving library prints a copy and makes it available to the reader.
6. Some libraries have transport facility under resource sharing agreement to allow readers of one library to go to the other library for reference purpose. The same transport is used for exchanging books and journal volumes under ILL. Some libraries engage a pilot for exchanging reading materials among libraries.

In some group of library for generation, handling and distribution of inter library loan demands an online system is created, where in such requests are received in library where they are scrutinised. Online union catalogue is referred and ILL requests are sent to respective libraries where the material is found to be available and thus needed material is obtained.

Some library groups hire the courier service for ILL transactions. However, it needs framing and following some rules and regulations. It is a general experience that if library accepts any of above ILL arrangement it is bound to increase work load on circulation staff. Secondly it also depends how other (lending) library responds to ILL loan request. If they positively respond then it would be successful. Thirdly, providing material on ILL to other libraries may bring some inconvenience to readers of lending library as they do not get the material for their use as it is issued to other libraries.

Sometimes a group of libraries accept to charge fees for ILL exchanging material in order to compensate expenses required to fulfill the requirement of other library as the concern staff need to pay some allowance who actually handle ILL transactions and one example in this context is given of OCLC library network where receiving library need to pay 43 cents where as for the library which lends the materials is paid 20 cents as royalty. The figures given are of old time and are just given as an example.

13.6.1.7. Electronic Document Delivery System

Electronic document delivery system is emerging as one of the useful tools for interlibrary exchange of information documents. Until this facility was available, libraries used to send copies of articles through fax or they would scan the document and send it as PDF as an attachment with e - Mail. Since in these modes documents are instantly exchanged it was saving time and money. Nowadays quite a considerable part of collection is available with the libraries in a digital form either on website or in digital library. Using these sources document in digital form and unless there is copy right restriction issue, the materials could be exchanged among libraries in a digital form only, which again saves library's time and money. An examples of electronic document delivery systems is as follows

Ariadne : The next generation electronic document delivery system has been established as Tilburg University, Which resemble with the old or first generation system called ADONIS evolved in the past. The standards followed with Ariadne Electronic Document delivery is ISO - ILL 10161 : 1991 for ILL request GEDI Group on Electronic Document Delivery systems FTAM = 1501988b for file transfer mechanisms.

Document Delivery : (www. documentsdelivered. com) It retrieves copyright complaint documents from the global library network with access to 288 million publications. They deliver the journal articles, book chapters and conference proceedings.

13.7. NETWORK ARCHITECTURE

13.7.1. Introduction

In networking environment it becomes possible to exchange information in digital format or data from one computer to another. This facilitates handling the information in different ways and presents it in the format acceptable to the customers. We have seen in the present chapter that in computer network computers are connected through telecom medium. Networks consists of nodes i. e. computer work stations terminals which are available at different locations. Normally the communication takes place by using telephone (Private or public companies) connectivity. Actual flow of signals takes place through optical fiber or coaxial wires, switched systems, satellites and through digital microwave/radio mechanism. The network could be local (LAN) or regional (WAN)

Developments and progresses in telecommunication and computer fields, need of networking. With the availability of expertise in establishing them and considering affordability and advantages in using network, during last 2-3 decades many networks have been emerged at various levels.

Networks are planned, formed and put into operations for various purposes like information exchange, sharing of library resource and providing various services. Generally reasons for network growth are given as:

1. Need of resource sharing
2. Need of communication and distribution of information
3. Sharing the communication infrastructure

Leaving concept, philosophy and management at ground level the network infrastructure consists of computers, peripherals, communication infrastructure, wiring, hardware and software equipments. All these equipments are manufactured by various companies and manufacturers. It is really difficult to assemble various equipments of different makes and establish flow of communication in the network set up. This becomes feasible only because of the protocols by which all the involved machinery equipment hardware and software respond positively with each other. In terms of networking terminology it is called compatibility and broadly it is called network architecture. There are various types of networks architectures. We are now going to understand about them.

13.7.2. Network Architecture: Protocol

Communication system design within a network is called network architecture. Communication system in a network is designed in such a way that computers at all nodes would properly communicate with each other. Computer manufacturer generally provide options in main and sub systems so that it matches with the network design making communication flow smooth.

In software sense network architecture is a group of instructions and rules which controls connecting of computers and they respond with each other. These rules consist of information format, protocols and proper structure of them. They make feasible the necessary communication with data processing system of network. When the layers in the network architecture divide the tasks of networking, the system is called as layered architecture

13.7.3. Network Architecture: Objectives

Network Architecture overlooks flow of signals, information, packets and fixes the protocols. This prompts manufactures to make the parts and peripheral which help in fulfilling objectives of network architecture. The list of network architecture objective would be as below :

1. Sensitivity : Each architectural hard ware and software parts posses built-in sensitivity to collaborate with the network architecture, which ensures smooth communication within the network.

2. Flexibility : Matching with the change in user trend and improving in technology and modification need not require costly programming or interfaces

3. Modularity : It promotes manufacturing of hardware and software in modules which can easily fit into the systems so also they could be useful in various technical subsystems.

4. Reliability : With the capability of finding faults and repairing them communication becomes accurate.

5. Simplicity : If the network is implemented in a simple manner then its installation, configuration and maintenance becomes easy.

6. Diversity of Network services : without knowing the complexity of network user must be able to use the system in a very simple way.

13.7.4. Layered Network Architecture

Important component of architecture design is the division of different communication systems. In order to fulfill the above objectives network architecture should ensure the following tasks :

1. Path of communication : All the technical components of network should possess communication capacity

2. Coding : Each signal going out of communication need to have tagged with specific code no.

3. Error correcting capability : Built in capacity of finding and correcting error ensures network to work smoothly and accurately

4. Data Transfer system : Data transfer system need to be capable and less costing

5. Path destination : It is necessary to provide path to each signal and its part which ensures their reaching to the destination correctly

6) Compatibility : Network technology should have discretional capacity to understand between sending and receiving signals.

Although all the above network objectives and its related task look easy and straight the network architectural design is difficult and complicated process in reality. To make protocols to understand network which signals would be receiving and outgoing and process them is the difficult task. In order to make it easy, layered architecture system is adopted which makes decentralise rules into the various layers. It also makes possible to make rules of each layer independent of others to maintain the security in their functioning which helps in improving quality in network functioning and incorporate new tasks in it.

Due to devising layered network protocols it makes it possible to manage complicated structure at one hand and also helps in improving process and bring in new tasks in it. It is considered open system inter connection the best example of layered network architecture (OSI).

Now let us try to know about OSI model into different layers and the software used to define various layers. The process involves division of network architecture layers in terms of their tasks and mechanisms. Considering these layer components different manufacturers try to manufacture the parts and accessories, for example if one of the companies is making modems then the use of modem is linked with particular layer of architecture. This layer is concerned with conversion of digital signal to analogue (modulation and demodulation). While manufacturing modem need to facilitate with protocol and compatibility about functioning of modem. In such case company need not worry about parts required for other layers. In network architecture particular layer is interfaced with immediate lower and upper layers.

13.7.4.1. Open System Inter Connection

Open system inter connection is a standardised mode for communication system. The meaning of open word in its title indicates capacity of flow of information two different systems is kept compatible to the respective system protocols. In another word it has the capability to maintain communication intact from communication hurdles. This mode ensures that which information is sent when is controlled by the respective system controller.

The main objective in adopting OSI modes is to connect computer peripheral which would be generally acceptable to all irrespective to how the system or its components are designed and manufactured. Most of major computer manufacturers have made such architecture available, for example IBM has devised its own system network architecture. This has made designing network easy otherwise in order to make different networking parts together one would have to do special program for it which would be costly affair. In order to avoid such conflicting situation, most network architecture components developers decide to accept universal communication standards in manufacturing. International standard organisation has prepared standards ISO-7998 in 1984 named as OSI reference model

13.7.4.2. OSI Reference Model

O. S. I reference model is one of the comprehensive models for network architecture. This model divides communication process in to smaller tasks. This makes each small component carry out its function independently. This model is a structure of seven layers. Each layer in this model handles particular type of communication. The main objective behind devising the standard for network architecture is to create specialisation in network architecture component manufacturing. This brings in lot of flexibility in universal use of these components or in exchanging components or to repair them. Now let us know how this seven layer architecture works.

Layer 7	Application
Layer 6	Presentation
Layer 5	Direction
Layer 4	Data Transfer
Layer 3	Networking
Layer 2	Data Link
Layer 1	Physical Connectivity

Index

A

Acquisition(Library) Policy 76
Automated Classification 95
Automating Librarian'S Office 140

B

Barcode In Library Management 248-252
    Advantages 253
Barcode Readers/ Scanners 256
Barcode Technology 248-249
Barcode Types 250
    QR Codes 258
    Smart/ Dumb Barcodes 254
BIBFRAME 165
    Bibliographic Data in Semantic Web 172
    BIBFlow 190
    Bibframe Project 158-169,170
    Bibframe Model 181
    Bibframe ,Aims 171
    Casalini Software with built-in Bibframe 184
    Converting MARC to Bibframe 171
    How to Bibframe 184
    Interlinking Bibliographic Data 175
    LD4L 190
    Library of Congress Initiative 158-169
    Linked Data Principles 172
    Need of- 170
    Organisation 181
    RDF Foundation 173
    RDA 181
    Zepheira Bibframe Contract 188
    Zepheira Training 189
Binary Storage Units 04
Book Acquisition
    Information Services 94
Budgeting, Library Management 80

C

Classification Systems(Library)
    Colon Classification(S.R.Ranganathan) 106
    DDC -Web Dewey 2.0- 96
    LC Online 97
    Online 96
    Subject Heading Tools(LCSH,SHE,Sears List etc.) 98
    UDC Online 96
Computer Accessories
    Parts 03
        CPU 06
        ALU
    Mother Boards 05
    Firmware 06
Computer Languages 04
Computer memory
    RAM/ROM 06
Computer Storage
    Internal/External 06,07
Computerisation Process 29-34
    Software Evaluation47
    System Performance 42
    System Development Life Cycle 35
    Systems Study,Analysis & Development 29, 30, 32, 33, 35, 39
Computerisation (Library) Ways and Means 44
    In-house Software 55
    Cloud Computing 71
    Commercial Software 48-49, 57

E- Granthalay 48
Librarian 49
Libsys 49
SLIM 49
SOUL 49
International softwares 50
VTLS 50
CDS-ISIS,J-ISIS& ABCD 52
Open Source Softwares 61
Koha 63-66
Newgenlib 69
Process 29
Service Provider's Help 72
Software Evaluation
Computerised Acquisition
Computerised Accession Registers 108
Donations Processing 84
E- Books Acquisition 85-88
Master Data 76-77
Online Suggestion Processing 79
Policy Statement 76
Pre-Acquisition Information Service 74
Purchase Orders
Procurement 81
Books on Approval 82
Cancellation 85
Direct Orders 84
E-Bidding /E- Procurement 91
Suggestions Handling 77
Computerised Circulation 109
Access Control System 121
BiometricAuthentication 120
Circulation Rules 110
Collection Location-in OPAC 120
Computerised Physical Verification138
Digital Signature Authentication 120
Instant Messaging 119
Issue/ Checking Out 111
Issue of E-Books 114
Issue of Non-book Materials 114
Master Data Creation 110
Messaging System117
No Due Charges 115
Overdue Charges 115
Self Checkout/ Online Renewals 119
Reservations/Claims 113
Retrospective Conversion(Database) 139-140
Return / Checking In
Tagging Status of Books 116
Virtual Browsing System 121
Computerised Classifications& Cataloguing 100
Authority File 95
Cataloguing of E-Books,E-Journals 106
MARC-21 Format 101
Marc Tags 101
Use of Expert Intelligence System 99
Computerised Physical Verification138
Computerised Serials Control 122
Accessioning, Classification & Cataloguing 128
Binding Process 127-128
Budgeting 124
Circulation of Journals 131
E-Journals Subscription 129-130
E-Journals Usage 131
Electronic Document Delivery System 134
Information Services 131-132
Journal Suggestion Handling 125
Master Data Creation 123
Non Receipt of Journal Issues-Actions 127
Physical Verification 128
Scheduling 126
Subscription & Renewals 125
Union Catalogue 133
Content Management Systems 230
List 232
Drupal 236-241
Joomla 236-241
CPU (Central Processing Unit) 03

D

Data 12
Data and Information 12
Data Network 272
Digital Preservation of Archives Materials 142

E

E- Bidding Book Procurement 91
E- Books Acquisition 85-89
E-Books Issue 114

E- Books, E-Journals Cataloguing 106
E-Journals Subscription 129-130
E-Journals Usage 131

I

ICT(Information and Communication Technology) 01
ICT Components
  Computer Technology 02
  Internet 07
  Telecommunication Technology 08
  Networking 11
Information and Data 12
Information Creation / Flow 16
Information Networks 278
  AGRIS 281
  INIS 281
  ISDN 284
Information Sources Types
  Primary 15
  Secondary 15
  Tertiary 16
Information Systems 13
Information Technology 07
Internet,Intranet and Extranet 08

L

Library Computerisation 19
  Acquisition 74
  Advanced Features 74
  Concept, Need and Background 19
  Cataloguing & Classification
  Circulation
  Economics 42
  Flowcharting 36
  Process
  Reference Service
  Role of Librarian 21
  Serials Control72
  System Study,Analysis & Development 29, 30, 32, 33, 35 & 39
  System Performance 42
  Training Needs (Librarian's) 22,25
  Ways and Means 44
Library Management Systems (LMS) 195
  Commercial Software 48-49, 57
  In-house Software Development 55
    E- Granthalay 48
    Librarian 49
    Libsys 49
    SLIM 49
    SOUL 49
  Innovative Feature 206
  International softwares 50
    VTLS 50
    CDS-ISIS,J-ISIS& ABCD 52
  Open Source Softwares 61
    Koha 63-66
    Newgenlib 69
  In-house
Library Resource Sharing 298-300
  Interlibrary Lending 300
  Electronic Document Delivery Systems 301
Library Networking
  Designing 150
Library Networks 287, 290
  CALIBNET 291
  DELNET 290
  INFLIBNET 292
Library Security
  Access Control 121
Library Websites 242
  Development Tools 250
  Mobile websites Development 242
LMS Migration 195
  Data Conversion 200-201
  Data Conversion Tools 203
  Innovative Features 206
  MARC Editor 204
Linked Data For Libraries LD4L 190

M

Management Of Library Computerisation 150
  Costing 151
  Drafting Proposal 154
  Manpower Needs 152
  System Maintenance 151
Migration of LMS 195
Mobile Library Websites
  Development 242

Examples 245
Guidelines
Multimedia Collection Handling 142

N

Network Architecture/ Protocol 303
OSI Ref.Model 305
Network Technology 264
Networks 270
Network Categories 273
Based on Geographical Areas 277
LAN, WAN and MAN 277
Based on Usage 273
Based on Topologies 274-276
Hybrid Topology 276
Loop Topology 275
Ring Topology 275
Star Topology 275
Tree Topology 275
Types 271
Data Network 272
Information Networks 278
Library Networks 287-290

P

Process of Library Computerisation 29

Q

Quality of Information 18

R

Reengineering Library Softwares 159
LMS Migration 195
Retrospective Conversion(Database) 139-140
RDA (Resource Description and Access) 181
RDF (Resource Description Framework)
Bibframe173

S

Scanning Technology 258
Colour Scanning 261
Scanners types 265
Switching Systems 269-270

T

Telecommunication Technology 266
Switching Systems 269-270
Telephony 267
Tools for Website Developments
AJAX 227
CSS(Cascading Style Sheets) 216
JAVA Scripts 224
HTML 21[illegible]
PHP 227

U

Union Catalogue 133

V

Virtual Reference Service 136
Question Point Software(OCLC) 137

W

Website Development
For Library 210
Mobile Library Websites242
Website Developments Tools
AJAX 227
Content Management Tools 230
List 232
Drupal 236-241
Joomla 236-241
CSS(Cascading Style Sheets) 216
JAVA Scripts 224
HTML 211
PHP 227